Marxism and Philosophy in the Twentieth Century

Marxism and Philosophy in the Twentieth Century

A DEFENSE OF VULGAR MARXISM

Richard Hudelson

PRAEGER

New York
Westport, Connecticut
London

Copyright Acknowledgments

The author and publisher gratefully acknowledge permission to reprint various material from the following:

Karl Marx. *Grundrisse.* Vintage Books, New York, 1973. Reprinted with permission.

Karl Marx. *Capital,* Vol. 1. International Publishers, New York, 1973. Reprinted with permission.

Karl Marx. *The German Ideology.* International Publishers, New York, 1966. Reprinted with permission.

Richard Hudelson. "Marxist Science as Ordinary Science." Reprinted by permission of the author and of the editor of NOÛS, Vol. 20 (1986): 53–63.

"Popper's Critique of Marx." *Philosophical Studies* 37 (1980): 259–270. Reprinted by permission of Kluwer Academic Publishers.

Richard Hudelson. "Marx's Empiricism." *Philosophy of the Social Sciences* 12 (1982): 241–253. Reprinted with permission.

Library of Congress Cataloging-in-Publication Data

Hudelson, Richard.
Marxism and philosophy in the twentieth century : a defense of vulgar Marxism / Richard Hudelson.
p. cm.
Includes bibliographical references.
ISBN 0–275–93593–0 (alk. paper)
1. Philosophy, Marxist. I. Title.
B809.8.H855 1990
335.4'11—dc20 90–32302

Library of Congress Catalog Card Number: 90–32302
ISBN: 0–275–93593–0

First published in 1990

Praeger Publishers, One Madison Avenue, New York, NY 10010
An imprint of Greenwood Publishing Group, Inc.

Printed in the United States of America

The paper used in this book complies with the Permanent Paper Standard issued by the National Information Standards Organization (Z39.48–1984).

10 9 8 7 6 5 4 3 2 1

To my parents,
Paul Hudelson and Charlotte Henry Hudelson

Contents

Preface ix

Introduction xi

I Historical Background

1 The Marxisms of the Second International 3

2 The Critique of Vulgar Marxism 29

II Analysis

3 The Theory of Capitalism 59

4 Historical Materialism 85

5 Epistemology 113

6 Metaphysics 143

7 Ethics 167

8 Politics 193

III Conclusions

9 Analytical Marxism and the History of Marxist Philosophy 211

Bibliography 239

Index 247

Preface

In 1982 I began work on this book. At that time, the universe of Marxist philosophy seemed to be exhaustively divided by two antagonistic claimants to the heritage of Marx: Marxist-Leninism and humanistic Marxism. In the ensuing years, this bipolar scheme of things has substantially given way. In part this is due to the inroads of analytical Marxism and the opening of both Marxist traditions to the tools and ideas of "bourgeois" social science. This loosening of the dominant traditions, and in particular of Marxist-Leninism, is in keeping with the theme of philosophical "convergence" considered in Part III.

But in recent months, these philosophical developments have been overshadowed by the dramatic political changes in Eastern Europe and the USSR. At first glance, it might appear that these developments are themselves consequences of the developments in philosophy. It is clear, for example, that independent intellectuals have played a significant role in the political ferment of these times. While I do not in the least wish to disparage the work of these intellectuals, if the analysis developed in this book is correct, there is no direct connection between the philosophical outlook of these intellectuals and their political orientations. From my point of view of the "independence of politics," it is also not surprising that the developing political movements have encompassed widely differing philosophical orientations. The passage from philosophy to policy depends upon a host of empirical assumptions that end up playing the primary part in the formation of policy prescriptions.

In the short run, at least, the dramatic political changes threaten to overwhelm the developments in philosophy. As these lines are written, we appear to be in the midst of a historical transformation perhaps as significant as the Bolshevik Revolution. At such times gray philosophy pales to insignificance. The turn to philosophy will appear after the political dust has settled. Just as in 1923, Georg Lukács and Karl Korsch set out to discover the philosophical revolution beneath the political revolution that had then transpired, I suspect that the current political revolution will give rise to its own subsequent revolution in philosophy. Already one can see signs of this. By this I do not mean the unseemly and ignorant self-congratulation of the Western establishment and some of its press. Rather, I have in mind the serious and informed rejection of Marxism that has been suggested by some Eastern European thinkers. I would certainly not want to proclaim the Marxism of Marx sacred and inviolate. It carries with it no guarantee of truth. But, again, if the analysis developed here is correct, it is a mistake to argue from the failure of Marxist politics to a sweeping rejection of Marxist philosophy. Perhaps this study, with its critical focus on the revolutionary philosophical break with "vulgar Marxism" that followed the October Revolution, can serve as a warning of the dangers involved in any coming revolutions in philosophy.

This work was given an important boost by a Summer Research Grant from the National Endowment for the Humanities in 1982 that enabled me to get a draft of a substantial part of the work off the ground. Even before that, important support for preliminary research work was provided by a grant from the Graduate School of the University of Minnesota. Jesús Guiral of the Department of Philosophy of the University of Montevideo provided both his considerable philosophical insight and translation of some materials from the Italian. Portions of the manuscript were read by Tom Moody and Steve Chilton, and I am grateful to them both for their philosophical and stylistic advice. I owe a special debt to Julius Sensat for his gentle criticisms of many of my philosophical errors. I would also like to acknowledge the late Dorothy Lemke of the University of Minnesota Duluth library, who assisted me in locating source material. And, finally, thanks to Eileen for quickly finishing her book and giving me lots of computer time.

Introduction

With the collapse of the Second International in the face of World War I, the international Marxist movement split into a variety of currents, each marked by its own subdivisions and crosscurrents. Of primary importance was the emergence of Marxist-Leninism as a coherent political and philosophical position. Because of the success of the revolution in Russia and the consequent admiration of the Bolsheviks outside of Russia, Marxist-Leninism gained a position of prominence. Activists throughout the world turned to Lenin for political leadership. They also turned to him for philosophical guidance.

Lenin argued that the Second International had been corrupted by bourgeois philosophy and that this philosophical corruption was largely responsible for the political failure of the Marxist parties in response to the war. The inroads of bourgeois thought were particularly clear in the position of Eduard Bernstein and other revisionists. Yet, Lenin argued, it would be wrong to think that Bernstein alone was responsible for the failure of the Social Democrats. After all, Bernstein's influence was mainly felt within the German Party, and even here his position was officially rejected. Yet the collapse of the Second International was an international phenomenon. Not only in Germany, but also in nearly all other European countries, Social Democrats abandoned Marxist internationalism in favor of social patriotism.

Restoration of the international Marxist movement required a thoroughgoing philosophical struggle to expose the sources of weakness and corruption in the Second International and to build the Third International on solid philosophical foundations. Lenin never claimed that philosophy could guarantee success in politics, but he did argue that mistaken views about philosophy could cause political failure. Philosophy was thus of great political importance. It formed the theoretical foundation upon which the political movement must be built. Without a solid foundation in philosophy, the international struggle of the proletariat would be wayward, inconsistent, open to corruption and misdirection, and uncertain in its results.

The philosophical outlook of Marxist-Leninism was clarified and developed in this philosophical struggle. Lenin was concerned both with exposing the particular errors of his contemporaries and with bringing to light the philosophical foundations already laid in the work of Marx and Engels. Marxist-Leninism was an application of Marxism to the conditions of the twentieth century. But in Lenin's view it was also a restoration of Marxism. It was a return to the philosophy of Marx and Engels, which had marked a definite advance in the history of philosophy, an advance that had been lost by the theoreticians of the Second International.

The political disaster that befell European socialism during the war also gave rise to another major current in Marxist philosophy, the humanistic Marxism of Georg Lukács and Karl Korsch. In many ways the works of Lukács and Korsch were motivated by the same concerns that motivated Lenin's attack on the Marxism of the Second International. Like Lenin, they were troubled by the failure of the European Social Democratic parties to carry through a revolutionary struggle in the objectively revolutionary conditions of capitalism in crisis and world war. Like Lenin, they blamed the leadership of the Second International for the political failure and traced the failure of leadership in part to the philosophical misconceptions of that leadership. And, like Lenin, Lukács and Korsch advanced a philosophical conception of Marxism that, they maintained, marked both an advance upon the philosophy of the Second International and a restoration of the Marxism of Marx.

Though similar to Leninism in its originating motivations, the understanding of the philosophy of Marxism developed by Lukács and Korsch differs fundamentally from the philosophical understanding of Lenin. The humanistic Marxism of Lukács and Korsch involves, contrary to Marxist-Leninism, rejections of the unity of science, the possibility of a social science, and the dialectics of nature.

Although Lukács officially renounced the position developed in *History and Class Consciousness*, the position formulated there has been of fundamental importance for the development of "Western Marxism" since the 1920s. It has been adopted as a theoretical starting point for a humanistic Marxism that is at once hostile to bourgeois philosophy and social science and to Marxist-Leninism. It is this humanistic Marxism that was incorporated into the outlook of the Frankfurt School and is found in a variety of Marxisms which have appeared in both Western and Eastern Europe.[1] Central to this understanding of Marxism is the theme of alienation and its attendant preoccupation with a normative theory of human nature. The publication of Marx's *Economic and Philosophical Man-*

uscripts of 1844, in German in the 1930s and in English translation after World War II, seemed to confirm the humanist reading of Marx. This, the emigration to the English-speaking countries of many of the representatives of the Frankfurt School, and the powerful influence of anti-Sovietism in the United States combined to promote the humanist reading of Marx to a position of dominance in the United States and much of the Western world. Such figures as Lukács, Korsch, Antonio Gramsci, Max Horkheimer, Herbert Marcuse, Erich Fromm, Theodor Adorno, Mihailo Markovic, Jean-Paul Sartre, Maurice Merleau-Ponty, and Jürgen Habermas, while certainly importantly different from one another, have all shared a humanistic interpretation of Marxism. Each of these theorists has attempted to work out a conception of Marxism that avoids both the vulgar Marxism of the Second International and the dialectical materialism of Marxist-Leninism.

Since the breakdown of the Second International, these two interpretations of Marxism, Marxist-Leninism and humanistic Marxism, have dominated Marxist philosophy. With the hegemony of humanistic Marxism in the West and Marxist-Leninism in the East, the Marxism of the Second International has appeared to be solely of historical interest. The central issues of Marxist philosophy have appeared to be framed by the great struggle between Soviet Marxist-Leninism and Western humanistic Marxism.

In recent years this bipolar scheme of things has weakened somewhat. In particular, in the West a challenge to the hegemony of humanistic Marxism has appeared with a resurgence of interest in "scientific" Marxism. The lead in this direction was provided by the Italian Marxists Galvano Della Volpe and Lucio Colletti. Also important were Louis Althusser's structuralist Marxism and his critique of humanistic Marxism. More recently, the humanist position has been challenged by the rise of analytic Marxism in English-language philosophy.

Of particular importance for this study is the new scientific Marxism that has appeared within analytic Marxism. In some respects it resembles the Marxism of the Second International. Contrary to humanistic Marxism, it defends the view of the Second International that Marxism is scientific socialism. Contrary to Marxist-Leninism, it defends the view of the Second International that this Marxist science does not depend upon a philosophy of dialectical materialism. Both Marxist-Leninism and humanistic Marxism grew out of the conviction that the Marxism of the Second International was philosophically impoverished and consequently politically impotent. At first glance, the new scientific Marxism bears a remarkable resemblance to the vulgar Marxism refuted years ago.

The central aim of this work is to investigate this new scientific Marxism within Western philosophy, with an eye to its historical setting. What were the central arguments against the Marxism of the Second International, and are these arguments applicable against the new scientific Marxism? Where are the central points of disagreement between the new scientific Marxism and the humanist and Leninist alternatives, and which position seems strongest in these disagreements?

These are questions that admit of no easy answer. Marxist-Leninism and humanistic Marxism are traditions that have built up extensive and rich bodies of writings. No single researcher can hope to cover all of this material. Inevitably, some selection of the important works and important arguments must be made. On the other hand, analytic Marxism is relatively new. Its content is not yet clear. Further, it has largely been developed without regard for historical antecedents.[2] In such circumstances it is perhaps premature to speculate on the historical significance of the resurgence of interest in scientific Marxism within analytic philosophy.

Nevertheless, it is just such speculation that is attempted here. If the criticisms of the scientific Marxism of the Second International provide serious objections to the new scientific Marxism, it would be well to remind ourselves of these criticisms now, before we become too deeply enmeshed in the errors of the past. If these criticisms do not apply, it would be well to determine why they do not, so that the new understanding of Marxism can avoid the vulgarizations of the past. It is my own view that developments within analytic philosophy of science have taken some of the sting out of the criticisms that, historically, seemed to undermine the outlook of the Second International. In saying this, I do not mean to suggest that I think the Neo-Kantian and positivist philosophies of science which were current within the Marxism of the Second International are adequate today. Rather, my argument is that in rejecting the vulgar Marxism of the Second International, humanistic Marxism and Marxist-Leninism constructed mistaken theories about the philosophical nature of Marxist thought. I believe that developments in contemporary philosophy of science allow us, along with the Marxists of the Second International, to appreciate the scientific nature of Marxism without recourse to these mistaken theories about the nature of Marxist thought. I also think that some of these same developments in the philosophy of science have made possible a fruitful exchange between analytic Marxism and Marxist-Leninism.

I shall try to clarify and defend these claims in the course of this study. I am convinced that what is most important in Marxism is social science, and that this social science does not depend upon any esoteric philosophical views. My attempt to defend these claims consists largely in an effort to show that contrary claims rest on bad arguments. Clearly this approach has its drawbacks. On the one hand, of course, there is the logical consideration that weakness in argument for *not p* is no argument for *p*. On the other hand, there is always the possibility that strong arguments against my favored positions have been overlooked. These are serious drawbacks. Nevertheless, if, as Marx said, the ideas of the past burden the minds of the present, there may be some emancipatory value in this critical examination of past debates.

This work is divided into three parts. In Part I, I present a historical introduction that attempts to identify positions and arguments that were historically significant. In Part II, I attempt to analyze the various arguments and determine where the strongest position lies. In Part III, I offer some concluding remarks on the significance of all of this for current directions within Marxist philosophy.

NOTES

1. "Humanistic Marxism" and "Western Marxism" are sometime used interchangeably to refer to a certain current in twentieth-century Marxist philosophy. Since some of the representatives of this current, such as the Yugoslav Praxis School and the Polish philosopher Leszek Kolakowski, have Eastern European roots, I prefer to use the term "humanistic Marxism" throughout this study.

2. Particularly striking is the lack of attention that has so far been shown to the work of the Italian Marxist Galvano Della Volpe. The first chapter of Russell Keat's *The Politics of Social Theory* (Chicago: University of Chicago Press, 1981) provides some of the historical setting needed to understand contemporary alternatives.

Part I

Historical Background

1

The Marxisms of the Second International

Late-nineteenth-century Social Democracy did not exist in an intellectual vacuum. Perhaps all social movements are sensitive in some degree to the world of ideas around them. Social Democracy was particularly sensitive to surrounding intellectual currents. The socialism of the Second International was avowedly Marxist. Marxism had been born out of the heady intellectual atmosphere of German culture before the incredible year of 1848. Marx had studied philosophy, finishing a Ph.D. in philosophy at Berlin in 1841. Unable to secure a teaching position because of his views and associates, he turned to journalism, writing for the *Deutsch-französische Jahrbücher* and the *Rheinische Zeitung* and serving briefly as editor for the latter. Engels, too, had studied philosophy at Berlin and had written for journals. The journalistic endeavors of Marx and Engels were part of the Left Hegelian effort to utilize philosophy to fight the reactionary Prussian regime. In these journals the most recent innovations in philosophy were applied directly to political issues. Marxism thus claimed to have its origins in the most advanced philosophical views. And, as scientific socialism, it claimed for itself the mantle of science. Because Marxism claimed to have its roots in the most advanced philosophy and science, the Marxists of the Second International were sensitive to any charges that either their science or their philosophy was deficient or out of date.

By the end of the nineteenth century, Marxist Social Democrats faced a number of challenges from the prevailing academic philosophies. Neo-Kantianism and positivism agreed in dismissing Marxist materialism as an outdated relic in metaphysics; in dismissing the Marxist epistemology of the reflection theory as naive and clearly untenable; and in dismissing the Hegelian currents in Marxist philosophy (and Hegelian dialectics in particular) as remnants of the worst excesses of an unscientific and empty philosophical approach to questions of reality. Neo-Kantians also raised doubts about the possibility of a science of historical development of the type that historical materialism claimed to be, and they agreed that Social Democracy as a political movement required an ethical justification of socialism that was entirely lacking in Marxism. While some positivists and Neo-Kantians were hostile to Social Democracy, other positivists and Neo-Kantians, the "Katheder" socialists, claimed to be friends of socialism. They offered to correct and supplement the discredited Marxism of Social Democracy, and so set the movement for socialism on a more acceptable intellectual basis.

Marxist Social Democrats reacted to these philosophical challenges in different ways. For some, the philosophical critique of Marxism showed the necessity for thoroughgoing revision of basic Party ideology. The revisionism debates of the turn of the century were, in part at least, motivated by these philosophical problems.[1] Others argued that the philosophical criticisms of Marxism rested upon mistaken views about what the philosophical foundations of Marxism really were. Such Marxists tried to show that Marxism really was not incompatible with the dominant academic philosophies. And, of course, some Marxists stood their ground, more or less firmly, and tried to defend Marxism from the criticisms raised against it. These different responses indicate different conceptions of Marxism within the Second International, though, as we shall see, there is also important common ground among them.

THE "ORTHODOX" MARXISM OF KARL KAUTSKY

Given his position as editor of *Die neue Zeit*, the leading theoretical journal of the German Party, Karl Kautsky played a central role in the theoretical disputes of the Second International. He both understood himself to be and was perceived by others as the leading champion of "orthodox" Marxism within the Second International. Central to Kautsky's view of Marxism was his conception of Marx's theories of capitalism and of history as social science. Kautsky thought that Marx had succeeded in showing the necessary course of evolution of capitalism and the inevitability of socialism.[2] He understood this necessity in terms of the subsumption of the social process under scientific laws that governed it. For him, Marxism was scientific socialism.

Kautsky contrasted this scientific socialism with the utopian socialism that had preceded it. The central point of this contrast lay in his conception of science as value free. The task of science is not to prescribe what ought to be, but to describe what is.[3] Earlier socialisms had sketched a vision of a just and free society and had prescribed this vision as something that ought to be pursued. In contrast, Kautsky thought, Marxism envisaged socialism as the inevitable outcome of existing social forces. To be sure, Kautsky recognized that Marx's writings bristled with moral indignation and moral judgments based upon a moral ideal. But, he argued, Marx "always endeavors and rightly to banish it [the ideal] where he can. Because the moral ideal becomes a source of error in science, when it takes it on itself to point out to it its aims. Science has only to do with the recognition of the necessary."[4]

This conception of Marxism as value-free social science became problematic during the debates with the revisionists at the turn of the century. Following the lead of the academic Neo-Kantian socialists, Eduard Bernstein and other prominent Social Democrats proposed basic revisions in the theoretical foundations of Social Democracy. They argued that Marxism required an independent grounding in moral theory. As a practical political program, Social Democracy maintained not only the necessity but also the desirability of socialism. Insofar as Marxism was value-free social science, it could not ground the judgment of the desirability of socialism. Hence, Bernstein and other revisionists turned to Kantian or utilitarian ethics to provide the needed foundation for the judgment of the moral desirability of socialism.

Kautsky resisted these efforts at providing a moral foundation for socialism in an ethical theory independent of Marxism. His thinking here is not altogether clear. On the one hand, he viewed the academic return to Kant as fundamentally motivated by a resistance to the social scientific perspective of historical materialism. He accused bourgeois philosophy of a schizophrenic dualism: materialism in the natural sciences and Kantianism in social theory.[5]

On the other hand, Kautsky appears to have thought that somehow historical materialism can provide all that is necessary for grounding the practical and political aims of Social Democracy. In *Ethics and the Materialist Conception of History*, he distinguishes between two component parts in moral experience. One of these parts is a natural social impulse that stirs in us a sense of duty and conscience. The other part is provided by some specific ideal state to which our sense of duty is attached. Kautsky sees the natural social impulse as a kind of instinct that has developed in us as a result of the evolutionary process. But for such an instinct to prompt us to some determinate course of action, it must be attached to a determinate ideal. The ideal itself is historically variable, its content determined by the material conditions of production.[6]

Ethical theories have traditionally dealt with problems about what makes something morally right or wrong and with problems pertaining to our motive to do what is right. Kautsky appears to be saying that our motive to do what is right is provided by the natural impulse arising in the evolutionary process, while it is the nature and level of development of the material conditions that make something morally right or wrong. But this latter point is open to at least two different readings. It can be understood as pertaining to the justification of the moral rightness of some social practices, or it can be understood as pertaining to the causation of the belief that such practices are right. In brief, it can be understood either as a normative justificatory account or as a descriptive theory in the sociology of moral beliefs.

Kautsky says, "Not from our moral ideal, but from distinct material conditions does the policy depend which the social development takes."[7] But it is not clear whether this "depend" involves a causal or a justificatory claim. Similarly, Kautsky says, "It was the materialist conception of history which has completely deposed the moral ideal as the directing factor of the social evolution, and has taught us to deduce our social aims solely from the knowledge of the material foundations."[8] Again, it is not clear whether this deduction involves the causal explanation of the aims in question or their moral justification.

Further confusion on this point is evident in the continuation of a passage quoted above as establishing Kautsky's acceptance of the fact/value distinction. Having said that moral ideals have no place in science, Kautsky goes on to say, "Science has only to do with the recognition of the necessary. It can certainly arrive at prescribing a shall, but this dare only come up as a consequence of the insight into the necessary. It must decline to discover a 'shall' which is not to be recognized as a necessity founded in the world of phenomena."[9] It is possible to read this as a naturalistic justificatory claim concerning the possibility of deriving a moral "ought" from a scientific "is." But this reading seems to contradict the distinction between descriptive theory and normative theory drawn in the preceding pages and also the idea that no nonnecessary "shall" is recognized by science. An alternative reading would understand the "shall" as a simple statement of future fact. This would fit better with the preceding pages and with the last quoted sentence, but it fails to make sense of Kautsky's view of this "shall" as prescriptive.

My own view is that in these passages Kautsky has in mind primarily a sociology of morals. He thinks that historical materialism provides a causal explanatory account of the content of our moral ideals as part of the ideological superstructure. But I say that this is "primary" because Kautsky also appears to hold that such a sociology of morals precludes the possibility of a Kantian (or any other) justification of a moral vision. He appears to have thought that once we see the inevitability of some ideal vision at a certain juncture in the historical process, nothing more remains to be said. There is no room for the autonomous moral subject of Kantian ethics, and hence no room for the kind of questions that arise with respect to the contemplation of such subjects.[10]

Although he saw the theory of capitalism and the materialist theory of history as the core doctrines of Marxism, Kautsky did not deny the philosophical dimension of Marxism, and he defended dialectical materialism against the criticisms of the Neo-Kantians and the positivists.[11] Before becoming a Marxist in 1870, Kautsky held a Darwinian materialism of the kind made popular by the scientific materialists of the mid-nineteenth century. His enthusiasm for Darwinian evolution remained with him throughout his life; indeed, he claimed that the Marxist theory of history was "nothing other than the application of Darwinism to social development."[12]

While his materialism had its roots in the natural scientific materialism of mid-century, Kautsky distinguished his Marxist dialectical materialism from this natural scientific materialism.[13] What distinguished Marxist materialism from natural scientific materialism was its antireductionist standpoint, which resisted any attempt to treat social systems in purely biological terms, and the specifically dialectical outlook that underlay this antireductionism.[14] While, as we shall see, some of the revisionists within Social Democracy followed the Neo-Kantians and positivists in rejecting the dialectic, Kautsky defended it: "What remains of Marxism if it is deprived of dialectics, its best working tool and its sharpest weapon?"[15]

Nevertheless, these philosophical matters were not of paramount importance for Kautsky's view of Marxism. For Kautsky, the vitally important elements of Marxism were the theory of capitalism and the materialist theory of history. As empirical sociology, both of these theories were compatible with either Neo-Kantian or positivist philosophy. In a letter to Plekhanov, Kautsky granted that "the economic and historical standpoint of Marx and Engels is, of necessity, also compatible with Neo-Kantianism."[16] And in a 1909 article in *Der Kampf*, the journal of the Austro-Marxists, he granted that the Marxist theory of capitalism and the Marxist theory of history were compatible with Machist positivism as well as with Neo-Kantianism.[17] In this same article Kautsky wrote, "I regard Marxism not as a philosophical doctrine but as an empirical science, as a special understanding of society."[18] Finally, for Kautsky the commitment to dialectics involved not the methodological principles of Hegel's science of reason but only an understanding of social processes in terms of conflicting forces and interests.[19] For Kautsky, the philosophical aspects of Marxism were relatively unimportant.

THE REVISIONIST MARXISM OF EDUARD BERNSTEIN

The revisionism of Eduard Bernstein has a historical importance that goes far beyond its theoretical contribution. Bernstein was representative of a major current within the Social Democracy of the Second International. His work was important then because it represented this current and not merely the viewpoint of one individual. Further, Bernstein's vision of a "democratic" and "evolutionary" socialism remains important as a vision for modern social democracy. In both theory and practice, the Bernsteinian vision continues to play a major role in European politics. In the conflict between Communists and Social Democrats today, one finds, as it were, an echo of the turn-of-the-century controversy.[20] My discussion of Bernstein will be focused on the philosophical aspects of his revisionism and on its connections with the academic challenge to Marxism. Thus, I will not be concerned with the question of the extent to which Bernstein's revisionism was the result of Fabian influences during his stay in England. Nor am I concerned with the claim that his revisionism was motivated by fear of revolution. I will not consider the sociological studies concerning the base revisionism found in various sectors of the Social Democratic Party. These questions are important and interesting in their own right, but I am interested in revisionism only insofar as it can be connected with certain philosophical conceptions.[21]

Bernstein's revisionism is rooted in the impact of theoretical developments outside the Social Democratic Movement on Bernstein's conception of Marxism. These developments were of two kinds: objections to the adequacy of Marxism as empirical science, and objections to the philosophical foundations of Marxism. The beginning point for Bernstein's revisionism was his conviction that Marxian claims about the development of capitalism had been refuted by the actual course of events. In particular, Bernstein claimed that the evidence showed that Marx was wrong in thinking that the development of capitalism would lead to the concentration and centralization of capital into fewer and fewer hands, to the elimination of the petite bourgeoisie, and to the polarization of the classes into two large classes of bourgeoisie and proletariat. He pointed to evidence showing that small businesses were persisting and capital ownership expanding to include more and more people. Further, he argued that, with the development of cartels and modern credit systems, capitalism had acquired the ability to adapt to fluctuations in the various markets and to avoid general crises. Finally, Bernstein argued that the trade union movement and parliamentary reforms had succeeded in ameliorating the worst abuses of capitalism, giving the working people some degree of security and some share in the increased production of wealth. Not the impoverishment of the working class predicted by Marx, but a modest, persistent gain in the condition of working people was the actual effect of the course of capitalist development.

Of particular importance for Bernstein's thinking was the cumulative effect of these changes on the Marxian prediction of socialism. Bernstein understood the Marxian theory as foreseeing socialism as the result of a general collapse of the capitalist system. Driven by misery, unemployment, and the general collapse of the system, the workers were supposed to overthrow the old order in a violent, revolutionary seizure of power. This insurrectionist model of the socialist revolution was, in Bernstein's view, no longer compatible with the facts of actual development. The economic causes that were supposed to lead to the revolution—misery and unemployment—were not the actual results of capitalist development. Further, given the gains that working people had achieved, a revolutionary uprising by organized Social Democracy would be dangerous and irresponsible.[22]

If one agreed with Bernstein's view of the facts, then one might very well decide that socialism simply was not to be expected. If the Marxian theory that socialism was the inevitable effect of the development of capitalism is wrong, then one might suspect that capitalism is here to stay. Bernstein does not quite draw this conclusion. Instead, he argues that socialism is to be understood not as a material necessity but as a moral necessity.[23] He remains committed to socialism as the ultimate end, but it is an end that is to be achieved as a result of the free, uncaused moral agency of human beings.

Bernstein's continued commitment to socialism is sometimes questioned. It is true that Bernstein said that for him the final aim of socialism is nothing and the movement is everything. This certainly does suggest that he abandoned the aim of socialism in favor of a program of reforms of capitalism. But Bernstein explicitly rejected this understanding of his words. He insisted that he was still committed to the basic transformation of the economic system from capitalism to socialism, and that he had not abandoned the goal of seizing power.[24] Nevertheless, consideration of what Bernstein has to say about how this transformation is to be achieved leads to a conception of the tasks of Social Democracy that is fundamentally reformist in its orientation.

To begin with, of course, Bernstein strongly rejects any insurrectionist model for the transformation of the economic order.[25] He appeals to three considerations here. First, the proletariat remains, contrary to what he saw as Marx's prediction, a minority class.[26] A revolutionary rising of the proletariat would face a hostile majority. Second, he argues that the proletariat is not ready to assume power because it lacks the technical, political, and moral qualities necessary to govern.[27] Third, the spread of democratic institutions creates the conditions for a lawful and orderly process of transformation and makes extralegal insurrection unnecessary.[28]

These arguments at best show the inadvisability of revolutionary insurrection under certain conditions. However, there are also two arguments to the effect that revolutionary insurrection is in general undesirable. The first of these is that, given the frailty of human understanding, a rapid and comprehensive transformation of the social order is almost certain to generate enormous difficulties and consequent human suffering: far better to undertake modest and limited changes with an experimental attitude. Radical transformation should be resisted on both prudential and moral grounds in favor of a slow, step-by-step process of change.[29] Finally, Bernstein argues that, as a matter of historical generality, no sudden historical changes can take place. While a revolutionary insurrection might appear to make a historical leap, in fact such insurrections are inevitably followed by the necessity to step backward and work through the process of change in a gradualist fashion.[30] For all these reasons, then, Bernstein is opposed to any revolutionary insurrection.

But Bernstein's revision of the socialist movement is not merely a rejection of insurrection. Bernstein also argues against any program of socialism calling for collective control of industry through the agency of a worker-controlled state. His argument here is largely based on the idea, mentioned above, that the working class lacks the qualities requisite to the management of such a planned economy. He also suggests that such a system is inherently undesirable because it demands a managerial capacity that is simply impossible for human beings.[31]

Given this assessment of the infeasibility of a centrally planned economy, Bernstein argues for a vague program of decentralized socialism. Thus, contrary to the dominant thinking in the German Party, he defended the ideas of cooperatives and municipal socialism not only as steps along the way but also as necessary components of the socialist future.[32] Through such localist structures Bernstein aimed at the development of self-governing skills and social values among the proletariat, and at the gradual construction of socialism within the capitalist system. It is clear that he saw some such decentralized system as the ultimate form socialism should take, and that he saw cooperatives and municipal governments as forms for the development of this system. But how socialism is to emerge in this way, and what shape it is to take, are never made clear.

In part Bernstein's vision lacks any sharp definition because he takes the position that the time for socialism is still a long way off. The current tasks of the movement, as Bernstein sees it, are the fight to preserve and deepen democracy, the broadening and strengthening of the trade union movement, legislative action to reform capitalism, and experimentation with cooperatives and municipal programs that will provide training in democratic self-management for working people and lay the foundations for fuller socialist development in the future.

Bernstein claimed that his program in reality was in no way different from the actual program-in-practice of German Social Democracy. He saw his writings as merely jettisoning aspects of Marxist "dogma" that had long been abandoned in practice by the Party. There is certainly some truth to this claim. No one in the German Party looked for the imminent collapse of capitalism, and insurrection was clearly not on the Party's agenda for either the near or the foreseeable future. Also, Bernstein's advocacy of a parliamentary struggle was clearly in line with the basic thrust of Party practice. Nevertheless, Bernstein's vision does represent a real departure from the outlook that had come to dominate the Social Democratic Movement. Of particular importance is his rejection of centralized socialism and his substitution for it of a vaguely formulated decentralized socialism. In this, and in his postponement of the conquest of power to the remote future, Bernstein in fact offered a program substantially different from the Marxist program of Social Democracy. Finally, in abandoning Marxian scientific socialism for ethical socialism, he clearly broke with the philosophical outlook of Marxian Social Democracy. I turn now to these philosophical considerations.

The influence of the Neo-Kantian movement on Bernstein is absolutely clear. He explicitly endorsed the "return to Kant" and saw his role in criticizing Marxism as similar to Kant's role in criticizing metaphysics.[33] He claimed that here was a dualism in Marx's thinking. On the one hand, Marx aimed at a scientific theory of capitalism and a scientific theory of history. On the other hand, he was fatally influenced by Hegelian metaphysics. In particular, Bernstein argued that Marx took over from Hegel a metaphysical principle of dialectics which looked for leaps, reversals, and qualitative jumps everywhere. Marx used this dialectical outlook in developing a schematic preconception of history as a dialectical struggle of opposites punctuated with periodic dialectical leaps from one mode of production to another. This metaphysical dialectics corrupted Marx's science in two ways: it led him to impose this preconception on his study of capitalist development in such a way as to ignore factual evidence that contradicted the preconceived schema, and it led him to embrace the insurrectionist model of the transformation from a capitalism to socialism.[34]

Bernstein saw himself as championing the "scientific" side of Marx against the metaphysical, dialectical side. His understanding of science was heavily influenced by his understanding of recent developments in the philosophy of science. The anti-metaphysical and anti-Hegelian stance were clearly part of this scientistic outlook, but only a part of it. Also important was a "positivistic" understanding of science as description of observable facts. At one point, Bernstein even calls himself a positivist.[35] In this appeal to positivism, he appears to contradict his expressed Neo-Kantianism.

In fact, what was of central importance for Bernstein was rejection of dialectical materialism as metaphysical pseudoscience, a theme that was common ground between positivists and Neo-Kantians. Bernstein thought of pure science as the formulation of regularities with regard to what is given in experience. A genuine scientific theory is one that "is capable of an objective proof based only on an experience and logic to which it conforms."[36] Thus, Bernstein sees in the persistence of small businesses, the rise of wages, and the absence of general economic crisis, "facts" that clearly refute the laws proclaimed by the Marxian theory of the development of capitalism. Under the influence of metaphysical preconceptions, Marxists were led to take Marx's genuine insights into tendencies within the capitalist system as fixed laws of historical development. Where in reality the tendencies discovered by Marx were dependent upon a host of external variables, Marx and his followers ignored this dependence and mistook what were merely tendencies of capitalism for genuine scientific laws.[37]

Kantian influences are also at work in Bernstein's rejection of the materialist conception of history. This is true in a twofold sense. Bernstein views materialism as implying that everything which happens is causally determined by matter in motion as governed by the laws of mechanics. Insofar as this mechanistic determinism is universal, it includes human ideas as phenomena ultimately determined by the motion of matter. Bernstein rejects this doctrine on the grounds that it rests upon a naive materialism which has been refuted by Kantian critical epistemology. He also rejects it on the Kantian grounds that it is incompatible with human moral responsibility.[38]

Bernstein also rejects any economic determinist theory of history. Such theories are sometimes taken as denying that ideas have any causal efficacy in the course of history. Such a view is patently false and is clearly denied by both Marx and Engels. A more plausible view of economic determinism would grant causal efficacy to ideas but also hold that ideas have economic causes and that, in some sense, these economic causes are primary. Bernstein goes to some lengths to show that Marx and Engels did not deny causal efficacy to ideas.[39] But where Marx and Engels appear to hold that ideas have economic causes and these economic causes are in some sense primary, Bernstein denies that human ideas are causally determined, or at least he holds that some ideas are not causally determined.[40]

This indeterminism is a direct consequence, in Bernstein's view, of human moral responsibility. It is here that we find a doctrine of free will and a dualistic conception of human beings at the center of Bernstein's ethical socialism.[41] But, even here, Bernstein is not altogether clear. He thinks that, in the past, the Marxist view of historical development was largely correct. But with the development of the productive powers of human beings, room is provided for ideas, and moral ideals in particular, to play a role in guiding the course of history.[42]

There appear to be a number of philosophical confusions in all of this. For one thing, a mechanistic determinism is assumed to be a clear consequence of the materialism of matter in motion. For another, there appears to be a confusion between the materialism of matter in motion and the materialism of an economic determinist theory of history. Bernstein seems to have thought that Marxism rested upon a philosophical materialism of matter in motion and that the determinism implicit in this view somehow underlies the determinism implicit in the economic theory of history. The connection is never made clear. That a universal determinism of matter in motion implies some deterministic view of history is plausible, but that it implies an economic determinism is not. It may be that the connecting link here is that both determinisms appear to deny the possibility of autonomous ideas influencing the course of history; but, of course, this does not establish any connection between the one determinism and the other. In any case, Bernstein rejects determinism and so rejects both.

Bernstein's position here has led some commentators to hold that he completely rejects the historical materialist conception of history as a law-governed process.[43] Bernstein professes to continue to believe in historical materialism, and he points to Marx's Preface of 1859, in which we find the classical statement of historical materialism, as the canonical text of Marxism.[44] Bernstein's flirtation with the Kantian idea of the autonomous moral agent did lead him to a position inconsistent with a deterministic understanding of historical materialism. And he clearly did think that Marx's argument for the inevitability of socialism failed.

Although just what remained of value in historical materialism in Bernstein's view is not altogether clear, his position is compatible with recognition of limits to what can be achieved by autonomous choice and with recognition of the historically variable nature of these limits. His position is compatible with historical materialism understood as a sensitivity to such historically variable constraints on human action. On such a view, the mode of production constrains but does not determine relations of production and ideological superstructures. That such a view was at work in Bernstein's understanding of the value of historical materialism is suggested by his argument against a revolutionary seizure of power. It it also suggested by his view, noted above, that an increase in the productive powers available brought with it increased room for autonomous moral choices.

Convinced that the Marxist idea of the inevitability of socialism rested on defective science and philosophical dogma, Bernstein sought to base socialism on moral imperatives rather than causal necessities. This is the fundamental idea of Bernstein's "ethical socialism," and in this respect he follows the lead of the "Kathedersozialismus" of the Neo-Kantians F. A. Lange and Hermann Cohen. But Bernstein's socialism differs from the "socialism" of Lange and Cohen in that, however much Bernstein champions the reformist road to socialism, unlike Lange and Cohen, he does not stop with the goal of a reformed capitalism. He remains committed to a fundamental change in the structure of the economic system—a change that would realize democratic control of the economy.[45]

Neither the details of the socialist economy of the future nor the ethical foundations that justify socialism are clearly spelled out by Bernstein. As we have seen, he defended cooperatives, unions, and municipalities as having a role in the socialist future. Broadly speaking, his ideal appears to have been a system in which necessary central authority is checked by a variety of mediating institutions. In ethics, Bernstein appealed to Kantian principles in making a moral case for socialism. His view of these Kantian moral principles as eternal and binding on all classes has led some opponents to charge him with abandoning a class viewpoint.[46] This is not altogether fair. Bernstein never denied the conflict of interest between the bourgeoisie and the proletariat, nor did he maintain that Kantian ethics opposed self-interested action by the proletariat. Rather, he argued that the eternal principles of Kantian morality supported proletarian demands. Nevertheless, in rejecting philosophical materialism, in rejecting the causal inevitability of socialism, in accepting the Kantian idea of an autonomous moral subject, and in making the coming of socialism depend upon the moral insight of such autonomous subjects, Bernstein had strayed far from orthodox Marxism.

AUSTRO-MARXISM

The revisionist position developed by Bernstein stands in a conscious relationship to Neo-Kantian philosophy and positivist philosophy of science. If Bernstein was led to revisionism by his belief that Marxist theory was contradicted by the facts, his understanding of this contradiction was shaped by the new critical philosophy of science that he saw in both Neo-Kantianism and positivism. His ethical socialism represented his attempt at reconciling the socialist movement with both the facts and modern philosophy. Austro-Marxism must also be understood as a coming to terms with late-nineteenth-century academic philosophy from within the Social Democratic Movement. However, the position developed by the Austrian Marxists differs from Bernsteinian revisionism both in philosophy and in political practice. In many respects Austro-Marxism is theoretically more sophisticated than Bernsteinian revisionism. If Bernstein moved from critical philosophy of science to ethical socialism, the logic of this movement is far from clearly thought out. In resisting this revisionism, Austro-

Marxism provides a theoretical alternative that both clarifies and complicates the philosophical and political issues involved.

Austro-Marxism shared with Bernstein an acceptance of the critical philosophy of science. By the end of the nineteenth century, philosophical materialism appeared to be discredited by modern epistemology. Positivists and Neo-Kantians alike rejected the materialism of mid-century on epistemic grounds. To postulate a world of material objects existing outside of consciousness appeared to be a metaphysical extravagance incompatible with a genuine scientific orientation. While positivists and Neo-Kantians might differ on the question of a priori sources for knowledge, they agreed that all knowledge was bounded by possible experience and that materialism transgressed this boundary. Insofar as it appeared to be a child of mid-century materialism, Marxism appeared to rest on an outmoded philosophical foundation. Like Bernstein, the Austro-Marxists accepted the critique of materialism in academic philosophy and the conception of science as bound to possible experience that was connected with it. Unlike Bernstein, they argued that Marxism was compatible with this philosophy of science.[47]

Like Bernstein and Kautsky, the Austro-Marxists saw Marxism as aiming at social science. Like Bernstein and Kautsky, they took the core of Marxism to be the theory of capitalism as a historically evolving mode of production. The heart of Marxian social science is the theory of the laws governing the evolution of capitalist economies. This theory was set within a more general theory of social development, the materialist theory of history. But where Bernstein seems to have thought that the critical philosophy of science in some way threatened the materialist theory of history, the Austro-Marxists maintained that this was not so. Max Adler and Otto Bauer both maintained that the materialist theory of history in no way depends upon philosophical materialism, and thus is not affected by the critical turn in epistemology and philosophy of science.[48]

The Austro-Marxists argued that the materialist theory of history is a theory which formulates laws governing the historical process. These laws are generalizations based upon experience that can be used to explain and predict observable phenomena. They are thus grounded in the experience of the subject, and are in principle testable by that experience. The materialist theory of history is empirical sociology. As such, it has nothing to say about the existence or nonexistence of mind-independent material objects. Nor does it make any assumption about the existence of such objects. As empirical theory, it is ontologically neutral between materialism and idealism. Confusion on this point derives from the fact that Marx and Engels called their viewpoint a "materialist" theory of history. However, all they mean by that is that their views are to be contrasted with the speculative, idealist theory of history developed by Hegel. For Marx, materialism is identified with the empirical and anti-speculative outlook. It is a simple verbal confusion to suppose that there is any connection between the positive sociology of Marxism and philosophical materialism.

Such, in outline, is the position developed by Max Adler, the philosophical spokesperson for Austro-Marxism. He maintained that Marxism is "empirical science," "the science of social life and its causal development," and that "consequently it aims to deduce the development of socialism from capitalism as a matter of causal necessity."[49] This view of Marxism as empirical social science was shared by Friedrich Adler, Otto Bauer, Rudolf Hilferding and Karl Renner as well.[50] While Max Adler, Bauer, and Hilferding looked to Neo-Kantianism for the philosophical foundations of this social science, Renner and Freidrich Adler looked to positivism to supply these foundations.[51] From their shared view of Marxism as a philosophically neutral social science, the philosophical differences between the positivists and the Neo-Kantians were not important. And, in fact, Max Adler could say of Marxism that it was "only a form of natural science positivism more or less in the manner of Ernst Mach."[52]

This view of Marxism as purely positive science placed the Austro-Marxists in opposition to Engels' view that Marxism stood with philosophical materialism. It was Max Adler's position that Engels' materialism was untenable, in light of the developments in the philosophy of science, but that nothing of importance in Marxism depended upon this.[53] This separation of the materialist theory of history from philosophical materialism, while it may prove ultimately untenable, is at least a step toward clarification of the issues. It surely is a theoretical confusion to think that the primacy of economic forces in determining the course of history implies or is implied by the philosophical thesis that nothing exists but material objects and their properties. The materialist theory of history can be interpreted as a theory about the phenomenal world of experience. This is in fact how the Austro-Marxists saw it. Given this view, there is nothing in the critical epistemology that threatens the Marxian theory of historical development.

If developments in the philosophy of science did not require revision of Marxism, neither, in the view of the Austro-Marxists, did the facts refute Marxism. If Bernstein's revisionism was motivated by what he understood to be the need for theoretical revision to accommodate the facts, this motivation presupposed a philosophy of science that was simplistic in its conception of the relationship between theory and facts. The Austro-Marxists held a more sophisticated view of the relationship between theory and facts, and worked to show that the theory of Marxism was not only consistent with the facts but, indeed, confirmed by them.

On at least one point the Austro-Marxists were in agreement with Bernstein: they, too, argued that the Marxist theory of the historical development of capitalism must be understood as a theory which discloses tendencies within capitalist economies that are dependent upon a host of variables both internal and external to the economic process.[54] Much of the valuable work done by the Austro-Marxists is empirical science aimed at developing the theory of Marxism in light of some of these variables that are exogenous to the model of capitalism developed by Marx. For example, Marx sets aside consideration of the effects of foreign trade on the general "law" of capitalist accumulation. However, the more or less constant expansion of overseas markets during the last quarter of the nineteenth century was, arguably, an important factor in accounting for the slow rise in wages and the absence of a general economic crisis. Where Bernstein pointed to the "facts" as obviously refuting Marx, Hilferding attempted to work out an analysis of the changed features of capitalism which showed that the basic Marxian theory was correct, and that the development of credit and cartels, far from falsifying Marxism, merely laid the foundations for worldwide crisis at a later time.[55]

Whether Bernstein or Hilferding was right is not the issue here. In fact, the subsequent years have been harsh on Bernstein's refutation of Marxism. All I want to argue here is that Bernstein's revisionism flowed not directly from the facts, but only from the facts placed within the philosophy of science that he had taken over from Neo-Kantian and positivist sources, as he understood it. Further, Bernstein's view of this modern philosophy of science was open to question.

Bernstein appears to have understood positive science in the manner of an extreme empiricism, which minimized the theoretical mediation of what was given in observation. What the Austro-Marxist response shows is that this reading of positive science is open to question. One can accept the view that science consists of law claims linking observable phenomena without also holding that this linkage is devoid of theoretical mediation. The importance of such mediations is made explicit in the post-positivist philosophy of science of Imre Lakatos. In effect, this was the direction taken in the development of Marxism by the Austro-Marxists; and, in this sense, their scientific practice was more sophisticated than their explicit philosophy of science. Given a complex view of the relationship between theory and facts, they tried to show that Marxist theory was compatible with the facts Bernstein cited to refute it. While Bernstein appears to have thought in terms of a simple falsificationism, the Austro-Marxists adopt a more sophisticated view of the relationship between theory and facts.[56]

Max Adler's philosophical defense of Marxism also differed from Bernstein's standpoint in its view of the dialectic. Bernstein saw the dialectic as a metrophysical schema, derived from Hegel, that infected Marxism with an a priori view of the course of historical development and an a priori insurrectionist model for the transition to socialism. Adler (or at least the early Adler) agreed with Bernstein in rejecting the dialectic as a principle of the Hegelian philosophy of nature.[57] However, he argues, for Marxism the dialectic is not a metaphysical law governing reality; rather, it is a methodological principle distinct from the Hegelian dialectic.

In saying that the dialectic is a principle of method, Adler seems to have in mind a principle concerning the development of science. A scientific theory is formed that then encounters its own limitation in certain persistent and fundamental problems. The problems constitute the negation of the theory. Development in the sciences consists in the elaboration of a more comprehensive theory in a higher theoretical perspective. So understood, the dialectic as method is compatible with the empiricist conception of scientific method elaborated within both Neo-Kantianism and positivism. The empiricist model of observation, abstraction, hypothesis formation, and experimental testing remains valid for each scientific theory. The dialectic pertains to the development of theory. It is a method of thought that seeks the partial truth contained in each fixed and one-sided theoretical grasp of things, and to combine these partial views into a more adequate conception of the whole. The dialectical method is a method of discovery, while the empiricist method serves as a method of justification.[58]

This view of the dialectic as method is, in a way, closer to Hegel's dialectic of concepts than is Engels' dialectics of nature. And it should be noted here that Adler clearly disagrees with Engels' conception of the dialectics of nature. There is, however, a point of disagreement with Hegel. Hegel presents the dialectic of concepts as moving by way of necessary connections immanent to thought itself. For Adler, the contradiction that moves science forward is a contradiction between theory and data. Further, for Hegel the dialectical science of reason is distinct from the empirical sciences of the understanding. In Adler's view, the dialectic exists as a partial philosophy of science, but not as an alternative to empirical science. For Adler, the dialectic is not a method that can be applied to solve theoretical difficulties. The advances in science characterized by the dialectic must be made on the basis of empirical observation and experimentation. There is no science of reason distinct from the sciences of the understanding.

Adler's philosophy of science was Neo-Kantian rather than positivist. Adler accepted the Kantian arguments for the necessity of a priori elements in the construction of a scientific theory. In this, his thinking appears to have been influenced by two kinds of considerations. First, he accepted the traditional Kantian arguments for the a priori character of the forms of sensibility and the categories as necessary to account for the possibility of scientific cognition. Second, he thought that Marxism rested upon an additional a priori category of social association. Adler argues that this category must be presupposed as given a priori if we are to account for the possibility of universal objective knowledge by the knowing subject and for the social nature of the individual consciousness.[59]

Adler's thinking here is obscure. He does not point to an explicit claim in Marx for the a priori nature of the concept of social association but, rather, claims that this concept functions as an a priori condition for social science. The basic idea seems to be that human experience is experience of a social world that cannot be reconstructed out of the atomistic experiences of individual subjects (witness the classical difficulties of the argument by analogy for other minds), and so must be assumed as given a priori to account for the social nature of experience.

The Austro-Marxists also accept Kantian moral theory as an a priori system of ethics.[60] But, unlike Bernstein, they do not use this moral theory as a foundation for an ethical socialism conceived an an alternative to Marxian scientific socialism. Bernstein's retreat to ethical socialism both followed from and supported his denial of scientific socialism. On the one hand, Bernstein had argued that the Marxian prediction of socialism had been empirically refuted by the facts. On the other hand, he held that moral responsibility presupposed a contra-causal freedom inconsistent with the historical materialist conception of history as a law-governed process. Bernstein's ethical socialism thus held both that socialism was impossible without the moral commitment of human beings to strive for it, and that this subjective factor was ignored by the materialistic theory of history presented by Marx.

Like many of the orthodox Marxist opponents of Bernsteinian revisionism, Adler argued that it was a simple misunderstanding of Marxism to suppose that it ignored the subjective role of ideas in bringing about socialism. The materialist theory of history was a positive theory of the coming of socialism. It sought to show that socialism was causally necessitated by the internal development of capitalism. However, it included the ideas of human beings as parts of the causal chain of events leading to socialism. In particular, the materialist theory of history recognized the class consciousness of the proletariat, with its ideological commitment to certain values and to socialism, as a necessary cause in the emergence of socialism from capitalism. The revisionist claim that Marxism ignored the subjective factor of human ideas was the result of supposing that the thesis of the ultimately determining role of economic forces precluded causal efficacy for human ideas. Supposing it is true that Marxism maintains that ideas are causally determined in the last resort by economic forces, this determinism is not a fatalistic determinism that would make history entirely independent of the ideas of human beings.[61]

This reply, based on the distinction between determinism in general and fatalistic determinism in particular, does get around the claim that Marxist theory ignores the causal role of ideas in history. However, it does not get around two deeper objections that were implicit in the revival of ethical socialism. The first is the traditional problem of the apparent incompatibility between determinism and moral responsibility. This traditional problem of philosophy is present within Marxism in terms of the tension between scientific socialism, as a causal theory of the inevitability of socialism, and revolutionism, as a moral commitment to bringing socialism about. In thinking that morality presupposes contra-causal freedom, Bernstein means to object not only to a fatalistic, but also to any deterministic, theory of history.

The second deeper problem concerns the moral justifiability of socialism. While socialism might be inevitable, as Marxian theory says it is, and while the proletariat may be causally determined to think that the coming of socialism is morally desirable, neither of these facts answers the question of whether socialism is morally valuable. Bernstein appears to have been bothered by both of these problems. Thus, he not only denies the Marxist theory of history but also demands a justification of the moral value of socialism.

The Austro-Marxists accepted the distinction between scientific claims and value claims that lies behind the second of these objections. They agreed that the causal prediction of socialism, and its being valued by the proletariat, say nothing about the true moral value of socialism. However, they did not accept the first objection, that morality precludes a causal theory of history. In taking this position the Austro-Marxists were closer to the historical Kant than Bernstein and others of the Neo-Kantians who rejected the possibility of a science of history. The historical Kant, of course, held that determinism rules the entirety of the phenomenal world, including the action of human subjects in history.[62] But it is not easy to see how the morally necessary freedom of the noumenal self is to be combined with the determinism of the decisions of the phenomenal self.

Though they reject the claim that morality precludes the historical materialist conception of history as a law-governed process, the Austro-Marxists nevertheless granted the need for some ethical supplementation of Marxism. They agreed with the Neo-Kantians and the positivists in drawing a sharp distinction between positive science and moral theory. As a positive science Marxism provided neither particular judgments of value nor a philosophical grounding for ethics.[63] Marxian science was of tremendous relevance for the key moral issues of the times, but this relevance presupposed a disposition to act morally and a commitment to some fundamental moral principle or principles. The Austro-Marxian conception of Kantian ethics is that it provides the fundamental moral framework necessary to supplement Marxism.

This point is brought out nicely in an example of Otto Bauer's.[64] Suppose, he said, that we are trying to persuade an unemployed worker not to function as a strikebreaker. We may appeal to the interests of the proletariat as a whole and argue that solidarity on the part of the workers is the only way to further the interests of the class within the context of a capitalist economy. The worker may understand this class interest and the need for solidarity, but may also argue that in this particular case, his interests are opposed to the interests of the class as a whole. Why, then, ought he to refrain from furthering his own interests in this particular case? Bauer argues that Marxism provides no answer to this question. On the other hand, the universalizability principle of Kantian ethics does give an answer.

While accepting the necessity of Kantian principles in accounting for the duty to be moral, the Austro-Marxists held that the Neo-Kantian socialists were wrong in thinking that Kantian ethics sufficed to show the moral value of socialism. In the first place, they pointed out that Kant himself surely did not argue for socialism as a consequence of his moral theory. The reason is that the value of socialism was not a question for Kant. It was not a question for Kant because the socio-historical development had not yet reached the stage at which that particular issue forced itself upon human consciousness. But even with the development of capitalism, and with it the development of the modern proletariat in its most distressed condition, without a scientific understanding of the causes of this distress, and the possibilities for its removal, the question of the moral value of socialism cannot be answered.

In short, granted the universal validity of the foundational moral principles proposed by Kant, moral questions remain historically relative to the whole socio-historical context. The key moral questions of a given time are determined by the specific human relations prevalent at that time and by the real possibilities for that historically specific stage of human development. As a science of history, Marxism clarifies the underlying class structure, the causes for the distress of the working class, and the possibilities for change. Given this understanding of the historical situation, socialism appears as the way to the realization of the Kantian command to treat everyone as an end. As a science, Marxism is not a moral theory. However, this science is clearly relevant to morality in the sense that without the kind of understanding it provides, moral theory remains a kind of empty and impotent wish for a better world. The key moral questions of the times—the distress of the working class, imperialism, and the threat of war—had their roots in the inner logic of capitalism. The tasks of moral education and moral improvement were better served by educating people to the scientific theory of Marxism than by educating them in the moral theory of Kant. In this sense, the Austro-Marxists staunchly resisted the effort of some revisionists to substitute the categorical imperative for the materialist theory of history.[65]

The Austro-Marxists' stress on the importance of Marxian science for questions of morality informs their political position. In particular, the Austro-Marxists remained committed to the necessity of a revolutionary transformation of the economic order. Having said this much, some clarification is needed as to just what is meant. A revolutionary transformation of the economic order might involve (a) a change in the dominant mode of production, (b) a rapid change in the dominant mode of production, or (c) a violent rapid change in the dominant mode of production. The revolutionary commitment of the Austro-Marxists (with the exception of Karl Renner) was to (a).[66] In effect this is a rejection of reformism as a goal for the movement.

The reformists thought that a program of reforms which left the private ownership of the means of production as the dominant mode of production would suffice to alleviate the suffering of the proletariat. Such a reform of capitalism was involved in the socialism of the Neo-Kantians Lange and Cohen.[67] It was also, in effect, the outcome of Bernsteinian revisionism that, while officially endorsing a fundamental change in the dominant mode of production as an ultimate end, put the achievement of that change in the distant future and directed the practice of the movement toward reformism and the development of a socialist base in cooperatives and trade unions. The Austro-Marxian political position differed from that of Bernstein and the reformists in placing the seizure of power by the proletariat for the purpose of imposing a change in the mode of production on the more or less current agenda of the movement. I say "more or less current agenda" because, first, no one among the Austro-Marxists thought that the gaining of power was imminent and, second, because the Austro-Marxists were open to the possibility that the revolutionary transformation of the mode of production might be a gradual, step-by-step process. Thus, for example, Otto Bauer talks about a "slow revolution" that would involve a patient construction of socialist institutions once the seizure of power had been achieved.[68]

This conception of a slow revolution has certain affinities with the viewpoint of Bernstein. Yet there are differences. We have already noted a difference with respect to the time frame involved. While both are gradualists, for the Austro-Marxists the basic transformation is nearer in time and essential for the formulation of what the socialist movement is about in the present. But there are other differences as well. For Bernstein, the gradual construction of socialism is approached through the development of cooperatives, trade unions, and municipal socialism, within the context of a dominant capitalist mode of production. For the Austro-Marxists, again with the exception of Renner, the gradual transformation is conceived as a process that occurs after the seizure of power by the proletariat.

Both Bernstein and the Austro-Marxists held a vision of some kind of decentralized socialism as the ultimate aim. But the Austro-Marxists, unlike Bernstein, saw such an ultimate socialism as following from, rather than preceding, the seizure of central power by the proletariat. Thus, while Bernstein flatly rejects the idea of a dictatorship of the proletariat, the Austro-Marxists continue to see the dictatorship of the proletariat as a necessary step for the construction of the socialist future. In part Bernstein's rejection of the dictatorship of the proletariat rests upon his understanding of "dictatorship" as incompatible with the principle of government by the people through elections based on universal suffrage.[69] The Austro-Marxists remain committed to such electoral forms of government, and consequently at least part of the difference here is a verbal disagreement.[70] But the issue goes deeper. Bernstein rejects the road to socialism via control of the central governmental power. It is precisely this road that the Austrians intend to follow.

Finally, the Austro-Marxist commitment to "revolution" differs from Bernstein in that the Austro-Marxists remain open to the possibility that the revolution would be a rapid or even a violent transformation. Where Bernstein's anti-dialectical viewpoint led him to argue against the possibility of a rapid transformation of the mode of production, and to reject revolutionary violence, the Austro-Marxists remained open to the possibility of historical leaps and to armed struggle, at least of a defensive nature.[71]

EMPIRIO-CRITICAL MARXISM

The revisionism of Bernstein and the Neo-Kantianism of Max Adler represent two responses of Social Democrats to developments in academic philosophy of science. Adler's philosophical position was adopted by Bauer and Hilferding, and for this reason can rightly be said to be the position of Austro-Marxism as a definite tendency within Marxist thought. The fundamental idea underlying this position was that Marxism, correctly understood as descriptive social science, was compatible with the modern critical philosophy of science.

This same fundamental conception lay at the foundation of empirio-critical Marxism. Where Max Adler had sought to supplement Marxian social science with Neo-Kantian philosophy of science, the empirio-critical Marxists sought to supplement Marxian social science with the empirio-critical, positivist philosophy of science of Ernst Mach and Richard Avenarius. Empirio-critical Marxism had its adherents within the Austrian party: Friedrich Adler in particular and, less clearly, Karl Renner.[72] But, as a tendency within the International Social Democratic Movement, empirio-critical Marxism was most strongly influential in Russia, where Aleksandr Bogdanov, Anatoly Lunacharsky, and V. A. Bazarov represented the position among the Bolsheviks and P. S. Yushkevich and N. V. Valentinov represented the position among the Mensheviks.

Empirio-critical Marxism was anti-metaphysical. Following Mach, it sought to avoid both materialism and idealism as metaphysical theories that went beyond the bounds of sensory experience. The epistemologically given consisted in the Machian "elements" of experience. A thing was simply an ordered group of such elements. Experience was ontologically neutral. The task of science was to develop descriptive laws concerning the regularities of experience that could be used in the explanation and prediction of experience. Scientific theories and the entities they introduced into our thinking were instrumentally useful for the prediction and control of our experiences, and hence for the satisfaction of our biological needs. They enabled us to bring together a mass of different experiences into an ordered pattern and thus satisfied the principle of economy of thought. However, our theory must not be thought to reflect any real objects existing external to and independent of experience. And, with the advance of science, the theories we now find useful would be set aside in favor of more comprehensive theories that better satisfy the principle of economy.

The empirio-critical Marxists argued that Marxian social science was fully compatible with the Machian philosophy of science. The materialist theory of history was viewed as independent from philosophical materialism, which asserted the existence of material objects external to and independent of experience. The Marxist theory of history, the specific theory of the historical development of capitalism, and the prediction of socialism were understood as theories about the world given in experience. The laws of capitalist development, and the general laws of historical development, were viewed as instrumentally useful organizations of our experience. As such a social science, Marxism was derived from experience and testable by experience, but also rooted in the biological needs of human beings, as is all science. In this biologically instrumentalist view of science, the empirio-critical Marxists claimed to find a point of contact between Machian philosophy of science and Marx. They pointed to the connection between theory and practice sketched by Marx in his "Theses on Feuerbach" as evidence for such an instrumentalist view of theory in Marx.[73]

Empirio-critical Marxism had much in common with Neo-Kantian Marxism. Both positions held that Marxism was descriptive social science, was not a philosophical position, and, in particular, did not depend upon philosophical materialism; that as social science Marxism did not provide nor depend upon a theory of ethics; that the laws constituting Marxian social science were derived from experience and were testable by experience; and that, consequently, Marxism was compatible with the critical epistemology of the then current philosophy of science. Where the empirio-critical Marxists differed from the Neo-Kantian Marxists was in their recourse to Mach rather than to Kant, and consequently in their rejection of the Kantian claims regarding the a priori status of the fundamental categories of science.

This empirio-critical Marxism had gained support within Bolshevism nearly from the time of its origins in the 1903 split in the Russian Social Democratic Labor Party (RSDLP). Early in 1904, Bogdanov published the first part of his *Empiriomonism*. He rejected the materialism of Georgi Plekhanov, and the dialectics of Hegel, as empty and prescientific metaphysics.[74] He saw the valuable core of Marxism in the social science of historical materialism, and he sought to supply a philosophical foundation for this social theory. The foundation he constructed drew from the empiriomonism of Mach and Avenarius. It claimed to provide a purely scientific framework, neutral with respect to the metaphysical question of materialism and idealism. It stressed the foundation of science in experience, and viewed science as the inductive search for instrumentally useful correlations between such neutral experiences. In fact, Bogdanov's philosophical system was his own original framework. In several respects, especially in its substitution of a social subject for the individual subject of Mach; in its claim that the Machists erred in seeing the subject as passive in experience; and in its claim that even natural laws were, in some sense, subject to the will of the social subject, Bogdanov's system significantly departed from the position of Mach.[75]

In fact, Bogdanov was only one of a number of leading Bolsheviks who were interested in updating Marxism with positivist philosophical foundations. He is important both for the importance of his theoretical works and for his relatively high position in Bolshevik affairs.[76] Among others, the new positivism appealed to the novelist Maxim Gorky and to Lunacharsky, who become the Bolshevik minister of culture during the 1920s. The importance of these positivist Bolsheviks can be seen from the fact that, together with Lenin, Gorky, Bogdanov, and Lunacharsky constituted the editorial board of the Bolshevik newspaper *Vperyod*, formed when the split in the RSDLP left the Mensheviks in control of the party newspaper, *Iskra*.[77]

SCIENTIFIC SOCIALISM AS THE MARXISM OF THE SECOND INTERNATIONAL

Bernsteinian revisionism, Austro-Marxism, and empirio-critical Marxism were responses within Social Democracy to developments in academic philosophy of science in the late nineteenth century. The rejection of philosophical materialism as metaphysics, by the critical philosophy of science common to Neo-Kantianism and empirio-critical positivism, threatened the orthodox Marxism of the day, which viewed Marxism as rooted in the mid-nineteenth-century materialism of Ludwig Feuerbach and the scientific materialists.[78] Bernstein agreed that Marxism was infected with a metaphysical philosophical dogma and concluded that it must be purged of this outdated philosophical baggage. The Austro-Marxists and the empirio-critical Marxists held that Marxism as science was independent of philosophical materialism, and hence resisted the revisionism of Bernstein.

With Bernstein, little if anything of Marxism remained. With the Austro-Marxists and the empirio-critical Marxists, Marxian economics and the materialist theory of history remained. In spite of differences in ethics, all three positions rejected philosophical materialism, accepted the new critical philosophy of science, thought that Marxism did not provide a philosophical position, and held that what was of value in Marxism was pure social science. In this last judgment, the three positions are also in agreement with the "orthodox" Marxism of Kautsky.

It is this shared view of what is valuable in Marxism as social science, and not philosophy, that forms the common ground of the various Marxisms of the Second International. This common ground was very much a product of the times. One has only to consider the highly philosophical interpretations of Marxism advanced by Engels in *Anti-Dühring* and *Ludwig Feuerbach* to see how quickly and to what an extent developments in philosophy were felt within the Social Democratic Movement. To be sure, Engels also considered Marxism as providing a positive social science, but he understood this within the context of dialectical materialism, as a philosophical viewpoint with its own perspective that is quite different from the critical philosophy of science of positivism and Neo-Kantianism.

It is from this perspective that Lenin developed his criticism of the Marxism of the Second International. He argued that it was incompatible with the philosophical position of Marx, that it was philosophically mistaken, that it was the result of the influence of bourgeois philosophy on Social Democracy, that it served the interests of the bourgeoisie, and that it led to serious political mistakes.

NOTES

1. For evidence of Neo-Kantian philosophical influences on revisionist Social Democrats, see Pierre Angel, *Eduard Bernstein et l'évolution du socialisme allemand* (Paris: Marcel Didier, 1961), p. 192. Also see Matthäus Klein et al., *Zur Geschichte der Marxistisch-Leninistischen Philosophie in Deutschland* (Berlin: Dietz Verlag, 1969), vol. 1.2, pp. 293ff.; Bo Gustafsson, *Marxismus and Revisionismus* (Frankfurt am Main: Europäische, 1972), p. 112; Erika Rilki, *Der Revisonismus* (Zurich: Girsberger, 1936), p. 115.

2. Here I refer to Kautsky's prewar views. In his *Karl Kautsky and the Socialist Revolution 1880–1938* (London: NLB, 1979), p. 15. Massimo Salvadori suggests that Kautsky changed his thinking on this after the war. (See pp. 30–34 for Kautsky's prewar views.)

3. Karl Kautsky, *Ethics and the Materialist Conception of History*, translated by John Askew, 4th ed. (Chicago: Charles Kerr), pp. 202–203.

4. Ibid.

5. Ibid., pp. 116–117.
6. Ibid., pp. 178–201.
7. Ibid., p. 201.
8. Ibid.
9. Ibid., pp. 202–203.
10. Kai Nielsen, "Introduction" in *Marx and Morality*, edited by Kai Nielsen and Steven Patten (Guelph: Canadian Association for Publishing in Philosophy, 1981), p. 4, says, "While both Kautsky and Plekhanov accepted the Kantian fact/value distinction, they, like Marx, resolutely refused to ground socialism in either moral philosophy or morality."
11. Kautsky, *Ethics*, pp. 116–117. For further background on this point, see Helena Sheehan, *Marxism and the Philosophy of Science* (Atlantic Highlands, NJ: Humanities, 1985), pp. 78–79.
12. Kautsky, *Das Werden eines Marxisten* (1930), quoted in Salvadori, *Karl Kautsky*, p. 23.
13. Kautsky, *Ethics*, p. 118.
14. Sheehan, *Marxism*, pp. 78–79.
15. Kautsky, quoted in Sheehan, *Marxism*, p. 78.
16. Klein et al., *Geschichte*, p. 316.
17. Sheehan, *Marxism*, pp. 79, 80.
18. Quoted in T. I. Oizerman. "The Problem of the Scientific Philosophical World-Outlook," in *Philosophy in the USSR: Problems of Dialectical Materialism* (Moscow: Progress, 1977), p. 22.
19. Salvadori, *Karl Kautsky*, p. 63.
20. For a discussion of the ideological significance of Bernstein in contemporary German politics, see Christoph Butterwege, "Der Bernstein-Boom in der SPD," *Blätter für deutsche and internationale Politik* 23, no. 5 (1978): 579–592.
21. Gustafsson, Angel, and Rilki agree in seeing a significant Fabian influence on Bernstein, as does Peter Gay, in his *The Dilemma of Democratic Socialism* (New York: Columbia University Press, 1952). Erika König. *Vom Revisionismus zum "Demokratischen Sozialismus"* (Berlin: Akadamie, 1964), p. 46, attributes Bernstein's philosophical revisionism to fear of the revolutionary consequences of the Hegelian dialectic. This is a common charge in Marxist-Leninist treatments of revisionism. Gustafsson *Marxismus*, (p. 317) claims that most of the revisionist intellectuals were of bourgeois origins. Rilki (*Revisionismus*, p. 25) claims that the intellectuals were divided between revisionists and radicals, and notes the popularity of revisionism among union, cooperative, and SPD functionaries of working class origins.
22. Eduard Bernstein, *Evolutionary Socialism* (New York: Schocken, 1963), pp. 196–197, 217–219.
23. Ibid., p. 49. Cf. Gustafsson, *Marxismus*, p. 110; Gay, *Dilemma*, p. 140; Angel, *Eduard Bernstein*, pp. 193–194.
24. Bernstein, *Evolutionary Socialism*, pp. xxviii, xxiv, xxix, 97, 147, 148.
25. Ibid., pp. xxvi–xxvii (quoting Engels), 164.
26. Ibid., pp. xxvi–xxvii, 106.
27. Ibid., pp. 161–165, 167, 216–219, 221.
28. Ibid., p. 145.
29. Ibid., pp. 144, 161, 196–197, 217–218.
30. Ibid., pp. xxviii–xxix, 125, 217 note.

31. Ibid., pp. 100, 101 (note on Parvus), 108.

32. Ibid., pp. 109–134, 135–165.

33. Bernstein explicitly endorsed the call for a return to Kant (Angel, *Eduard Bernstein*, p. 193). He appealed to "Kant against Cant" in rejecting the Hegelian "dogmatism" of Social Democracy, compared his own work to Kant's critical assessment of received opinion, and commented favorably on the work of the Neo-Kantian F. A. Lange (*Evolutionary Socialism*, pp. 200 ff., 223, 224).

34. Bernstein, *Evolutionary Socialism*, pp. 210–212, 209. Rilki (*Revisionismus*, p. 38) quotes Bernstein as saying that the working class today fights for emancipation under the banner of Kant—not Hegel. Later (p. 48), she quotes Bernstein as saying that dialectics is the root of all errors in Marx.

35. Angel, *Eduard Bernstein*, p. 194.

36. *Evolutionary Socialism*, p. 1.

37. Ibid., pp. 9, 204–205, 211–212.

38. On Bernstein's Kantian metaphysics, see Gustafsson, *Marxismus*, pp. 109–111; Angel, *Eduard Bernstein*, pp. 194–197.

39. *Evolutionary Socialism*, pp. 11–13; Angel, *Eduard Bernstein*, p. 188.

40. *Evolutionary Socialism*, p. 18.

41. Cf. Angel, *Eduard Bernstein*, p. 197.

42. *Evolutionary Socialism*, p. 15; A. Angel, *Eduard Bernstein*, pp. 186–187.

43. Gay, *Dilemma*, p. 140.

44. *Evolutionary Socialism*, p. 5.

45. Harry Van der Linden, *Kantian Ethics and Socialism* (Indianapolis: Hackett, 1988), maintains that Cohen clearly goes beyond liberalism in calling for "the transformation of the corporation into the cooperative." If Van der Linden is correct on Cohen's socialism, Bernstein is closer to Cohen than I thought when writing this.

46. Rosa Luxemburg, "Reform or Revolution?" in *Rosa Luxemburg Speaks*, edited by Mary-Alice Waters (New York: Pathfinder, 1970), pp. 84–85; cf. König, *Revisionismus*, p. 51, and Angel, *Eduard Bernstein*, p. 195. Angel (p. 197 n. 101) notes that Bernstein defended Kantian ethics against Anton Pannekoek's charge that it was a class-based morality.

47. In response to the charge of materialism, Max Adler, the most philosophical of the Austro-Marxists, maintained that "there is no need for us [Marxists] to become victims of naturalism," and held that "Marx stands in the same relation to Kant as does Newton." And, against Kautsky, the Austro-Marxist Otto Bauer argued that "we cannot renounce Kant's critique of reason; time and again it is able to protect us from the stream of scepticism unleashed by the enemies of the working class." *Austro-Marxism*, edited by Tom Bottomore and Patrick Goode (Oxford: Oxford University Press, 1978), pp. 75, 68, 84. For discussion of the Kantian epistemology of the Austro-Marxists, see Leszek Kolakowski, *Main Currents of Marxism* (Oxford: Oxford University Press, 1978), vol. 2, pp. 241, 258–268. See also Helga Grebing, *Der Revisionismus* (Munich: Beck, 1977), pp. 50–51.

48. Grebing, *Revisionismus*, p. 53; Kolakowski, *Main Currents*, vol. 2, p. 241.

49. Bottomore and Goode, eds., *Austro-Marxism*, pp. 72, 64.

50. Ibid., p. 83 on Bauer; pp. 25, 90 on Hilferding.

51. Horst Klein et al., *Philosophischer Revisionismus* (Berlin: Dietz, 1977), pp. 277–278.

52. Bottomore and Goode, eds., *Austro-Marxism*, p. 11. In a similar vein, Bauer

could speak of Kant and Mach as points of departure for Austro-Marxism (ibid., pp. 45, 50).

53. Kolakowski, *Main Currents*, vol. 2, pp. 268–269. On Bauer on modern science and materialism, see Bottomore and Goode, eds., *Austro-Marxism*, pp. 49–50.

54. Bottomore and Goode, eds., *Austro-Marxism*, pp. 48, 93.

55. Rudolph Hilferding, *Finance Capital* (New York: Routledge, Chapman and Hall, 1985).

56. Renner's discussion of state regulation of the economy provided another example of this kind of argument within the work of the Austro-Marxists. Renner understood his work as an application of true Marxist theory to a more complex empirical reality. See Bottomore and Goode, eds. *Austro-Marxism*, pp. 95–96, 93.

57. Grebing, *Revisionismus*, p. 55; Kolakowski, *Main Currents*, vol. 2, pp. 271–272.

58. Bottomore and Goode, eds., *Austro-Marxism*, pp. 75–76; Kolakowski, *Main Currents*, vol. 2, pp. 271–272; Grebing, *Revisionismus*, p. 55; Sheehan, *Marxism*, pp. 86–87.

59. Bottomore and Goode, eds., *Austro-Marxism*, pp. 16, 65–66, 70, 78; Grebing, *Revisionismus*, p. 50; Kolakowski, *Main Currents*, vol. 2, pp. 262–268.

60. Kolakowski, *Main Currents*, vol. 2, pp. 274–276.

61. Bottomore and Goode, eds., *Austro-Marxism*, pp. 67 (Adler), pp. 81–83 (Bauer).

62. Bauer makes this point himself (Bottomore and Goode, eds., *Austro-Marxism*, p. 83); Grebing, *Revisionismus*, p. 54.

63. The view of Marxism as value-free social science can be found in Hilferding's Preface to *Finance Capital* (quoted in Sheehan, *Marxism*, pp. 88–89). On Bauer, see Bottomore and Goode, eds., *Austro-Marxism*, pp. 81–83. Adler held the same view prior to the war but may have amended it after the war. Cf. Kolakowski, *Main Currents*, vol. 2, pp. 274–275; and Bottomore and Goode, eds., *Austro-Marxism*, p. 64.

64. Kolakowski, *Main Currents*, vol. 2, p. 275.

65. Bottomore and Goode, eds., *Austro-Marxism*, pp. 83–84.

66. Ibid., p. 6 note 18. On Renner's non-revolutionism, see also Kolakowski, *Main Currents*, vol. 2, p. 276.

67. Again, I must note Van der Linden's contrary view of Cohen. Still, the Austro-Marxists would share the orthodox Marxist rejection of Cohen's cooperativist socialism as a form of Lassalleanism.

68. Bottomore and Goode, eds., *Austro-Marxism*, pp. 26, 38–39.

69. *Evolutionary Socialism*, p. 146.

70. Kolakowski, *Main Currents*, vol. 2, pp. 243, 279.

71. See Bottomore and Goode's Introduction to *Austro-Marxism* (pp. 40–44) for a brief account of the failed civil war in Austria in 1933.

72. Friedrich Adler for a time taught physics at the University of Zurich before devoting himself full time to work for the Austrian SPD. He served briefly as editor of *Der Kampf*, the leading journal of the Austro-Marxists. An opponent of the war, he assassinated the wartime prime minister, Count Stürgkh. He wrote *Ernst Machs überwindung der mechanischen Materialismus* in 1918. On Adler and Renner, see the biographical notes in Bottomore and Goode, eds., *Austro-Marxism*. On positivist influences on them, see Horst Klein et al., *Philosophischer Revisionismus*, pp. 277–278.

73. For overviews of the basic ideas of empirio-critical Marxism, see Kolakowski, *Main Currents*, vol. 2, pp. 432–441; Sheehan, *Marxism*, pp. 124–126; and S. V. Utechin, "Philosophy and Society: Alexander Bogdanov," in *Revisionism: Essays on the*

History of Marxist Ideas, edited by Leopold Labedz (New York: Praeger, 1962), pp. 118–125. For a more detailed study of the empirio-critical Marxism of Bogdanov, see K. M. Jensen, *Beyond Marx and Mach: Aleksandr Bogdanov's Philosophy of Living Experience* (Dordrecht: Reidel, 1978). It should also be noted that Neo-Kantianism found support among some Russian Marxists, including Struve, Mikhail Bulgakov, and Nikolai Berdiaev. On these Russian Neo-Kantian Marxists, see Kolakowski, *Main Currents*, vol. 2, pp. 362–373; Gustafsson, *Marxismus*, pp. 291–312; and Christian Gneuss, "The Precursor: Eduard Bernstein," in *Revisionism*, edited by Leopold Labedz (New York: Praeger, 1962), pp. 38–41.

74. Jensen, *Beyond Marx and Mach*, pp. 102–109. George Katkov, "Lenin as Philosopher," in *Lenin: The Man, the Theorist, the Leader*, edited by Leonard Schapiro, Peter Reddaway, and Paul Rosta (New York: Praeger, 1967), pp. 72–73, cites even earlier work by Bogdanov.

75. Ibid., pp. 120–121 on voluntarism; p. 49 on individualism; pp. 78–79, 124, 143 on activist epistemology.

76. According to Katkov ("Lenin as Philosopher," p. 76), he shared control of certain illegal Bolshevik funds with Lenin and L. B. Krasin.

77. Richard Appignanesi and Oscar Zarate, *Lenin for Beginners* (New York: Pantheon, 1978), p. 73.

78. David Riazanov, writing in the 1920s, remarked that Wilhelm Liebknecht, the leader of the German SPD, perhaps personally closest to Marx, constantly confused the materialism of Marx with the materialism of Ludwig Büchner and Jacob Moleschott (Sheehan, *Marxism*, p. 105). See Frederick Gregory, *Scientific Materialism in Nineteenth Century Germany* (Dordrecht: Reidel, 1977), for a study of this mid-century materialism.

2

The Critique of Vulgar Marxism

> Bourgeois professors of philosophy reassured each other that Marxism had no philosophical content of its own—and thought they were saying something important *against* it. Orthodox Marxists also reassured each other that their Marxism by its very nature had nothing to do with philosophy—and thought they were saying something important *in favour* of it. There was a third trend. . . . It consisted of those "philosophizing socialists" of various kinds who saw their task as that of "supplementing" the Marxist system with ideas from *Kulturphilosophie* or with notions from Kant, Dietzgen or Mach, or other philosophies. Yet precisely because they thought that the Marxist system needed philosophical supplements, they made it quite clear that in their eyes too Marxism in itself lacked philosophical content.[1]

With these words, Karl Korsch describes the Marxism of the Second International. His description fits with the analysis of the Marxisms of the Second International developed in Chapter 1. What was common to orthodox Marxists, revisionists, supplementationists, and external critics of Marxism alike was the conviction that Marxism stood as (good or bad) social science and that, in itself, it was devoid of philosophical content. Korsch deplored this narrowing of Marxism to social science. The scientific Marxism of the Second International was a vulgar Marxism. Its truncated Marxism was incapable of understanding the world around it, and thus incapable of wisely guiding political practice. Vulgar Marxism was theoretically degenerate and politically disastrous.

In the period immediately following World War I and the October Revolution, a number of Marxist thinkers developed similar criticisms of the vulgar Marxism of the Second International. In the Great War, it was argued, capitalism confirmed its Marxist critics. Unable to survive without imperialist expansion, the various capitalist states, each in the service of indigenous capital, launched a war of unprecedented barbarism. Objectively the conditions were ripe for proletarian revolution. What was lacking was the political leadership necessary for such a revolutionary struggle. In the revolutionary crisis, the leaders of the Second International were lost and impotent. Whatever their subjective intentions may have been, objectively speaking, their lack of leadership was a betrayal of the working class.

How was this failure of leadership to be understood? Critics of vulgar Marxism argued that the wholesale failure of leadership could not be explained as the result of accidental or individual circumstances. They argued that, in part at least, this political failure had roots in the philosophical shortcomings of vulgar Marxism. In this attempt to trace the political failure of the Second International to its philosophical roots, the critics of vulgar Marxism were in fundamental agreement. But, in their analysis of the philosophical sources of the political error, there was fundamental disagreement among the critics.

Basically, two understandings of the failure of vulgar Marxism developed in the period following 1920. One of these is the understanding of Marxist-Leninism. The contours of this Leninist critique of vulgar Marxism were clearly and sharply developed in the writings of Lenin and in the political struggles associated with the formation of the Third International. The other understanding of the failure of vulgar Marxism grows out of a tendency in Marxist philosophy that I have called "humanistic Marxism." The nature of humanistic Marxism, its differences from Marxist-Leninism, and the distinctive nature of its critique of vulgar Marxism are less clearly defined. In part this is due to the fact that humanistic Marxism, which grows out of the work of several thinkers, lacks the authoritative hand of a single author. In part, too, this lack of clarity can be traced to the efforts of two of the leading humanistic Marxists, Georg Lukács, and Antonio Gramsci, to remain within the Marxist-Leninist fold of the Third International. Nevertheless, by now it is apparent that humanistic Marxism exists as a distinctive current within twentieth-century Marxist philosophy. It is my view that Marxist-Leninism and humanistic Marxism have provided the major alternatives in Marxist philosophy in the period since World War I. Each has its origins in the postwar critique of vulgar Marxism. Understanding the nature of these origins throws light on the basic features of each standpoint.

THE LENINIST CRITIQUE OF THE MARXISM OF THE SECOND INTERNATIONAL

As we have seen, Central European attempts to synthesize Marxism with the most up-to-date currents in academic philosophy of science had their influence on the development of Marxism in czarist Russia. Neo-Kantianism formed an element in the "legal Marxism" of Nikolai Berdiaev and Peter Struve, who opposed the populism of the Narodniks as a reactionary utopianism ruled out by the scientific laws of historical development elaborated in Marx's historical materialism. And, as we have seen, positivism made significant inroads into both Menshevism and Bolshevism. It was the popularity of this positivistic Marxism that prompted Lenin to write his *Materialism and Empirio-Criticism*. And it is this work that stands as the central text in the Leninist critique of positivism.

Lenin's book appeared in 1909. It was intended as a Marxist and philosophical criticism of the positivism supported by other leading Bolsheviks. One central claim of the book is that the fashionable positivism of Ernst Mach and Richard Avenarius is, its claims of metaphysical neutrality notwithstanding, nothing more than a warmed-over version of the idealism of Berkeley and Hume. In addition, Lenin argues that this empiricist idealism cannot make sense of the elementary physiology of the organs of perception or of the dependence of consciousness upon states of the brain; that it is inconsistent with the scientifically established truth of the existence of the natural world prior to the existence of conscious beings; that only materialism can make sense of the growth of human knowledge; that the principle of simplicity favors materialism; and that positivism cannot make sense of the very idea of science as the attempt to discover the truth of the world outside us. Finally, Lenin argues that the new positivism leads to fideism in that it adopts an agnostic rather than an atheistic position with respect to the existence of a God transcedent to human experience. And for this reason, since belief in divine providence is apt to undermine revolutionary fervor, Lenin thought that positivism was politically reactionary.

In *Materialism and Empirio-Criticism*, Lenin's critique of positivism is focused on a refutation of the anti-materialist sensationalism of the positivists. The book purports to be a defense of materialism. A number of Lenin's critics have attempted to dismiss it as resting on an amateurish confusion of materialism and realism. To be sure, much of what Lenin has to say is primarily directed at realism and not at materialism. And there are some passages in which he appears to reduce materialism to realism: "For the *sole* 'property' of matter with whose recognition philosophical materialism is bound up is the property of *being an objective reality*, of existing outside our mind." And "The concept of matter . . . epistemologically implies *nothing but* objective reality existing independently of the human mind and reflected by it."[2] Numerous critics have pointed out that, on this criterion, Berkeley's God and Hegel's Absolute count as material objects.

Supposing that this is so, there is nonetheless an important disagreement with positivism implicit in the thesis of realism alone, since it marks a rejection of the instrumentalism of the positivists. However, a more sympathetic reading of *Materialism and Empirio-Criticism* suggests that for Lenin, material existence counted as the only plausible form of real existence outside human consciousness, and that a defense of realism was thus equivalent to a defense of materialism.

The chapter of *Materialism and Empirio-Criticism* dealing with the revolution in natural science and the supposed dematerialization of physics clearly involves a richer conception of matter than mere realism. I will consider whether the lines of argument mentioned above lay the basis for a reasoned defense of materialism in Part II.

In addition to his attack on positivism for its idealist metaphysics, a second line of attack on positivism stems from Lenin's conception of dialectics. In the unpublished *Philosophical Notebooks*, Lenin maintains that it is absolutely impossible to understand Marx's *Capital* without thoroughly understanding Hegel's *Logic*.[3] He sees the core ideas of Hegel's dialectic as the idea of the necessary connectedness of all aspects of the phenomena, and the idea of development by way of the necessary immanent emergence of new forms.[4] Lenin thinks that an understanding of this dialectical outlook is necessary in order to understand Marx's theory of capitalism because he sees Marx as showing how the fully developed contradictions of capitalism dialectically emerge out of his analysis of exchange.[5] Lenin thus sees Marx's scientific theory of capitalism as methodologically based on a distinctly dialectical derivation of the more fully developed contradictions from more elementary forms. In this respect, Lenin's analysis of Marxist science distinguishes this science from ordinary, nondialectical science.

Lenin also holds that a dialectical core distinguishes Marxist philosophy and politics from non-Marxist philosophy and politics. He sees dialectics as distinguishing Marxist materialism from the metaphysical materialism of his predecessors. Thus he says that the fundamental weakness of metaphysical materialism is its inability to apply dialectics to the theory of knowledge and to the reflection theory in particular.[6] In the Hegelian philosophy, Kant's sharp distinction between the world of appearance and the world of reality is denied. Reality appears in the appearance and the appearance is an appearance of reality. Lenin sees this as a way of avoiding the skepticism of Kantianism and of rescuing materialism from the Kantian critique of it. He conceives of the "phenomenal" appearance as an appearance of the material thing rather than as a subjective process entirely removed from the object. "Hegel perceives scepticism here in the fact that Hume and Kant do not see the *appearing* Thing-in-itself in 'phenomena,' divorce phenomena from objective truth, doubt the objectivity of cognition, remove, weglassen alles Empirische from the Ding-an-sich. . . ."[7] Metaphysical materialism is guilty of this separation of Thing-in-itself and appearance. Its realism is naive. Only a materialism that recognizes the dialectical connection between the material object and its reflection in consciousness is epistemically defensible.[8]

Lenin also connects the metaphysical weakness of a nondialectical perspective with political shortcomings. In the *Notebooks* this connection is made in terms of the earlier critique of empirio-criticism. This is the idea that positivism and Neo-Kantianism are fundamentally skeptical philosophies, and that this skepticism supports political reaction. Both maintain that the only possible knowledge is knowledge of appearances. Both deny the possibility of knowledge of an external, mind-independent reality. Lenin sees this skepticism as protecting religion from scientific criticism, however much the positivists might deny this.[9]

Another sort of connection between philosophical dialectics and politics is made in Lenin's criticisms of his political opponents, after the October Revolution, for their lack of a properly dialectical perspective. For example, in his reply to Karl Kautsky's criticism of the Bolshevik Revolution, Lenin attributes Kautsky's political rigidity, in clinging to electoral politics, to his undialectical perspective.[10] In Lenin's view, Kautsky had become trapped by the image of an electoral revolution to be accomplished by a gradual increase in electoral support for the party. He was unable to consider alternative paths to social democracy and, in particular, failed to see the necessity of revolutionary repression in the circumstances of the Bolshevik Revolution. While not denying that a peaceful electoral path to socialism might be correct in some circumstances, Lenin insisted that a properly dialectical point of view would understand that the correctness of the electoral path depends upon circumstances that might change. The dialectician would not fixate upon any one strategy. The dialectician would understand that the general laws of historical development discovered by Marxist social science are only models which are subject to the peculiarities of actual historical situations.[11] To be sure, the proletarian revolution marked an extension of democracy. But it was undialectically rigid and "one-sided" to interpret this general law as precluding revolutionary repression.[12]

In "Our Revolution," one of the last works he dictated before his death, Lenin presents this lack of dialectics as the fundamental theoretical weakness of "all the heroes of the Second International": "They all call themselves Marxists, but their conception of Marxism is impossibly pedantic. They have completely failed to understand what is decisive in Marxism, namely, its revolutionary dialectics."[13] Lenin goes on to consider the common charge that the Bolshevik Revolution in backward Russia violates Marx's law of historical development from feudalism to capitalism to socialism. He insists that this "law" must be "taken as a model only *mutatis mutandis*, only with certain amendments (quite insignificant from the standpoint of the general development of world history)."[14]

Lenin saw the opposition of Kautsky and other of the leaders of the Second International to the course of the Bolshevik Revolution as growing out of their undialectically rigid, and hence one-sided, conception of the working of this general law of historical development. The specific criticism raised here, that the "law" should be understood as conditional, illustrates part of what Lenin had in mind in criticizing the leaders of the Second International for their lack of revolutionary dialectics. A dialectical viewpoint would recognize the conditional status of the law. Failure to see this is due to the undialectically rigid manner of thinking that dominated the leaders of the Second International. Even here there are complications, since Lenin also appears to think that the law holds unconditionally for world development as a whole.

But there is another aspect of the matter as well. The dialectic is a "revolutionary" dialectic. A dialectical view of historical development comprehends the process as consisting in continuous evolutionary change, at times spurred rapidly ahead with qualitative leaps and discontinuities. In effect, Lenin agrees with those anti-Hegelian revisionists who see in Marx's Hegelian dialectics a dangerous revolutionism.[15] Whereas the revisionists sought to eliminate the dialectic, which gives rise to this revolutionism, Lenin sought to preserve it at all costs.

Lenin thus sees two fundamental threats to good Marxist politics deriving from academic philosophy of science. Neo-Kantianism and positivism had infected Social Democracy, with idealism on the one hand and with an undialectical perspective on the other. In *Materialism and Empirio-Criticism*, the threat of idealism is foremost in Lenin's mind, while in the later works the political dangers of an undialectical outlook are chief among his concerns.

A number of commentators have seen in this contrast not merely a difference of interest but also a fundamental and unresolvable difference in philosophical outlooks.[16] On this view, *Materialism and Empirio-Criticism* is read as a defense of a nondialectical, natural scientific materialism, and the *Philosophical Notebooks* as a dialectical humanism incompatible with the materialism of the earlier work. The contrast between these two views is thought to be particularly sharp with respect to questions of epistemology. In *Materialism and Empirio-Criticism*, Lenin adopts the reflection theory, which views the subject as essentially passive. In the *Philosophical Notebooks*, it is argued, Lenin recognizes the active role of the subject in the process of cognition, and that this recognition makes untenable any materialism of the sort defended in the earlier work.

It is certainly true that dialectics plays a more prominent role in the *Notebooks*, and there is even one passage in them in which Lenin says, "Plekhanov criticizes Kantianism (agnosticism in general) more from a vulgar-materialistic standpoint than from a dialectical-materialist standpoint," then goes on to suggest that in general "Marxists criticized (at the beginning of the twentieth century) the Kantians and Humists more in the manner of Feuerbach (and Büchner) than of Hegel."[17] It is possible that Lenin did mean to include his own earlier *Empirio-Criticism* in this remark. Further, in commenting on the difference between a vulgar-materialistic and a dialectical-materialistic criticism, he remarks that the former merely rejects Kantianism and agnosticism, while the later corrects them in the fashion of Hegel, "deepening, generalizing and extending them."[18] On the "two Lenins" thesis, what dialectical materialism recognizes as true in the Kantian system is its insistence on the active role of the subject in constituting the world of experience. But, it is argued, this activist epistemology is fundamentally at odds with the reflection theory and the concomitant materialism of *Empirio-Criticism*. The "two Lenins" thesis thus leads to the conclusion that the Lenin of the *Notebooks* came to reject the vulgar materialism of the Lenin of *Empirio-Criticism*.

Within Western Marxism, this version of the "two Lenins" thesis has been used to attack Soviet philosophy as un-Leninist, as un-Marxist, and as philosophically inadequate. Soviet philosophy is held to be un-Leninist because it fails to ascend to the philosophical level of the *Notebooks* and remains mired in the vulgar materialism of *Empirio-Criticism*. It is held to be un-Marxist because, it is argued, the philosophical insight achieved by Lenin in the *Notebooks* repeats the philosophical insight achieved by Marx in the first of the *Theses on Feuerbach*. It is held to be inadequate because, it is argued, it cannot be defended against Kantian epistemic criticisms of naive materialism.[19]

I will return to the question of whether Marx accepted the viewpoint of an activist epistemology and to the question of the philosophical adequacy of the reflection theory below.[20] Here I would like to comment briefly on the idea that the Lenin of the *Notebooks* rejects the Lenin of the *Empirio-Criticism*. The argument, as I have summarized it, turns upon construing the difference between a dialectical materialism and a vulgar materialism in terms of dialectical materialism's recognition of the active role of the subject in cognition and its rejection of the reflection theory. But there are a number of problems with this as an interpretation of the Lenin of the *Notebooks*. In the first place, if epistemological activism extends to the constitution of all possible objects of knowledge, it is difficult to see what materialism is left for dialectical materialism. For his part, Lenin seems committed to a robust materialism even in the *Notebooks*. There he clearly does adopt a dialectics of nature, which accepts the Hegelian law of the unity of opposites, and also endorses the view of change as arising out of the self-development of matter.[21] Second, nowhere in the *Notebooks* does Lenin explicitly reject the reflection theory. Indeed, he continues to defend it. He appears to endorse the empiricist theory of the origin of ideas.[22] He also offers a gloss on a passage from Hegel as profound and clever for showing that the laws of logic are the reflections of the object in the subject.[23] To be sure, there are warnings against an undialectical understanding of the reflection theory. It is said to be a mark of vulgar materialism that it fails to apply dialectics to the reflection theory.[24] But this is not a rejection of the reflection theory itself. "Cognition is the eternal, endless approximation of thought to the object. The *reflection* of nature in man's thought must be understood not "lifelessly," not "abstractly," *not devoid of movement*, *not without contradictions*, but in the eternal *process* of movement, the arising of contradictions and solution."[25] In this passage, both the concept of reflection and the concept of a nature that is reflected are retained. In this, and in the appeal to the idea of approximation of thought to object, the *Notebooks* remains in fundamental agreement with the earlier *Empirio-Criticism*.

There can be no doubt that Lenin thought dialectics of utmost importance. He called it the "essence" of the Marxist theory of knowledge.[26] But, as we have seen, Lenin did not believe that dialectics required a rejection of the reflection theory or of materialism. Nor is Lenin's appreciation of the Hegelian-inspired dialectic of Marxism limited to the late and unpublished parts of the *Notebooks*. In the early *What Is To Be Done?* he quotes a passage from Engels which states that without Hegel there would be no scientific socialism.[27] In *Marxism and Revisionism*, which was written in 1908, the same year that the earlier comments on Abel Rey in the *Notebooks* show Lenin dismissing criticism of the reflection theory, Lenin traces the philosophical roots of revisionism to the rejection of Hegelian dialectics.[28] Here the connecting link between the political error of the revisionists and their philosophical error turns on the distinction between revolutionary dialectics and evolutionary anti-Hegelianism. This is the same connection that we have encountered repeatedly in other theorists of the Second International, including Eduard Bernstein.

So, contrary to the "two Lenins" thesis, it cannot be argued that Lenin's appreciation of dialectics is a late insight, spurred perhaps by his meditation on the failure of the leadership of the Second International. It is true that Lenin did trace that failure to the undialectical perspective of that leadership. But this is, in effect, an extension of his own earlier analysis of the philosophical roots of revisionism to Kautsky and the centrists as well. For Lenin the disastrous failure of leadership was an unhappy confirmation of views he had developed earlier.

THE HUMANIST CRITIQUE OF VULGAR MARXISM

Lenin had tried to trace the roots of the political failure of the leadership of the Second International to its philosophical deficiencies. Humanistic Marxism originates in a similar attempt to come to terms with that failure. Like Lenin, the humanistic Marxists see this political failure as rooted in philosophical error. Like Lenin, humanistic Marxism locates the error in the regression from Hegelian dialectics to vulgar materialism, Neo-Kantianism, and positivism in philosophy. However, in its understanding of dialectics and the relation of dialectics to other philosophical problems, humanistic Marxism differs sharply from Leninism on a number of basic philosophical issues.

The classic works of humanistic Marxism are *History and Class Consciousness* by Georg Lukács, and *Marxism and Philosophy* by Karl Korsch. Both works appeared in 1923, and each attempted to take stock of the crisis and failure of German Social Democracy. Though they were outwardly supportive of Leninism and the politics of the Third International, both adopted positions that were at odds with Leninism on fundamental questions of philosophy. A third work, the *Prison Notebooks* of Antonio Gramsci, though written somewhat later (between 1929 and 1935), might also be considered a classic source of humanistic Marxism because of its independent origins and because of the similarity of its point of view to the earlier works by Lukács and Korsch. While there are some differences between the three works, there is clearly considerable common ground. It is this common ground that I understand as humanistic Marxism and that has influenced subsequent schools of Marxist thought, such as critical theory, praxis Marxism, and existential Marxism. In this section I will sketch some of the basic ideas of humanistic Marxism. In Part II, I will consider the relevant arguments in more detail.

Central to the humanistic critique of the "vulgar Marxism" of the Second

International is a rejection of the materialism of Kautsky and Georgi Plekhanov as a regression to a pre-Marxist form of materialism, untenable in the world of post-critical philosophy.[29] In this, the humanistic Marxists agreed with Neo-Kantian and positivist criticism of Marxism, and with those Marxists who rejected the scientific materialism of "orthodox" Marxism. But unlike the Neo-Kantian and positivist elements inside and outside the Marxist fold, the humanistic Marxists rejected the Neo-Kantian and positivist frameworks as philosophically unsatisfactory.

Unlike the Neo-Kantians and the positivists, the humanistic Marxists insisted on the value of the philosophy of Hegel. For the humanists, it was the abandonment of Hegel by the Second International that lay at the bottom of its degeneracy. The Hegelian philosophy was important for the humanists because they saw it as overcoming the opposition of half-truths that formed the terrain for bourgeois thought. Thus, for example, humanists thought that in Hegel the traditional opposition between idealism and materialism was overcome, at least implicitly. For Hegel the distinctions between being and consciousness, object and subject, are overcome in the philosophy of objective idealism. To be sure, in Hegel's own work this objective idealism is interpreted in terms of the coming to self-consciousness of Absolute Spirit. What was needed, and what Marx supplied, was an interpretation of Hegel's system in which the real subject/object of the historical process was humankind rather than Absolute Spirit. For the humanistic Marxists, it is this interpretation of the Hegelian Absolute in terms of humankind that distinguishes Marx's "materialism" from Hegel's idealism.[30] To interpret this materialism in terms of the ontological thesis of the real existence of an external material world is to miss completely the philosophical outlook of Marxism.

This interpretation of the Hegelian philosophy of history in human terms is basic to humanistic Marxism. As we have seen, at the ontological level this involves an attempt to transcend the whole debate between idealism and materialism as traditionally understood. Neither being nor consciousness, but rather the dialectical union of being and consciousness involved in human praxis, becomes the philosophical starting point for humanistic Marxism.

Adoption of this starting point leads humanistic Marxism to distinctive positions on a number of issues. Epistemically, it leads to an abandonment of a correspondence theory of truth in general, and in particular to an abandonment of the Leninist version of the correspondence theory in terms of reflection.[31] A correspondence theory of truth assumes a distinction between subjective conception and external object. But it is this naive separation of thought and being that humanistic Marxism rejects. Further, on the correspondence theory, truth becomes an either/or property of thought. Following Hegel, the humanistic Marxists favor a theory of truth that will allow for partial truths and degrees of truth. In developing his system, Hegel had tried to show what was true in each of the great philosophies that had preceded him, and how the truth of each of these was preserved in his own system. These elements of Hegelian epistemology are preserved within humanistic Marxism in the theory of the role of ideas in history.

Within the historical process, human beings have constructed different types of social structures, such as ancient slavery, feudalism, and capitalism. In each of these, human beings are cast in different roles with different duties, benefits, and expectations. Such social systems are meaningful wholes. The various specialized roles fit together. They presuppose each other and would not make sense in isolation from one another. A conscious recognition of the duties, benefits, and expectations connected with these roles, and a conscious acceptance of these roles as legitimate or unavoidable, are necessary for the social system to exist and reproduce itself. Thus, it is a mistake to separate social being and consciousness of that being. Consciousness is not something that exists outside social existence and corresponds or fails to correspond to that social existence. Rather, it is a necessary component of social existence itself. A historical mode of existence exists as a totality.[32] A genuine Marxist approach to understanding a social formation sees it in this way and understands the "truth" of the social consciousness that sustains the social formation in terms of its functional value for the total system. But, of course, this "truth" is a limited truth. It is historically determinate. In the revolutionary transformation of the social system as a whole, the limited nature of this truth is recognized and placed within the more adequate outlook of a more developed social consciousness.

Another idea common to the humanistic Marxists is a rejection of the view that these historically determinate "truths" are products of the material foundation of the social system. Humanistic Marxists are united in opposition to any form of economic determinism. In their view, one of the principal errors of vulgar Marxism is the view that the economic base causally determines the ideological superstructure. Such a view is mistaken for two reasons. First, it falsely distinguishes an "economic" realm and an "idealogical" realm as if these were self-subsistent entities when in fact that ideologized economy exists as a single totality.[33] Second, such views invariably mistakenly denigrate the role of ideas in history. The ideological superstructure becomes a kind of epiphenomenon that accompanies the real processes at work in the economic base. Such a conception leads to a fatalistic understanding of the historical process as independent of conscious human direction.[34]

The political consequences of this economic determinism are disastrous. The economic determinist believes that the historical process is completely determined by economic factors which are independent of human consciousness. Consciousness trails along as a kind of echo in men's minds of the real historical process. The coming of socialism is thus made independent of human consciousness. History is an automatic pilot. One need only wait for the economic forces to do their work. No direct struggle on the ideological terrain is necessary. Humanistic Marxists see this neglect of the "subjective" side as one of the central political failures of the Marxism of the Second International.[35]

Another political criticism of the Marxism of the Second International stems from a related philosophical conception of the dialectic. Like Lenin, the humanistic Marxists criticized vulgar Marxism for its undialectical perspective. On the surface, the humanist criticism on this point looks very much like the Leninist criticism. Like Lenin, the humanists contrast the revolutionary dialectic with the evolutionary outlook of Neo-Kantianism and positivism.[36] But whereas Lenin interprets the dialectic in terms of general laws governing all processes in natural and social systems, humanists reject the idea of a pure dialectics of nature.

This can be understood in both a weak and a strong sense. On the strong reading, dialectics is understood as pertaining only to the interaction between the subject and object poles in the historical process of human self-creation. This appears to be the position adopted by Lukács, at least in *History and Class Consciousness*. There he criticizes Engels' account of dialectics in *Anti-Dühring* for leaving out "the most vital interaction, namely the *dialectical relation between subject and object in the historical process*," and expressly rejects Engels' dialectics of nature.[37]

On the weaker reading, humanists reject a pure dialectics of nature only in the sense that their ontology rejects a pure nature existing independently of human consciousness. On this weaker reading, dialectic pertains to processes studied by the natural sciences, as well as to processes studied by social theory, but only because both social and natural processes exist as part of the same historical process. This appears to have been the position of Gramsci when, for example, he suggests that, out of opposition to the mechanistic understanding of Nikolai Bukharin, Lukács has fallen into the error of idealism in separating the natural and social sciences.[38] Korsch appears to hold a position similar to Gramsci's. He defends Engels against the charge of naturalistic materialism, but only by insisting that Engels consistently opposed any "wholly naturalistic" outlook which would naively accept the idea of a separation between thought and being.[39] Korsch appears to think that with adoption of a thoroughly dialectical outlook, even the natural sciences will be transformed.[40]

Although allowing for a dialectics of nature, Gramsci and Korsch agree with Lukács in seeing philosophically important differences between natural science and social theory, and this, too, distinguishes the humanist position from the Leninist unity-of (dialectical)-science position. The humanists advance a number of arguments designed to show that the method of the natural sciences is inappropriate for the development of social theory. It is claimed that social theory is statistical rather than causal, and that this precludes the natural scientific approach.[41] Also, it is argued that the method of the natural sciences is appropriate only to nonhistorical phenomena. Social systems are historical in character. They have definite origins, they undergo change, and they pass away. The method of the natural sciences, which seeks universal laws, is inapplicable to such historical realities.[42] It is argued that, unlike natural science, social theory is reflective in character. That is, the understanding of human beings about the social world is, as we have already seen, itself a part of the social system. Thus, social theory must account for itself in order to fully know its object, and in arriving at this account it fundamentally alters the object of its study.[43]

At bottom, the humanists' rejection of the model of the natural sciences rests on their conception of human beings as free agents. Determinism is false. Any view that sees human action as causally determined, whether by material and biological causes or by environmental forces, represents an alienated self-conception of the human being. Humanistic Marxism is a philosophy of praxis. The practical engagement in the world of human beings as agents in the historical process is the starting point for all philosophical reflection. It is this fundamental conception that underlies the humanist rejection of the method of the natural sciences as inappropriate for purposes of social theory.[44]

The agency theory at the heart of humanistic Marxism also provides the basis for its rejection of the fact/value distinction. For the Neo-Kantian and the positivist, there is a sharp distinction between trying to say how the world is and trying to say how the world ought to be. Descriptive theory, which tries to say how the world is, is grounded in factual claims that can be empirically confirmed. Normative theory, which tries to say how the world ought to be, cannot be empirically confirmed. It is either subjective and void of truth value, as it is with the positivists, or it requires a transcendental grounding, as in Neo-Kantianism.

From the viewpoint of humanistic Marxism, both of these standpoints rest upon an abstract separation of the subject and object that makes the practical-normative aspect of human existence inconceivable. If, as with the positivists, human beings are mere objects causally determined in their every behavior, then it becomes inconceivable how the moral "ought" can have any standing whatsoever. If, on the other hand, as with the Kantians, moral consciousness is relegated to a subject outside or behind the natural order of objects, it becomes inconceivable how the transcendental subject and the natural object become united in one person. The humanistic Marxists follow Hegel in seeing this whole problem as derivative from an abstract separation of subject and object. If we begin with the human being as free practical agent, the humanist maintains, the whole problem can be avoided.[45]

We will examine the various issues raised by this humanist critique in Part II of this study. My aim here has been simply to sketch some of the fundamental ideas of humanistic Marxism as it presents itself within the history of Marxist philosophy. From what has been said, it is clear that this current represents a way of understanding Marxism and the world that is fundamentally at odds with both Leninism and the Marxism of the Second International. For humanistic Marxism, the philosophical roots of Marxism lie in certain aspects of the philosophy of Hegel. But, for all of its hostility to scientistic Neo-Kantianism, humanistic Marxism also draws heavily upon the nonscientistic Neo-Kantianism of the Heidelberg School. This is clearly true of Lukács, who studies at Heidelberg in 1913 and 1914.[46] Similar influences were at work on Gramsci with his indebtedness to the philosophy of Benedetto Croce.

SCIENTIFIC MARXISM AND THE POSITIVIST CRITIQUE OF SCIENTIFIC SOCIALISM

With the formation of the Third International, based on the principles of Marxist-Leninism, Lenin's critique of the Marxism of the Second International acquired institutional significance. The splits in the socialist movement resulting from the war were perpetuated, deepened, and given different interpretations. At an institutional level, of course, the fundamental split was between the new Communist parties affiliated with the Third International and various non-Communist parties outside the Third International. For the most part, theoretical argument turned on the nature of the Bolshevik Revolution and the new Soviet system. Questions of political structure and of the proper understanding of a genuinely Marxist conception of the dictatorship of the proletariat were foremost. The connection of these political questions with philosophical positions was tenuous at best. Nevertheless, philosophical discussion persisted and in various quarters "scientific Marxist" alternatives to Marxist-Leninism continued to be voiced.

The more philosophically inclined leaders of the Second International maintained their philosophical convictions despite the Leninist critique. To the best of my knowledge, no attempt was made to respond to the charge that the political errors of the Second International stemmed from foundational errors in philosophy. Kautsky defended the positions he had taken during the war and blamed the political disaster on the intransigent positions of both the right and left wings of the SPD, which had forced the disastrous split in the Party. Though increasingly critical of the undemocratic politics of the Communists, he did not attempt to trace this political regression to philosophical mistakes of Lenin or his followers.[47] In a similar vein, other theorists of the Second International criticized the politics of the Communists without responding to the philosophical criticisms raised by Lenin. For the philosophical response to the Leninist critique, we must turn to other sources.

Science and the Socialism of Workers' Councils

Perhaps the clearest philosophical defense of positivistic Marxism is provided by the Dutch Marxist Anton Pannekoek, who is best known for his "left" opposition, along with Hermann Gorter and Henriette Roland-Holst, to the politics of the Comintern. While agreeing with the Leninists in rejecting trade unions and parliaments as the basic institutions of revolutionary struggle or socialist construction, the left-oppositionists also rejected the Leninist model, which gave the Communist Party supremacy in both processes. Instead of unions, parliaments, or the Party, the left-oppositionists looked to workers' councils, modeled on the Soviets of the Russian revolutionary experience, as the basic institutional units for socialist politics. But Pannekoek also wrote a sharp criticism of Lenin's philosophical views.

In *Lenin as Philosopher*, Pannekoek, who was trained as an astronomer, defends Mach and Avenarius against Lenin's criticisms of them in *Materialism and Empirio-Criticism*. He distinguishes between Marxist materialism and what he calls "middle-class materialism." Middle-class materialism is an ontological position characterized by the claim that nothing exists but matter, by the consequent denial of any truth to religion, and by a reductionist account of consciousness in terms of material processes in the brain. Marxist materialism is understood by Pannekoek as involving the social scientific perspective of historical materialism in which consciousness is socially determined. He views Lenin and Plekhanov as middle-class materialists rather than as Marxists: "The alleged Marxism of Lenin and the Bolshevist party is nothing but a legend. Lenin never knew real Marxism."[48]

Pannekoek sees Lenin's effort to defend middle-class materialism not only as un-Marxist but also as mistaken. He tries to show that Lenin's arguments for the most part turn on distortion and misunderstanding of his opponents. He accepts the view that materialism is epistemically naive, and follows Mach in adopting an instrumentalist view of scientific theory. He agrees with the viewpoint of Wilhelm Ostwald's energetics that modern physics has broken with ontological materialism. In place of the outmoded ontology of materialism, he adopts the "neutral" experientialism of Mach, which views both materialism and idealism as metaphysical transgressions against science. He construes relativity theory as confirmation of Mach's philosophy of science.[49]

Pannekoek does not dispute Lenin's claim that Machism and related doctrines in the philosophy of science serve reactionary interests: "The tendency of Machism, somehow parallel to revisionism in Germany, was to break the radicalism of struggle and solid unity of the party, in theory and in practice."[50] He offers an account of this in terms of the class position of the natural scientists and "the anti-materialist trends in the ruling class."[51] But Pannekoek does not take this reactionary import as evidence for the falsity of the new theory of knowledge: "Valuable progress in the theory of knowledge is garbed in mystical and idealistic forms."[52] Like Lenin, Pannekoek thinks it is important to attack reactionary interpretations of the new epistemology. However, he sees Lenin's attack as pre-Marxist. Whereas Lenin tries to defend an indefensible ontology, Pannekoek looks to recognition of the social determination of consciousness as a more effective antidote to mysticism. He argues that Engels' attempt, echoed by Plekhanov and Lenin, to refute Kant by appeal to technological success fails. Pannekoek claims that the real refutation of Kant lies in the historical materialist account of moral consciousness as a product of the social environment.[53]

Pannekoek's Marxism thus agrees with the Marxism of the Second International in its insistence upon the social science of the theory of capitalism and of historical materialism as the core elements of Marxism. Whereas middle-class materialism is primarily an ontological doctrine, "historical materialism is primarily the science of society."[54] And this social science is compatible with the neutralistic ontology and instrumentalist epistemology of Machian positivism.

Positivism and Soviet Philosophy in the 1920s

We have already noted the popularity of Machism within the Bolshevik ranks before the revolution. Despite Lenin's criticism of this tendency, its representatives continued to play a significant role in the philosophical controversies after the revolution. Aleksandr Bogdanov and V. A. Bazarov, two of the prominent targets of Lenin's attack, were members of the post-revolutionary Communist Academy. Anatoly Lunacharsky served as commissar of education. M. N. Pokrovsky was the first director of the Institute of Red Professors, and M. N. Liadov was appointed rector of Sverdlov Communist University.[55] Machism also appealed to many of the non-Marxist natural scientists within the Soviet Union. Thus the viewpoint continued to be publicly defended throughout the 1920s, both within the Bolshevik Party and outside it.[56]

To a large extent, the debate over Machism both inside and outside the Party was a continuation of the pre-revolutionary debate between the Machists and their materialist opponents. One new issue concerned the philosophical interpretation of relativity physics. Like Pannekoek, the Bolshevik Machists saw the new physics as a confirmation of Machian philosophy of science.[57] Some of their materialist opponents resisted relativity theory, in part because they agreed that it led to Machism. Other materialists, however, defended relativity theory, both in its own right as a physical theory and as fully consistent with philosophical materialism.[58] In general, the debates among the Marxists on this point reflected similar debates within the philosophical communities outside the Soviet Union.

Machism is the most clearly positivist of the contending points of view within Marxist philosophy in the Soviet Union in the 1920s. But other "positivistic" tendencies were present as well. S. Minin, lecturer at the Sverdlov Communist University, maintained that all philosophy was repressive ideology, advocated a complete elimination of it in favor of the special sciences, and called mention of "the philosophy of Marxism" by Plekhanov and Lenin slips of the pen.[59] Minin appealed to Comte to support his anti-philosophical viewpoint. An equally sweeping rejection of all philosophy, and of dialectical materialism in particular, was advocated by E. Enchmen on the basis of an appeal to Pavlov and physiological psychology.[60] While Enchmen appears to have been a materialist, Minin's position explicitly appeals to positivism for its foundations. And, in a broad sense, both positions are positivistic in their admiration for science and their hostility to philosophy. Neither gained much support from philosophers or natural scientists inside or outside the Party, though both were published in Bolshevik organs and Minin's position was commended in the *Bulletin of the Central Committee of the Ukrainian Communist Party*.[61]

Much more influential was the viewpoint of mechanistic materialism, which found support among both philosophers and natural scientists, and among both Marxists and non-Marxists. David Joravsky calls this the dominant position in Soviet philosophy in the early 1920s.[62] The mechanists were in agreement on a number of basic points. They were materialists. They were determinists. They maintained that the scientific method was the only path to knowledge. They maintained that the sciences were self-sufficient, and that nothing remained for philosophy but an attempt to sum up and integrate the results of the special sciences. And they maintained a reductionist stance in seeing all phenomena as ultimately determined by physical causes. Gustav Wetter, Joravsky, and Helena Sheehan each characterize this mechanistic materialism as a ''positivist'' position.[63] Of course, insofar as it is a materialism, the position is not ''positivist'' in the Machian sense, as Joravsky points out. However, it is clear that it shares a number of positions with the various historical formulations of positivism.

Of particular interest for our purposes is the position of the mechanists on the dialectic. I. I. Stepanov, editor of *Izvestiya* and a Central Committee member within the Bolshevik Party as well as a leading mechanist, identified a dialectical understanding of nature with a reductionist viewpoint.[64] Another leading mechanist, physicist and Party member, A. K. Timiriazev, understood dialectics in terms of a model of conflicting forces and the disturbance and restoration of equilibrium. In this he agreed with the Machist Bogdanov and the mechanist Nikolai Bukharin, who was, after Lenin, the chief theoretician of the Bolsheviks.[65] This mechanistic understanding of the dialectic is similar to the view of it held by Kautsky.

In the mid–1920s, this mechanistic materialism came under attack by the philosopher A. M. Deborin and others. Deborin had been a Menshevik philosopher before the revolution. At that time, he had criticized the Bolsheviks for their Machism and had defended the dialectical materialism of Plekhanov. After the revolution, he and another prominent Menshevik philosopher, L. I. Axelrod, were appointed to positions in philosophy at Sverdlov Communist University. During the 1920s, they were the most prominent philosophers in the Soviet Union.[66]

The central point of Deborin's critique of the mechanists was that they failed to appreciate the importance of the materialistically transformed Hegelian dialectic in the philosophical foundations of dialectical materialism. Deborin viewed the materialism of the mechanists as a regression to pre-Marxist versions of materialism. In this, at least, he agreed with the Machist Pannekoek. But whereas Pannekoek objected to the materialism of the mechanists, Deborin objected to the absence of the dialectic in their position. Deborin agreed with Hegel in viewing the special sciences as dependent upon a system of categories that could receive their grounding only in a purely philosophical and dialectical elaboration. In this sense he rejected as philosophically naive both the empiricist attempt to ground science in sensations and the positivist view of the sciences as self-sufficient.[67]

The mechanists replied to this critique with an attack of their own on the value of Hegelian dialectics. The positivist flavor of this critique is evident in a comment by Deborin's chief philosophical adversary, L. I. Axelrod: "Deborin says, for example: purposefulness is *transcended* by causality. This sounds chic and entirely Hegelian. But such terminology binds one to nothing and suggests no questions."[68] Another sort of positivist criticism of Hegel is made by Stepanov when he presents the contrast between the mechanists and the Deborinites as a struggle between empirical science and a priori scholasticism.[69] In a similar vein, Bukharin found a "theological flavor inevitably connected with the Hegelian formulation" of the dialectic and resisted the Deborinite appeal to Hegel.[70]

The debate raged throughout the second half of the 1920s. The termination of the debate in favor of the Deborinites was in part a function of factors other than the force of philosophical argument. The publication of Engels' *Dialectics of Nature* in 1925, and Lenin's *Philosophical Notebooks* in 1929, tended to support the Deborinite side in that each work stressed the distinction between dialectical and mechanistic materialism and each praised Hegel. However, neither of these publications was decisive. Mechanists were able to appeal to them and, in some cases, were willing to suggest that Engels' views were outmoded.[71] Another factor of some importance was Bolshevik distrust of non-Marxist scientists, who tended to side with the mechanist faction. The mechanists appeared to be pandering to bourgeois viewpoints rather than "drawing the line" against them.

The defeat of the mechanists was sealed in April 1929 at the Second All-Union Conference of Marxist-Leninist Scientific Institutions. There a resolution was adopted that supported Deborin's position and condemned mechanism for "substituting for revolutionary materialist dialectics a vulgar evolutionism, and for materialism, positivism."[72] The mention here of "vulgar evolutionism" foreshadows a political criticism of mechanism that became popular later. In December 1929, Stalin delivered a speech in which he connected his political struggle against the "right wing" policies of Bukharin and his followers with the philosophical struggle against the mechanists.[73] Bukharin had become the chief defender of the New Economic Policy (NEP) policies within the Party. He was particularly concerned to prevent any attempt to force the peasantry into collective farming, on the grounds that to do so would threaten the political alliance between the proletariat and the peasantry that was vital to the political survival of Soviet power.[74] In the course of defending his position, Bukharin had worked out an analysis of how socialism would gradually emerge out of the institutions of NEP life.

This gradualist evolutionism was opposed by the "left wing," which argued that action must be taken to build socialist institutions immediately. In 1929 the die was cast in favor of the policies of the left. After that time, the position of the Bukharinites became known as "rightist deviationism," and an argument was developed to link this political policy with the mechanistic philosophy. Essentially the argument said that mechanism lacked a dialectical perspective, and hence could not support sudden qualitative leaps in any developmental process. In contrast, a dialectical perspective would countenance such revolutionary leaps. Hence mechanism led to political evolutionism, and dialectics led to political revolutionism. The political turn adopted in 1929 was seen as just such a revolutionary advance.

Marxism Within the Vienna Circle

One of the central concerns of some of the logical positivists was the attempt to demarcate science from pseudoscience. A number of the proposed criteria of demarcation have been used to relegate Marxism to the latter category. We will consider some such criticisms below. However, not all of the logical positivists shared this view of Marxism. For some, Marxism fell on the side of genuine science. Some even went so far as to see a rational connection between the philosophical outlook of logical positivism and the political agenda of Marxism. For the most part, after World War II, the positivist critique of Marxism prevailed and the Marxism of the Vienna Circle was forgotten.

In a study of the Vienna Circle, Douglas Carr distinguishes between "right" and "left" wings. Moritz Schlick, Friedrich Waismann, Richard von Mises, Gustav Bergmann, and Victor Kraft formed the "right" wing, with Hans Hahn, Rudolf Carnap, and Otto Neurath on the "left."[75] It was Neurath who functioned as the political leader of the "left" wing, and it was he who was most clearly Marxist in his politics. His involvement in Marxist politics preceded his connection with the Vienna Circle. He was an active participant in the Spartacist movement in 1919.[76] In 1924 he organized the Verein Ernst Mach, which brought together scientists from various fields who were interested in social problems. Neurath supported the cogency of Marxism within this group.[77] When he and others from the Verein Ernst Mach entered the Vienna Circle, Neurath continued to support Marxism.

Two points are central to Neurath's position. First, Neurath considered Marxism as offering a genuinely scientific view of social processes. He held that "Of all the attempts at creating a strictly scientific unmetaphysical physicalist sociology, Marxism is the most complete," and that "Marxism is, to a higher degree than any other present-day sociological theory, a system of empirical sociology."[78] Second, Neurath argued for a connection between positivism in philosophy and Marxism in politics:

> "The opposition of the ruling classes [to logical empiricism], which usually finds support in the universities of capitalist countries, is explained sociologically above all, by the fact that empirical sociology, through its non-metaphysical attitude, reveals the meaninglessness of such expressions as "categorical imperative," "divine injunction," "moral idea," "superpersonal state," etc. In doing this it undermines important doctrines which are useful in the maintenance of the prevailing order.[79]

At best this argument shows that philosophical positivism leads to a denial of some alternatives to Marxism in social and political theory. To get from positivism in philosophy to Marxism in social science one needs, of course, the additional premise that Marxism is the best available empirical theory of society. As we have seen, Neurath defended the truth of this premise.

Neurath's Marxism resembles the Marxism of Bogdanov and Pannekoek in that it involves an explicit appeal to the positivism of Mach and an attempt to combine this positivism with Marxism understood as empirical social science. There is, however, one important point of difference. Whereas Bogdanov followed Mach's attempt to build science upon sensationalistic foundations, Neurath consistently rejected the phenomenalism implicit in this sensationalism. The debate with Carnap over *protokollsätze* is one side of this opposition to phenomenalistic sensationalism. In fact, Neurath's position in this regard did undergo some movement. For some time Neurath defended materialism in opposition to phenomenalism. Later, he became persuaded that materialism was itself a metaphysical thesis and adopted a physicalist alternative to materialism and phenomenalistic sensationalism, in which the central idea is that the empirical foundations of science are to be found in statements about physical objects that are metaphysically neutral.[80]

The extent to which others within the "left wing" of the Vienna Circle shared Neurath's Marxism is unclear. In some brief autobiographical remarks, Carnap describes his own views before World War I as "perhaps also socialist."[81] Several people who knew Carnap have testified to the influence of Neurath's political views on him. Maria Neurath, Neurath's widow, quotes Carnap as saying that his views in the 1920s were the same as Neurath's.[82] However, Carnap never publicly proclaimed any allegiance to Marxism, and his political actions are consistent with either Marxist or non-Marxist beliefs. Ludwig Wittgenstein is reported to have intended to move to the Soviet Union in the early 1930s, but this in itself provides no reason to think that he had any philosophical allegiance to Marxism.[83]

Positivist Criticism of Marxism

While most of the philosophers within the Vienna Circle refrained from following Neurath in his endorsement of Marxism, it is worth mentioning that, to the best of my knowledge, none of the philosophers within the Vienna Circle expressed public criticism of Marxism. The "positivist" identification of Marxism as one of the pseudosciences is a criticism made by philosophers outside the Circle. The "right wing" position within the Circle was primarily identified by its resistance to Neurath's claim that positivism in philosophy supported Marxism in social theory.[84] All that is necessary for this view is doubt as to the clear superiority of Marxism over all alternative social theories.

Of the various versions of the pseudoscience criticism, probably the most important is the critique of Marxism by Karl Popper, who, of course, rejects the verifiability condition as a solution to the demarcation problem in favor of the falsifiability condition. On the basis of this general solution to the demarcation problem, he formulates an argument for rejection of Marxism as pseudoscience. The argument is fairly straightforward. Popper sees Marx as arguing for the inevitability of socialism on the basis of his acceptance of a dialectical law governing all processes of development. He refers to a passage near the end of volume 1 of *Capital* where Marx says:

> The capitalist mode of appropriation, the result of the capitalist mode of production, produces capitalist private property. This is the first negation of individual private property, as founded on the labour of the proprietor. But capitalist production begets with the inexorability of a law of nature, its own negation. It is the negation of the negation.[85]

What follows capitalism is here characterized as the "possession in common of the land and of the means of production."[86] Popper sees Marx as here arguing for the inevitability of socialism by subsuming capitalist development under a dialectical law which claims that all developmental processes proceed by way of negation and negation of the negation. But, Popper argues, this supposed dialectical law is defective because it is unfalsifiable. "Any development whatsoever will fit the dialectic scheme; *the dialectician need never be afraid of refutation by forthcoming experiences.*"[87]

Popper mounts a more complex argument against Marxism in his critique of historicism. There Popper's critique turns not upon the importation of Hegelian metaphysics into Marxism but upon a methodological confusion underlying the whole of Marx's historical materialism. In his somewhat idiosyncratic conception of historicism, Popper distinguishes between anti-naturalistic historicists who deny the applicability of the methods of the natural sciences to social systems, and pro-naturalistic historicists who attempt to apply the method of the natural sciences to social processes. Popper views Marx as a pro-naturalistic historicist. In this regard, his interpretation of Marx is fundamentally at odds with humanistic Marxism. Nevertheless, while granting that Marx aims at social science, Popper argues that Marx is confused about the nature of empirical laws, and so fails in his effort to construct a genuinely scientific theory.

In particular, Popper argues that Marx confuses laws and trends.[88] A trend statement asserts the existence of some tendency over time, such as a tendency for population to grow. It is existential in its logical form. A law statement, on the other hand, is universal in its logical form. It makes no existential assertions. It "asserts the impossibility of something or other."[89] One should not conclude from this that trends are of no importance or interest to science. The explanation of trends is a proper aim for theory. An explained trend is a kind of empirical law. Thus, a law of the form "If conditions of kind *c* obtain, then there will be a trend of kind *t*" is perfectly acceptable to Popper.[90] His criticism of Marx is that Marx fails to understand that trends are dependent upon *c* conditions and hence confuses trends with laws:

There is, for example, a trend towards "an accumulation of means of production" (as Marx puts it). But we should hardly expect it to persist in a population which is rapidly decreasing; and such a decrease may in turn depend upon extra-economic conditions, for example, on chance inventions or conceivably on the direct physiological (perhaps biochemical) impact of an industrial environment.[91]

Popper argues that since Marx's whole theory of historical materialism rests upon the assumption of autonomous accumulation of means of production as a universal law of history, the theory of historical materialism is defective at its roots and cannot pass for genuine science.

Another positivist-inspired criticism of historical materialism has been advanced by H. B. Acton. Here the central complaint is that the key terms of historical materialism are so vaguely defined as to make the theory untestable.[92]

A related argument is that Marx's claim that the ideological superstructure is determined by the economic base is untestable, and hence defective as science, since historical materialism appears to make it true by definition. The economic base is identified by the means of production and relations of production that constitute it. Relations of production are defined in terms of ownership of the means of production. But "ownership" is a legal term, and legal relationships are supposed to belong in the ideological superstructure, according to Marx. If relations of production are defined as those which instantiate a certain legal relationship, then it will be trivially true by definition that an economic base including such relations of production will have an ideological superstructure in which the key legal relationships are recognized and maintained.[93]

Yet another positivist-inspired criticism aims at revealing the fundamentally religious and unscientific character of Marx's theory of history.[94] Fundamental to all of these views is the attribution to Marx of a Hegelian teleological perspective, which finds in the historical process a continual movement toward the goal of human emancipation. Where Hegel describes the movement of Absolute Spirit from primal, unmediated unity, through alienation, to unalienated, mediated self-awareness, Marx substitutes the sequence from primitive communism, through alienated class societies, to the overcoming of alienation in socialism. Marx's pretensions to science notwithstanding, his critics maintain that in Marx, just as in Hegel, what underlies this view of history is not science or any rational foundation, but a religious yearning for salvation. Marxism is at bottom a matter of irrational faith.

The criticisms I have considered so far have focused on the theory of history and in particular on the prediction of socialism. Other positivist-inspired criticisms have focused on the economics, in particular on the labor theory of value. One such criticism was advanced by Joan Robinson, who was in other respects quite sympathetic with Marxist economics. She argued that the labor theory of value was not a proper scientific theory at all. Rather, it was a metaphysical theory that had no significance for genuine science nor for what was valuable in Marx's own economics. Her position is most clearly stated in this passage in which she considers Marx's concept of value:

What is value and where does it come from? It does not mean usefulness—the good that goods do us. It does not mean market prices . . . nor is it a historical average of actual prices. Indeed, it is not simply a price; it is something which will explain how prices come to be what they are. What is it? Where shall we find it? Like all metaphysical concepts, when you try to pin it down it turns out to be just a word.[95]

The influence of logical positivism is apparent here, both in the general aim of distinguishing science from metaphysics and in the appeal to a theory of meaning to accomplish this.

A somewhat different criticism of Marx's theory of value aims at revoking the scientific credentials of his economics on the grounds that it violates the positivist distinction between descriptive science and normative theory. A clear example of this kind of criticism is provided by William Riker:

The inclusion of normative elements in a descriptive theory renders it scientifically unfit. This, for example, is where Marx's endeavor to be scientific went astray. The main proposition of *Capital* can be summarized as "Capitalism is theft"; and since theft, when divorced from a positive legal system, is a normative notion, verification of this sentence as a description of nature is impossible.[96]

Again, the positivist roots of this criticism in the idea of the nonverifiability of normative "judgments" is apparent.

MARXISM AT MID-CENTURY

With the renewal of the positivist critique of Marxism in the 1930s, 1940s, and early 1950s now directed at supposed Marxist science rather than philosophical materialism, the conception of Marxism as scientific socialism appeared to have been vanquished. In the socialist world, this positivist criticism was met with a philosophical critique of the adequacy of positivist philosophy of science. Marxist-Leninists defended the claim that Marxism was scientific socialism, but insisted that it was a kind of science both different from and superior to the kind advocated by positivist philosophy of science.

In the West, the defense of Marxism against positivist criticism was largely based upon the humanistic interpretation of Marxism according to which the positivist critique was fundamentally misplaced. The positivist critique viewed Marxism as defective science. The humanist reply was that Marxism was not defective science because it was not science at all. Rather, the humanists understood Marxism as emancipatory social theory. Unlike the Leninists, the humanistic Marxists did not contest the adequacy of the positivist philosophy of science. The humanists accepted this account as an adequate theory of the natural sciences and of social science modeled on the natural sciences. For the humanists, the error of the positivists was in maintaining that the only path to knowledge followed the method of the natural sciences. Emancipatory social theory did not conform to the method of the natural sciences, but it did provide knowledge. And, in the field of social theory, the method of emancipatory social theory was superior to the method of natural science.

By mid-century, Marxist-Leninism and humanistic Marxism were established as the basic alternative interpretations of Marxism. Each claimed to be the authentic interpretation of Marx, and each saw the other as a perversion of authentic Marxism. Each claimed superiority over the other on grounds of philosophical adequacy as well. This philosophical polarization largely corresponded with the geopolitical contest between the socialist East and the capitalist West. To be sure, there were isolated philosophical infections from the enemy camp on each side of the political boundaries. In the West, Marxist-Leninist views continued to be published, though usually only in the Party presses and hardly ever in the academic journals. In the East, humanistic Marxism found some support among individuals and even in some academic institutions and journals in some of the Eastern European countries. This was especially true in Poland, Czechoslovakia, and Yugoslavia. But, though sometimes tolerated, these tendencies on several occasions met with resistance from political authorities. By and large, at mid-century, Marxist-Leninism stood as orthodoxy in the East and humanistic Marxism stood as orthodoxy in the West.

NOTES

1. Karl Korsch, *Marxism and Philosophy* (New York: Monthly Review Press, 1970), p. 33.
2. Lenin, *Materialism and Empirio-Criticism* (New York: International, 1972) pp. 267, 268.
3. Lenin, *Collected Works*, vol. 38 (Moscow: Foreign Languages Publishing House, 1963), p. 180.
4. Ibid., p. 97.
5. Ibid., pp. 360–361.
6. Ibid., p. 362.
7. Ibid., p. 205.
8. Ibid., p. 277; cf. p. 114.
9. Ibid. See p. 401 for the claim that positivist agnosticism is a source of political reaction. In his comments on Rey (p. 422), Lenin mentions religion in particular in this regard, in spite of Rey's opposition to Bergsonian fideism as rationally indefensible.
10. " 'Left-Wing' Communism—An Infantile Disorder," in *Collected Works*, vol. 31, p. 102.
11. Ibid., pp. 98–99. Cf. Lenin's remarks in *Our Revolution*, January 1923.
12. Ibid., p. 102, for the use of "one-sidedness" to describe the fixation on the electoral path.
13. *Against Revisionism* (Moscow: Progress, 1976), p. 547.
14. Ibid., p. 548.
15. See Chapter 1, section "The 'Orthodox' Marxism of Karl Kautsky." For Lenin's

view of the evolutionary/revolutionary distinction and its philosophical roots in dialectics, see "Marxism and Revisionism," in *Against Revisionism*, p. 112.

16. Ernst Fischer and Roger Garaudy have both defended this viewpoint. For Marxist-Leninist responses to their views here, see Robert Steigerwald, *Anti-Communist Myths in Left Disguise* (New York: International, 1977), p. 18; and S. I. Popov, *Der moderne Revisionismus* (Berlin: Deutscher Veriag der Wissenschaften, 1975), pp. 42–43.

17. Lenin, *Collected Works*, vol. 38, p. 179.

18. Ibid.

19. See, e.g., George Lichtheim's claim that Lenin never fully grasped the importance of his own turn to Hegel with respect to overcoming his earlier work. *George Lukács* (New York: Viking, 1970), p. 57.

20. Chapter 5, section "The Reflection Theory" and Chapter 6, section "The Philosophy of Praxis and the Critique of Vulgar Materialism."

21. *Collected Works*, vol. 38, pp. 359, 380–383.

22. Ibid., pp. 290–291 (on the source of cognition and the concept).

23. Ibid., p. 183.

24. Ibid., p. 362.

25. Ibid., p. 195.

26. Ibid., p. 362.

27. Lenin, *What Is To Be Done?* (Moscow: Progress, 1973), p. 27.

28. *Against Revisionism*, p. 112.

29. Korsch, *Marxism and Philosophy*, pp. 86–88; Georg Lukács, *History and Class Consciousness* (Cambridge, MA: MIT Press, 1971), pp. 111–112 (on classical philosophy) and 202 (on materialism). In a 1971 interview, Lukács said, "In the twenties, Korsch, Gramsci and I tried in our different ways to come to grips with the problem of social necessity and the mechanistic interpretation of it that was the heritage of the Second International" (*New Left Review*, no. 68 [July–August 1971]: 51). In *The Young Lukács and the Origins of Western Marxism* (New York: Seabury Press, 1971), p. 173. Andrew Arato and Paul Breines see the humanistic Marxism of Lukács and Korsch as rooted in opposition to "a recrudescent positivism and mechanistic materialism within communism itself." For Gramsci's critique of "crude and banal" materialism, see Antonio Gramsci, *Prison Notebooks* (New York: International, 1971), pp. 390, 444, 446, 455.

30. See Korsch, *Marxism and Philosophy*, p. 90, on Hegel's secret materialism; and Gramsci, *Prison Notebooks*, pp. 399–402, 449–450, where the speculative immanence of Hegel is contrasted with the historical or realist immanence of Marxism. For Lukács, of course, it is the proletariat that replaces Hegel's Absolute as the subject/object of history (Lukács, *History and Class Consciousness*, pp. 145–149).

31. Korsch, *Marxism and Philosophy*, p. 95; Lukács, *History and Class Consciousness*, pp. 189, 200, 202–204.

32. The concept of "totality" is central to Lukács. See, e.g., *History and Class Consciousness*, pp. 9, 25, 39, 151, 164, 230. The concept is also present in Korsch (*Marxism and Philosophy*, p. 96), and I believe also in Gramsci's idea of the historical bloc (*Prison Notebooks*, p. 377) as a concrete totality.

33. Lukács, *History . . .*, pp. 12–13; Korsch, *Marxism . . .*, pp. 80–81, 88–89, 96. Cf. Leszek Kolakowski, *Main Currents of Marxism* (Oxford: Oxford University Press, 1978), vol. 3, pp. 268–269.

34. Lukács, *History . . .*, pp. 195–197, 208–209, 241–245; Korsch, *Marxism . . .*, pp. 80–81; Gramsci, . . . *Notebooks*, p. 407.

35. Lukács, *History* . . . , pp. 195–197, 208–209; Korsch, *Marxism* . . . , pp. 12, 73, 80; Gramsci, . . . *Notebooks*, p. 437.
36. Lukács, *History* . . . , pp. 179, 239, 245, 249; Korsch, *Marxism* . . . , pp. 65, 68; Gramsci, . . . *Notebooks*, pp. 426, 437.
37. Lukács, *History* . . . , pp. 3, 24 n. 6. (In "Reification and the Consciousness of the Proletariat," an essay in *History and Class Consciousness*, Lukács appears to allow for distinct dialectics of nature and society.)
38. Gramsci, . . . *Notebooks*, p. 448.
39. Korsch, *Marxism* . . . , pp. 91–92.
40. Ibid., p. 69.
41. Lukács, *History* . . . , pp. 6–7; Gramsci, . . . *Notebooks*, p. 428.
42. Lukács, *History* . . . , pp. 7–8; Gramsci, . . . *Notebooks*, pp. 401, 410–412.
43. Lukács, *History* . . . , pp. 150, 169, 175, 178, 199.
44. Ibid., pp. 208–209.
45. Ibid., pp. 160–161; Korsch, *Marxism* . . . , pp. 89, 94.
46. Lichtheim, *George Lukács*, p. 2. See ibid., p. 27, for Lukács' comments on Heidelberg Neo-Kantianism.
47. See Massimo Salvadori, *Karl Kautsky* . . . (London: NLB, 1979), chs. 8–10, for an account of Kautsky's criticism of the Bolshevik Revolution and the Bolshevik model.
48. Anton Pannekoek, *Lenin as Philosopher* (New York: Breakout Press, 1975), p. 97.
49. Ibid., p. 56.
50. Ibid., p. 99.
51. Ibid., p. 45.
52. Ibid.
53. Ibid., p. 18.
54. Ibid., p. 28.
55. Helena Sheehan, *Marxism and the Philosophy of Science* (Atlantic Highlands, NJ: Humanities, 1985), p. 161.
56. David Joravsky, *Soviet Marxism and Natural Science* (New York: Columbia University Press, 1961), p. 283.
57. Ibid.
58. See ibid., p. 279 on Timiriazev's opposition to relativity theory. On the position of Semkovskii, who passed from mechanism to Deborinism, in part because of the interpretation of relativity physics, see ibid., pp. 160, 284.
59. On Minin, see Sheehan, *Marxism* . . . , p. 166; Joravsky, *Soviet Marxism*, p. 95; and Gustav Wetter, *Dialectical Materialism* (New York: Praeger, 1961), pp. 129–130.
60. Joravsky, *Soviet Marxism*, pp. 93–94; Sheehan, *Marxism* . . . , pp. 165–166.
61. Wetter, *Dialectical Materialism*, p. 130.
62. Joravsky, *Soviet Marxism*, p. 93.
63. Wetter, *Dialectical Materialism*, p. 139; Joravsky, *Soviet Marxism*, p. 167; Sheehan, *Marxism* . . . , p. 167.
64. Sheehan, *Marxism* . . . , p. 177.
65. Ibid., pp. 168, 177–178. Cf. Stephen Cohen, *Bukharin and the Bolshevik Revolution* (Oxford: Oxford University Press, 1980), p. 116.
66. Joravsky, *Soviet Marxism*, p. 109; on Deborin, see Wetter, *Dialectical Materialism*, pp. 159–166.
67. Joravsky, *Soviet Marxism*, pp. 170–183; Sheehan, *Marxism* . . . , pp. 179–181; Wetter, *Dialectical Materialism*, pp. 159–166.

68. Quoted in Joravsky, *Soviet Marxism*, p. 140.

69. Sheehan, *Marxism . . .*, p. 183.

70. Ibid., p. 168.

71. See Stepanov's comments on Engels and electron theory in Wetter, *Dialectical Materialism*, p. 130.

72. Sheehan, *Marxism . . .*, p. 187.

73. Wetter, *Dialectical Materialism*, p. 133.

74. Cohen, *Bukharin . . .*, pp. 165–166.

75. Douglas Carr, "Tolerant Empiricism: An Essay on the Philosophy of the Vienna Circle" (unpublished M.A. thesis, University of Alberta, Edmonton, 1977), pp. 25–26. Cf. p. 28, on Kraft.

76. Ibid., p. 27; Sheehan, *Marxism . . .*, p. 246; Alec Nove, *The Economics of Feasible Socialism* (London: George Allen and Unwin, 1983), p. 198, gives a brief account of Neurath's economic and political vision, which was close to that of Kautsky—central planning with national elections.

77. Carr, "Tolerant Empiricism," p. 28.

78. The first quotation is from "Empirical Sociology," in Otto Neurath, *Empiricism and Sociology* (Dordrecht: Reidel, 1973), p. 349. The second quotation is from Neurath, "Sociology and Physicalism," in *Logical Positivism*, edited by A. J. Ayer (New York: Free Press, 1959, p. 309.

79. Neurath, "Sociology and Physicalism," p. 316; cf. Sheehan, *Marxism . . .*, p. 403.

80. Carr, "Tolerant Empiricism," pp. 43–45; Sheehan, *Marxism . . .*, p. 404.

81. *The Philosophy of Rudolf Carnap*, edited by P. A. Schilpp (La Salle, IL: Open Court, 1963), p. 9.

82. Carr, "Tolerant Empiricism," p. 67. Cf. H. Feigel, "Memoir of Rudolf Carnap," in *Boston Studies in the Philosophy of Science*, edited by Roger Buck and Robert Cohen, vol. 8 (Dordrecht: Reidel, 1971). p. xv.

83. G. H. von Wright, "Ludwig Wittgenstein, A Biographical Sketch," *Philosophical Review* 69 (1955): 540, mentions the plan to move to the USSR. F. Rossi-Landi, "Towards a Marxian Use of Wittgenstein," in ed. J. C. Nyiri, *Austrian Philosophy: Studies and Texts* (Munich: Philosophia, 1981), pp. 113–149, attempts to uncover philosophical affinities between Marx and Wittgenstein.

84. Carr, "Tolerant Empiricism," pp. 22–26.

85. Karl Marx, *Capital* (New York: International, 1973), vol. 1, p. 763; for the German text see *Marx Engels Werke* (Berlin: Dietz Verlag, 1968), vol. 23, p. 791 (hereafter *MEW*). For Popper's discussion of this passage, see "What Is Dialectic?" *Mind* 49 (1940): 403–426.

86. *Capital*, vol. 1, p. 763; *MEW*, vol. 23, p. 791.

87. Popper, "What Is Dialectic?" p. 424.

88. Karl Popper, *The Poverty of Historicism* (New York: Harper, 1964), pp. 128–129.

89. Ibid., p. 115.

90. Ibid., p. 129 n. 1.

91. Ibid., p. 129.

92. H. B. Acton, *The Illusion of the Epoch* (London: Cohen and West, 1955), pp. 150ff.

93. Ibid., pp. 159–168. See also John Piamenetz, *German Marxism and Russian Communism* (London: Longman's Green, 1954), p. 21–28.

94. Edmund Wilson, *To The Finland Station* (Garden City, NY: Anchor, 1940), pp. 194–197. See also Max Eastman, *Marxism: Is It Science?* (London: George Allen and Unwin, 1941); J. L. Talmon, *The Origins of Totalitarian Democracy* (Boston: Beacon Press, 1952); and Robert Tucker, *Philosophy and Myth in Karl Marx* (Cambridge: Cambridge University Press, 1961).

95. Joan Robinson, *Economic Philosophy* (Chicago: Aldine, 1962), p. 26.

96. William Riker, *Theory of Political Coalitions* (New Haven: Yale University Press, 1965), p. 5.

Part II

Analysis

3

The Theory of Capitalism

Marxism is scientific socialism—or so it has claimed to be. But the nature of this Marxist science is a matter of contention among Marxists, both as an issue of interpretation and as an issue of substance. As we have seen, within the period of the Second International, there was near unanimity among Marxists in seeing the central contribution of Marx to be his scientific theory of capitalism and his scientific theory of historical development. During the revisionism debate, the adequacy of this Marxist social science was at issue, but its nature as a scientific theory was not. Eduard Bernstein did claim that Marx's science was contaminated with Hegelian philosophy on certain points, but he seemed to regard this contamination as fundamentally at odds with the spirit of Marxist science.

Further, the thinkers of the Second International were prone to see this Marxist science as fully conformable to the leading philosophies of science of the late nineteenth and early twentieth centuries. There were differences of opinion as to which among the contending philosophies of science was most plausible. Where Max Adler appealed to Neo-Kantian theory, Aleksandr Bogdanov appealed to positivism, Bernstein appealed to both, and Karl Kautsky rejected the new theories and stuck doggedly to the scientific materialism of the mid-nineteenth century. But what is interesting, from our point of view, is that none of the leading thinkers of the Second International, with the exception of Lenin, thought that Marxist science differed in nature from bourgeois science. For the Marxists of the Second International, Marxist science was ordinary science. This conception of Marx's work was, of course, strongly contested by both Marxist-

Leninists and humanistic Marxists. Marxist-Leninists maintained that while Marx's work was scientific, it was a distinctive and superior kind of science. Humanistic Marxists denied that Marx's work should be viewed as a science at all. In this chapter I will attempt to make as strong a case as I can for the view that Marxist science is ordinary science. I will then consider objections to this view from both the Marxist-Leninist and the humanist interpretations of Marxism. I will begin by focusing on the theory of capitalism, since this is clearly the paradigm case of Marxist social science. In Chapter 4 I will consider some of the special problems raised by Marx's materialist conception of history.

THE SCIENTIFIC THEORY OF CAPITALISM

A reader familiar with the work of Adam Smith or David Ricardo would find in *Capital* a comprehensible theory of economics. There is a substantial overlap between Marx's work and the work of his classical predecessors. This is true with respect to central theoretical concepts, to problems, and to the method of analysis. Like his classical predecessors, Marx aims at laying bare the inner workings of capitalist economies. A central theoretical tool is the labor theory of value, which holds that the value of a commodity is proportional to the labor time socially necessary to produce it. This theory of value was one of several theories of value present in Smith's *Wealth of Nations*. The theory was given a more rigorous and consistent development in Ricardo's *Principles*. Marx's own theory of capitalism builds upon the work of Ricardo in particular.

The labor theory of value is central to this classical tradition in two respects. First, it serves as the foundation for an equilibrium theory of prices. Second, the theory provides a measure of value, labor time, which can be aggregated and hence can serve as the basis for the analysis of growth and distribution. Marx's commitment to the labor theory was a result of his respect for the fruitfulness of the theory in Ricardo's hands and his appreciation of the difficulties facing alternative contemporary theories of value.

Marx is not unaware of problems with the labor theory and tries to repair certain inadequacies in Ricardo's formulation of it. He recognizes the inconsistency of Ricardo's theory of prices and his assumption of a normal rate of profit, with the existence of differing capital/labor ratios in different industries, and attempts to get around this by making the labor values only indirectly determinate of relative prices.[1] He recognizes the prima facie incompatibility of the labor theory with phenomena of scarcity, but believed Ricardo had laid the basis for a solution to these problems with his theory of rent.[2] Finally, Marx recognizes the existence of "curious examples" that seem incompatible with the labor theory about which he has nothing to say (the classic case here, one that troubled Ricardo as well, is that of the wine in the cellar which increases in value with no additional labor).[3]

In his earliest work in political economy, Marx rejected the labor theory of value, in part because he thought it was incompatible with the supposition that in a free market all exchanges would involve equivalent values. How is it, Marx wondered, that if all exchanges involve equivalents, and the labor theory of value is true, the value received by the worker is less than the value of his product, as it is in Ricardo's system? At this point, too, Marx accepted Jean Baptiste Say's criticism of Ricardo's labor theory for failing to grasp the role of demand in determining exchange values. Following Say and other opponents of the labor theory, Marx sought to develop a theory of prices on the basis of the concepts of supply and demand.[4]

Marx's conversion to the labor theory followed his later close study of Ricardo. Marx was persuaded that the concepts of supply and demand could not alone provide an adequate foundation for a theory of prices. Changes in relative prices could be explained by shifts in demand or supply, but these concepts could not explain why goods tended to exchange in the ratios they did. Without the labor theory it was impossible at that time to develop an equilibrium theory of prices or an account of distribution of income between land, labor, and capital. Attempts to develop such a theory without the labor theory had all proven to be circular or patently question begging.[5]

Further, with his own distinction between "labor" and "labor power," Marx found the means of reconciling the exchange of equivalents assumed by the labor theory of value with the exploitation theory of profit as advanced by Smith and Ricardo. While Marx notes that the distinction is implicitly drawn by Ricardo, he considers his explicit formulation of it to be one of his major improvements on Ricardo's version of the labor theory.[6] Far from being the motivation for adopting the labor theory, for Marx the exploitation of labor served, initially at least, as an obstacle to the labor theory. The attraction of the labor theory was its power as a theory of prices and a theory of factor distribution.

In Marx's theory of capitalism, the labor theory continues to play a central role in his accounts of relative prices and of factor distribution. However, it would be a mistake to think that his theory of capitalism flows from the labor theory alone. It is fairly simple to see that this is not the case. As an analytic device in the construction of his theory of capitalism, Marx considers a system of "simple commodity production" which is like capitalism except that it does not include labor power as a commodity. Marx uses the labor theory of value in analyzing how such a system would work, but this analysis cannot lead to an analysis of capitalism without the assumption of labor markets. The presence of a market for labor power is a basic feature of capitalism. So, too, are a number of other features—such as the existence of competitive markets, production for sale in such markets, and private ownership of the means of production—that are shared with systems of simple commodity production. At bottom, it is the presence of such basic social arrangements that makes a system capitalist. The labor theory of value provides a tool for analyzing what happens in capitalist systems built on these basic institutional arrangements. But a theory of capitalism can be built in this way only on the basis of a clear understanding of such basic institutional features.

Further, there are grounds for thinking that the labor theory of value is a dispensible tool of analysis. In the late 1930s, both Oskar Lange and Joan Robinson argued that nothing of importance in Marx's theory of capitalism depended upon his labor theory of value.[7] More recent work by Ian Steedman, John Roemer, and others supports this claim.[8] It is the analyses of the basic institutional features of capitalism rather than the labor theory of value that provide the real foundation of Marx's theory of capitalism.[9]

In this respect, Marx's theory stands squarely within the classical tradition of political economy. But, in Marx's hands, the method of analysis developed by the classical economists grounds a deeply pessimistic prognosis for the future of capitalism. Marx tries to show how the economics of Smith and Ricardo, consistently developed, leads not only to conclusions concerning a tendency for a declining rate of profit (a tendency assumed by many of the classical economists) but also to such tendencies as increasing unemployment, centralization and concentration of capital, polarization of classes, and recurring crises of increasing frequency and intensity. Marx tries to show how these tendencies are products of the inner workings of capitalism. The kind of explanation he offers for these tendencies is similar to that offered by Smith and Ricardo. They are the unintended consequences of individual actions within the framework of the basic structures of capitalist economies. With Smith the invisible hand is benevolent; with Marx it is malevolent.[10]

Like Smith and Ricardo, Marx reaches his conclusions through deductive chains of reasoning beginning with certain basic, defining features of capitalist economies. As Joan Robinson put it, "Marx had learned from Ricardo the trick of setting up what we now call a model—stating the assumptions and drawing the conclusions."[11] This model is an example of what Leszek Nowak called an "idealization."[12] That is, in certain respects the model is oversimplified. It has a certain unreality about it. Through "successive concretization" it begins to approximate reality more and more closely.[13] Marx is self-conscious of this process. Thus, in the first volume of *Capital*, he warns his readers that the theory presented there assumes that prices are equivalent to values, and he promises to remove this oversimplification in the later volumes.[14]

To the extent that any theory involves this structure of idealization, its connection with actual processes is problematic. Nevertheless, some sort of idealization seems to be present in all scientific theorizing. Questions of empirical applicability must always be addressed in a context informed by knowledge of just what simplifying assumptions have been made, and how those assumptions stand with respect to the actual processes under investigation. Idealization may be more or less distorting of reality. In any case, it is clear that Marx took both classical economics and his own economic theory to be empirically applicable. Given a theoretical structure of the kind in question, it was possible to deduce general law claims that could be used in the explanation and prediction of observable phenomena. Despite his criticisms of specific chains of deductive reasoning in the works of the classical economists, as in his criticism of Smith's account of expanded reproduction, Marx clearly believed it to be the great merit of the economics of Smith and Ricardo that with such idealized modeling, it had achieved a genuinely scientific comprehension of capitalism. In the *Grundrisse* Marx contrasts the scientific theory of the classical economists with the work of their predecessors:

The economists of the seventeenth century, e.g. always begin with the living whole, with population, nation, state, several states, etc.; but they always conclude by discovering through analysis a small number of determinant, abstract general relations such as division of labour, money, value, etc. As soon as these individual moments had been more or less firmly established and abstracted, there began the economic systems which ascended from the simple relations, such as labour, division of labour, need, exchange value, to the level of the state, exchange between nations and the world market. The latter is obviously the scientifically correct method.[15]

Marx's understanding of classical economics and of his own economic theory are reflected in his comments on the nature of science and scientific economics. Marx thought that the world of experience was a surface governed by a deeper structure. The task of science was to uncover this hidden nature of things, and to show how this hidden nature produces the world given in experience.[16] By force of abstraction, the theorist arrives at a model of the essential features of the hidden structure. By deductive reasoning the theorist shows how the features found in the surface experience of things follow from the essential features given in the model. The whole thus gains the appearance of a purely a priori construction, though in fact the essential features of the model are the result of abstraction, rooted in observation, and of analysis of what is given in observation.[17]

It is this movement "from abstract definitions by way of reasoning to the reproduction of the concrete situation" that Marx takes to be the method of Smith and Ricardo, and it is this procedure that, as we saw in the passage quoted from the *Grundrisse* above, Marx takes to be "manifestly the scientifically correct method." This identification of the correct approach to a science of economics with the economic theory of Smith and Ricardo is repeated in the discussion of method in the Afterword to the second German edition of *Capital*. There Marx quotes with approval the remark of a reviewer who says, "The method of Marx is the deductive method of the whole English school."[18]

Given such a theory, it is possible to formulate nomothetic laws that can be used in the explanation and prediction of the surface phenomena given in ordinary experience. Marx believed that he had produced such a theory with his theory of capitalism. Volume 1 of *Capital* provides an analysis of the central concepts of the theory of capitalist economies, and applies these concepts to the analysis of the accumulation of capital. In the unfinished volumes, Marx intended to extend the analysis to include a more empirically adequate theory of prices, a theory of expanded reproduction, and a theory of the periodic crisis of overproduction, among other things. So, in this sense, the theory of capitalism that

Marx actually achieved is incomplete and open-ended. Nevertheless, it is clear that he believed the foundations for the theory of capitalism had been laid.

Further, Marx conceived of this method as common to both the natural and the social sciences. In the Preface to the first German edition of *Capital* he says, "It is the ultimate aim of this work to lay bare the economic laws of motion of modern society"; calls these laws "natural laws"; and draws analogies between his own work in economics and work in chemistry of physics. Marx thus appears to hold that his theory of capitalism is similar in nature to both the theories of the classical economists and the theories of the natural sciences.

This conception of Marxist science as ordinary science was widely held at the time of the Second International. From this point of view, what distinguished Marxist science from other science was not form or method, but content. The revolutionary nature of Marxist science was due not to a revolution in epistemology and philosophy of science but to the implications of Marx's theory of capital for the law-governed development of capitalist economies. The conception of Marxist social theory as offering a philosophically different kind of theory is a phenomenon of the twentieth century. Moreover, there is considerable disagreement about the nature of this Marxist social theory and how it differs from ordinary science. In the rest of this chapter I will consider some of the alternative conceptions of Marx's theory of capitalism that have been advanced.

MARXISM AS EMANCIPATORY SOCIAL THEORY

> Let us assume for the sake of argument that recent research had disproved once and for all every one of Marx's individual theses. Even if this were to be proved, every serious "orthodox" Marxist would still be able to accept all such modern findings without reservation and hence dismiss all of Marx's theses *in toto*—without having to renounce his orthodoxy for a single moment. Orthodox Marxism, therefore, does not imply the uncritical acceptance of the results of Marx's investigations. It is not the "belief" in this or that thesis, nor the exegesis of a "sacred" book. On the contrary, orthodoxy refers exclusively to *method*.[19]

This thesis, which appears on the first page of Georg Lukács' *History and Class Consciousness* (1923), has had a profound influence on Western Marxism. In it, and the interpretation of Marxism that underlies and surrounds it, is found what Paul Piccone has aptly called "the Grand Central Station of present day Marxism."[20] Though I would amend this to say "the Grand Central Station of Western Marxism," I would agree with Piccone's assessment of the importance of Lukács' *History and Class Consciousness* for Western Marxism. Fundamental to this Western Marxism is the idea of Marxism as a new kind of emancipatory social theory, fundamentally different in kind from natural scientific theory. It is in this context that Lukács' claim, that what is important in Marxism is method, must be understood.

The idea that Marxism involves a new method, distinct from the method of bourgeois natural science, has become widely accepted.[21] But, though widely accepted, there has been no consensus as to the nature of this method, and there has been considerable unclarity in attempts to explain it. In a sense, then, the search for a method has been the central theme of Western Marxism.[22] But if this search remains unconsummated, if the nature of this method remains in important respects quite unclear, nonetheless certain basic features are well known and have been well known since the work of Lukács. If we cannot say precisely what this method is, we can nonetheless say with certainty what it is not, and in this negative characterization there is at least the beginning of an account of the method. And further, while this definition by negation is quite limited and unsatisfactory, the negative theses are themselves of considerable philosophical importance, both as interpretational claims about Marx and as substantive philosophical claims.

In fact, this self-definition through negation is present in humanistic Marxism from the beginning. Above all, Lukács formulated his position as a critical alternative to the scientistic Marxism that had dominated the Second International. Central to his position, and the humanistic Marxism that derives from it, are the views that there cannot be a social science modeled on the natural sciences, as was imagined by the Marxists of the Second International; that this is so because human social behavior is not causally determined; and that Marxist social theory represents a new kind of thought, with its own critical task and its own standards of rational adequacy.

A convenient point of entry into this Lukácsian reinterpretation of Marxism is by way of the question of the role of ideas in history. According to one common popular exposition of Marxism, Marx was an economic determinist who saw the coming of socialism as the inevitable outcome of economic forces. Contrary to idealism, which stressed the role of ideas in history, the Marxist economic theory denied causal efficacy to ideas. On this view, the coming of socialism is a result of purely "objective" forces, and the "subjective" reflection of these forces in human consciousness is a purely epiphenomenal by-product.

Such an economic determinism is surely mistaken, and humanistic Marxism is surely correct in rejecting it. But such an epiphenomenalist economic determinism is a "straw man" position. In particular, it does not accurately represent the orthodox Marxism of the Second International. As was seen in Part I, Kautsky, the champion of orthodoxy, granted the causal efficacy of ideas, and in particular of moral beliefs, in the historical transition to socialism. In contrast with this crude epiphenomenalist determinism, there is a more sophisticated version of economic determinism that would allow causal efficacy to ideas, and yet holds that these ideas are themselves effects of economic causes. In this version ideas play a role in the historical process. They are necessary links in the causal chain that has socialism as its outcome. It is this theory that Kautsky embraced, along with Georgi Plekhanov, the Austro-Marxists, and the empiriocritical Marxists. Ideas are historically efficacious but also historically determined.

Lukács' criticism of the Marxism of the Second International is sometimes directed against an epiphenomenalist economic determinism, and his alternative interpretation of Marxism is sometimes summarized in terms of an insistence on the importance of subjective consciousness in the revolutionary process. However, it is important to see that Lukács' position is also a critique of the more sophisticated version of economic determinism. It is not just that Lukács insists that consciousness plays a role in the revolutionary processes; that much both the sophisticated representatives of the Second International and Lukács' Leninist critics can grant. Philosophically more important is the way Lukács understands the role of consciousness in history.

Economic determinism, in either its epiphenomenalist or its interactionist form, objectivizes the historical process. That is, it treats the historical process as an objective, law-governed process similar to purely natural processes as they are understood by the natural sciences. Lukács rejects any such objectivization as a false consciousness. The social world and the historical process are not objectively given parts of the natural order, but products of free human creation. To see the social world in an objectivist fashion is to misperceive the social as the natural. It is an alienated form of consciousness in that what is in fact a product of human freedom is understood as an independent reality constraining human freedom. This is the fundamental error of bourgeois social science. Marx's critique of political economy tore away the naturalist mask covering the social world. He showed how the bourgeois economists systematically mispresented the social for the natural, and in doing so he awakened a nonalienated, revolutionary, proletarian consciousness.

But why could there not be an objective science of the socio-historical process of human creation? Why could not one grant that the social world is nonnatural, in the sense of being the product of human action, and yet hold that this process is itself governed by objective laws? This is, in effect, the position of "interactionist" (as opposed to epiphenomenalist) economic determinism.

Lukács offers some arguments to show that there cannot be an objectivist science of socio-historical processes.[23] His comments are specifically directed against the pretensions of economics to be such an objectivist social science. Each of these arguments turns on the "historical character" of economic theory. His first argument turns on what he takes to be the statistical nature of economic theory:

> The unscientific nature of this seemingly so scientific method consists, then, in its failure to see and take account of the *historical character* of the facts on which it is based. This is the source of more than one error. . . . The nature of this source of error is that statistics and the exact economic theory based upon them always lag behind actual developments.[24]

This argument is a failure from every point of view. For one thing, it rests on a basic misunderstanding of economic theory as fundamentally a statistical social science. However, even granting that all social science is statistical in nature, the argument fails. That the data of an economic science are historical in nature does not undermine the project of a social science based upon such data. The theory might, for example, explicitly recognize the historical parameters. Or the historical process may be so slow as to leave the theory applicable, for all practical purposes, for an extended time period. Or in some cases the nature of the "lag" may itself be a predictable result of the data. Consider, for example, a study of racial attitudes, based on statistical surveys, that shows both a tendency toward racial integration and a correlation between degree of integration and decline of racism.

A second argument turns on Lukács' assumption that bourgeois economics, like the natural science on which it models itself, rests on the view that "the manner in which data immediately present themselves is an adequate foundation of scientific conceptualization." Lukács goes on to argue that because of this assumption, bourgeois economics uncritically accepts the social order as unalterable.[25] This argument seems to rest on an absurd confusion of epistemic claims with attitudes toward the object of investigation. A medical investigation, committed to the principle that the manner in which the data present themselves is adequate for science, is not thereby committed to the view that disease is inevitable and untreatable. It should also be noted that Marx does not share Lukács' assumption that bourgeois economics and natural science rest on the epistemic principle of the adequacy of the immediately given for purposes of science. As was seen above, in Marx's view, all science is the attempt to uncover the hidden essences behind the data of experience, and it is the great merit of Smith and Ricardo to have succeeded in doing so.

Terence Ball offers yet another argument to support the Lukácsian claim that the historical character of social formations precludes a social science modeled on the natural sciences. In the social sciences, he says:

> Such "laws" as are available to us . . . are *historical* laws of temporally restricted scope; they hold true only for situations, relations, and event-types of particular social formations and modes of production. Such historically restricted generalizations cannot qualify as general laws of a Humean or Hempelian sort.[26]

This argument seems to trade on a simple confusion of the sense in which law claims are understood to be universal in the Hempelian model of science. On that model, law claims are universal in their logical form. However, this is compatible with the restriction of their applicability to events of a certain kind. On the Hempelian analysis, law claims take the following form: "Given conditions $c_1 \ldots c_n$, if an event of kind E_1 occurs, an event of kind E_2 will follow." This is consistent with historical or other restrictions on the occurrence of the relevant conditions. Scientific law claims are universal in the sense of applying to all events of a certain kind, but this does not imply that the law applies to all events. The Hempelian analysis is perfectly consistent with recognition of historical laws of temporally restricted scope.

Neither Lukács' arguments nor Ball's supporting argument succeeds in showing any formal distinction between social theory and natural science. And so we are back to the possibility of a social science modeled on the natural sciences. Is this not in fact achieved in economic theory? Granted that the classical economists tended to overlook the historically restricted scope of the theories they presented, did they not give us scientific theories of capitalist economies? And is this not, in fact, the aim of Marx's theory of capitalism?

Lukács acknowledges that there is a certain truth to these remarks. Classical economics does resemble theories in the natural sciences, but this is so because capitalism exists as a system of reified human relations. What is peculiar about capitalism is that it is a system of social relations which relinquishes control of social life to market relationships that escape control of human agents. Lukács says, "The purest, indeed one might say the only pure form of the control of society by its natural laws is found in capitalist production."[27] For him, classical economics as a social science is possible only because capitalism exists as the pervasive alienation of human freedom.

In the same way, Marx's theory of capitalism approximates in appearance certain formal properties of classical economics and the natural sciences. But it would be a serious mistake to be misled by the approximation in appearance into thinking of Marxist social theory as social science modeled on the natural sciences. For the whole aim of *Capital* is to dispel the illusion of naturalism, to reveal the capitalist system as a historical product of human freedom and as subject to revolutionary transformation. *Capital*, subtitled *A Critique of Political Economy*, is at bottom an emancipatory awakening of revolutionary consciousness.

As a way of explicating one possible understanding of what such emanicpatory theory might be, let us return to the question of the role of ideas in history. In the interactionist version of economic determinism, ideas do have causal efficacy, but they are themselves causally determined by economic forces. On this view, Marxism is understood as objective social science modeled on the natural sciences. Part of this social science is the theory of ideology, which provides a descriptive account of the various ideas that in turn play a role in the historical process. But, of course, as one idea among others, the Marxist theory appears as a part of the social process theorized about. And, of course, this is true of social theory in general. Insofar as theory construction is a social activity, it appears as part of its own object domain. Hence, social theory is said to be reflective in nature.[28]

It is not obvious that all social theory is reflective. Though of course there could be a reflective anthropology, concerning itself in part with the practices of anthropologists, usually the anthropologist's theory does not appear within its own domain. It may well be that much of social theory is nonreflective. But Marxism, and especially its component theory of the ideological superstructure, does appear to be reflective in nature. However, it is not clear just what this reflectivity, where it does exist, implies concerning the proper method of theory construction. That a social theory is reflective, and in this sense different from natural scientific theories, is not itself sufficient to establish that it requires a method different in kind from the method of the natural sciences. In what ways does reflectivity produce methodological problems?

At least three sorts of difficulties present themselves. One sort of difficulty that might arise is a problem concerning self-fulfilling theories. A widely accepted racist theory may find itself empirically verified. But this empirical verification may arise only because the theory is widely accepted and internalized. The social theorist, unlike the natural scientist, must be wary of such difficulties. Second, wide acceptance of a theory may lead to its falsification. For example, widespread acceptance of the theory that the most common cause of divorce is early marriage might lead to postponement of marriage as a general practice and so to the undermining of the theory. Third, a theory may be in some way self-undermining. For example, a theory which held that all social theories are delusional would undermine itself whether or not anyone believed it. Do these sorts of problems have any importance for the conception of Marxism as an emancipatory social theory?

The basic idea of a critical theory is of a social theory which aims at the emancipation of some social group from some oppressive social order by showing the members of the group that some belief of the group which sustains that social order is false. Criticism of self-fulfilling theories would provide one clear example of such a critical theory. Conviction within a group of its own racial inferiority may work to sustain an oppressive social order. Exposure of this belief as false undermines at least one of the supports for the oppressive social order. Something like this is involved in Marx's critique of the political economists for claiming that capitalist social structures were natural for any social system. Widespread acceptance of this false belief within the working class would work to sustain the social order oppressive of that class, and in that way make the theory's claim of unremediable naturalness appear to be true. Unlike the natural sciences, which are independent of the object of study, classical political economy appears to be a reflective social theory that affects the social order it investigates.

But, how does Marxism achieve the liberation from this illusion of naturalness? It is by pointing out features of the capitalist era that are unlike features of earlier social existence—by showing the difference between the wage laborer and the peasant, on the one hand, and the difference between the capitalist and the feudal lord, on the other. And are the reasoning and evidence involved here different in kind from the reasoning and evidence involved in showing that two chemicals or two geological strata are different? The issue seems to be a question of empirical fact. Though classical political economy can be seen as a self-fulfilling reflective social theory, and the critique of political economy can be understood as aimed at emancipation from this self-fulfilling illusion, it does not appear that the way this emancipation is achieved involves a kind of rationality, or kind of evidence, distinct from the kind of reasoning or evidence involved in the natural sciences. In short, the reflectivity of social theory has not yet been shown to involve social theory in any methodology distinct from the methodology of the natural sciences.

The exposure of the false naturalism of classical economics is clearly part of Marx's critique of political economy. However, it would be a mistake to think that this is all that is involved. Consider, for example, Marx's critique of Adam Smith. Although wary of the capitalist masters' incentives to prevent competition, Smith is basically optimistic about the effects of free-market capitalist economies on the well-being of the working class. He thinks that the uncorrupted system, left to itself, will achieve stable growth and maximum prosperity for all. Of course Marx presents quite a different picture. He sees capitalism as crisis prone, limited in its capacity to utilize the growing productive forces, and prone to increasing unemployment and the relative impoverishment of the working class. Given normal human ends, acceptance of the Smithian theory works to sustain capitalist patterns of social organization. The promotion of such patterns was, after all, one of Smith's aims. In this sense Smith's social theory is not independent of the object of its study. But does this have any methodological significance for economics?

First, note that here the relationship involved does not turn on any reflective properties of Smithian social theory. It is not because Smith's theory is a part of its own object domain that it has the effect that it does. Given normal human ends, identification of an insect as a disease carrier may lead to attempts to exterminate that insect, but this is not because of the reflective nature of entomology. And so here there does not appear to be any prospect of tracing the need for a distinctive methodological approach to the formal property of reflectivity.

More important, an examination of the evidence and reasoning involved in Marx's critique of Smith does not show any method distinct from the method of the natural sciences. Marx focuses on Smith's account of expanded reproduction and shows that his system rests on the mistaken assumption that total value produced in a given period will equal total revenues for that period.[29] From Marx's point of view, what is involved here is Smith's faulty deduction from shared assumptions. It is this gap between value produced and revenue that eventually leads, by way of a long and complicated analysis, to the tendencies Marx attributes to capitalist economies. The point thus has tremendous practical importance. However, the methodology involved is ordinary deductive reasoning.

Thus we see that on at least two levels Marx's critique of political economy rests on features of ordinary positive science. The exposure of the historical nature of capitalism and the critique of Smithian optimism turn, respectively, on ordinary empirical claims and on the correction of faulty deductive reasoning. It is thus possible to make sense of the critical nature of Marx's enterprise without appeal to cognitive procedures foreign to positive science.

I would also argue that it is impossible to make sense of Marx's critique of political economy without recognition of the central role of corrections of fact and ordinary deduction in the formulation of that critique. Lukács' claim that what is of lasting importance in Marxism would remain even if all of Marx's factual claims were to prove false, is profoundly mistaken. The hold of bourgeois ideology on the working class is not devoid of content. At bottom, the central legitimating claims of bourgeois ideology are that capitalism is unavoidable and that it delivers the goods. It is by challenging the truth of these claims that *Capital* promotes the emancipation of the working class. If *Capital* does serve as emancipatory critical theory, the way in which this emancipation is achieved is precisely by showing the error of the assumption of naturalness and the errors underlying Smith's optimistic prognosis. Empirical evidence and deductive reasoning are the ways in which those errors are shown and corrected.

Of course, all this shows is that empirical observation and deductive reasoning are necessary components of Marx's critique of political economy and that such methods suffice for emancipatory critical theory of a sort. So understood, critical theory is compatible with positivist philosophy of science.[30] The view of Marxism as critical theory thus faces two tasks. First, it must allow for the role that empirical observation and deductive reason clearly play in Marx's critique of political economy. Lukács' claim, cited above, that Marx's emancipatory critique does not rest on the correctness of any substantive claim, fails in this regard. Second, critical theorists must make clear what methods, in addition to these elements of empirical and deductive reasoning, are involved in a distinctly Marxist emancipatory social theory. Neither the historical nature of the laws of capitalism nor the reflective nature of social theory has been shown to require an abandonment of the methods of ordinary science.

One other possible way of identifying what is unique to Marxist social theory, which is central to Lukács' account, is his characterization of Marx's critique of political economy as self-consciously totalizing theory. Lukács argues that a social system is a meaningful organic whole in which the significance of the parts arises out of their interconnections with the total social system. This being so, he argues, social theory must grasp the social system as a totality. Attempts to apply the method of the natural sciences to the understanding of social life fail because the analytic method of the natural sciences seeks to understand the various aspects of social life individually, separated from one another and from the totality within which their real significance arises.

This criticism of positivist social science involves two claims: that social life is a meaningful totality, and that this fact requires of social theory a method distinct from the natural sciences. One way of understanding the claim that social life is a meaningful totality is in terms of a strong version of the theory of internal relations. On this view, each aspect of social life is related to every other aspect; each of these relations is essential to the identity of each aspect; and a change in any one of these relations involves a change in every aspect of the whole. Marx clearly rejects such a strong version of the theory of internal relations, as we shall see below in considering his criticism of the method of speculative construction.[31] There are some accidental properties of individual parts of the social whole that cannot be derived from a clear conception of the social totality. Nevertheless, it is clear that Marx does think that certain parts of the capitalist system can be understood only in the context of their relation to other parts and to the system as a whole. For example, he tells us that capital presupposes wage labor, and that the cotton gin becomes capital only within the context of a whole ensemble of social relations.[32]

This limited contextualism does not, however, distinguish Marx's economics from non-Marxist economics. Within bourgeois economics the same object can have different significations depending upon its relation to other objects and to the social system as a whole. A sack of grain ground and consumed as bread is not capital, while the same grain used as seed is capital. Nor does this limited contextualism distinguish social theory from natural science. The animal heart presupposes the other parts of the circulatory system and acquires it significance only as part of the organic totality. Even the simple lever presupposes its fulcrum and can exist as a lever only in relation to it. If Lukács' claim that social systems are totalities involves a commitment to the strong thesis of internal relations, it seems to be a claim that Marx rightly rejected. If the claim is only the weaker thesis that the significance of at least some parts of the social system depend upon relations between those parts and other parts of the whole, then this weaker claim does not succeed in distinguishing social systems from other systems or in showing the need for a distinct method in social theory.

Lukács' conception of the social system as a totality, and his worries about the adequacy of the method of the natural sciences for social theory, are connected with his conception of the empiricism of the natural sciences. Lukács seems to think of empirical positive science as fundamentally a matter of noting statistical correlations between distinct observed phenomena. At least part of what is involved in his rejection of this empiricism as a method for social theory is his conviction that such an empiricism can never grasp the significant structure within which social phenomena occur. Only observation that is theory laden, that is guided by a conception of the totality within which the phenomena occur, can see the real significance of the individual phenomena.

In this respect I think Lukács is clearly correct. Observation requires a theoretical context if it is to give us any understanding of the world around us. The logical positivist dream of science built upon uncontaminated observation cannot be realized. However, the correctness of Lukács' insight on this point does not have the consequences he seems to attach to it. For, on the one hand, it does not distinguish Marxist social theory from non-Marxist social theory, and, on the other hand, it does not distinguish social theory from natural science. And it certainly does not justify a view of social theory that would make theory immune to factual refutation.

One possible reason for thinking that social theory is radically distinct from natural science turns on the supposed value ladenness of social theory. And one reason for thinking that social theory is value laden is an argument based on the recognition that all observation is theory laden. If there is no theory-neutral observation, then all comprehension of reality presupposes the adoption of some theoretical framework not dictated by observation itself. Given the selection of one theoretical framework, certain problems and certain "facts" acquire a central importance. Given the selection of an alternative framework, these same problems and "facts" may fall into the shadowy periphery of thought while other problems and other "facts" assume a central importance. In adopting one framework rather than another, the thinker is guided by moral and pragmatic considerations as to what is important for theory to comprehend. Hence, all theoretical comprehension is necessarily normative. Comprehension rests upon moral commitments, and there is no morally neutral test to decide between conflicting theories.[33]

I do not believe this argument succeeds. While all theory does involve selection of certain phenomena as significant, either as explananda or as explanandum, such selection is implicit in all science, including the natural sciences. Hence, the argument does not establish the normative nature of social theory as distinct from natural science. Second, the selection of one framework rather than another need not be guided by moral considerations or moral commitments. Religious, metaphysical, or aesthetic considerations, rather than moral considerations, may guide the selection of a framework. Further, where this selection is guided by moral considerations, this does not preclude a morally independent evaluation of the theory as a descriptive, explanatory theory. Empirical adequacy remains a basic requirement. Finally, there is no reason to think that the kind of insight Marx's theory of capital contained requires any moral commitments for its comprehension. There is no contradiction in thinking that *Capital* is right and at the same time lamenting that fact on (to my mind mistaken) moral grounds. A profound moral pessimist might be led to adopt whatever framework most highlighted evidence of moral decline. If the thinker also saw in socialism evidence of moral decline, the thinker might be led to adopt a "Marxist" view of the coming of socialism even though he or she refrained from revolutionary furtherance of socialism.[34]

Lukács' conception of social theory is developed, as was noted at the beginning of this section, largely by negation. It is defined by what it is not. A central weakness of his position, which persists in later versions of critical theory, is that it rests on an inadequate conception of the method of the empirical natural sciences. Post-positivist philosophy of science has undermined the view of the natural sciences against which the conception of Marxism as a distinctive kind of emancipatory social theory was developed.

DIALECTICAL DERIVATION IN *CAPITAL*

In his book *The Logic of Marx*, Jindřich Zelený contends that in Marxism one finds "a scientific rationality of a new sort."[35] In his claim that Marxism involves a new kind of rationality, Zelený appears to agree with Lukács, but the agreement is only apparent. Where Lukács rejects the possibility of social science, and understands Marx's theory of capitalism as a critical theory directed toward the emancipation of free human subjects, Zeleńy comprehends Marx's theory of capitalism as a social science in which law claims are grounded in a new way. In contrast with Lukács' humanistic reading of *Capital*, Zeleńy advances a Marxist-Leninist interpretation in which what is new in Marxist science is its use of a distinctive dialectical grounding of law claims. Zeleńy does not deny that scientific work of the kind described by the hypothetico-deductive model of science is present in Marx's theory of capital. What is wrong with this model as an interpretation of Marx's scientific practice, in Zeleńy's view, is that it leaves out what is both original and of decisive importance for Marx's theory of capitalism.

Zeleńy sees Marx as holding a dialectical materialist ontology according to which reality is conceived as a self-developing whole. The task of science is to provide a theoretical reflection of this real process. Accordingly, any adequate theory of a mode of production, such as capitalism, must take on a structural-genetic character. That is, it must accurately display the essential structural conditions of the mode of production as a determinate social form, but it must also grasp the inner trajectory of development that gives rise to this social form and governs its passing away. What distinguishes the science of Marx from the science of Ricardo is that whereas Ricardo treats the essential features of capitalism as fixes categories, and attempts to trace out the laws governing the distribution of the social product within a mode of production defined by those categories, Marx comprehends the essential features of capitalism as relatively stable structures thrown up by a self-developing process. For Marx the scientific enterprise cannot rest with the analysis of the structures governing a determinate mode of production, but must go on to grasp those structures as part of a law-governed, self-developing process.

The scientific knowledge of the developmental trajectory of these structures involves a kind of rationality distinct from that appropriate for the analysis of a set of structures as defining a relatively fixed and stable mode of production. For the latter task, the hypothetical-deductive mode of analysis is appropriate. Knowledge of the developmental trajectories requires a dialectical mode of analysis. Such a dialectical analysis seeks to grasp the "inner necessary connections" between the various determinate forms that arise in the course of historical development.[36] The necessary connections discovered in this way are distinct from the causal regularities of Humean empiricism, distinct from the deductive connections of Aristotelian logic, and distinct from the conceptual connections of the Hegelian dialectic. They are the determining conditions of the independent real process of development. Their conception involves a new conception of "necessity," a new version of "determinism," a new conception of "causality," a "new mode of abstraction," and a new method of "dialectical derivation."[37]

These are large claims which give substantial content to the idea that Marxist social theory involves a method distinct from the method of pre-Marxist science. But are they true? Zeleńy's argument for these claims turns on his analysis of the theoretical practice exhibited in *Capital*. As a way of testing Zelený's claim, let us consider an example of such a dialectical derivation at work in *Capital*. Zelený claims that it is in Marx's exposition of the transitions from one value form to another "at which the departure from traditional derivation and the use of a new method of derivation have come to light in the *clearest* way."[38]

In volume 1 of *Capital*, in the opening chapter on commodities, Marx distinguishes between four forms of value: the elementary form, the expanded form, the general form, and the money form. In the elementary form, a certain quantity of one commodity is claimed to be equivalent to a certain quantity of another commodity:

elementary form:

x commodity A = y commodity B
(e.g., 20 yards of linen = 1 coat).

In the expanded form, a definite quantity of one commodity is claimed to be equivalent to definite quantities of each of the other commodities with which it can be exchanged in this fashion:

expanded form:

z commodity A = u com. B or = v com. C or
= w Com. D or = x Com. E or = etc.

The general form of value simply reverses this expanded form:

1 coat
10 lbs. of tea
40 lbs. of coffee
general form:
1 quarter of corn = 20 yds. of linen
2 ounces of gold
1/2 a ton of iron
x com. A., etc.

The money form is identical to the general form except that the place filled by the 20 yards of linen is taken by a particular commodity that is socially identified as the universal equivalent for purposes of exchange, in this case, by 2 ounces of gold:

1 coat
10 lbs. of tea
40 lbs. of coffee
money form:
1 quarter of corn = 2 ounces of gold

2 ounces of gold
1/2 a ton of iron
x com. *A*., etc.

It is in the transitions from one value form to another that Zelený finds the clearest example of dialectical derivation in Marx. He notes that Marx uses a dialectically charged terminology to describe these relations. For example, in discussing the elementary value form, Marx characterizes the left-hand side of the equation as the active, relative side and the right-hand side of the equation as the passive, equivalent side. He says of these two sides, "The relative form and the equivalent form are two intimately connected, mutually dependent and inseparable elements of the expression of value; but, at the same time, are mutually exclusive, antagonistic extremes—*i.e.*, poles of the same expression."[39] Marx also tells us that though a commodity appears at first sight to be a very trivial thing, in reality it abounds in "metaphysical subtleties and theological niceties."[40] Nevertheless, I do not think examination of Marx's argument supports the claim that he here relies on a distinctly dialectical mode of derivation.

To begin with, neither of the comments from Marx quoted here pertains to the derivation of one value form from another. The first is a dialectical gloss on the elementary value form itself. The second pertains to the fetishistic appearance that these equivalences somehow reside in the things themselves rather than in the equivalence of the labor time socially necessary to produce them, as an examination of the text that follows the quoted passage will show. We need, then, to focus on the reasoning that takes us from one value form to the next.

The transition from the elementary to the expanded form occurs in a passage at the end of the section on the elementary value form:

> Nevertheless, the elementary form of value passes by an easy transition into a more complete form. It is true that by means of the elementary form, the value of a commodity A, becomes expressed in terms of one, and only one, other commodity. But that one may be a commodity of any kind, coat, iron, corn, or anything else. Therefore, according as A is placed in relation with one or the other, we get for one and the same commodity different elementary expressions of value. The number of such possible expressions is limited only by the number of the different kinds of commodities distinct from it. The isolated expression of A's value, is therefore convertible into a series, prolonged to any length, of the different elementary expressions of that value.[41]

Here the crucial transition seems to rest on the appeal to the fact that any commodity can appear as the equivalent in the elementary value form. Contrary to Zelený, this appeal does not rest upon some dialectical development of the elementary form itself but, rather, upon "external" background knowledge about the exchangeability of commodities in a market economy. The analysis is here appealing to one of the structurally defining features of a capitalist economy.

The second transition, from the expanded to the general form of value, is even less mysterious than the first. It is, in fact, a simple case of the transition from $a=b$ to $b=a$, as Marx notes at the end of the section on the expanded form.

We are left, then, with the transition from the general form to the money form as the remaining case to be considered and, indeed, it is this case that Zelený features in his discussion of dialectical derivations in *Capital*. There is something peculiar about the transition to the money form. The first three value forms are all attainable by analysis of the structurally defining characteristic of capitalist economies as market economies in which all commodities are interchangeable. From this it follows that a given quantity of any one commodity can be expressed as equivalent to any other, individually or in a series of disjunctions. However, that this universal equivalence should take a money form is not itself analytically derivable from the structural characteristic of universal exchangeability. There is no logical impossibility in a barter economy. Marx notes that the transition from the general form to the money form differs from the transitions involved in passing from the elementary to the expanded to the general form.[42] Zelený, too, focuses on this transition. Having raised the question as to the nature of the *necessity* involved in the transition from one value form to another, Zelený claims that these transitions involve neither Kantian analytical necessity nor Hegelian dialectical necessity. He then focuses on the transition from the general form to the value form and quotes a passage from Chapter 2 of Volume 1 of *Capital* that comments on the necessary appearance of money:

> Money is a crystal formed of necessity in the course of the exchanges, whereby different products of labour are practically equated to one another and thus by practice converted into commodities. The historical progress and extension of exchanges develops the contrast, latent in commodities, between use-value and value. The necessity for giving an external expression to this contrast for the purposes of commercial intercourse, urges on the establishment of an independent form of value, and finds no rest until it is once for all satisfied by the differentiation of commodities into commodities and money. At the same rate, then, as the conversion of products into commodities is being accomplished, so also is the conversion of one special commodity into money.[43]

I think that Zelený is right in saying that what we find here is a sense of necessity distinct from Kantian analytical necessity and Hegelian dialectical necessity. But I do not think that what we see here is a new Marxian dialectical necessity; rather, it is practical necessity. An exchange economy needs some one commodity to serve as the money form because this facilitates commercial exchange. It is a necessity "for purposes of commercial intercourse." Thus, in the passage mentioned above, where Marx distinguishes the transition from the general form to the money form from previous transitions in the analysis of value, he says that the money form emerges as a result of "social custom."[44]

I do not think Marx's account of the emergence of the money form need involve him in any controversial methodological procedures or force us to attribute to him any nonstandard concepts of abstraction, necessity, or causation.

Since this transition is central to Zelený's argument, I conclude that his claims for these nonstandard concepts, and for a distinctive dialectical form of derivation in Marx's social science, fail.[45]

Like Zelený, Jon Elster finds in Marx's theory of capitalism instances of "dialectical deduction" that distinguish Marx's science from ordinary science. Unlike Zelený, who regards such dialectical derivation as a contribution to the advancement of science, Elster regards Marx's use of dialectical deduction as "fundamentally misguided reasoning."[46] He quotes the following passage from Marx's *Grundrisse*:

> We have already seen, in the case of money, how value, having become independent as such—or the general form of wealth—is capable of no other motion than a quantitative one; to increase itself. It is according to its concept the quintessence of all use values; but, since it is always only a definite amount of money (here, capital), its quantitative limit is in contradiction with its quality. It is therefore inherent in its nature constantly to drive beyond its own barrier. . . . Already for that reason, value which insists on itself as value preserves itself through increase; and it preserves itself precisely only by constantly driving beyond its quantitative barrier, which contradicts its character as form, its inner generality.[47]

Elster comments on this as follows:

> Marx here tries to perform with a conceptual sleight of hand the task to which Max Weber devoted vast empirical studies: to explain the emergence of the reinvestment motive in early capitalism. No short-cut, however, is possible—unless one already has the answer. The explanation of saving and investment must be found in the motives of individual economic agents. It cannot be derived from a conceptual analysis of money.[48]

Though hostile to such "deductions," Elster does not claim that their presence in Marx's work vitiates the scientific value of that work. The reason for this is that Elster sees such dialectical deductions as lying alongside an independently grounded scientific theory of capitalism in Marx's works. In his account of Marx's genuine scientific theory, Elster offers a view of the theory of capitalism that is, in its broad outlines, similar to the account offered above in terms of the working out of the unintended consequences of individual actions within the basic social structures defining a capitalist system of production.[49]

For Elster, dialectical deductions in Marx's works are pseudoscientific excrescences on an otherwise healthy body of science. In a sense, then, he agrees with the view that what is of value in Marxist science is ordinary science. Elster's approach has been criticized by some readers who see in it a highly selective reading of Marx. To some it appears that Elster has thrown away the distinctly valuable methodology of Marx's work. On the contrary, it seems to me that Elster is too quick to charge Marx with occasional lapses into dialectical nonsense.

Elster contrasts the dialectical pseudoscience of Marx with the empirical research of Max Weber. He complains that a dialectic of concepts cannot provide a shortcut to such empirical research. The chosen example of such dialectical deduction in Marx's works is the passage from the *Grundrisse* quoted above. Julius Sensat has raised a number of questions about Elster's claim to find such dialectical derivations in Marx.[50] Elster's case relies heavily on what Marx says in unpublished manuscripts and popular journalistic writings. The *Grundrisse* is one of these works not published in Marx's lifetime—it was an early draft of Marx's work in political economy. Further, in a parenthetical remark within the *Grundrisse*, Marx cautions himself concerning such dialectical derivations. He says, in a different but similarly "dialectical" context, that it will be necessary to correct "the idealist manner of presentation, which makes it seem as if it were merely a matter of conceptual determinations and of the dialectic of those concepts."[51] Similar cautions against the dialectic of concepts appear elsewhere, in a discussion of method in the *Grundrisse* and in the Afterword to the second German edition of *Capital*.[52] Elster construes these remarks as expressions of Marx's bad conscience over reliance on dialectical deductions. Sensat suggests—rightly, in my view—that these remarks "express a criticism not of an actual assertion of conceptual self-realization but rather of the use of certain expressions for wrongly suggesting that such an assertion is intended."[53]

Caution in the use of unpublished drafts, such as the *Grundrisse*, and Sensat's specific comments on Elster's reading of Marx's self-criticism in regard to the appearance of dialectical conceptual derivations seem to me to be confirmed by looking more closely at what Marx has to say on the same topic in *Capital*. In his citation of the example of dialectical deduction in the *Grundrisse*, Elster directs us, without further comment and without quotation, to this passage in *Capital* where Marx discusses the same point:

> The circulation of money as capital is, on the contrary, an end in itself, for the expansion of value takes place only within this constantly renewed movement. The circulation of capital has therefore no limits.
>
> As the conscious representative of this movement, the possessor of money becomes a capitalist. His person, or rather his pocket, is the point from which the money starts and to which it returns. The expansion of value, which is the objective basis or main-spring of the circulation M-C-M, becomes his subjective aim, and it is only in so far as the appropriation of ever more and more wealth in the abstract becomes the sole motive of his operations, that he functions as a capitalist, that is, as capital personified and endowed with consciousness and a will.[54]

The distinction between the simple money form and the form of money as capital remains, as does the idea that capital aims at unlimited expansion of value. However, here the idea of a dialectic of concepts appears to vanish. In his comments on the draft discussion in the *Grundrisse*, Elster insists that "The explanation of savings and investment must be found in the motives of individual economic agents. It cannot be derived from a conceptual analysis of money."[55] In the discussion of the matter in *Capital*, Marx, too, insists that "it is only in so far as the appropriation of ever more and more wealth in the abstract becomes the sole motive of his operations, that he functions as a capitalist." Capitalist behavior depends upon the presence of certain motives in individual economic agents. Marx says nothing here about the origins of those motives. He is saying that to act as a capitalist is to aim at unlimited expansion of value. He is not attempting to explain the origins of this behavior by deduction from the concept of money. In *Capital*, Marx has corrected the misleading suggestion of a dialectical conceptual account of the form of value as capital. Instead, he clearly indicates the dependence of this form on individual motives that are not derived in a dialectic of concepts.

The problem of dialectical derivations will recur in the content of my discussion of historical materialism. In discussing historical materialism, I will also comment on Elster's criticisms of functionalist explanation in Marx's works, and on some related issues pertaining to methodological individualism. My aim here has been to focus on the question of dialectical derivations in Marx's theory of capitalism. Like Elster, I see this theory of capitalism as an account built around the analysis of the unintended outcomes of individual action within the institutional framework of capitalism. Where Elster sees Marx as lapsing into a dialectical pseudoscience, I am inclined to follow Sensat's more sympathetic reading of the significance of the passages in question in Marx's works.

NOTES

1. In his classic critique of Marx's economic theory, *Karl Marx and the Close of His System* (1896), Eugen von Böhm-Bawerk argued that Marx's attempt to reconcile the labor theory of value with both a uniform rate of profit and differing capital/labor ratios in different industries failed. For a discussion of the issue sympathetic to Marx and the labor theory, see Maurice Dobb, *Theories of Value and Distribution* (Cambridge: Cambridge University Press, 1973), pp. 158–161. For a discussion sympathetic to Böhm-Bawerk's criticism, see Gottfried Haberler, "Marxist Economics in Retrospect and Prospect," in *Marxist Ideology in the Contemporary World*, edited by Milorad M. Drachkovitch (New York: Praeger, 1966). Marx clearly anticipates the difficulty, even in the volume 1 exposition of the labor theory. See *Capital* (New York: International, 1973), vol. 1, p. 220 n.1; Karl Marx and Friedrich Engels, *Marx Engels Werke* (Berlin: Dietz Verlag, 1968), vol. 23, p. 234 n.31a (hereafter *MEW*).

2. *Capital*, vol. 3, pt. 6. For recognition of the prima facie incompatibility, see p. 623; *MEW*, vol. 25, p. 636. On the debt to Ricardo, see *Capital*, vol. 3, p. 648; *MEW*, vol. 25, pp. 662–663.

3. Marx, *Contribution to the Critique of Political Economy* (New York: International, 1970), p. 63. Cf. *Capital*, vol. 3, p. 633.

4. Ernest Mandel, *The Formation of the Economic Thought of Karl Marx* (New York: Monthly Review Press, 1971), pp. 40–41.

5. Marx, *Theories of Surplus Value*, (Moscow: Progress, 1968), vol. 2, pp. 216–217; *MEW*, vol. 26, pt. 2, pp. 214–215. See also *Theories*, vol. 1, pp. 95–97; *MEW*, vol. 26, pt. 1, pp. 66–69.

6. *Theories*, vol. 2, pp. 399–401; *MEW*, vol. 26, pt. 2, pp. 402–402.

7. Oskar Lange, "Marxian Economics and Modern Economic Theory" (1935), repr. in *Marx and Modern Economics*, edited by David Horowitz (New York: Monthly Review Press, 1968), pp. 76–77; Joan Robinson, "The Labor Theory of Value," in her *Collected Economic Papers* (Oxford: Basil Blackwell, 1951), p. 148. Attempts to replace the labor theory with a marginal utility theory of value had been made by some of the turn-of-the-century revisionists and by the English Fabians. See Bo Gustafsson, *Marxismus*, pp. 318, 324.

8. See Daniel Little, *The Scientific Marx* (Minneapolis: University of Minnesota Press, 1986), pp. 82–91, for a review of some of this work.

9. In this respect, I agree with Little's account of the foundations of Marx's theory of capitalism in chapter 1 of *The Scientific Marx*. However, I reject Little's view that Marx's science, and perhaps all of social science, rests upon a methodology that is philosophically different in important ways from the methodology of the natural sciences. On this, see Richard Hudelson's review of *The Scientific Marx* in *The Philosophical Review*, July 1989, pp. 421–423.

10. The role of this kind of explanation in Marx's theory of capitalism is stressed by Little in his conception of the "logic of institutions" (*Scientific Marx*, pp. 33–37). It is also central to Jon Elster's account of Marx's economic theory in his *Making Sense of Marx* (Cambridge: Cambridge University Press, 1985), pp. 3, 22–27.

11. Joan Robinson, *Economic Philosophy* (Chicago: Aldine, 1962), p. 37.

12. Leszek Nowak, *The Structure of Idealization* (Dordrecht: Reidel, 1980).

13. The phrase is from Oskar Lange, *Political Economy* (New York: Pergamon Press, 1963), vol. 1, pp. 117–118. A similar conception of Marx's theory can be found in Ronald Meek, *Economics and Ideology and Other Essays* (London: Chapman and Hall, 1967), pp. 93–94.

14. *Capital*, vol. 1, p. 220 n.1; *MEW*, vol. 23, p. 234.

15. Marx, *Grundrisse* (New York: Vintage, 1973), pp. 100–101; *MEW*, vol. 13, p. 632.

16. *Capital*, vol. 3, p. 817; *MEW*, vol. 25, p. 825; Marx to Kugelmann, July 11, 1868; *MEW*, vol. 32, p. 553. G. A. Cohen has rightly stressed the importance of the essence/appearance distinction for Marx's philosophy of science. In "Karl Marx and the Withering Away of Social Science," *Philosophy and Public Affairs* 1(2) (Winter 1972), he cites a number of other references to the distinction in Marx's work. For a response to the idea of the withering of social science under socialism, see Richard Hudelson, "Marxist Science as Ordinary Science," *Noûs* 20 (1) (Spring 1986): 59–60.

17. *Capital*, vol. 1, p. 19; *MEW*, vol. 23, p. 12.

18. *Capital*, vol. 1, *MEW*, vol. 23, p. 25.

19. Georg Lukács, *History and Class Consciousness* (Cambridge, MA: MIT Press, 1971), p. 1.

20. Quoted in Helena Sheehan, *Marxism and the Philosophy of Science* (Atlantic Highlands, NJ: Humanities, 1985), p. 280.

21. Among others, by G. D. H. Cole, *The Meaning of Marxism* (Ann Arbor, MI: Ann Arbor Paperbacks, 1948); George Lichtheim, *Marxism* (New York: Praeger, 1961); Louis Dupré, *The Philosophical Foundations of Marxism* (New York: Harcourt Brace and World, 1966); Bertell Ollman, *Alienation* (Cambridge: Cambridge University Press, 1971); Schlomo Avineri, *The Social and Political Thought of Karl Marx* (Cambridge: Cambridge University Press, 1971); and Istvan Meszaros, *Marx's Theory of Alienation* (New York: Harper Torchbook, 1972). For an overview of some recent perspectives, see

David McLellan, "Elusive Foundations: Recent Work on Marx and Marxism," *Philosophy* 57 (219) (January 1982). McLellan accepts the distinctive method view (p. 119).

22. Here and above I use the term "Western Marxism." Insofar as the family of interpretations of Marx under consideration here has dominated "Western" alternatives to "Eastern" Marxist-Leninism, there is a certain validity to this. But, insofar as several influential Eastern European interpretations of Marx—for example, those of the Polish philosopher Leszek Kolakowski and the Yugoslav philosopher Mihailo Markovic—also belong to the family of interpretations stemming from the work of Lukács, I prefer the designation "humanistic Marxism," which is not geographically misleading, for the family of views in question.

23. The following discussion of these arguments and the argument of Ball discussed below, are largely taken from Hudelson's "Marxist Science as Ordinary Science" and are used here by permission of the editor of *Noûs* 20 (1) (1986): 53–63.

24. Lukács, *History and Class Consciousness*, pp. 6–7.

25. Ibid., p. 7.

26. Terence Ball, "Marxian Science and Positivist Politics," in *After Marx*, edited by Terence Ball and James Farr (Cambridge: Cambridge University Press, 1984), p. 249.

27. Lukács, *History and Class Consciousness*, p. 233.

28. On the reflective nature of critical social theory, see Raymond Geuss, *The Idea of a Critical Theory: Habermas and the Frankfurt School* (Cambridge: Cambridge University Press, 1981), p. 55. Though I shall make no attempt to follow Geuss' close analysis of the various possibilities involved in the idea of critical theory, the discussion that follows is obviously indebted to his work. That this reflective aspect of social theory makes for an important qualitative difference between social theory and natural science is central to the claim that Marx offers a new kind of science in Roy Edgley, "Marx's Revolutionary Science," in *Issues in Marxist Philosophy*, edited by John Mepham and David-Hillel Ruben (Atlantic Highlands, NJ: Humanities Press, 1979), pp. 5–26.

29. *Capital*, vol. 1, pp. 588–591; *MEW*, vol. 23, pp. 614–617.

30. Cf. Geuss, *Idea*, pp. 26–31. Neurath, of course, believed in the emancipatory power of positivism. On this, see Carr, "Tolerant Empiricism" (unpublished M.A. thesis, University of Alberta, Edmonton, 1977), p. 39.

31. Chapter 5.

32. Bertell Ollman uses these examples in making his case for a theory of internal relations in Marx in *Alienation*, p. 15 nn. 12, 13. In Richard Hudelson, "Marx and the Theory of Internal Relations: A Critical Note on Ollman's Interpretation of Marx," *Philosophy of the Social Sciences* 14 (December 1984): 505–507, I argue against Ollman's view of the significance of these passages.

33. This argument appears in Lucio Colletti, *From Rousseau to Lenin* (New York: Monthly Review Press, 1972), pp. 74–76. A similar argument appears in Alan Garfinkel, *Forms of Explanation* (New Haven: Yale University Press, 1981), ch. 5.

34. This may have been the case with Joseph Schumpeter.

35. Jindřich Zeleńy, *The Logic of Marx* (Totowa, NJ: Rowman and Littlefield, 1980), p. 114.

36. Ibid., pp. 52, 97.

37. Ibid: "necessity," p. 78; "determinism," p. 39; "causality," pp. 71, 75, 77; "abstraction," p. 105; "derivation," p. 47.

38. Ibid., p. 56. In focusing on these value forms, Zeleńy may be following the lead of Lenin, who pointed to Marx's analysis of commodities as exemplary of dialectical

analysis in *Capital*. Cf. Lenin, *Philosophical Notebooks*, in *Collected Works* (Moscow: Foreign Languages Publishing House, 1963), vol. 38, pp. 360–361.

39. Marx, *Capital*, vol. 1, p. 48; *MEW*, vol. 23, p. 63; Zelený, *Logic of Marx*, p. 48.

40. *Capital*, vol. 1, p. 71; *MEW*, vol. 23, p. 85.

41. *Capital*, vol. 1, p. 62; *MEW*, vol. 23, p. 76, Zelený, *Logic of Marx*, pp. 48–49.

42. *Capital*, vol. 1, p. 70; *MEW*, vol. 23, p. 84.

43. *Capital*, vol. 1, pp. 86–87; *MEW*, vol. 23, pp. 101–102; Zelený, *Logic of Marx*, p. 50.

44. *Capital*, vol. 1, p. 70; *MEW*, vol. 23, p. 84. Cf. further discussion of this in *Capital*, vol. 1, pp. 86–89; *MEW*, vol. 23, pp. 101–104.

45. See Ulrich Steinvorth, *Eine analytische Interpretation der Marxschen Dialektik* (Maisenheim am Glan: Anton Hain, 1977), pp. 53–58, for a discussion of the "dialectic" of value forms in Marx that also disputes the kind of reading advanced by Zelený.

46. Elster, *Making Sense of Marx*, p. 39.

47. Ibid., quoting Marx, *Grundrisse*, p. 270.

48. Elster, *Making Sense of Marx*, p. 39.

49. Ibid., pp. 3–5.

50. Julius Sensat, "Methodological Individualism and Marxism," *Economics and Philosophy* 4 (2) (October 1988): 203–209.

51. Marx, *Grundrisse*, p. 151.

52. Ibid., p. 101; *Capital*, vol. 1, p. 19.

53. Sensat, "Methodological Individualism," p. 207.

54. *Capital*, vol. 1, pp. 151–152.

55. Elster, *Making Sense of Marx*, p. 39.

4

Historical Materialism

My examination of the theory of capitalism has shown no reason why Marxist social theory must be understood as fundamentally different from ordinary science in its method. No compelling case for either the Lukácsian humanistic Marx or the Leninist dialectical Marx emerged from consideration of the theory of capitalism. The view of Marxist science as ordinary science seems confirmed by the examination of the paradigm case of Marxist social theory. Nevertheless, serious difficulties remain. In particular, Marx's materialist conception of history raises a number of difficulties for the view of Marxist science as ordinary science.

The canonical expression of this materialistic conception of history appears in the famous Preface to the *Contribution to the Critique of Political Economy* of 1859. There Marx seems to assert, among other things, that in all societies the economic base determines the ideological superstructure, that all societies go through a certain sequence of distinct modes of production, and that the transition from one mode of production to another is a result of the developing forces of production bursting asunder the relations of production that fetter them.[1]

These claims have been subjected to two lines of criticism: either they are manifestly false or else they are so vague and ambiguous as to be of no value as empirical social science. Thus, for example, it has been argued that it is clearly impossible to account for the religion, law, and art of a society, all of which are part of its ideological superstructure, solely in terms of the characteristics of its economic base. Or it has been argued that it is clearly false that all societies have to progress through a definite sequence of modes of production, as the Russian and Chinese revolutions, which bypassed capitalism, have made apparent. Or it is argued that the origins of capitalism, even on Marx's account, contradict his theory that the autonomous factor in historical change is the development of the productive forces. I shall return to these charges later in this chapter. However, I would like to begin with consideration of an argument by Karl Popper that rests on philosophical objections to the possibility of a scientific theory of history. Popper has argued that the very idea of historical laws of development rests on a confusion about the nature of scientific laws.[2]

ON THE POSSIBILITY OF A SCIENCE OF HISTORY

Popper raises a number of distinct objections to any claim to know laws of historical development. Here I shall consider the two of his objections that seem to me most persuasive.[3] Popper begins with an argument designed to show that it is impossible to predict the future. The argument goes as follows:

1. The course of human history is strongly influenced by the growth of human knowledge. (The truth of this premise must be admitted even by those who see in our ideas, including our scientific ideas, merely the by-products of material developments of some kind or other.)
2. We cannot predict, by rational or scientific methods, the future growth of our scientific knowledge. (This assertion can be logically proved by considerations that are sketched below.)
3. We cannot, therefore, predict the future course of human history.[4]

Popper argues that the second premise is the decisive premise in the argument and claims that it is provable on strictly logical grounds. Granted that this is so, what of the first premise?

Elsewhere in *The Poverty of Historicism* Popper talks about what he calls the "Oedipus effect."[5] This effect involves the influence, either positive or negative, of a prediction upon the predicted event. As we have seen, such influences are especially problematic in the social sciences. But does the problem of the Oedipus effect render all predictions in the social sciences impossible? Popper himself does not draw this strong conclusion. Following his formulation of the argument for the impossibility of predicting the course of history, Popper comments:

> The argument does not, of course, refute the possibility of every kind of social prediction; on the contrary, it is perfectly compatible with the possibility of testing social theories—for example, economic theories—by . . . predicting that certain developments will take place under certain conditions. It only refutes the possibility of predicting historical developments to the extent to which they may be influenced by the growth of our knowledge.[6]

The question, then, is to what extent Marx's historical predictions are strongly influenced by the growth of human knowledge. On the face of it, it would appear that Marx's historical predictions are especially vulnerable to Oedipus effects. For example, his prediction of the coming of socialism hinges on his identification of tendencies inherent in capitalism that work to create a revolutionary overthrow of the system. But, it might be argued, by the very act of bringing these tendencies to the light of day, Marx makes possible action by the ruling class to dampen them. Legislative control of laissez-faire capitalism through the legalization of trade unions and the institution of welfare state measures, in part informed by Marx's theories, may have worked to save capitalism from its predicted fate.

I believe that there is considerable truth in his view of the effect of socialist theory on capitalism. Others would argue that the revolution-producing tendencies of capitalism are not manageable. One way of looking at these tendencies is to see them as the unintended social outcome of self-interested individual behavior within the framework of capitalism. If this is so, then, having read Marx, each individual capitalist could know the revolutionary social outcome, yet have no motive to alter his individual behavior. If others change and he does not, then he reaps super profits and there is no revolution. If he changes and others do not, then he reaps super losses and still there is a revolution. In short, each individual, even knowing the predicted outcome, may be rationally motivated to persist in the socially destructive behavior. Further, social legislation may succeed in containing these destructive pressures on one point, only to have them emerge again on another. From this point of view, Marx's predictions are relatively immune to the Oedipus effect because of the disparity between individual and social rationality built into capitalism.

While I am inclined to think that socialist theory has influenced the evolution of capitalism at the level of public policy, and while I am not convinced that it is impossible to contain the revolution-producing tendencies of capitalism, I shall not attempt to defend these beliefs here. The point I want to make is that Popper's argument against the possibility of historical predictions rests upon the empirical truth of the first premise: that history is strongly influenced by the growth of knowledge, with respect to all relevant historical predictions. While I am inclined to agree with Popper that Marx's theories have influenced the behavior of the object of study, I do not think this must always be true of every historical prediction. Hence, I do not think that Popper's argument succeeds in showing that historical predictions are all impossible.

There is another sense in which I think Popper's argument, as a criticism of Marxisim, is misdirected. In the passage quoted above, in which he allows for the possibility of some social predictions, Popper cites as permissible, predictions made by economic theories which predict that certain developments will take place under certain conditions. It is arguable that Marx's predictions are of exactly this sort. They rest on tendencies inherent in capitalism and, hence, are conditional upon the continued existence of the conditions of capitalist production that give rise to them. This understanding of Marx's "laws" of capitalist development and of his "laws" of historical development as "tendencies" has become a standard part of Marxist-Leninist literature and offers a way of understanding these law claims that avoids the kind of criticism advanced by Popper.[7]

However, Popper advances another argument which tries to show that there is a serious misunderstanding of the nature of genuine science in Marxism's claim to know the laws of historical development. In particular, he argues that Marxism confuses genuine scientific laws with mere empirical trends. This criticism needs to be considered before the understanding of Marx's law claims as tendencies can be assessed.

Popper draws the distinction between trends and laws in the following way. A trend statement asserts the existence of some tendency over time, such as a tendency for population to grow. A trend statement is existential in its logical form. A law statement, on the other hand, is universal in its logical form. It makes no existential assertions. It "asserts the impossibility of something or other."[8]

One should not conclude from this that trends are of no importance or interest to science. The explanation of trends is a proper aim for theory. An explained trend is a kind of empirical law. Thus, a law of the form "if conditions of kind *c* obtain, then there will be a trend of kind *t*"is acceptable to Popper.[9] The historicist's error, of which Marx is guilty, according to Popper, consists in the failure to recognize that empirically observed trends rest on such *c* conditions. As Popper sees it, the historicist simply notes some pattern in history and projects this pattern into the future as an "absolute trend."[10] Thus, he criticizes Marx for failing to understand that trends are dependent upon *c* conditions and, hence, for confusing trends with laws:

> There is, for example, a trend towards "an accumulation of means of production" (as Marx puts it). But we should hardly expect it to persist in a population which is rapidly decreasing; and such a decrease may in turn depend upon extra-economic conditions, for example, on chance inventions, or conceivably on the direct physiological (perhaps biochemical) impact of an industrial environment.[11]

This is the only specific example Popper offers of this central fallacy of historicism at work in Marx's thought. I believe the example seriously distorts what is going on in Marx. Marx did believe that there is a tendency for the means of production to accumulate. This is true both as a belief about the course of human history as a whole and as a belief in a tendency for an accelerated accumulation of means of production as a characteristic of capitalism. But in neither case does the belief rest simply on a projection of a tendency observed to hold in the past.

The general tendency for accumulation rests on Marx's account of human need satisfaction. People, like all animals, have certain needs that must be satisfied if they are to survive and reproduce. Unlike other animals, which simply follow instinctive behavior patterns in satisfying their needs, human beings use their heads to devise new, more reliable, and more productive means for satisfying needs. And they pass on these artificially developed means to succeeding generations. Further, Marx notes that this tendency for accumulation depends on commerce and that it can be retarded or reversed by warfare.[12]

The specific tendency for an accelerated accumulation under capitalism rests on Marx's analysis of the behavior of individual capitalists under conditions of a competitive struggle for survival. Further, Marx realized that the rate of accumulation is dependent upon a number of factors. He explicitly mentions the effects of the degree of exploitation, the productivity of labor, the ratio of capital consumed to capital employed in a given time period, and the magnitude of capital advanced.[13] Marx made some effort to trace out the effects of these variables. He also recognized the dependence of the rate of accumulation upon the ratio of investment to revenues consumed by the capitalist, and foreign trade and investment, the effects of which he made no attempt to analyze.

Insofar as Marx recognized that both the existence of the trend toward accumulation and the specific rate of that trend depend upon conditions which he attempts to formulate, it does not seem to be the case that he confuses trends with laws. Popper comments: "But what about those who see that trends depend on conditions, and who try to find these conditions and to formulate them explicitly? My answer is that I have no quarrel with them."[14] However, a different interpretation of Popper is possible. On this interpretation, Popper's claim is that an explained trend is to qualify as an empirical law only if *all* the conditions upon which the trend is dependent are explicitly formulated in the antecedent conditions of the assumed law: "If we succeed in determining the *complete* or sufficient conditions *c* of a singular trend, *t*, then we can formulate the universal law: 'Whenever there are conditions of the kind *c* there will be a trend of the kind *t*'."[15] Since it is true that Marx neglects to state the dependency of the tendency toward accumulation upon rate and direction of change in population size, and since it is possible that this tendency would fail to obtain if there were, say, a sharp decline in size of population, Popper seems to conclude that the supposed laws are not laws and are, in fact, indicative of methodological confusion.

This conclusion is unwarranted. In the first place, Popper seems to confuse questions of truth with questions of method. An explained trend can be expressed as a law of the form "If conditions $c_1 \ldots c_n$ obtain, then there will be a tendency of kind *t*." This hypothetical statement is false only if there is some set of circumstances such that $c_1 \ldots c_n$ obtain and trend *t* does not obtain. But if there is some such set of circumstances, then $c_1 \ldots c_n$ cannot be a full statement of all the conditions upon which the trend is dependent. As a methodological principle, Popper's requirement that formulation of the law include *all* conditions upon which the trend is dependent has the consequence that any false explained trend law claim is *methodologically* unsound.

Further, scientific practice often fails to conform to Popper's methodological principle. An explanation may be elliptically formulated so that specific steps in a proof, assumptions, or laws necessary for a model explanation are omitted.

Or a proposed explanation may in fact be only an explanation sketch that presents the outlines for a complete explanation, the full presentation of which would require considerable elaboration and supplementation. If we accept Popper's principle, such forms of explanatory incompleteness must be seen as indicative of methodological confusion.

In short, Popper's demand that all conditions upon which a trend depends must be explicitly formulated seems too strong, while his weaker claim, that one must recognize the dependence of trends on some conditions, allows Marx's claim for a trend toward accumulation to escape his methodological criticism of historicism.

HISTORICAL MATERIALISM AS SOCIAL SCIENCE

Supposing, then, that Popper's attempt to show the impossibility of a science of history fails, let us turn to consideration of historical materialism as claimant to the status of such a science. At the beginning of this chapter, we noted the charge that the central claims of historical materialism are manifestly false. Marxist replies to such charges have produced various attempts to get around them. Thus, for example, Engels responded to the charge that, contrary to historical materialism, ideas influenced the course of history by conceding that ideological factors may depend upon noneconomic factors as well, and may even play a determining role with respect to the economic base. However, Engels also says that economic factors are the "*ultimately* determining factor."[16] Humanistic Marxists have offered an alternative response in which they entirely reject the economic determinist aspects of historical materialism and the idea of laws of historical development. They have sought to comprehend the social system as an organic totality of dialectically interacting parts.[17] These and similar attempts to avoid charges of manifest falseness exposed Marxists to the positivistically inspired charge that historical materialism was defective as scientific theory because it had become so vague and ambiguous in its content as to be empirically immune to refutation, and consequently was empirically empty.

Since about 1977, a number of works have appeared that attempt to defend the scientific value of historical materialism against such charges.[18] G. A. Cohen's *Karl Marx's Theory of History: A Defence* provides a strategic point of entry for the consideration of this work. On Cohen's account, the central elements in Marx's theory of history are the productive forces, the productive relations, and the superstructure built upon the production relations. Productive forces include the physical and intellectual powers of labor, raw materials, and the machinery and tools of labor.[19] Production relations include patterns of cooperation and interaction among people employed in production, and the relations of power and control over productive forces within which production takes place.[20] Cohen devotes considerable attention to the problems attendant upon the definitions of these key terms with the aim of avoiding the charges of vagueness and ambiguity mentioned above. The result is a formulation of historical materialism as a theory containing law claims capable of generating empirically testable explanations of some historical processes and some social institutions.

Cohen presents the theoretical core of Marx's historical materialism as a functionalist theory of history and society. On this account, "production relations have the character that they do because, in virtue of that character, they promote the development of the productive forces" and "the superstructure has the character it does because, in virtue of that character, it confers stability on the production relations."[21] Having worked out this formulation of the theory of historical materialism, Cohen goes on to try to show that the theory is textually well grounded as an interpretation of Marx, and to try to defend this view of the theory against philosophical objections to functionalist explanation in general, and against Marx's functional explanations in particular.

There are a number of threads in Cohen's defense of functionalist explanation that are important for my purposes. First, Cohen does not see the kind of functionalist theory offered by Marx as unique to Marxist social theory. Rather, he sees Marx's historical materialism as sharing a common structure with functionalist theories in such areas as biology and anthropology. Second, while Cohen distinguishes functionalist from nonfunctionalist theories, he tries to show that functionalist theories satisfy those formal properties of nonfunctionalist theories thought to be important by positivist philosophers of science. Thus, for example, functionalist theories contain universal law claims, and these law claims can be used to generate explanations that satisfy the requirements of Carl Hempel's D-N model of explanation. This is not to say that Cohen endorses the adequacy of the Hempelian model; it is just to say that, insofar as this model does point to important features of scientific explanation, it is satisfied by historical materialism as Cohen interprets it.[22]

Cohen's defense of Marx's theory of history seeks to rescue the theory from attacks growing out of positivist philosophy of science. The strategy behind his defense is one of accommodation rather than confrontation with this philosophy of science. In this sense, his reading of Marx falls within the camp of positivistic Marxism. The acclaim that Cohen's interpretation has received rests on its subtle analysis of the basic categories of historical materialism, its success in formulating a statement of historical materialism that both avoids many of the standard criticisms of it and at the same time remains remarkably close to Marx's own formulations of the theory, and its defense of functional explanation in general. Nevertheless, Cohen's defense has met with criticisms that point to persistent difficulties with historical materialism as viewed from the perspective of positivist philosophy of science. There are two difficulties that I want to consider here. The first deals with a new version of the positivist rejection of functional explanations. The second pertains to the adequacy of Cohen's version of historical materialism to deal with the actual historical process, even as described by Marx.

In his book *Analyzing Marx*, Richard Miller provides both a critique and an alternative to the interpretation of historical materialism proposed by Cohen.

While conceding that Cohen's interpretation does find support in Marx's writings, Miller goes on to say that "there is no plausible argument that Marx, so interpreted, is right."[23] Given a principle of charity in interpretation, the obvious wrongness of a doctrine is in itself reason to doubt its adequacy as interpretation. In this case, Cohen's interpretation is further weakened by Marx's expression of contrary views about a number of concrete historical and political events.

Cohen's interpretation is one of a number of technological determinist readings of historical materialism. Its historical materialism is a technological determinist account of social systems because it makes the productive forces the independent variable that determines both the productive relations and, ultimately, the superstructural institutions. It is a technological determinist account of the historical process because it makes change in productive forces the independent motor for historical change in the social system. It is a technological determinism because it defines productive forces in terms of the technical inputs in the production process. Of particular importance for Miller's critique is technological determinism's denial of political factors as independent causes of fundamental changes in social structures. On the technological determinist view, historical change is, as Engels would say, ultimately the result of autonomous changes in the productive forces. If a point is reached at which the most efficient use of the new productive forces requires a change in the production relations and corresponding superstructural institutions, then such a change in production relations will take place. Political changes are ultimately caused by independent changes in productive forces.[24]

Miller calls attention to a significant number of cases where Marx's comments on historical events suggest a more significant role for political factors. For example, Marx's account of the change from feudalism to capitalism, which should be a paradigm example of the kind of change historical materialism is meant to consider, stresses the importance of a number of political and economic factors other than change in productive forces as the key causes of the development of capitalism. Increase in productive forces appears more as a result rather than as a cause of these political and economic factors. Miller considers a range of examples of this sort from a variety of Marx's writings and in addition cites passages where Marx seems to attribute explanatory primacy to such political factors.[25] These considerations form the basis for his alternative interpretation of Marx's historical materialism.

As an alternative, Miller advances a "mode of production" interpretation of Marx's historical materialism. A mode of production is, roughly, a socially organized way of producing goods and services. It consists of productive forces, in the technological sense, supplemented by work relations as patterns of cooperation in the use of purely technical capacities, and relations of production.[26] The "mode of production" theory is similar to technological determinism in at least two respects. First, it views the mode of production as determining the nature of the institutional superstructure. Second, it views historical change as a product of internal change in the mode of production rather than as the outcome of independent cultural or ideological processes.[27] But the "mode of production" theory differs from the technological determinist reading of historical materialism in at least two other respects. First, it is not a technological determinism because it includes within the forces of production not only technology but also social forms of cooperation in the use of technology. Second, it is not an economic determinism because it holds that relations of production cannot be understood without consideration of factors of an explicitly political nature.

Marx identifies five distinct modes of production: socialism, capitalism, feudalism, ancient slavery, and the Asiatic mode. The essential feature of each is the distinctive dominant relation of production it employs: employer/employee, lord/serf, owner/slave, and landlord-state/direct producer, respectively for the pre-socialist modes. The technological determinist version of historical materialism defines relations of production in terms of control over means of production. But how are we to differentiate the distinct relations Marx takes to be determinant of distinct modes of production? Technological determinism seems forced to identify distinct relations of production in terms of distinct objects of control, distinct forces of production.

If I understand Miller correctly, his central objection to technological determinism is that this way of understanding relations of production does not do justice to the key role of these relations in Marx's understanding of historical and social processes. What is central for Marx is not the object controlled but the way in which that control is exercised. Thus, capitalist oilmen and capitalist automakers stand in the same relation of production even though they exercise control over distinct objects, while a capitalist farmer and a feudal lord exist within different relations of production even though they exercise control (at different times) over the same land. Miller thinks that if we try to make clear the specific nature of the distinct ways of exercising control over the means of production embodied in these distinct relations of production, we will be forced to appeal to features such as the legal and political institutions through which this control is exercised and maintained. It is this sense, then, that Miller contends that relations of production cannot be understood independently of "relatively superstructural" considerations.[28]

But if Miller is correct in this contention, then once again we face objections to historical materialism from the direction of positivist philosophy of science. In *The Illusion of the Epoch*, published in 1955, H. B. Acton had argued that the Marxist claim that the economic base determines the legal superstructure failed to meet a basic requirement of scientific adequacy in that it provided no means for identifying the economic base independent of the legal superstructure it was supposed to explain. If we cannot identify an economic base as a mode of production of a certain kind without identifying it in terms of the legal superstructure that accompanies it, then the claim that an economic base of that kind gives rise to a legal superstructure of a certain kind involves a kind of circularity which renders it empirically unfalsifiable and hence empirically vacuous.[29]

Cohen's defense avoided this charge by offering a means of independent identification of forces, relations, and the superstructural institutions determined by them. If Miller's criticism of Cohen is correct, and if fair interpretation of Marx forces us to adopt the "mode of production" version of historical materialism, with its non-eliminable appeal to superstructural factors in identifying relations of production, then we confront once again the kind of criticism raised by Acton.

Whereas Cohen sought to defend Marx by bringing the theory of historical materialism within the confines of "positivist" philosophy of science, Miller insists on the need for changes in the philosophy of science that would allow for theories of the kind put forth by his "mode of production" reading of Marx. As a starting point in this endeavor, he takes issue with an assumption underlying Acton's charge of circularity.

The charge of circularity arises out of the fact that historical materialism seems to assert both definitional and causal connections between relations of production and superstructural political institutions. However, Miller maintains, this kind of circularity is common in science. By way of example he points to the distinction between true compounds and mere mixtures that was put forth in Dalton's atomic theory. Given the atomic theory, chemical compounds could occur only in certain fixed ratios of elements. If presented with an apparent counterexample to this claim, the Daltonians replied that what was involved was merely a mixture. However, there was no theory-independent way of distinguishing compounds and mixtures.[30] Miller concludes from this that isolated law claims made by a theory are often empirically untestable because of the way key terms are defined within the theory. But, he argues, the theory as a whole may nonetheless be empirically testable. If this is so, that the theory makes certain law claims true by definition is not in itself reason to reject the theory.

Miller's reply to the specific charge of empirical vacuousness, due to definitional guarantee of law claims, attacks the issue from the point of view of general philosophy of science. That is, on Miller's reply, the supposed defect does not interestingly distinguish historical materialism from other sciences, and is not a defect. Nonetheless, Miller does seem to think that historical materialism differs from at least some other sciences in philosophically interesting ways.

On Cohen's functionalist technological determinism, the relations of production defining a mode of production will be replaced by alternative relations of production if changes in the productive forces make new relations more efficient than the old. This allows for the possibility of theoretically grounded predictions of historical change. On Miller's "mode of production" interpretation, in which the forces are not independent of politics, all that can be said is that change will occur when the forces for change outweigh the forces for stability. But the theory has no resources for saying when such a point will be reached. Hence, on the "mode of production" interpretation, historical materialism lacks the capacity for making empirically testable predictions. And, insofar as the D-N model takes a capacity for predictive power and a capacity for explanatory power as formally equivalent, it follows that on the "positivist" Hempelian view of the nature of scientific explanation, historical materialism lacks explanatory power as well.[31]

Miller's reply again takes the form of an attack on the assumptions of positivist philosophy of science. Here he takes issue with the idea that a capacity for predictive success (or failure) is a necessary condition for a theory to be capable of providing a genuine scientific explanation. Miller's argument against this claim gets embedded within a broader critique of positivist philosophy of science. I will not attempt to follow this critique or the arguments for it in detail here. Rather, I will touch upon some of what seem to me to be the basic ideas.

The Hempelian "covering law" model of explanation and prediction serves as the initial target for criticism. By now it has become clear that not everything which most of us would intuitively take for a scientific theory is capable of generating empirically testable predictions in the fashion required by Hempel's model. Miller points to Darwinian biology and plate tectonics as examples of non-predictive theories. How should we respond to this? One strategy, in keeping with the spirit of positivism, would be to try to revise the formal requirements put forth by the Hempelian model in favor of some other formal requirements that would successfully demarcate scientifically acceptable explanations from non-science. Miller rejects this approach, arguing that the attempt to find some purely formal criteria for judging scientific theories is misguided. Rather, he insists, the value of a proffered explanation, or in general the value of a scientific theory, must be assessed in terms of the relative success of the theory vis-à-vis its competitors within its own theoretical environment. Judgments of the relative worth of competing scientific theories thus depend more upon knowledge of the data, previous work, and problems within a particular field than upon philosophically elaborated criteria that apply to all fields at all times.[32] Miller thinks that, from this point of view, the "mode of production" theory has proven itself a valuable framework for scientific research.

Miller's work raises a host of interesting and important questions adequate treatment of which is impossible here. However, I would like to comment briefly on the direction of his work and to raise some questions I have concerning it.

First, a brief remark on the direction of his work. It is clear that Miller thinks we must abandon much of positivist philosophy of science. Yet, in some ways, his position is closer to the positivist and Neo-Kantian currents within Marxism than it is to either Marxist-Leninism or humanistic Marxism. My reasons for saying that are these. First, Miller views Marxism from the point of view of a "unity of science" position. While he does think that historical materialism differs from some sciences in its lack of predictive power, Miller does not see this as unique to historical materialism, nor as indicative of a split between, say, the natural sciences and social theory.[33] Miller sees Marx as offering a scientific theory that is like the kinds of scientific theories offered by scientists in other areas. He sees Marxist science as ordinary science. Thus, it would be incorrect to locate Miller within the tradition of Lukácsian humanism.

On the other hand, Miller's break with positivist philosophy of science does not rest on any of the central ideas of Marxist-Leninism. He does not reject positivism because of its idealism. Nor does he see the Marxist alternative to positivism as in any interesting way turning upon a dialectical point of view. Indeed, insofar as he sees a Hegelian influence on Marx, he sees it leading toward a technical determinism.[34] For Miller, Marxism offers genuine social science that is not understood as resting upon some deeply distinctive methodological principles. In this sense, Miller's position shares common ground with the ''scientific socialism'' of the Second International, though of course his position is informed by a more sophisticated philosophy of science. In this basic outlook, Miller's work is representative of what has come to be called analytic Marxism. (I shall return to this theme in Part III.)

So much for remarks on the direction of Miller's work. I want now to raise a few questions about it. Miller suggests that we ought to replace purely formal and universal criteria of adequacy with empirically informed comparative judgments between competing theories within a given field. I am not optimistic about prospects for finding adequate universal formal criteria of evaluation, but I am reluctant to abandon all of formalist, ''positivist'' philosophy of science.

Consider a situation in which we are comparing rival theories in some field. How do we decide between them? It is clear by now that there are diverse criteria which could be employed here, and that it is possible to give diverse weightings to these criteria. Among these criteria is something that might very roughly be called overall empirical adequacy. Other things being equal, if one theory seems to do a better job, on the whole, of fitting the facts thought to be relevant, then that theory is preferable. Thus, something like empirical testing, confirmation, verification, and falsification does go on, even within this comparative context. Further, some of the other formal criteria that philosophers have proposed might be relevant here—consider fruitfulness in this regard. I don't think Miller would disagree with this. Historical materialism is subject to a test of overall empirical adequacy, and it is only in a context in which this judgment of overall empirical adequacy, along with other criteria, plays a significant role that a case for historical materialism could be made. It is also true that, even on Miller's ''mode of production'' reading, historical materialism could lose out in the competition with rival theories. Indeed, Miller sketches a scenario in which a Weberian theory might win out over a ''mode of production'' theory.[35]

If we can conceive of a scenario in which a Weberian theory would prevail over a ''mode of production'' theory, then we can imagine a situation in which something like falsification, or a suitably weakened analogue, takes place. And, if this is so, then it must be in virtue of the relative predictive failure of the ''mode of production'' theory. Of course things may not be as clear-cut as positivists once thought they could be, but the basic parameters of evaluation identified by positivist philosophy of science remain. Again, I think Miller would agree with this. Empirical confirmation and falsification remain as possible fates for the ''mode of production'' theory. While Miller would insist that judgments concerning these matters can be made only within the comparative context, and within that context they take on a somewhat more tenuous and provisional character than is realized within positivist philosophy of science, there remains a grain of truth in the positivist framework.[36]

There is one other worry about Miller's alternative to positivism that I would like to mention briefly. His stress on the comparative aspects of theory evaluation leads to a relative devaluation of the various formal criteria that have been proposed by philosophers of science. But, in at least one context, he suggests a consideration that may indicate the continued importance of some noncomparative criteria. In discussing the issue of scientific realism, Miller suggests that in fields where no one theory has established a pattern of success in handling the problems of the field, and where frequent paradigm shifts occur, the assumption of scientific realism with respect to the ''best theory'' is not rational.[37] I agree with Miller's conclusion here, but it seems to me that what this points to is the continued importance of a noncomparative criterion of empirical adequacy. A certain minimum level of explanatory and predictive success remains a necessary condition for the rational acceptability of a theory.

HISTORICAL MATERIALISM AS PHILOSOPHY

While Cohen and Miller differ concerning the interpretation of Marx and the necessary features of a genuine scientific theory, they agree in seeing historical materialism as a scientific theory. This understanding of historical materialism has been questioned by Daniel Little, who accepts Miller's objections to the technological determinist reading of historical materialism.[38] However, he is less sanguine than Miller about the scientific status of historical materialism:

> Historical materialism provides a hypothesis about the process of historical change generally: that the economic structure ''determines'' noneconomic structure. And it embraces a variety of more specific hypotheses as well—theories of class, politics, ideology, religion, and so forth. But none of these is a theory in the full sense relevant to science, and consequently Marx has no scientific theory of history.[39]

Little contrasts the undeveloped state of historical materialism with the much richer analysis of the theory of capitalism. He concludes that whereas the theory of capitalism is a full-fledged scientific theory, historical materialism is best understood as a family of research hypotheses, in the sense in which this is understood in the work of Thomas Kuhn, Imre Lakatos, and Larry Laudan.[40] Such hypotheses provide a fruitful conception that can guide further research, but they are not themselves scientific theories. ''They are not sufficiently elaborated to constitute explanations, and they are not precise enough to have definite empirical consequences.''[41]

I believe that Little is right to stress the different statuses of the theory of capitalism and historical materialism. Further, I think that keeping this different status clear goes some way toward at least muting the difficulties presented by historical materialism. My own view is that the family of claims advanced by historical materialism is best understood not as science, nor even primarily as research hypotheses, but as philosophical claims.

Marx worked on the economic theory of capitalism for some forty years. In the course of this work, he produced the lengthy *Grundrisse*, the published *Contribution* of 1859, the published volume 1 of *Capital*, the various unpublished parts of *Capital* that we now know as volumes 2 and 3 of *Capital*, and the three volumes of the *Theories of Surplus Value*. There is no even remotely comparable corpus in which historical materialism finds a careful and systematic expression. The classical expression of historical materialism, in the Preface of 1859, is only a page and a half long. In addition to this, there is a sketch of historical materialism in Marx and Engels' *German Ideology*, and some scattered passages in the rest of Marx's corpus. While it is true that some inferences can be made on the basis of what Marx says about historical events, as in the short works on politics in France, what is said in these works is often open to conflicting interpretations, and there is nothing comparable with the systematic theory of capitalism to guide interpretation in these cases. In short, it is tempting to say that the only social science Marx leaves us is the theory of capitalism, and that insofar as we want to inquire concerning the nature of Marxist social theory, it is to the economics that we must turn.

The archetypal formulation of historical materialism occurs in the Preface to the *Contribution to the Critique of Political Economy* of 1859. There Marx briefly recounts how he was led to the study of political economy and what approach he was led to adopt. He tells us that he reached a "general conclusion" that became the "guiding principle" of his studies. He then presents a brief page-and-a-half summary of this guiding principle. It is this summary that has become the central formulation of historical materialism. It is my contention that we miss the point of what Marx is saying in this text if we interpret the formulation of historical materialism as a scientific theory on a par with the theory of capital. Instead, I contend, the passage plays a philosophical rather than a scientific role.

That the formulation of historical materialism presented here is not a scientific theory on a par with the theory of capital is evident from its location within the *Contribution*. It occurs as a short passage in the Preface to a substantial piece of work in theoretical economics. This fact alone should indicate that the formulation is not intended as a full-fledged scientific theory.

The philosophical role of the statement of historical materialism in the Preface of 1859 begins to appear when we look at the context surrounding it in the Preface, and then view the Preface in light of the German philosophical scene in the mid-nineteenth century. Having explained how he was led to consider French socialist theories, Marx tells us that the first step in this consideration was, for him, a reconsideration of Hegel's political philosophy. He then says, "My inquiry led me to the conclusion that neither legal relations nor political forms could be comprehended whether by themselves or on the basis of a so-called general development of the human mind, but that on the contrary they originate in the material conditions of life . . . ,'' the anatomy of which is provided by political economy.[42] Marx goes on to provide the summary of the general conclusion he reached on the basis of his study of political economy, then returns to the recounting of the development of his views. He tells us that he became aware of the work of Engels, that Engels independently arrived at the same result as he, and that ''we decided to set forth together our conception as opposed to the ideological one of German philosophy, in fact to settle accounts with our former philosophical conscience.'' This settling of accounts was accomplished in *The German Ideology*, which has become generally accepted as the first formulation of historical materialism. This settling of accounts was a *philosophical* one. Historical materialism arose in opposition to the philosophical views of the post-Hegelian philosophers.[43]

Thus we see that Marx himself conceived of historical materialism as having philosophical significance, and that this significance pertained to his break with the dominant outlook of post-Hegelian philosophy in Germany. Within the milieu of post-Hegelian philosophy, philosophy played an exalted role. The philosophical development of the categories led the historical transformation of the world. World history was a reflection of philosophical history. When Marx says, in the Preface in 1859, ''It is not the consciousness of men that determines their existence, but their social existence that determines their consciousness,'' he is rejecting this post-Hegelian view of the role of philosophy. There is no independent dialectic of the categories that leads the actual historical process. For Marx, philosophy plays a more modest and mundane role. I believe that this is the central point of historical materialism. To interpret the passage about existence and consciousness as an assertion of economic determinism, or as a denial that ideas play a role in history, is to miss the specific philosophical target against which the outlook of Marx and Engels is directed.

Further evidence for the philosophical status of historical materialism can be found in *The German Ideology*. In the section of that work in which the concepts and claims typical of historical materialism are most extensively developed, Marx claims that as ''positive science'' develops its ''representation'' of reality, ''Philosophy as an independent branch of activity loses its medium existence.'' Immediately following this observation, he comments as follows:

> At the best its [philosophy's] place can only be taken by a summing-up of the most general results, abstractions which arise from the observation of the historical development of men. Viewed apart from real history, these abstractions have in themselves no value whatsoever. They can only serve to facilitate the arrangement of historical material, to indicate the sequence of the separate strata. But, they by no means afford a recipe or schema, as does philosophy, for neatly trimming the epochs of history. On the contrary, our difficulties begin only when we set about the observation and arrangement—the real depiction—of our historical material whether of a past epoch or of the present. The removal of these difficulties is governed by premises which it is quite impossible to state

here, but which only the study of the actual life-process and the activity of the individuals of each epoch will make evident. We shall select here some of these abstractions, which we use to refute the ideologists, and shall illustrate them by historical examples.[44]

In this introduction, Marx identifies the claims that follow as abstractions which arise from observation of the historical development of men. They are intended as refutations of the German ideologists, who hold that ideas lead history, in the specific sense of the philosophical theories of history of the Left Hegelians.[45] These abstractions are said to take the place of philosophy. They are, as it were, the last vestiges of philosophy. But they are not themselves part of positive science, nor do they offer a substitute for positive science. ''Our difficulties only begin when we set about the observation and arrangement—the real depiction—of our historical material.''

Marx's comments here support Little's claim that historical materialism is not a scientific theory. Marx also claims some sort of heuristic role for these abstractions about historical development. They are said to ''serve to facilitate the arrangement of historical material.''[46] In playing such a heuristic role, these abstractions function somewhat like research hypotheses in the sense intended by Little. However, there is a difference between the role played by the claims of historical materialism and research hypotheses. Research hypotheses typically provide a simple model of processes at work in the field of study. The scientific theory appears as a filling out, deepening, and correcting of this simple model. But the relationship between historical materialism and the theory of capitalism does not appear to be quite like that, and the relationship between historical materialism and Marx's account of the rise of capitalism and the coming of socialism does not appear to be quite like that either. The theory of capitalism builds around the analysis of unintended outcomes of individual behaviors within a capitalist institutional framework. The categories of theory construction are quite different from the categories of forces and relations of production found in historical materialism. Similarly, the myriad considerations that go into Marx's account of the rise of capitalism, though perhaps consistent with a ''mode of production'' interpretation of historical materialism, do not seem to draw any inspiration from the categories of historical materialism.

How, then, can this claim for a heuristic role be understood? In directing historical research away from the post-Hegelian pursuit of the idea at work in history, Marx's historical materialism plays a weak heuristic role. It is a philosophical claim about the kind of research appropriate to understanding a social system and its history. A social system is not be understood as the realization of an idea, and its historical trajectory cannot be grasped through the dialectic of ideas. As the passage from *The German Ideology* concludes, these ideas are used ''to refute the ideologists.''

This reading of historical materialism as a philosophical critique of post-Hegelian philosophy of history is not without its difficulties. For one thing, in the Preface of 1859 Marx does not stop with saying that social existence determines consciousness. He goes on to provide a more specific account of this determination in terms of forces and relations of production and forms of social consciousness that correspond to these forces and relations. Second, Marx claims that he arrived at his "general conclusion" or "guiding principle" as a result of a study of political economy. This seems to locate historical materialism within the domain of empirical science.

The second objection is not a serious difficulty. While a study of the political economy of the times may have been the occasion for Marx's discovery of historical materialism, or may have confirmed the conclusion reached on the basis of Marx's critical re-examination of Hegel's philosophy of law, it cannot have been the source of the ideas present in the summary of the Preface, since this deals with matters such as ancient economies, historical development, philosophy of law, and philosophy of religion quite foreign to political economy.

The specific categories of forces and relations of production provide a more serious difficulty for my interpretation of historical materialism. Rejection of post-Hegelian views about philosophy and history need not lead us to these categories. What links the critique of post-Hegelian philosophy with these categories is the idea of the logic of unintended consequences. In the first sentence of his summary in the Preface of 1859, Marx says, "in the social production of their existence, men inevitably enter into definite relations, which are independent of their will, namely relations of production which are appropriate to a given stage in the development of their material forces of production." Within these relations, human beings conduct their affairs. Human beings are conscious, and their actions have conscious aims. But within the web of relations in which they act, these conscious actions produce unintended consequences. History happens "behind men's backs."[47] This vision is directly opposed to the philosophical-historical theories of the post-Hegelian philosophers. The categories of forces and relations of production, and their dominance over law, religion, and philosophy, serve to illustrate this conception. The vagueness, inconsistency, and brevity of the various statements involving these categories is a mark of their primarily illustrative intent.

I must confess that I am not satisfied with this treatment of historical materialism as philosophical opposition to post-Hegelian philosophy. The recurrence of such categories as forces, relations, modes, and superstructures throughout Marx's works suggests that these categories had more than illustrative significance for Marx. Nevertheless, while I do not think the account of historical materialism offered here is ultimately adequate, I do think some significant results have been achieved. First, I think that it is the theory of capitalism, and not historical materialism, that must be taken as the paradigm of a Marxist science. Second, I think it is clear that historical materialism has a philosophical significance, and that this significance is connected with Marx's rejection of post-Hegelian German philosophy. Third, and more specifically, I think that historical materialism must be understood as opposed to the specific conception of the role of philosophy in post-Hegelian philosophy of history. Fourth, the various comments made by Marx about the role of ideas in history must be approached with this philosophical context in mind.

THE HUMANIST CRITIQUE OF ECONOMIC FATALISM

On one reading, historical materialism appears to contain a scientific theory of the course of historical development. On this reading, it is a law of history that every society progresses from feudalism to capitalism to socialism. Further, it appears that this progression from one stage to the next is determined by economic forces which are independent of conscious human action. Such an understanding of historical materialism is fatalistic, in that it views each stage in the sequence as the inevitable outcome of the stage that preceded it, regardless of human actions. It is an economic fatalism because it views the historical progression as determined by economic forces. Humanistic Marxism rejects this economic fatalist interpretation of historical materialism.

In his essay "The Changing Function of Historical Materialism," Lukács argues that this economic fatalism is approximately valid only as a theory of capitalism. Only under capitalism has the social order been completely subordinated to the blind control of economic forces. In pre-capitalist societies, economic forces are themselves subordinated to the control of tradition, politics, or religion. Under socialism the economic forces are subordinated to the conscious, rational will of the proletariat. It is for this reason that historical materialism cannot be applied to non-capitalist societies without significant alteration. Historical materialism is the "self-knowledge of capitalist society."[48] Even as a theory of capitalism, economic fatalism is of limited validity. Under normal circumstances, the economic laws of motion of capitalism govern the fates of men. However, during times of crisis, these laws break down, and it is only by the forceful intervention of the ruling class that the system can be restarted.[49] And, even under normal conditions, the validity of economic fatalism is merely apparent. For, in reality, the entire system of capitalism is a product of human making. It is only because this dependence is forgotten, only because of the alienated objectification and reification of the social system, that the whole appears to be subject to the impersonal control of economic forces.[50]

Lukács' interpretation of historical materialism rejects both aspects of the economic fatalist view of historical development. It restricts the rule of economic forces to capitalism, and it comprehends fatalism as the false consciousness of capitalism. In place of an economic theory of history and social systems, Lukács advances a view of social systems as totalities of interdependent parts. It is this insight, and not the specific understanding of capitalism as a totality in which economic forces play the dominant role, that Lukács sees as the methodological breakthrough of historical materialism.[51] The understanding of historical materialism as a fatalistic theory of historical development grows out of the vulgar Marxist enchantment with the economic model of capitalism. The vulgar Marxist illegitmately extends this conception of a social system dominated by autonomous economic forces outside the historical boundaries of capitalism.[52] In doing so, he or she commits two errors. First, he or she assumes that economic forces dominate in all social systems. Second, he or she fails to understand that each social totality is the product of human making. In the case of the transition from capitalism to socialism, this human production of the social system becomes, for the first time, a matter of collective deliberation.[53] On Lukács' reading, historical materialism supports neither an economic theory of history nor a fatalistic theory of history. For him, the decisive turning points from one type of social system to another involve the free actions of human beings, and the transition to socialism requires the direction of proletarian class consciousness.

In considering the interpretations of Cohen and Miller, we have already touched upon problems pertaining to the economic interpretation of history. Cohen's technological determinism and Miller's "mode of production" theory each accord a certain preeminence to the economic sphere, though of course on Miller's reading distinct political relations are fundamental aspects of distinct modes of production. Lukács reading of historical materialism entirely excludes any economic theory of history. On his view, economic determinism has a kind of limited validity only as the self-consciousness of capitalism. This is not without its difficulties as a reading of Marx. In Marx's formulations of it, the priority of the economic base over the ideological superstructure seems to hold in pre-capitalist modes of production as well as in capitalism.[54] Subsequent efforts within humanistic Marxism to work out an interpretation of historical materialism more faithful to Marx have adopted Lukács' notion of social systems as totalities of interdependent parts where the mode of production plays a dominant, but not causally determining, role not only in capitalism but in pre-capitalist social systems as well.[55]

Such interpretations accord better with Marx's emphasis on the importance of the mode of production in pre-capitalist social systems, and they escape the difficulties of technological determinism. But, though they avoid a narrow technological determinism, such holistic theories remain compatible with deterministic theories of the historical process as a whole. That is to say, it might well be that feudalism, as a totality of interacting economic, political, and ideological spheres, might inevitably give rise to capitalism as a system of interacting parts, and capitalism inevitably give rise to socialism as yet another totality of interacting parts. Rejection of economic determinism is not necessarily rejection of determinism.

The humanist tradition has not carefully distinguished between determinist, economic determinist, and economic fatalist theories of history.[56] Economic fatalist theories of history would hold that the course of historical development is determined by economic forces independent of human consciousness. Economic determinist theories of history would hold that the course of historical development is determined by economic forces and, in part at least, by the human consciousness caused by those forces. Determinist theories of historical development would simply hold that each step in the course of historical development is causally determined without specifying the nature of the causes involved. Too often humanist arguments against the Marxism of the Second International rest on confusing the economic determinism of the Second International with economic fatalism.[57] Or arguments slide from the rejection of fatalism to the rejection of determinism.[58] In fact, the humanist critique of fatalism was a "straw man" argument from the beginning, since neither Karl Kautsky nor Georgi Plekhanov rejected the historical efficacy of ideas. Both adopted a deterministic framework in which ideas appear as (causally determined) historical forces. In a similar vein, Lenin adopted the view that causally determined ideas influence history.[59]

Lukács' position on the question of human freedom is not as clear as it might be. While I would agree with the assessment of George Lichtheim that Lukács is committed to the "doctrine that free, autonomous, emancipated man is both the presupposition of philosophy and the true goal of all human activity," Lukács' comments on human freedom are more likely to take the form of a contrast between the unfreedom of historical development up to the point of the proletarian revolution and the freedom of historical development subsequent to that point.[60] The connection between these two conceptions of human freedom is not apparent. Indeed, there is an apparent inconsistency between them. If human freedom is an ontological condition, then it cannot erupt at a particular point in the course of human history. The inconsistency is, I think, merely apparent. From Lukács' point of view, freedom is an ontological condition of human existence. The unfreedom of all previous historical development is merely apparent, arising from the alienation of human freedom and the fetishistic appearance of human institutions.

However, if the inconsistency is merely apparent, the reason for thinking that ontological freedom pertains to human nature is not clear. The distinction between a historical period of unfreedom and a historical period of freedom does not require ontological freedom as a condition of human nature. The historical distinction can be understood in terms of the difference between consciously directed and not consciously directed development. But this distinction can be granted by nonfatalist versions of determinism—even by economic determinist versions of determinism.

A somewhat different approach to the question of human freedom within the tradition of humanistic Marxism turns on the importance of Marx's claim that "men make their own history."[61] Humanistic Marxists have found in this claim a foundation for their rejection of any deterministic theory of history. Thus, for example, in introducing the thinking behind the Praxis Group in Yogoslav philosophy, which held that the central category of Marxist philosophy was the category of "free, human, creative activity," Mihailo Markovic points to questions about determinism: "How are we to reconcile the principle of determinism, according to which historical processes are governed by laws independent of human consciousness and will, with the principle of freedom according to which it is men who make their own history?"[62] The way the question is posed here illustrates the inattention to the distinction between fatalistic and nonfatalistic versions of determinism mentioned above. For determinism in general does not maintain that historical processes are independent of human consciousness and will. That men make their own history is perfectly consistent with complete determinism of men's actions—even with economic determinism of those actions.

A more careful version of the humanist appeal to the principle that men make their history is found in the work of Richard Schmitt. Like Markovic and other humanist Marxists, Schmitt takes a capacity for human collective self-creation of social life forms as the central idea of Marxist philosophy. He contrasts this viewpoint, which emphasizes the human capacity to make our own history, with the viewpoint of traditional Marxism, which emphasizes the determining influence of material conditions on human consciousness.[63] Schmitt does not claim any incompatibility between his own and the traditional viewpoint; he introduces the distinction solely as a difference of emphasis. Further, he holds that his view is consistent with recognition of "laws" of development for capitalism, where these laws are understood as resulting from the unintended consequences of individual actions within the institutional framework of capitalism. Schmitt concludes that, consequently, "it is consistent to argue that human beings shape their worlds and that these worlds are subject to laws discoverable by science."[64]

In this conclusion I believe that Schmitt is correct, and I believe that this insight is important because it shows that not even from the humanistic perspective is it necessary to argue against the scientific status of the theory of capitalism. However, as to the question of the scientific status of the theory of historical materialism, or of the possibility of a scientific theory of history, Schmitt is not altogether clear. At one point, having argued that people's beliefs and actions are "shaped in significant ways by the practices characteristic of their societies," he insists that "nothing said so far implies that human choices are necessitated by social contexts, or that human beings are not free agents."[65] It appears that Schmitt regards social conditions as necessary, but not causally sufficient, conditions for human actions. Thus, he appears to regard the fundamental human capacity for self-creation as involving a kind of freedom incompatible with determinism. However, no argument for this assumption is presented. Understood as a capacity for creating life forms distinct from the life forms of our ancestors, human freedom does not require a rejection of determinism. The contrast between Schmitt's view and the traditional view is only one of emphasis. Within the traditional debates over free will, only the fatalist would deny that men make their own history.

It appears, then, that there is no theoretical difficulty in reconciling historical materialism, understood as a determinist theory of history, with Marx's claim that men make their own history, or with the Marxist idea of the dawning of an age of freedom. Neither idea presupposes the ontological freedom involved in the traditional conception of free will. Where ontological freedom does enter the picture, perhaps, is in the understanding of ethics and political life. Thus, for example, Markovic's philosophy of praxis is driven to ontological freedom, not because men make their own history but because Markovic conceives this making as normatively directed:

Praxis has to be distinguished from the purely epistemological category of *practice*. The latter refers simply to any Subject's activity of changing an object and this activity can be alienated. The former is a normative concept and refers to an ideal, specifically human activity which is an end in itself, a statement of basic values and at the same time a standard of criticism of all other forms of activity.[66]

It may be that consideration of the nature of morality will require rejection of determinism, and hence rejection of historical materialism as a determinist theory of history. We will consider this matter in Chapter 8.

THE INEVITABILITY OF SOCIALISM

There can be no doubt that Marx and Engels sometimes seem to claim to have demonstrated the inevitability of socialism. One illustration of this kind of claim is the passage, from volume 1 of *Capital*, where Marx claims that "capitalist production begets, with the inexorability of a law of Nature, its own negation."[67] There are a number of different ways to understand this claim. On the one hand, it might be viewed as a simple consequence of a philosophical law of dialectics.[68] A second interpretation, consistent with but not implying the first, might view the passage as a consequence of a general law of historical development to the effect that all societies pass through a sequence of stages, from feudalism to capitalism to socialism. Marx appears to reject this second understanding of his claim. In reply to Russian worries about whether Russia had to pass through a capitalist stage, he denies the view that his own theories require this. In doing so, he insists that his sketch of the development of capitalism in Western Europe had been misconstrued as a general philosophical theory of historical development. Marx denies that any such general theory of history is possible, and he insists that one must examine the particular causes at work in every distinct historical situation. Accordingly, he says that his remark about capitalism begetting its own negation was only a way of summing up the entire argument of *Capital*.[69] This suggests a third way of understanding the inevitability of socialism. On this understanding, what grounds the prediction is not a philosophical law of dialectics or a general theory of history but, rather, the theory of capitalism.

There are problems with Marx's self-understanding here. It appears to rest on the view that Marx has succeeded in showing certain laws of capitalist development that lead to increasing unemployment, concentration of capital, polarization of classes, decline in the rate of profit, and increasing frequency and amplitude of crises. These claims are all controversial. On the whole, it appears that at best Marx has shown that there are inherent tendencies within capitalist systems which support the claims about economic development under capitalism. Whether these tendencies can be offset by countervailing forces or controlled by public policy is another matter. I shall not attempt an assessment of the questions of economic science involved here except to say that the historical experience seems to me to support Marx's claims on the whole.

In addition Marx appears to assume that these economic developments will also lead to the formation of a revolutionary, class-conscious proletariat. This assumption is also controversial. Resolution of the issue would involve at least consideration of the theory of imperialism and of the role of intellectuals in developing revolutionary class consciousness. Though I think that, from the appropriate global perspective, Marx's assumption is historically confirmed, I shall not press this point here. Rather, the point I want to make concerns the issue of determinism as it relates to Marx's prediction of socialism.

It seems to me that Marx's prediction of socialism is independent of the issue of determinism and free will. As we have seen, what grounds the prediction of socialism is not a law of philosophical dialectics nor a general law of historical development. What grounds the prediction of socialism is the analysis of the developmental tendencies within capitalism, and the assumption that the proletariat will gain an understanding of these tendencies and act in its interest to remedy them. No assumption of determinism need be made.

As it is usually presented, the humanistic conception of men making history appears to be an "agency theory" version of free will. On any such view, our actions flow from our character and our understanding of the world around us, though not as effects of causes. Any reasonable theory of human action must assume such connectedness between the agent's character and his or her actions. So also, any reasonable theory of human action must assume that there is some connectedness between the agent's understanding of the world around him or her and the actual state of the surrounding world. We all do get things wrong sometimes, but surely, for the most part, changes in the world around us do influence our beliefs. Connectedness of this sort is all that Marx's prediction of socialism requires.[70] While it may be that philosophical problems pertaining to the apparent incompatibility of determinism and moral responsibility require us to abandon determinism, from the point of view of the theory of history, determinism is not the issue.

DETERMINISM AND EMANCIPATORY THEORY

In the letter on the Russian situation mentioned above, Marx directly addressed the question of whether it might be possible for Russia to skip capitalism and pass directly from its largely pre-capitalist institutions to some form of socialism: "I have arrived at this conclusion: If Russia continues to pursue the path she has followed since 1861, she will lose the finest chance ever offered by history to a people and undergo all the fatal vicissitudes of the capitalist regime."[71] This is, of course, in accord with Marx's denial that he had discovered any general law of historical development, as was mentioned above. Here, I would like to focus on the implications of this passage for our understanding of emancipatory theory.

With the October Revolution, Russia embarked on a course of historical development that deviated from the "natural" sequence of feudalism, capitalism, and socialism. At least part of the reason for this was that the Russians had the benefit of experience of Western capitalism and of the theoretical knowledge provided by Marx's theory of capitalism. By bringing the tendencies of capitalist development into the open, this theory made possible the choice for a different course of development. In doing so, Marx's theory served as an emancipatory theory. In a sense there is also to be found here an illustration of the "Oedipus effect" identified by Popper. In identifying a theretofore unintended sequence of development as "natural," Marx's theory affected the course of events in a way that appears to contradict the theory. Both Popper and the humanistic Marxists argue that this sort of interaction between theory and the social world precludes a deterministic conception of historical development.

I am not convinced that this is so. Why could it not be the case that economic developments caused Marx to have the insights that he did have, and these insights in turn caused the Russian revolutionaries to attempt to bypass capitalism? Although, as I stated above, I do not think historical materialism needs to assume determinism, I see no reason why recognition of the emancipatory role of Marxist social theory requires abandonment of determinism.

NOTES

1. Some more recent accounts of Marx's theory of history can be found in Allen Wood, *Karl Marx* (London: Routledge & Kegan Paul, 1981), pt. 2; Gerald Cohen, *Karl Marx's Theory of History: A Defence* (Princeton: Princeton University Press, 1978); John McMurtry, *The Structure of Marx's World View* (Princeton: Princeton University Press, 1977); William Shaw, Marx's *Theory of History* (Stanford, CA: Stanford University Press, 1978); Melvin Rader, *Marx's Interpretation of History* (Oxford: Oxford University Press, 1979). Wood, Cohen, McMurtry, and Shaw treat historical materialism as descriptive social science; Rader offers a humanistic interpretation.

2. Karl Popper, *The Poverty of Historicism* (New York: Harper, 1964); *The Open Society and Its Enemies*, vol. 2 (Princeton: Princeton University Press, 1963); "Prediction and Prophecy in the Social Sciences," in his *Conjectures and Refutations* (New York: Basic Books, 1962), pp. 336–346.

3. For a fuller consideration of Popper's position, see Richard Hudelson, "Popper's Critique of Marx," *Philosophical Studies* 37 (1980): 259–270.

4. *Poverty of Historicism*, pp. vi–vii.

5. Ibid., pp. 15–16.

6. Ibid, p. vii.

7. See for example, Heinz Pepperle, "Der Determinismus der materialistischen Geschichtsauffassung und die moderne bürgerliche Philosophie," *Deutsche Zeitschrift für Philosophie* 34 (1986): 434–442.

8. *Poverty of Historicism*, p. 115. (My discussion of this argument is taken from my

"Popper's Critique of Marx." I am grateful to *Philosophical Studies* for permission to use this material here.)

9. Ibid., p. 129 n.1.

10. Ibid., p. 128. Note the distinction between prophecies and predictions Popper uses here. This distinction ultimately proves to be of no importance. Prophecies derived from genuine laws are acceptable in the social sciences (cf. *Conjectures and Refutations*, p. 339). The real issue is whether Marx's predictions are based on laws or are simply projections of observed trends.

11. *Poverty of Historicism*, p. 129.

12. My attempt at construing Marx's trend toward accumulation as an explained trend rests on what Marx has to say about human production as free and universal in *The Economic and Philosophical Manuscripts of 1844*, in *Karl Marx: Early Writings*, edited by T. B. Bottomore (New York: McGraw-Hill, 1964), pp. 127–129. Also in Marx and Engels, *Marx Engels Werke* (Berlin: Dietz Verlag, 1968), vol. 1, pt. 1, pp. 515–517. (Hereafter *MEW*.) Marx's comments on commerce and war can be found in *The German Ideology*, in Marx and Engels, *Collected Works*, vol. 5 (New York: International, 1975), p. 67; *MEW*, vol. 3, p. 54.

13. *Capital*, vol. 1, pp. 592, 599–608; *MEW*, vol. 23, pp. 618, 625–636.

14. *Poverty of Historicism*, p. 128.

15. *ibid.*, p. 129 n.1

16. Engels to Joseph Bloch, Sept. 21–22, 1890. *Marx/Engels Selected Correspondence* (Moscow: Progress, 1975), pp. 394–395, *MEW*, vol. 39, p. 36.

17. Lukács, Korsch, and Gramsci adopt such a view. Modern defenses of a humanistic reading of historical materialism can be found in Rader, *Marx's Interpretation of History* and in Richard Schmitt, *Introduction to Marx and Engels: A Critical Reconstruction* (Boulder, CO: Westview, 1987).

18. Laird Addis, *The Logic of Society* (Minneapolis: University of Minnesota Press, 1975); Cohen, *Karl Marx's Theory of History*; Daniel Gandy, *Marx and History* (Austin: University of Texas Press, 1979); Daniel Little, *The Scientific Marx* (Minneapolis: University of Minnesota Press, 1986); J. McMurtry, *The Structure of Marx's World View*; Richard Miller, *Analyzing Marx* (Princeton: Princeton University Press, 1984); Shaw, Marx's *Theory of History*; Wood, *Karl Marx*.

19. Cohen, *Marx's Theory*, p. 32. See p. 55 for his somewhat more complex final account.

20. Ibid., pp. 31, 34–35.

21. Ibid., p. 249.

22. Ibid., pp. 272–277.

23. Miller, *Analyzing Marx*, p. 253; cf. Jon Elster, *Making Sense of Marx*, Cambridge University Press, Cambridge, 1985, p. 31; Little, *Scientific Marx*, p. 57, on Cohen's, but not McMurtry's, version of functionalism.

24. See Cohen, *Marx's Theory*, p. 250, where functionalist determination of political change is characterized as a special type of causality.

25. Miller, *Analyzing Marx*, pp. 188–189, 210–213.

26. Ibid., p. 205.

27. Ibid., pp. 221–226, 256–257.

28. Ibid., p. 197. Miller appears to include political institutions within the superstructure. See pp. 229, 258, where Miller contrasts social relations of production with "political superstructures."

29. Miller provides a summary of the argument on pp. 202–205.

30. Ibid., pp. 203–204.

31. Ibid., p. 273. On Miller's view, similar problems infect Marx's theory of the state, theory of ideology, and economics.

32. Ibid., pp. 283–304. A fuller account of this alternative framework in the philosophy of science is offered in Miller's *Fact and Method* (Princeton: Princeton University Press, 1987).

33. See Miller, *Analyzing Marx*, p. 274.

34. Ibid., p. 218. In his review of *Analyzing Marx*, Steven Smith comments that Miller's account eliminates "the crucial elements of contradiction and dialectic in Marx's account of change" (*Political Theory*, Nov. 1985, p. 625).

35. Miller, *Analyzing Marx*, pp. 237–238.

36. Ibid., p. 296.

37. Ibid.

38. Little, *Scientific Marx*, pp. 49–51.

39. Ibid., p. 66. Joseph Schumpeter, *History of Economic Analysis* (Oxford: Oxford University Press, 1954), p. 441, takes a similar view of historical materialism. Denial of the status of scientific theory to historical materialism is also found in Perry Anderson, *Considerations on Western Marxism* (London: NLB, 1976), p. 4 Cf. Derek Sayer, *Marx's Method* (Brighton, England: Harvester Press, 1979), p. 81.

40. Little, *Scientific Marx*, p. 66.

41. Ibid.

42. The quotations from the Preface of 1859 are from the Ryazanskaya translation, *A Contribution to the Critique of Political Economy* (New York: International, 1970), pp. 19–23.

43. Consider, too, that *The Poverty of Philosophy* is directed against the philosophical pretensions of Pierre Proudhon. As in *The German Ideology*, Marx's formulation of historical materialism arises in opposition to Left Hegelian philosophy of history.

44. *The German Ideology* (New York: International, 1966), pp. 15–16; *MEW*, Vol. 3, p. 27.

45. Cf. Wood, *Karl Marx*, p. 117.

46. The Preface of 1859 speaks of the "guiding principle."

47. Marx, *Capital*, vol. 1, p. 44; *Grundrisse*, p. 225. See also Engels' letter to Joseph Bloch, in *Marx/Engels Selected Correspondence*, pp. 395–396.

48. Georg Luckács, *History and Class Consciousness* (Cambridge, MA: MIT Press, 1971), p. 229; cf. pp. 232–233, 238.

49. Ibid., p. 243.

50. Ibid., pp. 232, 240.

51. Ibid., p. 230.

52. Ibid., pp. 238–239.

53. Ibid., p. 247 (quotation from Engels).

54. See, e.g., Marx's reply to the objection that politics ruled the ancient world and religion the feudal world. *Capital*, Vol. 1, pp. 81–82 n.1; *MEW*, vol. 23, p. 96 n.33.

55. Rader, *Marx's Interpretation of History*, adopts an organic totality model of history that distinguishes between the mode of production, which is the most *determinant* aspect of the whole, and religion, which was the *dominant* aspect of life in the Middle Ages.

A weakness of this approach is its failure to explain the sense in which the mode of production can be the chief determinant (but not dominant) part of the social totality. Rader employs an analogy (p. 78) in which the heart is said to play the most determinant role within the human body. The reason for this is that "no organ can operate without the heart." But insofar as this is true of the heart (artificial hearts?) it appears to be true of the brain, lungs, and kidneys as well.

56. Failure to make these distinctions also infected turn-of-the-century philosophical discussion of Marxism. Thus, like Rader, Eduard Bernstein thought that there was a contradiction between Marxist determinism and Marxist revolutionism (Pierre Angel, *Eduard Bernstein et l'évolution du socialisme allemand* [Paris: Marcel Didier, 1961] pp. 190–191). The extent of confusion of fatalism and determinism is indicated by Rilki's characterization of the debate between Marxists and idealists in terms of a debate between fatalism and agency theory on one page and between determinism and agency theory on the next (Erika Rilki, *Der Revisionismus* [Zurich: Girsberger, 1936], pp. 34–35).

57. Thus, for example, Rader (p. 5 n.4) claims that Lenin's political activism marked a rejection of the "mechanistic determinism of Kautsky, Plekhanov, and other theorists of the Second International," and Frederick Gregory seems to accept the view that Karl Vogt's romantic revolutionism contradicted his materialistic determinism (*Scientific Materialism in Nineteenth Century Germany* [Dordrecht: Reidel, 1977], pp. 61, 68, 90).

58. Thus, Dick Howard, *The Marxian Legacy* (New York: Urizen Books, 1977), pp. 6–7, appears to argue from the dependence of a social structure on human will to some sort of "essential" (ontological?) freedom as the necessary condition of this. Z. A. Jordan, *Philosophy and Ideology* (Dordrecht: Reidel, 1963), p. 55, argues from the efficacy of human action to a rejection of mechanistic materialism. And Andrew Arato and Paul Breines, *The Young Lukács and the Origins of Western Marxism* (New York: Seabury Press, 1977), pp. 202–203, appear to endorse an argument from acceptance of the vital role of supereconomic forces in history to a rejection of vulgar materialism.

59. On Lenin, see O. G. Drobnitskii, "Marxist Philosophy and the Problem of Value," *Soviet Studies in Philosophy* 5 (1966–67): 19. Laird Addis, *The Logic of Society*, pp. 185–186, has a discussion of the differences between fatalistic and determinist versions of historical materialism. On Plekhanov's position and the shallowness of much of the critique of "vulgar Marxism," see Andrew Collier, "Truth and Practice," *Radical Philosophy* 5 (1973): 14.

60. George Lichtheim, *Georg Lukács* (New York: Viking Press, 1970), p. 70; Lukács, "Die Rolle der Moral in der kommunistischen Geschichtsauffassung und die moderne bürgerliche Philosophie," quoted in Heinz Pepperle, "Der Determinismus der materialistischen Geschichtsauffassung," p. 439.

61. Marx, *The 18th Brumaire of Louis Bonaparte* (New York: International, 1963), p. 15; *MEW*, vol. 8, p. 115.

62. Mihailo Markovic, *The Rise and Fall of Socialist Humanism* (Nottingham: Spokesman Books, 1975), pp. 18–19, 22.

63. Schmitt, *Introduction to Marx and Engels*, p. xv.

64. Ibid., p. 29.

65. Ibid., p. 20.

66. Markovic, *The Rise and Fall of Socialist Humanism*, p. 32.

67. *Capital*, Vol. 1, p. 763; *MEW*, vol. 23, p. 791.

68. See Chapter 7 of this volume.

69. Marx, "Letter to the Editorial Board of the Otechestvenniye Zapiski," in Marx and Engels, *Basic Writings on Politics and Philosophy*, edited by Lewis Feuer (Garden City, NY: Anchor, 1959), p. 440.

70. Wood, *Karl Marx* (pp. 114–115), presents a similar argument for the view that Marx's theory of history is compatible with a libertarian rejection of determinism.

71. "Letter to Editorial Board," p. 439.

5

Epistemology

Having considered the nature of Marx's science, my aim in this chapter is to examine his philosophical understanding of how knowledge of this kind is possible and to examine the normative constraints on scientific theorizing embedded in that philosophical understanding. As before, I will move back and forth between what Marx says about these issues and what epistemic stance is implicit in his own scientific practice. I will begin with a discussion of Marx's critique of Hegel, since I believe this critique serves to locate Marx's epistemology within the history of philosophy. I will then turn to some features of Marx's conception of science that are sufficiently general to function as epistemological theses. Finally, I will consider a number of distinct problems that emerged in the consideration of the history of Marxism in Part 1.

MARX'S CRITIQUE OF HEGELIAN EPISTEMOLOGY

In his various attempts to settle accounts with the philosophy of Hegel, Marx makes a number of points that reveal his thinking about the nature of scientific method.[1] Hegel distinguishes between the sciences of the understanding and the science of reason.[2] Sciences such as astronomy and physics were examples of sciences of the understanding. Such sciences sought general laws that could be used to explain, predict, and control the phenomena of ordinary experience. They were not merely empirical in nature. They appealed to hidden forces and hidden entities not immediately given in experience. The formulation of these theories involved concepts that, as Kant had shown, could not be derived from experience. And the sciences so developed worked at a level of abstraction that sometimes involved considerable distortion of the world as given in experience. Nevertheless, these sciences of the understanding were for Hegel, as they were for Kant, empirical sciences. If some of the key concepts of such theories could not be derived from experience, the particular content these concepts acquired depended upon experience. If, for example, the concept of "force" was not derived from anything given in experience, the particular values attributed to gravitational forces in Newtonian physics were based on experience. It was not reason alone that gave us Kepler's laws but observation of the movement of the heavenly bodies. In the sciences of the understanding, reason could suggest a hypothesis, but empirical observation was necessary to confirm or disconfirm it.

The science of reason was quite different from these sciences of the understanding. It, at least on Marx's understanding of Hegel, involved a purely a priori dialectic of concepts. Marx viewed the *Science of Logic* as an attempt to work out this purely philosophical science. In it there is a train of concepts that begins with the most abstract and works its way through one concept after another in a direction of increasing differentiation and specificity. This development is internally directed. Each concept leads to its successor as the necessary step in the development of self-conscious thought. The task of the logic, the immanent and necessary development of the concepts, the science of reason, is for Hegel the fundamental task of philosophy. It is a higher science than the sciences of the understanding. It is higher because in it the concepts, such as force, that are taken for granted in the sciences of the understanding are given a rational foundation. It is also higher because, whereas the results of the sciences of the understanding are only contingent, the results of the science of reason are necessary. The science of reason is all-encompassing. In it every conceptualization of both the natural and the human world finds its place. The movement of thought, by its own immanent and necessary development from one concept to the next, is the Hegelian dialectic. It is, in the context of Hegel's objective idealism, with its principle of the identity of thought and being, both the method proper to philosophy and the subject matter of philosophy.

In *The Holy Family* Marx ridicules "the mystery of *speculative*, of *Hegelian construction.*" In a short, four-page discussion he tries to capture and parody the Hegelian method "in general":

> If from real apples, pears, strawberries and almonds I form the general idea "*Fruit*", if I go further and *imagine* that my abstract idea "*Fruit*", derived from real fruit, is an entity existing outside me, is indeed the *true* essence of the pear, the apple, etc., then—in the *language of speculative* philosophy—I am declaring that "*Fruit*" is the "*Substance*" of the pear, the apple, the almond, etc.[3]

Having in this way arrived at an attribution of substantiality to concepts, the speculative philosopher goes on to deny that individual fruits are truly real:

"Particular real fruits are no more than *semblances* whose true essence is '*the* substance'—'*Fruit.*' "[4] The problem for the speculative philosopher now becomes one of showing why the substantial concept manifests itself in diverse ways as various particular fruits. The answer is that the substantial concept is also subject:

This, answers the speculative philosopher, is because "*the* Fruit" is not dead, undifferentiated, motionless, but a living, self-differentiating, moving essence. The diversity of the ordinary fruits is significant not only for *my* sensuous understanding, but also for "*the* Fruit" itself and for speculative reason. The different ordinary fruits are different manifestations of the life of the "*one* Fruit"; they are crystallizations of "*the* Fruit" itself.[5]

And, Marx adds, "In the speculative way of speaking, this operation is called comprehending *Substance as Subject*, as an *inner process*, as an *Absolute Person*, and this comprehension constitutes the essential character of Hegel's method."[6] The speculative method thus consists of three sorts of moves. First, general concepts are treated as substantial, and particular instances of the things to which the concept applies are seen as appearances or manifestations of the concept. Second, substantive concepts are treated as moments of a subjective process. Third, this subject is conceived as a supernatural subject, Absolute Mind.

This summation of the speculative method encapsulizes similar presentations of it in the *Critique of Hegel's Philosophy of Right* and the *Economic and Philosophical Manuscripts of 1844*. The criticisms of Hegel developed in these works indicate the foundations for the epistemology and metaphysics of the mature Marx.

In the first place, Marx objects to the speculative philosopher's treatment of general ideas as substantial. In the words of *The Holy Family* quoted above, the speculative philosopher "imagines" that the general idea is "an entity existing outside me." The same point is made in the *Critique of Hegel's Philosophy of Right:* "Instead of considering them to be predicates of their subjects Hegel makes the predicates independent and then lets them be subsequently and mysteriously converted into their subjects."[7] For Marx, individual entities are the substantial bearers of predicates and not the manifestations of substantive concepts:

Precisely because Hegel starts from the predicates of universal determination instead of the real *Ens* (ὑποχείμενον, subject), and because there must be a bearer of this determination, the mystical Idea becomes this bearer. This is the dualism: Hegel does not consider the universal to be the actual essence of the actual, finite thing, i.e., of the existing determinate thing, nor the real *Ens* to be the true subject of the infinite.[8]

The same point is made in the *Manuscripts*: "Real man and real nature become mere predicates—symbols of this esoteric, unreal man and of this unreal nature. Subject and predicate are therefore related to each other in absolute reversal."[9]

No doubt it is passages such as these that prompt some philosophers to characterize Marx's method as consisting of a reversal of the position of subject and predicate in Hegel's philosophy.[10] Insofar as Marx treated those things which Hegel saw as manifestations of substantial concepts as independent, substantial entities, and also treated universal ideas as predicates of those entities, there is truth in this characterization of his method. However, it would be a mistake to think that this "reversal" somehow constitutes the fundamental nature of Marx's method. The immediate point in this reversal of Hegel is an ontological rather than a methodological issue. Certainly this ontological issue has some bearing on the question of methodology, but to see Marx's method as consisting solely in such a systematic reversal is to suggest the absurd view that Marx simply rewrote Hegel, transposing the positions of subject and predicate as he did so. On this view one should expect the Hegelian subject, Absolute Mind, to appear in Marx's works as a predicate, which of course it does not. Rather, this characterization of Marx's method as a "reversal" of Hegel simply skims the surface of Marx's critique of Hegel. In particular, it fails to bring out an important element of empiricism that emerges from Marx's critique of Hegel.

From the speculative point of view, particular entities and events are manifestations of concepts as they develop in pure Absolute Consciousness. On this view, to have knowledge with respect to such a particular is to have traced out the development of the concept of which it is a manifestation. This development is not a matter of logical deduction, but it is considered a kind of "logic" in which, to use Marx's term, concepts are "constructed" as necessary steps in the dialectic of concepts. In commenting on the use of the speculative method by Herr Szeliga, whom he ridicules as a transparent imitator of Hegel, Marx observes:

> In Herr Szeliga we also see a brilliant illustration of how speculation on the one hand apparently freely creates its object *a priori* out of itself and, on the other hand, precisely because it wishes to get rid by sophistry of the rational and natural dependence on the *object*, falls into the most irrational and unnatural *bondage* to the object, whose most accidental and most individual attributes it is obliged to construe as absolutely necessary and general.[11]

The Hegelian science of reason requires the comprehension of each concept as necessarily given by the immanent development of thought. In identifying the real with the idea, this science is forced to deny that there are any accidental properties. Every property of a thing must somehow be connected with the essence of the thing.

Marx's ridicule of this approach reveals a number of things about his own conception of what is going on in the scientific cognition of a thing. In the first place, it is important to note that Marx takes for granted that some of the properties of a thing are accidental. This point presents a difficulty for those interpretations of Marx which attribute to him a strong, Hegelian version of the theory of internal relations, according to which all relations of a thing are necessary to its identity as the thing it is.[12]

Second, in rejecting this *a priorism* as involving an unnatural bondage to the object, Marx also rejects the claim for reason's ability to comprehend the thing in this way. There is no rational connection by which all of the properties of a thing can be grasped a priori. It is sophistry to deny the empirical dependence upon the object as a necessary component in any scientific cognition of a thing. This same point is made in the *Critique of Hegel's Philosophy of Right*, which is a paragraph-by-paragraph criticism of a portion of Hegel's *Philosophy of Right*. There Marx takes up Hegel's effort to grasp the German constitution as a manifestation of the concept of organism. Like many of Hegel's readers, Marx finds a completely arbitrary connection passing itself off as a necessary development of the dialectic. "Why then is he [Hegel] entitled to conclude that 'this organism is the constitution of the state'? Why not 'this organism is the solar system'?"[13] So far the criticism only points to a weakness in a particular example of speculative science. However, it is clear that Marx believes this example illustrates an inherent defect in the very idea of the speculative science of reason:

> What Hegel wants to achieve is the determination of the organism as the constitution of the state. But there is no bridge by which one can pass from the universal ideal of the organism to the particular idea of the state or the constitution of the state, nor will there ever be.[14]

Here Marx is saying not just that Hegel's execution of the dialectic of reason breaks down at a certain point, but also that no dialectical transition of the sort the science of reason requires is possible. In the same way Marx argues in *The Holy Family* that it is impossible to move, by a pure dialectic of reason, from general concepts to particular objects.[15] The commitment at the heart of the science of reason—to comprehend everything within the immanent dialectic of concepts—is doomed to failure. Matters of fact cannot be comprehended by a pure logic of concepts.

Marx sees observation, sense experience, as a necessary component in any genuine science. Thus, in the *Critique of Hegel's Philosophy of Right*, we find him criticizing Hegel on the grounds that "The fact, which is the starting point, is not conceived to be such but rather to be the mystical result."[16] And, in *The Holy Family*, Marx criticizes Hegel for hiding the role of sensory experience in the historical development of thought: "Hegel with masterly sophistry is able to present as a process of the imagined creation of the mind itself, of the Absolute Subject, the process by which the philosopher through sensory perception and imagination passes from one subject to another."[17] If Hegel is a master of sophistry, it is nonetheless true that Marx sees the speculative science of reason as a kind of sophistry. It provides no genuine knowledge but only a "mystical" interpretation of the world.[18] The mineralogist who adopted the speculative method "would be a mineralogist in *his imagination*."[19] Hegel's speculative science is a "pseudoscience."[20]

Marx's rejection of the possibility of a Hegelian science of reason is coupled with his affirmation of the method of the sciences of the understanding as the only method appropriate for science. He approvingly summarizes the Baconian conception of science as based on sensory experience: "All science is based on *experience*, and consists in subjecting the data furnished by the senses to a *rational method* of investigation. Induction, analysis, comparison, observation, experiment, are the principal forms of such a rational method."[21] And it is clear that Marx saw empirical observation as lying at the foundation of his social theory. In the *Manuscrips* he assures the reader that his results are attained by the means of "a wholly empirical analysis."[22] Similar assurances accompany the introduction of his materialist view of history in *The German Ideology*, where Marx assures us that his anlaysis begins with premises susceptible of empirical verification. There, too, he advances the strong claim that from the viewpoint of this materialist theory of history, every problem of philosophy is "resolved . . . quite simply into an empirical fact."[23]

What these passages show is that Marx's critique of Hegel involves much more than a critique of Hegel's idealism. In the Afterword to the second German edition of *Capital*, there is a famous passage in which Marx says, "The mystification which dialectic suffers in Hegel's hands, by no means prevents him from being the first to present its general form of working in a comprehensive and conscious manner. With him it is standing on its head. It must be turned right side up again, if you would discover the rational kernel within the mystical shell."[24] It is tempting to think of the dialectical method as the "rational kernel" that must be stripped of its "mystical" (idealistic) shell. But this is entirely too simple. Marx's critique of the philosophy of Hegel involves not only a rejection of his idealism but also a rejection of the whole project of a science of reason distinct from the sciences of the understanding. Such a science is a "pseudoscience." In opposition to the Hegelian project, Marx insists that the Baconian model applies to all genuine science. This rejection of a science of reason has important implications for the understanding of Marx's method and consequently for the understanding of Marxist science. What these remarks suggest is that, at least in his early critique of Hegel, Marx did not think of his own scientific work as methodologically distinct from other science. In contrast with the Hegelian science of reason, Marxist science appears as science of the understanding.

MARX'S PHILOSOPHY OF SCIENCE

Marx's critique of the Hegelian science of reason provides an important element in his own philosophy of science. I want to turn now to Marx's view of the nature of science. The most famous passage in this regard is the "Introduction to the Critique of Political Economy," which was unpublished in Marx's lifetime and appears now as the Introduction to the *Grundrisse*. In it Marx offers some comments about the nature of economic science. The passage of central importance is as follows:

> The economists of the seventeenth century, e.g., always started out with the living aggregate: population, nation, state, several states, etc., but in the end they invariably arrived, by means of anlaysis, at certain leading, abstract general principles such as division of labor, money, value, etc. As soon as these separate elements had been more or less established by abstract reasoning, there arose the systems of political economy which start from simple conceptions, such as labor, division of labor, demand, exchange value, and conclude with state, international exchange, and world market. The latter is manifestly the scientifically correct method. . . . The first procedure attenuates meaningful images to abstract definitions, the second leads from abstract definitions by way of reasoning to the reproduction of the concrete situation.[25]

In this passage Marx is contrasting the economics of the seventeenth century with the later scientific systems of political economy, such as the systems of Adam Smith and David Ricardo. Whereas the economists of the seventeenth century begin with the concrete and end with the abstract, the later, scientific economists begin with the abstract and end with the concrete. This point of contrast has led some commentators to find in Marx's characterization of science here an important rejection of his earlier empiricism. Thus, for example, Louis Althusser claims to find in this passage the clearest expression of the epistemological break between the empiricism of the young Marx and the dialectical materialism of the mature Marx.[26] For Althusser the method of the seventeenth-century economists, which moves from the concrete to the abstract, is the method of empiricism, which Marx contrasts with the genuine scientific approach that begins with the abstract and ends with the concrete.

I do not think such a conclusion is warranted. Marx's remarks in the passage in question might be construed as a rejection of a crude empiricism that sees science as somehow emerging directly, without the intervention of theory, out of a mass of observations to higher and higher levels of abstraction. It is such an anti-theoretical empiricism that Althusser has in mind. But not all empiricism is so crude, and I see no reason to think that Marx's earlier empiricism was so crude.[27]

In its classical formulations in Locke and Hume, empiricism is a thesis about the origins of ideas. As was noted above, Marx seems to affirm this origins thesis in his critique of Hegel. Contrary to Althusser, there is nothing in the passage from the *Grundrisse* which would indicate that Marx rejects the origins thesis. Indeed, Marx there seems to affirm that the abstract concepts, with which the scientific systems of economics began, have their origins in the analysis of the observations of earlier economists.

In its more modern formulations, empiricism is a thesis about the justification of theory by observational test, confirmation, or verification. This justificatory version of empiricism is also present in Marx's critique of Hegel, as I noted above in relation to Marx's claim that the premises with which he begins are empirically verifiable. There is nothing in the passage from the *Grundrisse* that implies Marx's rejection of this justificatory thesis of empiricism. The claim that a theory begins with abstract concepts and arrives at a replication in theory of the concrete situation given in experience does not preclude acceptance of empirical observation as a justificatory test of theory. Indeed, I have already argued that Marx's theory of capitalism remains open to the test of empirical observation.

The *Grundrisse* passage does indicate that Marx conceived of abstraction and abstract concepts as playing a central role in the construction of a genuine scientific theory. The scientific economics of Smith and Ricardo are built upon certain abstract concepts. By use of such concepts, the scientist constructs a theoretical model of the real world process. By analyzing these concepts and their interconnections, the scientist can trace out, by deductive reason, the consequences of changes in some aspect of the system throughout the theoretical model. As has already been seen, such models provide us with a simplification or idealization of the real world process. Gradually the theory is enriched by the introduction of modifications of the model that bring it closer and closer to an adequate representation of the actual social process. This is the movement characterized by Marx in the key *Grundrisse* passage as the movement "from abstract definitions by way of reasoning to the reproduction of the concrete situation." In a fully developed theory of this sort, Marx tells us, empirically observable processes appear to be derivable in a purely *a priori* fashion.[28] But this appearance of *a prioriticity* is mere appearance since, as Little's work stresses, the abstract core of the theory is itself derived by analysis from experience. And further the concrete processes derived from this core in the process of the theoretical reproduction of the concrete remain open to empirical testing.

As I have interpreted them, Marx's comments on the role of abstract concepts in the genuine scientific treatment of a subject matter point to what we would now call the elaboration of a theoretical model. These abstractions stand in a complex relationship to the real world. They are drawn from observation, and in this sense reflect the real world; but at the same time, as abstractions, these concepts select certain aspects of reality as theoretically more significant than others, and leave certain aspects of the real process outside the network of concepts that constitute the core of the scientific theory. Models both model and distort. The aim of a model is to represent in a clear way significant processes that are at work in the real world. Given such a model, it is possible to trace out by deductive reason the consequences of changes in certain variables on other variables within the model.

Hence, such a model makes possible the formulation of law claims for the following form: Given conditions C_1 and $C_2 \ldots C_n$, if an event of kind K_1 occurs, then an event of kind K_2 will follow. Here the C conditions specify the core defining features of the model, and the K factors specify kinds of events that can occur within these defining conditions. A genuine scientific presentation of a subject matter seeks to formulate laws of this type that govern the behavior of objects within the domain of study which the theory claims to model. The

Grundrisse passage makes no explicit mention of scientific laws in its characterization of science, but the possibility of such law claims is implicit in the characterization it does present in the fashion described above. And Marx explicitly endorses the importance of law claims elsewhere in his characterization of genuine science.[29] Given an abstract model of the real world process and some empirical assumptions, it is possible, by deductive reasoning, to develop explanations for what has occurred and predictions concerning what will occur. It is this deductive movement that we saw realized in Marx's own theory of capitalism, and it is this same deductive movement that Marx described in the passage from the *Grundrisse*.

Another theme in Marx's philosophy of science involves a distinction between hidden essence and surface appearance. This distinction appears repeatedly in Marx's comments on science.[30] A genuine scientific treatment of a subject matter penetrates beneath the surface appearance of things to get at the essential processes beneath this surface that governed the behavior of the objects within the field of study. The relationship between essence and appearance is epistemically complex. The surface appearance is the appearance of the hidden essence, and in this sense it is a revelation of the inner reality of things. However, the surface appearance is not epistemically adequate. It omits, obscures, and distorts features of the real objects that produce it. Knowledge of the hidden essences of things is reached by way of abstraction and analysis of the surface appearances. In this sense, the phenomenal appearance is epistemically primary. However, as we have seen in the key passage from the *Grundrisse*, the genuine scientific treatment of a field of study only begins with the results obtained by such a process of abstraction and analysis, and aims at a replication, by way of deductive theory, of the surface appearance of things. The economics of Ricardo is Marx's paradigm example of a scientific economics. Beginning with certain abstract concepts that define the hidden inner structures of capitalist economies, Ricardo is able, by analysis and deductive reasoning, to account for the surface appearances of economic life.[31]

Marx conceives of science as an attempt to grasp the inner essence that governs the surface appearances of things. By abstraction and analysis of what is given in the surface appearance of things, the thinker arrives at certain abstract concepts that are used to construct a simplified model of actual processes. By deductive reason and the progressive enrichment of the model, the scientist is able to reproduce in thought a more or less adequate picture of the complex world given in the surface appearance of things. In a successful scientific theory, reality, both as inner essence and as surface phenomena produced by that inner essence, is reflected in thought "as in a mirror." Scientific consciousness is the reflection in thought of a reality external to consciousness. The distinction between essence and appearance in Marx's philosophy of science is linked to both a scientific realism and the reflection theory of knowledge.

We have already seen, in Part 1, how the epistemological currents of late-nineteenth-century philosophy seemed to threaten both scientific realism and the reflection theory of knowledge. In the attempt to avoid both the excesses of Hegelian metaphysics and the naiveté of the scientific materialists, philosophers turned to either Neo-Kantianism or positivism, both of which rejected realism as an epistemically untenable transgression of the boundaries of human knowledge.

For the Neo-Kantians, the objects of scientific knowledge existed only within the phenomenal world, as constituted by the transcendental subject. The reflection theory thus failed, not only because it naively presupposed the knowability of objects existing independently of consciousness, but also because it failed to recognize the active role of consciousness in the constitution of the object. While not invoking any doctrine of the transcendental constitution of the objects of scientific study, the positivists rejected the reflection theory, because of its apparent commitment to an untenable realism, in favor of an instrumentalist philosophy of science. As was seen in Part 1, each of these epistemological positions found support from some Marxists of the Second International. Both Marxist-Leninism and humanistic Marxism have their origins, in part, in response to this epistemic crisis in the Marxism of the Second International. However, it is an indication of the radical divergence of these two trends in Marxist philosophy that while Leninists defended scientific realism and the reflection theory, Lukácsian humanists rejected them.

THE EPISTEMOLOGY OF PRACTICE

The question whether objective truth is an attribute of human thought—is not a theoretical but a *practical* question. Man must prove the truth, i.e. the reality and power, the "this-sidedness" of his thinking in practice. The dispute over the reality or non-reality of thinking that is isolated from practice is a purely *scholastic* question.

Marx, *Theses on Feuerbach* II

All social life is essentially *practical*. All the mysteries which urge theory into mysticism find their rational solution in human practice and in the comprehension of this practice.

Marx, *Theses on Feuerbach* VIII

Some philosophers have found in these remarks a radical alternative to previous approaches in epistemology. Accordingly, they have argued that Marxism rests on an epistemology of practice or, more profoundly still, that Marxism is best understood as a philosophy of praxis. The nature of this philosophy of praxis, and the relationship between praxis and practice, have been subject to a number of different interpretations. As a way of entry into these issues, I would like to begin with two different interpretations of the idea of an epistemology of practice.

Roughly put, the two interpretations differ as to whether successful practice is a criterion of truth, or whether it just is what is meant by truth. On the first interpretation Marx's theses on Feuerbach are taken as asserting that successful application of a theory in some practical matter is an indication or sign or proof of the truth of the theory, where truth is understood in terms of a relation of correspondence, or reflection, between the theory and the external world. On the second interpretation, Marx's theses are taken as asserting that the whole concept of truth is meaningless when it is applied outside the sphere of practical application. The first interpretation understands Marxism as adopting a scientific realism, with practical success as evidence that the theory correctly reflects the external world. The second interpretation understands Marxism as adopting an instrumentalist theory of science according to which "truth" means "works in practice."

The instrumentalist interpretation, as we have seen, was embraced by Aleksandr Bogdanov, Anton Pannekoek, and other Marxist followers of Ernst Mach.[32] Whatever the merits of instrumentalism as a philosophy of science, the position fails as an interpretation of Marx. In the first place, Marx frequently talks about thought reflecting an external reality, and this seems incompatible with an instrumentalist theory of science.[33] Second, Marx's distinction between the hidden essences of things made known by scientific theories and the surface phenomena present in empirical experience makes difficult a purely instrumentalist conception of science.[34] Let us turn, then, to the interpretation of practice as evidence for truth as correspondence.

In *Ludwig Feuerbach and the End of Classical German Philosophy*, Engels cites the industrial production of alizarin, a naturally occurring dye, as proof of the theories of organic chemistry that made this production possible and further as refutation of the skeptical philosophies of Hume and Kant.[35] In a similar vein, Lenin cites human practice as proving the objective correctness of thought.[36] Both Engels and Lenin construe correctness of theory in terms of its reflection of an independently existing external reality. They take successful practical application of a theory as establishing that such a reflective relationship holds.

Marxist critics of Engel's argument, such as the Neo-Kantian Konrad Schmidt and the positivist Anton Pannekoek, argue that this appeal to successful practice fails.[37] On one plausible reading, Engels' argument is patently fallacious. Engels appears to be arguing that if the organic chemistry were true, then certain practical applications would succeed. The practical applications did succeed; therefore the organic chemistry was true. This, of course, is an instance of the fallacy of affirming the consequent. It is, at the same time, an illustration of the kind of difficulty faced by any empiricist philosophy of science struggling with the problems of confirmation and verification.

A more charitable interpretation of Engels' argument, and one more in keeping with his own view of the tentative and revisable nature of all scientific theory, would understand the appeal to practice to establish the truth of theories in terms of the best-explanation accounts of scientific success. It may well be that practical success is logically compatible with the falsity of the theory leading to that success, but the at least approximate truth of the theory may nonetheless be the most reasonable account of the success of the theory. Some such best-explanation approach seems to be at work in Georgi Plekhanov's discussion of Engels' argument. For example, Plekhanov says that it is useless to try to *prove* the subjective idealism of Hume and Berkeley to be false, and he tries to refute the Kantian alternative to materialism by showing that its attempt to account for the practical success of scientific theories involves it in serious difficulties.[38]

The best explanation of the success defense of scientific realism remains a much-discussed option in post-positivist analytic philosophy of science. I shall not attempt a survey of this literature here. Whatever problems the argument may have, it stands as one of the common arguments in the recent resurgence of scientific realism within analytical philosophy of science. Insofar as the Marxist-Leninist epistemology of practice is understood in this way, it does not appear to represent a radical alternative to contemporary analytic epistemology.

THE EPISTEMOLOGY OF PRAXIS

I have so far considered Marx's appeal to practice solely from the point of view of technical application of theory. Some such view of the appeal to practice seems to be found in the discussions of Engels, Plekhanov, and Lenin. However, within the framework of humanistic Marxism, a technological construal of practice is itself symptomatic of a basic misunderstanding of Marxism. The humanistic understanding of Marxism as the philosophy of praxis insists that the kind of knowledge gained by Marxism, and the method by which this knowledge is acquired, differ fundamentally from the technocratic knowledge and the technocratic method of the natural sciences.

Though the epistemic difficulties of pre-critical materialism play a foundational role in Lukács' humanistic critique of the dialectical materialism of Engels, and of the Marxism of the Second International, these difficulties are only part of what is involved in the epistemic revolution in Marxist philosophy effected by Lukács' work. To see this, it is enough to contrast the viewpoint of Lukács with the viewpoints of the Neo-Kantianism of Adler and the positivism of Bogdanov. All agree in rejecting materialism as a metaphysical doctrine that cannot survive the critical revolution in epistemology. But whereas Max Adler and Aleksandr Bogdanov retain a view of Marxism as essentially a scientific theory analogous to the theories of the natural sciences, Lukács rejects this view. For Lukács, Marxism is a social theory that is fundamentally distinct from the kind of theories found in the natural sciences. The conception of Marxist social theory as distinct in kind from natural science does not follow from the purely epistemic revolution of post-Kantian critical philosophy alone, although, as we shall see, this distinctive conception of Marxist social theory sometimes appears to be linked to the epistemic revolution of critical philosophy.

Consider, for example, the concept of "constitution" that plays a central role in Kantian epistemology and in the conception of social theory advanced by Lukács. Kantians maintain that, in some sense, the world of ordinary experience is, at least in part, constituted by the knowing subject. But, for the Kantian, this is true of the moon and stars as much as it is true of the social world. Further, "constitution" in this Kantian sense does not preclude the existence of universal laws that govern the behavior of the objects of knowledge, nor does it preclude the objectivity of knowledge understood as the search for these universal laws.

Marxist-Leninists sometimes argue that Kantian or positivist attempts to sever historical materialism from ontological materialism involve them in denying any objective foundation to historical laws, and hence also in denying the objectivity of historical materialism.[39] This argument appears to confuse the idea of an objective law-governed process with the materialistic explanation of such processes. If successful, it would work against the possibility of Kantian or positivist physics as well. Neo-Kantian opposition to historical materialism derived more from Kantian doctrines of ethical autonomy than from Kantian epistemology. In this respect, Heidelberg Neo-Kantianism, with its stress on the difference between natural science and social theory, did play, and continues to play, a more significant role in resistance to determinist theories of history than do the purely epistemic theories of Kant. From a purely metaphysical point of view, the Neo-Kantian Konrad Schmidt is surely right in saying that historical materialism is consistent with either materialism or idealism.[40]

Within Kant's own critical philosophy, the constitution of the world by the subject does not lay the basis for a distinction between social theory and natural science. However, within the humanistic Marxism of Lukács, "constitution" does serve to distinguish social theory from "objectifying" natural science. The idea seems to be that whereas the natures of the objects of study of natural science do not depend upon social consciousness, the "objects" of study of social theory do depend upon social consciousness for their natures. Thus, widespread acceptance of divine right may be necessary for the existence of monarchical forms of government. In this sense, a form of social existence may be said to be, at least in part, constituted by a form of social consciousness, in a way that the objects of study of the natural sciences are not so constituted. And, insofar as this is true, alteration of consciousness may be sufficient to alter the form of social life. In this sense, "constitution" of the social world is what grounds the reflective nature of social theory discussed in Chapter 3.

Clearly there are two distinct conceptions of "constitution" at work here. One could accept either without accepting the other. While I believe that Lukács himself accepted both senses of "constitution," the distinctive features of the epistemology of humanistic Marxism appear to lie more in the sense of "constitution" involving the role of social consciousness in forms of social life rather than in the strictly Kantian conception of the constitution of the world of experience by a transcendental subjectivity. But it is not at all clear that constitution of the social world by the human subject is an epistemic process at all.

One version of the philosophy of praxis grounds all forms of rationality in a praxiological relationship to the world. So understood, praxis Marxism partakes of a current within European philosophy since Kant, running through such diverse figures as Fichte, Hegel, Schopenhauer, Nietzsche, Heidegger, and Sartre, that stresses the primacy of the practical over the theoretical relationship to the world.

On this view, the conception of the subject as passive in cognition, and even the separation between subject and object—both presupposed, it is claimed, in the epistemology of the reflection theory—are untenable. On this interpretation of the philosophy of praxis, all cognition is determined by the needs of human agents. These needs, and the categories and preconceptions built on the basis of them, play an active role in all cognition. Marxism, unlike Aristotelian realism, does not see the categories of human knowledge as reflecting forms inherent in external objects but, rather, as expressions of human needs. The world we experience is a product of these need-based categories of human cognition.[41]

There are two ways of understanding such claims. On one reading, these claims take on an ontological or metaphysical significance. So understood, they deny the existence, or at least the knowability, of any reality distinct from human subjects. Kolakowski says, "The world of things exists for man only as a totality of possible satisfactions of his needs."[42] Kolakowski also holds that existence in itself cannot be an object of human cognition. In a similar vein, Z. A. Jordan argues that the reflection theory of knowledge is incompatible with Marx's epistemology, which recognizes the active role of the subject in constituting the object of cognition.[43] On this reading, every possible object of cognition, even the objects of a natural science, is existentially dependent upon the activity of the human agent.

An alternative reading of the philosophy of praxis would distinguish between the world of nature, which is existentially independent of human agency, and the artificial world of social systems and produced artifacts, which is existentially dependent upon the activity of the human agent. I will call this a sociological reading of the philosophy of praxis to distinguish it from the metaphysical reading. It is clear that the kind of dependence claimed here is quite different from the kind of dependence claimed by the metaphysical interpretation. The metaphysical interpretation clearly does have epistemological implications. It appears to be inconsistent with the reflection theory in at least two respects: it insists on the active role of the subject in the process of cognition, and it denies the existence of a reality independent of consciousness that could be reflected in consciousness. On the other hand, it is not at all clear that the sociological interpretation does have any epistemological consequences. For the active role attributed to the human agent pertains to the creation of objects, not to their cognition, and the sociological interpretation does not deny the existence of objects, natural and artificial, external to the consciousness of the human knower.

This brings us back to the two senses of "constitution" mentioned above. The metaphysical interpretation of the philosophy of praxis seems to turn on a Kantian sense of "constitution," while the sociological version turns on the sense of "constitution" involving the human production of the social environment. As was said above, Lukács is somewhat unclear about whether he is endorsing the metaphysical or the sociological version of the philosophy of praxis. In one passage, he appears clearly to endorse the metaphysical position:

Nature is a societal category. That is to say, whatever is held to be natural at any given stage of social development, however this nature is related to man and whatever form his involvement with it takes, i.e. nature's form, its content, its range and its objectivity are all socially conditioned.[44]

While many of Lukács' commentators have taken this as a clear statement of the metaphysical interpretation, Andrew Feenberg has correctly pointed out that Lukács says only that whatever is *held* to be natural is socially conditioned, and not that nature itself is socially constituted.[45] Feenberg argues for the sociological construal of Lukács' position, both on the grounds of the interpretation of this passage and on the grounds that only the sociological construal makes sense of Lukács' distinction between the natural sciences and social theory. My own (uncertain) view is that Lukács is best understood as maintaining a kind of double constitution of the social. On the one hand, on general philosophical grounds, he, rejects the idea of a reality external to consciousness as naive and untenable. He rejects the dichotomy of thought and being.[46] In addition, he holds the sociological thesis, that social forms existentially depend upon the consciousness of human beings.

I shall postpone discussion of the metaphysical version of the philosophy of praxis until Chapter 6. This leaves us with the question of what, if any, are the epistemological implications of the sociological interpretation of the philosophy of praxis.

The most plausible way of connecting the sociological interpretation to the domain of epistemology is via the argument that since the existence of social relations depends upon the acceptance of those relations by humans bound by those relations, it follows that social theory, unlike theory in the natural sciences, influences the objects within its domain of study. This argument is supposed to show that the methodology of the social sciences must be different from the methodology of the natural sciences. It is also supposed to show that the reflection theory fails, at least for social theory, because consciousness, unlike a reflected image, can alter the object it supposedly reflects. We have already faced this argument in considering the nature of Marx's theory of capitalism. As was said there, I think the importance of this line of argument for the social sciences is less than is often claimed. While it is no doubt true that consciousness can influence the world, and social theorists need to be attentive to self-fulfilling and self-defeating consequences of this sort, this truth does not justify a sharp distinction between the social sciences in general and the natural sciences in general. Nor does it require a radically different epistemology or methodology for the social sciences. From the point of view of methodology, the key thing is to recognize that all law claims pertain only to objects of a certain kind. From the point of view of epistemology, the interaction between theory and object is irrelevant.

An alternative normative version of the philosophy of praxis has played a significant role within humanistic Marxism. The Yugoslav philosopher Mihailo Markovic writes:

> *Praxis* has to be distinguished from the purely epistemological category of *practice*. The latter refers simply to any Subject's activity of changing an object and this activity can be alienated. The former is a normative concept and refers to an ideal, specifically human activity which is an end in itself, a statement of basic values and at the same time a standard of criticism of all other forms of activity.[47]

Here Markovic appears to be locating the concept of praxis outside the bounds of epistemology altogether. But this is not in fact the case. Rather, Markovic argues, the philosophy of praxis does require a modification of traditional epistemology:

> On these grounds [the presuppositions of the philosophy of praxis] it becomes possible to distinguish between *true, genuine needs* and *false, artificial* ones, or between a true and an illusory *self-realization*. The concept of truth in this context is much more general than the customary epistemological concept. One of its dimensions is adequacy to actual reality (the descriptive concept of truth). Another dimension is adequacy to an ideal standard, to an essential possibility (the normative concept of truth).[48]

Here, then, the distinctive epistemic feature of the Marxist philosophy of praxis appears to involve the grounding of normative claims.

Markovic makes no effort to draw such a grounding out of Marx's philosophical writings, and his own effort falls far short of providing such a grounding. In the passages quoted, Markovic tells us that praxis is a normative ideal and that this ideal can be used to distinguish true needs from false needs. But how is the ideal of praxis itself to be justified? Markovic tells us that "values" do not exist "in themselves" as some sort of denizens of a Husserlian or Popperian "third world." Rather, values exist only as a result of human penetration into the world. "Objects and processes become values only when they are relative to human needs, which again in their turn are a product of the whole of preceding history."[49]

However, this account appears to have a circularity built into it. On the one hand, it grounds values on human needs, and on the other, it appeals to ideals (values) to distinguish true needs from false. It may well be that some account of this process can be developed which makes this circularity nonvicious. Perhaps, for example, a kind of Rawlsian reflective equilibrium of needs and ideals could be worked out. But, as it stands, Markovic's philosophy of praxis fails to provide the epistemic theory it requires.

Markovic's conception of the philosophy of praxis involves a distinction between the technocratic rationality of natural science, which is the object of study for traditional epistemology, and the normative rationality of praxis, for which a distinct epistemology is required. Such a distinction between different kinds of rationality is common to much of the literature of Western Marxism. It is a basic theme for the Frankfurt School, with its distinction between traditional and critical theory. A central difficulty for this conception of praxis has been the problem of justification of normative judgments. In contrast with traditional epistemology, which has viewed normative judgments as involving nonrational commitments, this conception of the philosophy of praxis has attempted to work out an epistemology of normative claims according to which such claims are capable of a distinctive sort of rational grounding.

The most promising attempt to develop such an epistemic foundation is found in the work of Jürgen Habermas. He argues for three distinct kinds of knowledge, each growing out of distinct human interests: empirical science, aiming at technical mastery of nature; hermeneutics, which aims at an understanding of the meaning of social life forms; and critical theory, which aims at human emancipation.[50]

The specific grounding of normative critical theory is based on norms that Habermas claims to find implicit in the nature of language. In speaking a language we attempt to communicate something to others within the language community. This attempt presupposes an intention to convey some truth to others. Commands, deception, and fiction are parasitic on this more fundamental intention to convey the truth. However, the fundamental intention to convey the truth carries with it a vulnerability to requests for clarification, objections, and the like. Habermas develops an analysis of the conditions presupposed by the fundamental intention of language use as a set of ideal speech conditions that function as necessary conditions for free, full, and unconstrained discourse. Given this analysis, he argues that critical social theory works by showing how existing social arrangements depend upon violations of the ideal speech conditions. What grounds these ideal speech conditions is their inherence as necessary presuppositions of language use. The underlying strategy is strikingly formulated in this passage from Habermas' "Frankfurt Inaugural Address" of 1965:

> The human interest in autonomy and responsibility is not mere fancy, for it can be apprehended a priori. What raises us out of nature is the only thing whose nature we can know: *language*. Through its structure, autonomy and responsibility are posited for us. Our first sentence expresses unequivocally the intention of universal and unconstrained consensus.[51]

Habermas' attempt to supply epistemic foundations for the normative critical theory of humanistic Marxism faces a number of difficulties. To begin with, such a strategy is nowhere indicated in the works of Marx himself. Habermas argues that, though Marx's works do at times implicitly presuppose a distinct kind of critical knowledge, Marx's explicit understanding of his own work fails to take into account the distinctive nature of this kind of critical knowledge. The result is a "positivist atrophy of epistemology" in which Marx understands his own work on the model of positivist natural science.[52] While an argument of this form might be successful if the discrepancy between what Marx is doing and his understanding of what he is doing were great enough, it is not at all clear that this is so. Indeed, I shall argue in Chapter 9 that the critique of political economy can be understood without recourse to the epistemic apparatus of Habermas' universal pragmatics. If that is so, it would be rash to adopt Habermas' epistemology of critical theory as a Marxist epistemology.

Habermas does not maintain that his position is true Marxism. Rather, he appears to hold his position as an improvement on traditional Marxism.[53] While it is interesting and worthy of serious consideration, there are serious substantive difficulties with Habermas' attempted grounding of critical theory. At least three sorts of criticisms suggest themselves. First, granted that the norms implicit in the ideal speech conditions are presupposed by all language use, it need not be the case that these same conditions are morally ideal. Language use is only one of many human practices. Why should the presuppositions of this human practice be morally paramount? Second, it is not obvious that social arrangements reached in accordance with Habermas' ideal speech conditions would be morally satisfactory. It may be that human deliberation is sufficiently susceptible to nonrational forces to make any connection between the social arrangements actually reached under Habermas' ideal speech conditions and morally acceptable arrangements purely fortuitous. Finally, it is not at all clear that language use does presuppose the ideal speech conditions elaborated by Habermas. Surely we can imagine language arising under circumstances where these conditions are not actually realized (presumably they have never been actually realized). And, if language is possible without actual realization of these conditions, then it is difficult to see just how these conditions or their normative relevance is presupposed by language.

THE REFLECTION THEORY

The reflection theory is a particular version of correspondence theories of truth. It holds that there is a correspondence between external objects and their representation within the consciousness of the human knower. In addition, the reflection theory suggests a number of other features about the relationship between the external object and the representation that corresponds to it. It suggests that the external object causes the representation in consciousness, just as the object causes its reflection in some medium. Further, the reflection theory suggests that the representation in consciousness more or less accurately pictures the external object, just as a reflection more or less accurately pictures the object of which it is a reflection. Finally, the reflection theory suggests that the human being is basically passive in knowing the object, just as the medium in which the reflection occurs is basically passive with respect to the features of the reflection appearing within it.

Each of these features of the reflection theory has been criticized. Attacks on the correspondence component have been framed in terms of the metaphorical nature of the supposed relation of correspondence and in terms of philosophical problems in metaphysics and philosophy of language. Within the Marxist tradition, the most common attack on the correspondence features has come from the metaphysical versions of the philosophy of praxis that deny the existence of an external world with which representations in human knowers could correspond. As indicated above, I will reserve consideration of such criticisms to Chapter 6.

The causal component of the reflection theory appears to imply an empiricist theory of the origin of our ideas. While it might be that external objects cause representations in us by some means other than the senses, it is difficult to see what this mechanism could be. Within the history of Marxism, the principal challenge to the origins thesis of empiricism have come from Neo-Kantian arguments for a priori concepts. A similar sort of challenge is made in Louis Althusser's structuralist Marxism, which directly denies the origins thesis. I have already argued that Marx's philosophy of science commits him to the empiricist account of the origin of our ideas in sensory observation. (In addition to the origins version of empiricism, the causal component of the reflection theory also holds that it is mind-independent objects which cause the representations in us. In this, too, it is subject to criticisms growing out of the metaphysical interpretations of the philosophy of praxis that will be considered below.)

But further difficulties remain. As was noted above, to say that thought in consciousness is a reflection of the object external to consciousness suggests that the representation in consciousness more or less accurately pictures the external object. However, this is clearly not the case with respect to all of our ideas. Some beliefs are false. This falsity can be a matter of highly specific detail, as when we form a mistaken belief about someone's eye color. Or the false belief may have a global significance within our world view—as, for example, is the case with religious beliefs that support a network of beliefs constituting political and moral ideologies. Marxists themselves have claimed that whole systems of belief are illusory in this way. How can this be reconciled with the simple epistemology of the reflection theory?

Some headway can be made toward replying to this objection by attending to the "more or less" qualification of the claim that representations in consciousness accurately reflect the external object. A reflecting medium can be more or less successful in representing an object. Mirrors are better than rippling streams, and both of these are better than the sides of automobiles. Distortion and error can appear as a result of the nature of the reflecting medium. But this surely does not get at the kind of illusion involved in false beliefs. It is the same man who masters metallurgical engineering who believes he has an immortal soul. The rippling stream and the car door distort uniformly. The man combines accurate knowledge with the wildest fantasies. A capacity for distortion and error must somehow lie in the human mind, which is the medium of reflection, but this capacity cannot alone account for false beliefs.

A more promising account of error within the Marxist framework comes from pointing to misrepresentations by the object itself. Thus, Marx argued that various mistaken beliefs about capitalism arise because capitalist systems present a surface appearance that conceals the true nature of their inner workings. The mistaken beliefs reflect the surface appearance rather than the hidden essential structure. Similarly, the panda appears to be a bear but is not. The belief that pandas are bears reflects real features of the world, but they are features that are misleading.

This account of error is powerful in some cases, but it is not clear that it will work in all cases. Consider Marx's claim that under feudalism exploitation is apparent, while under capitalism it is hidden beneath a surface of free exchanges. This may account for the illusory belief that capitalism fosters human freedom, but it suggests a different account will be needed for the false beliefs necessary for religious legitimation of exploitation under feudalism. And, indeed, Marx does give a different sort of account here, one that is couched in terms of the functional role of religious legitimation within the feudal mode of production. But how is this functional account of illusory beliefs related to the reflection theory? There is no simple inconsistency between the two, but there is no obvious connection either. And, in the case of the transparent feudal relations of production, it is hard to see what features of the external object, the feudal mode of production, could be responsible for the causation of the appropriate false religious beliefs.

To be sure, there are mechanisms of socialization that may have led the feudal peasants to "see" a divine sanction for relations of exploitation and domination in aspects of the mundane world they experienced—in patterns of deference, speech, dress, and so on. But in doing this the peasants are not simply reflecting what is there. In this kind of "seeing" they play an active role. They bring to their experience a whole network of beliefs and connected dispositions to interpret the mundane world from the point of view of their religious world view. They are the bearers of cultural prejudices. Their experience is theory laden.

This brings us to the objection to the reflection theory on grounds that in knowing the world we play an active role, rather than the purely passive role suggested by the reflection theory. To my mind, this is the most serious objection facing the reflection theory. The point has been forcefully pressed by the hermeneutic perspective, and finally acknowledged even within the camp of empiricist philosophy of science. Humanistic Marxists have appealed to the theory ladenness of all observation as a decisive objection to the reflection theory. Marxist-Leninists have countered with the claim that a course Lenin did not mean to deny the active role of the subject in acquiring knowledge of the world. They have insisted that the reflection theory must be understood as one aspect of a dialectical interaction between subject and object.[54]

While I am not convinced of the usefulness of the appeal to dialectics here, I am in sympathy with the Marxist-Leninist response. In the first place, I think it is important to keep in mind the central point Lenin was trying to make with his use of the reflection theory. Clearly, for Lenin, the central issue was the issue of realism versus some form of phenomenalistic instrumentalism. Empirio-criticism appeared to dissolve the external object and leave nothing but the internal representation. The reflection theory was fundamentally an insistence on the real existence of the external object. For Lenin, "reflection" was a metaphor for bringing out this aspect of the knowledge relationship. The objection that reflection ignores the active role of the subject, like the objection that reflection obscures the possibility of false beliefs, trades on connotations of the reflection metaphor that are not central to Lenin's position. What is vital to Lenin's reflection theory, realism, can be preserved without denying the active role of consciousness in the act of cognition.[55] We construct our theories partly out of materials we receive in the process of socialization, partly out of ideas that result from our own experience of the world, and partly, perhaps, out of our own inventiveness. But this does not preclude our theory from more or less accurately representing external objects. The painter acts—even the realistic representationalist painter.

IS HISTORICAL MATERIALISM SELF-DEFEATING?

Historical materialism appears to claim that the ideological superstructure is determined by the economic base. That is to say, that the beliefs people hold are determined by the social environment, in particular the mode of production, in which they find themselves. Several critics have argued that any such position is self-defeating. A clear formulation of the argument is presented by Tom W. Goff:

> If it is held that the intellectual sphere is totally rooted in "existential" factors and therefore that it can and must be "extrinsically" interpreted or explained, then all statements of "fact" must be regarded as but relative statements of opinion or simple rationalizations, statements which reflect the social biography, social location and social interests of an individual or group. If this is true, then clearly even those statements about social conditioning uttered by the sociologist of knowledge must themselves be reflections of a particular social biography. If the status of fact, of objectivity or of truth is claimed for such statements, then they are self-contradictory. Either such statements are true, thereby refuting their own claims about existential conditioning, or they are false and the position is obviously refuted.[56]

In part, the difficulty here pertains to the idea of that our beliefs are causally determined. The argument is an old one. Epicurus formulated it succinctly: "He who says that all things happen of necessity cannot criticize another who says that not all things happen of necessity. For he has to admit that the assertion also happens of necessity."[57] Goff's sociologist of knowledge is in the position of Epicurus' necessitarian.

The standard determinist response to this argument is that there is no reason why a belief cannot be both causally determined and epistemically justified. The distinction between explanation and justification helps to disarm the argument. If I ask a student why he/she believes in God, I may get two different kinds of answers.

A student may say that he/she believes in God because he/she was raised in a Christian home, or because the world is so well ordered it must have had an intelligent designer. The first answer provides a causal explanation for the belief. It says nothing about whether there is reason to believe that God exists. The second answer provides a justification for the belief in the existence of God, grounds for thinking that God exists is true. With this distinction in mind, Goff's version of the argument is less persuasive. From the fact that a belief is explained by social causes, it does not follow that it is mere opinion or rationalization. The causal explanation says nothing, in itself, about the justifiability of the belief. A historical materialist claim that superstructural beliefs are causally determined by modes of production does not, of itself, preclude the rational justifiability of beliefs.[58]

Karl Popper concedes that a belief could be both causally determined and rationally justified. But, he claims, if we assume determinism to be true, we could never be justified in claiming to know that our beliefs are rationally justified.[59] Just why Popper thinks this is not altogether clear. His argument is cast in the form of a dialogue between a materialistic determinist and a dualistic indeterminist. Popper seems to think that claims to be rationally justified presuppose some standard of justification that cannot be reduced to some material object, and that justification involves appeal to some such standard. His reason for thinking that rational justification involves appeal to some nonmaterial standard is that any material standard could go wrong (misprints, warping, shrinkage, and the like). Our recognition that this is so presupposes some standard of judgment which is immune to such failures. The objects that play this role are objective ideas—concepts, theories, principles, and the like. Rational justification involves autonomous recognition of the satisfaction of this ideational standard. The judgment of satisfaction is autonomous presumably because such ideas, having no existence in space or time, cannot function in causal relations.

There are a number of difficulties with this view. In the first place, if it proves anything at all, it seems to prove not just that we cannot know our beliefs to be both causally determined and rationally justified but also that beliefs cannot be both causally determined and rationally justified. If rational justification involves autonomous recognition of the satisfaction of ideational standards, then, if determinism is true and is inconsistent with such autonomy, there cannot be justified beliefs. But Popper denies that this is his position.

Second, there is a classic difficulty concerning the nature of the autonomous judgment the argument presupposes. Some version of agency theory seems required, but just what is involved here remains a major problem for any such theory.

Third, it is not clear how it helps solve the kind of problems Popper sees in materialism to postulate nonmaterial standards of rationality. It is true that material standards can go wrong, but cannot ideas go wrong also? Definitions can be too narrow or too broad, "proofs" can involve errors, and so on. It will not help to say that recognition of such mistakes presupposes some standard in virtue of which the mistake can be recognized as a mistake. The question is whether recognition of error presupposes some fixed and errorproof standard, and it is not obvious that this is so or that any such standard is possible. I conclude, then, that the argument that claims of determinism preclude claims to rational justification fails, and that there is no incoherence in saying that a belief is both caused and justified.

Now suppose that I am standing ten feet from a tree and suppose that, as a result of a normal perceptual experience, I form the belief that there is a tree there. It seems perfectly reasonable to say both that my belief was caused and that it is justified. Indeed, in this case, it seems reasonable to think that part of what justifies my belief in the existence of the tree is that this belief was formed as a result of a reliable causal process. I am justified in thinking that a belief formed in this way is probably true, whereas I would be much less justified in thinking that a belief formed as a result of my being hypnotized by a stage-show hypnotist is true. What is relevant to the question of justification is not whether there were causes for the formation of the belief but, rather, the reliability of the kind of causal processes involved. If I were to discover that some belief of mine stood in no causal relation whatsoever to the world around me, surely this would tend to undermine rather than support my justification in holding the belief.

ARE THERE EPISTEMOLOGICALLY FAVORED CLASSES?

I have argued that the mere fact that a belief is causally determined does not preclude that same belief being justified, nor does it preclude the possibility that the subject holding the belief will make well-founded judgments as to the epistemic warrant of the belief. There is, however, somewhat more involved in the worry about the epistemology of historical materialism than just the problem pertaining to causation of beliefs in general. On some readings of it, historical materialism seems to claim that beliefs held by members of distinct classes are determined by their class position. Further, historical materialism seems to hold, according to some readings of it, that beliefs held by non-proletarian classes are defective because of their class origins, and proletarian beliefs are non-defective because of their class origins. This epistemic favoritism seems to rest on a confusion of the origins of a belief with the justifiability of that belief. In short, the claim that the beliefs of the proletariat are epistemically favored seems to be an instance of the genetic fallacy.[60]

A claim for the epistemically favored position of the proletariat need not involve the genetic fallacy. If there is some reason to believe that the members of the proletariat are in a better position to see the truth of the matter, then the claim that a proletarian belief is more likely to be true than a conflicting belief held by members of some other class is not an instance of the genetic fallacy. In this case, proletarian beliefs would be favored because there is reason to believe that they result from a more reliable process than beliefs formed by other classes.

A number of reasons have been given for thinking that proletarian beliefs are epistemically privileged. Following Lukács, humanistic Marxists have argued that bourgeois consciousness is necessarily deluded in order to mask self-awareness of the fact of exploitation. Only the proletariat can gaze upon the full truth without a painful conscience.[61]

Another argument, also offered by Lukács, turns on the superior nature of the dialectical outlook of the proletariat. Central to the dialectical outlook, according to Lukács, is the ability to view social systems as totalities. The outlook of the bourgeois sciences, which consider aspects of the social system in isolation from their connections to the system as a whole, cannot comprehend the fuller truth attainable by the dialectical outlook. The bourgeoisie, as a particular class, remains wedded to the viewpoint of isolated aspects. Only the proletariat, the universal class, can adopt the totalistic perspective of the dialectical viewpoint. Thus, Lukács argues, the bourgeois economists were unable to make the distinction between constant and variable capital, which is discoverable "only through the dialectical method."[62]

A third argument appeals to the location of the proletariat in the course of historical development apparently claimed by historical materialism. Ernest Untermann, a German Social Democrat who emigrated to the United States, suggests an argument for the epistemically privileged position of the proletariat in this comment on proletarian science:

> Proletarian science is the Declaration of Independence of the proletarian mind from the control of the capitalist mind. And since the proletariat is historically the most revolutionary class in society, and the future man in embryo, proletarian science is the most revolutionary science and the embryo of the future world philosophy.[63]

The clear assumption here is that the revolutionary science of the future is an improvement over the science of the past. This sort of argument, from the later position of the proletariat in the sequence of the historical appearance of the various classes to the superiority of its ideas, lay behind the "prolekult" movement of the early period of Bolshevik rule, and also served to support the replacement of bourgeois scientists with Red scientists in Stalin's attack on the intelligentsia in the early 1930s.

In my view none of these arguments succeeds in showing a priviledged epistemic status for the proletariat. While it may be that it is psychologically difficult for the bourgeoisie to admit to exploitation, this need not imply distinct class-based epistemologies. The connection between epistemology and particular truth claims is mediated by a host of background assumptions with respect to general laws and particular judgments of fact. An unpleasant consequence can be avoided by placing different weight on any one of these factors. If, as is reasonable to believe, epistemic principles are relatively central to the web of belief, then one would expect such psychological factors to influence changes in the mediating links between the unpleasant "fact" and the epistemic principles rather than in the epistemic principles themselves. Nor is it obvious that members of the bourgeoisie are necessarily blinded by their class positions. Marx clearly believes that it is possible for members of the bourgeoisie to cross over to the side of the proletariat. Further, he quotes the economist Heinrich Storch, who has this to say about the proletariat:

> The progress of social wealth begets this useful class of society . . . which performs the most wearisome, the vilest, the most disgusting functions, which takes, in a word, on its shoulders all that is disagreeable and servile in life, and procures thus for other classes leisure, serenity of mind and conventional dignity of character.[64]

Storch's robust conscience squarely faces the fact of exploitation, and accordingly would appear not to require the blinkered epistemology of bourgeois thought.

The argument from the totalistic viewpoint of proletarian dialectics fares no better as an interpretation of Marx. Marx holds that revolutionary proletarian consciousness can arise in other classes from observation of the situation of the proletariat.[65] And Lukács' claim that the distinction between constant and variable capital cannot be recognized by an economics committed to the method of the bourgeois sciences is a claim denied by Marx. He cites the bourgeois economists John Barton, David Ricardo, Richard Jones, and George Ramsey as having conjectured the effect of change in the composition of capital on the demand for labor, and credits Ramsey with having drawn the distinction and with recognizing the weakness it exposes in Adam Smith's account of accumulation.[66] Since it is clear that bourgeois social science has enriched its models in this way, the argument that it cannot do so because of lack of dialectics is clearly false.

The third argument for the epistemically privileged status of the proletariat stems from its late appearance in the course of historical development. The underlying assumption of this argument is that later is better. However, it is not obvious that this is so. Indeed, there are those who would argue that Stalin's "proletarian science" was a setback for the Soviet Union.

Underlying all of these arguments is the assumption that proletarian science is epistemically different from bourgeois science. Historical materialism seems to imply that this is so, since it holds that the ideological superstructure is determined by the mode of production. Proletarian science, which is produced by a socialist mode of production, thus differs from bourgeois science, which is produced by a capitalist mode of production.[67] Since I have argued that Marxist science does not differ methodologically or epistemologically from bourgeois science, some response to this argument is needed here.

In the first place, even supposing that Marxist science does differ from bourgeois science, it does not follow that this difference must appear at the level of methodology or epistemology. It might be that the difference appears in the content of theories (as I have argued with respect to the difference between Marxist economics and the classical economics of Smith and Ricardo). Or it might be that the difference would appear in terms of the institutional commitments to promote certain research programs rather than others.

However, it is not clear that historical materialism does require any difference between proletarian and bourgeois science. For one thing, different causes can give rise to the same effect. Granted that capitalism and socialism are different modes of production, it does not follow that the science produced by them must be different. For another thing, it is not clear that historical materialism assigns science to the ideological superstructure. The argument from historical materialism to the "two sciences" conclusion rests on the assumption that science is superstructural. In his careful interpretation of historical materialism, Gerald Cohen is led to reject the superstructural status of science.[68] If Cohen is right, then the argument fails on this ground as well.

Finally, of course, in my own view the argument fails because it mistakenly construes historical materialism as a historico-sociological social science.

NOTES

1. The principal sources for Marx's critique of Hegel are *Critique of Hegel's Philosophy of Right* (1843), *The Holy Family* (1844), *The Economic and Philosophical Manuscripts* (1844), and *The German Ideology* (1845). The discussion of Marx's critique of Hegel that follows is largely taken from Richard Hudelson, "Marx's Empiricism," *Philosophy of the Social Sciences* 12 (1982): 241–253. I am grateful to the editor of *Philosophy of the Social Sciences* for permission to use this material here.

2. Hegel, *Science of Logic* (London: Allen and Unwin, 1966), vol. 1, pp. 55–64.

3. Marx, in Marx and Engels, *The Holy Family,* in Karl Marx and Frederick Engels, *Collected Works*, vol. 4 (New York: International, 1975), pp. 57–58.

4. Ibid., p. 58.

5. Ibid., pp. 58–59.

6. Ibid., p. 60.

7. Marx, *Critique of Hegel's Philosophy of Right* (Cambridge: Cambridge University Press, 1970), p. 23.

8. Ibid., p. 24.

9. Marx, *The Economic and Philosophical Manuscripts of 1844* (New York: International, 1973), p. 188; *Marx Engels Werke* (Berlin: Dietz Verlag, 1968), supp. vol., pt. 1, p. 584. (Hereafter *MEW.*)

10. The view that Marx's method consists in a "reversal" of Hegel which preserves a fundamentally Hegelian and non-empiricist philosophical foundation can be found in Robert Tucker, *Philosophy and Myth in Karl Marx* (Cambridge: Cambridge University Press, 1961); and in Shlomo Avineri, *The Social and Political Thought of Karl Marx* (Cambridge: Cambridge University Press, 1971).

11. Marx and Engels, *The Holy Family*, p. 61.

12. See Richard Hudelson, "Marx and the Theory of Internal Relations: A Critical Note on Ollman's Interpretation of Marx," *Philosophy of the Social Sciences* 14 (March 1984): 505–507.

13. *Critique of Hegel's Philosophy of Right*, p. 14.

14. Ibid.

15. *The Holy Family*, p. 58.
16. *Critique of Hegel's Philosophy of Right*, p. 9.
17. *The Holy Family*, pp. 60–61.
18. Ibid., p. 60.
19. Ibid., p. 58.
20. Ibid., p. 127.
21. Ibid., p. 128.
22. *Economic and Philosophical Manuscripts of 1844*, p. 63; *MEW*, supp. vol., pt. 1, p. 467.
23. Marx and Engels, *The German Ideology* (New York: International, 1966), p. 15; *MEW*, vol. 3, p. 27.
24. *Capital* (New York: International, 1973), vol. 1, pp. 19–20; *MEW*, vol. 23, p. 27.
25. Marx, *Grundrisse* (New York: Vintage, 1973), pp. 100–101; *MEW*, vol. 13, p. 632.
26. Louis Althusser, *For Marx* (New York: Vintage, 1969), pp. 21–39, 190.
27. In *Marx's Method, Epistemology and Humanism: A Study in the Development of His Thought* (Dordrecht: Reidel, 1986), Philip Kain also finds in Marx's stress on the role of abstractions in the *Grundrisse* a break with the empiricism of an earlier stage in his thought. However, Kain's understanding of Marx's mature science is closer to my view than it is to Althusser. Where I differ with Kain is in the interpretation of the critique of abstraction in the earlier works and in *The German Ideology* in particular. I read the critique of abstraction as a critique of certain forms of philosophical abstraction and not as a critique of abstraction in science.
28. *Capital*, vol. 1, p. 19; *MEW*, vol. 23, p. 12.
29. For example, in the prefaces to the first and second German editions of *Capital*.
30. *Capital*, vol. 3, p. 817; *MEW*, vol. 25, p. 825. See also Marx to Kugelmann, July 11, 1868; *MEW*, vol. 32, p. 553.
31. Marx, *The Poverty of Philosophy* (New York: International, 1973) p. 49; *MEW*, vol. 4, pp. 81–82.
32. On Bogdanov, see K. M. Jensen, *Beyond Marx and Mach* (Dordrecht: Reidel, 1978), p. 79. On Pannekoek, see Anton Pannekoek, *Lenin as Philosopher* (New York: Breakout Press, 1975), p. 74. More recently, the instrumentalist interpretation of Marx has been defended by Z. A. Jordan, *The Evolution of Dialectical Materialism* (New York: St. Martin's Press, 1967), p. xi. Jordan seems to see instrumentalism as following from Marx's activist epistemology. About this, see below.
33. In the Afterword to the second German edition of *Capital*, Marx says that, in a successful theory, "the life of the subject matter is ideally reflected." *Capital*, vol. 1, p. 19; *MEW*, vol. 23, p. 27. For further evidence of Marx's commitment to the reflection theory, see Kain, *Marx's Method*, pp. 84, 85, 87.
34. But it is not impossible. See Chapter 7 of this volume.
35. Engels, *Ludwig Feuerbach and the End of Classical German Philosophy* (Peking: Foreign Languages Press, 1976), p. 19.
36. Lenin, *Philosophical Notebooks*, in his *Collected Works* (Moscow: Foreign Languages Publishing House, 1963), vol. 38, p. 191.
37. Pannekoek, *Lenin as Philosopher*, p. 18; On Schmidt, see Plekhanov's notes to Engels, *Ludwig Feuerbach*, p. 154.
38. Plekhanov, Introduction to Engels, *Ludwig Feuerbach*, pp. 154–155.

39. Robert Steigerwald, *Bügerliche Philosophie und Revisionismus im imperialistischen Deutschland* (Frankurt am Main: Marxistische Blätter, 1980), p. 38.
40. See Karl Vorländer, *Marx und Kant* (Tübingen: J.C.B. Mohr, 1926), p. 155.
41. A classica statement of this view can be found in Leszek Kolakowski, "Karl Marx and the Classical Definition of Truth," in his *Marxism and Beyond* (London: Pall Mall, 1969), pp. 63–67.
42. Ibid., p. 63.
43. Jordan, *The Evolution of Dialectical Materialism*, pp. 9, 34.
44. Georg Lukács, *History and Class Consciousness* (Cambridge, MA: MIT Press, 1971), p. 234.
45. Andrew Feenberg, *Lukács, Marx, and the Sources of Critical Theory* (Totowa, NJ: Rowman and Littlefield, 1981), p. 207.
46. Lukács, *History and Class Consciousness*, pp. 16, 111 ff, 142, 200–203.
47. Mihailo Markovic, *The Rise and Fall of Socialist Humanism* (Nottingham: Spokesman Books, 1975), p. 32.
48. Ibid., p. 33.
49. Ibid., pp. 35–36.
50. Jürgen Habermas, *Knowledge and Human Interests* (Boston: Beacon Press, 1971).
51. This appears as an appendix to ibid., p. 314.
52. The quote is found in Thomas McCarthy, *The Critical Theory of Jürgen Habermas* (Cambridge, MA: MIT Press, 1978), p. 84. Cf.Julius Sensat, *Habermas and Marxism* (Beverly Hills, CA: Sage, 1979), ch. 6, for a defense of Marx against this line of criticism in Habermas.
53. Rüdiger Bubner, *Modern German Philosophy* (Cambridge: Cambridge University Press, 1981), p. 183, provides evidence of Habermas's explicit rejection of traditional Marxism.
54. For a valuable Marxist-Leninist contribution to the recent discussion of the reflection theory, see Alfred Kosing, "Recent Problems of Marxist Epistemology," *Revolutionary World* 27 (1978): 69–74.
55. Lenin recognized the creative role of the thinker and degrees of correspondence with the object in his discussion of the reflection theory in the *Philosophical Notebooks* (*Collected Works*, vol. 38, p. 182). For a defense of Lenin's reflection theory, see Frank Cunningham and Dan Goldstick, "Marxism and Epistemological Relativism," *Social Praxis* 6 (1979): 237–254.
56. Tom Goff, *Marx and Mead* (London: Routledge & Kegan Paul, 1980), p. 4. Similar worries about self-refuting dangers in historical materialism have been expressed by Andrew Arato and Paul Breines, *The Young Lukács* (New York: Seabury, 1971), p. 204; Roy Edgley, "Marx's Revolutionary Science," in *Issues in Marxist Philosophy*, edited by John Mepham and D.-H. Ruben, vol. 2 (Atlantic Highlands, NJ: Humanities, 1979), pp. 24–25; and Tom Rockmore, "Lukács on Classical German Philosophy and Marx," *Idealistic Studies* 10, no. 3 (September 1980): 209–232.
57. Quoted in Karl Popper and John Eccles, *The Self and Its Brain* (New York: Springer Verlag, 1977), p. 75.
58. See Andrew Collier, "Truth and Practice," *Radical Philosophy* 5 (1973): 11.
59. Popper and Eccles, *The Self and Its Brain*, pp. 75–81.
60. Cf. Goff, *Marx and Mead*, p. 4.
61. Lukács, *History and Class Consciousness*, p. 225.
62. Ibid., p. 14.

63. Quoted in Diane Paul, "Marxism, Darwinism, and the Theory of Two Sciences," *Marxist Perspectives* (Spring 1979): 136.

64. Quoted by Marx in *Capital*, 1, p. 647; *MEW*, vol. 23, p. 677.

65. See the selection from *The German Ideology* in *Karl Marx: Selected Writings in Sociology and Social Philosophy*, edited by T. B. Bottomore (New York: McGraw-Hill, 1964), p. 65.

66. Marx, *Capital*, vol. 1, p. 631 n.1; *MEW*, vol. 23, p. 660 n. 79. Also *Capital*, vol. 2, pp. 389–390; *MEW*, vol. 24, p. 389.

67. Paul, "Marxism . . . Two Sciences," worries that this argument deeply commits Marxism to the view that proletarian science is different from bourgeois science.

68. Gerald Cohen, *Karl Marx's Theory of History* (Princeton: Princeton University Press, 1978), pp. 45–47.

6

Metaphysics

One possible view is that Marxist social science has no connection with any metaphysics whatsoever. This is, in fact, the position adopted by many of the theorists of the Second International in response to the philosophical critique of materialism in the last third of the nineteenth century. Neo-Kantian and positivist revisionists deplored the confusion of historical materialism as a social science with materialism as a doctrine in philosophy. They argued that Marxism was not a philosophical doctrine at all, and sought in Kantianism or positivism the philosophical foundation for Marxist economics and theory of history. Karl Kautsky, the champion of orthodoxy in the debate, insisted that Marxism did include its own philosophical foundation in dialectical materialism. But, though he defended this Marxist materialism, he also held that what was most important in Marxism was the economic theory of capitalism and the theory of history. And he held that these central scientific theories were compatible with alternative philosophical foundations. Thus, all sides in the revisionism debates of the turn of the century agreed in thinking that (1) what was most important in Marxism was its social science, and (2) this social science was philosophically neutral.

In the period following the war, these same issues continued to be debated. Lenin argued that dialectical materialism, historical materialism, and Marxian economics must be understood as parts of a coherent and comprehensive whole "forged from a single piece of steel," and rejected any attempt to separate Marxist science from its philosophical foundations.[1] Other Marxists, such as Aleksandr Bogdanov and Anton Pannekoek, continued to argue for the positivistic position that sought to combine Marxist science with positivist philosophical foundations.

More important for Western Marxism was the interpretation of Marxism developed by Georg Lukács and Karl Korsch, which agreed with Lenin in seeing Marx's social theory as inseparably connected to its own philosophical foundation, but rejected the Leninist interpretation of Marxist philosophy as dialectical materialism. On the humanistic view of Lukács and Korsch, it is a mistake to think that Marx was a materialist at all. Such a reading of Marx represents, in their view, a regression to a pre-critical philosophical position. While the Lukácsian position is in many ways original, in this respect at least Lukács and Korsch both show the influence of the Neo-Kantian critique of materialism on their thinking, and thus represent a kind of continuation of the prewar debates.[2]

The positivist and Lukácsian rejection of materialism implies, of course, a rejection of dialectical materialism. And this requires an alternative to the Leninist interpretation of dialectics. We are thus left with a number of distinct but interconnected questions. Some of these are interpretational questions: Was Marx a materialist? Was Marx a dialectical materialist? What is the relation between Marx's philosophical views and his social theory? In addition to these interpretational questions there are the substantive questions: Is materialism true? Is dialectical materialism true? Is there any connection between materialism or dialectical materialism and Marxist social theory?

MARX'S MATERIALISM

Let us begin with the question of whether Marx is a materialist. The claim that he is not has been widely accepted in Western Marxism.[3] On this view, the Leninist reading of Marx as a materialist and a dialectical materialist stems from an uncritical acceptance of the later works of Engels as correctly presenting the philosophical views of Marx. One of the basic arguments for the view that Marx is not a materialist is that nowhere does he say that he is. The claims advanced by Engels do not appear in Marx's own works.

One possible reply here is that, even supposing no explicit endorsement of Engels' views in Marx's writings, it does not follow that Marx diagreed with those views. So the argument is at best inconclusive. But a stronger objection can be made. In some of his writings Marx does appear to identify himself as a materialist in at least some sense. Just what his identification of himself as a materialist does involve is complex and, in crucial respects, open to differing interpretations. I want to begin to address this issue by considering some comments Marx made in his criticisms of Hegel.

Following Hegel, Marx saw materialism and metaphysics as antagonistic philosophical views.[4] Like Hegel, he identified the materialist outlook with "the philosophy of common sense" that underlies the positive sciences.[5] For both Hegel and Marx the history of the seventeenth and eighteenth centuries is seen as a process whereby metaphysics gradually gave way to the viewpoint of common sense and positive science.[6] Also like Hegel, Marx identified materialism with the emergence of an atheistic philosophical view.[7] Where Marx and Hegel diverged was in their response to this assessment of the history of philosophy. Where Hegel sought to restore metaphysics and theology, with his speculative science of reason, Marx rejected the speculative method and defended the materialist tradition against the onslaught of Hegelian philosophy. Marx locates criticism of Hegel within the longer philosophical struggle between materialism and metaphysics.[8] In doing so, he locates himself within the materialist tradition in philosophy.

For Marx, successful criticism of Hegel's speculative philosophy was virtually tantamount to a restoration of materialism as he, Marx, understood it. I say "virtually" tantamount because the restoration of materialism involved not only the overthrow of speculative philosophy but also the development of materialism to meet the speculative criticism of it. I say materialism "as Marx understood it" because it is important to keep in mind just what is involved here. Both Marx and Hegel include in "materialism" what might best be called "empiricism" in the terminology of contemporary analytic philosophy. The struggle between materialism and metaphysics is understood in methodological terms. The materialist sees sense perception as the indispensable foundation for all knowledge claims while the metaphysician attempts to ground philosophical knowledge by means of *a priori* reason. Thus, Marx refers to Bacon as "the real progenitor of *English materialism* and all *modern experimental* science," and views Locke as the great theorist of materialism in modern philosophy.[9]

But Marx's materialism involves more than this empiricism. For one thing, it also involves atheism. In Marx's view, the struggle of seventeenth- and eighteenth-century materialism against metaphysics was also a struggle against theology. He saw materialism as implying atheism. Thus, according to Marx, while the materialism of Bacon was corrupted by "inconsistencies imported from theology" and deistic theology was for materialists "but an easy-going way of getting rid of religion," in the French materialism of the eighteenth century, the atheism implicit in materialism became explicit.[10]

What is the connection here? Why did Marx link "materialism," understood as a methodological claim concerning the indispensable role of sense perception in all knowledge, with atheism? The connection appears in his discussion of Hobbes. Summarizing Hobbes's systematization of Bacon, Marx cites Hobbes's view that "Only material things being perceptible, knowable to us, we cannot know *anything* about the existence of God."[11] Though he criticizes Hobbes for failing to provide "proof" for "Bacon's fundamental principle" that "the origin of all human knowledge" is "from the world of the senses," Marx clearly agrees with Hobbes's dictum and sees Locke as providing the proof that was lacking in Hobbes.[12] While some of the arguments for God's existence relied upon empirical premises, by the end of the eighteenth century these arguments were discredited, and the nineteenth–century defense of theology came to rest on the Hegelian effort to restore metaphysics. Hence, in Marx's view, the "materialist" criticism of Hegel's science of reason led to atheism.[13]

In addition to empiricism and atheism, Marx's materialist criticism of Hegel also involved realism: the assertion of the existence of the world external to or independent of consciousness. This realism is implicit in Marx's approval of the Hobbesian dictum, quoted above, that only material things are perceptible. Marx makes his commitment to this realism explicit in his comments on the egoist who imagines himself independent of any external reality. He follows Feuerbach in thinking that both sensory experience and practical need force the egoist to acknowledge the existence of this external reality: "Each of his senses compels him to believe in the existence of the world and of individuals outside him, and even his *profane* stomach reminds him every day that the world *outside* him is not *empty,* but is what really fills."[14] Whether it is possible to prove the existence of an external material world by appeal to such "profane" needs, we need not consider here. Here my point is that Marx's materialism involves a commitment to realism—to the existence of an independent reality external to consciousness.[15]

Yet another component of Marx's materialism involves the idea that consciousness is a product of the material body. The denial of an immaterial soul is implicit in his endorsement of Hobbes's dictum, since there is no empirical basis for belief in souls. Or, at least, as in the case of the existence of God, the dictum claims that we are not justified in asserting the existence of a soul. This sort of argument against the plausibility of belief in souls was common in the eighteenth-century French materialism with which Marx aligns himself. But Marx also makes his acceptance of a materialist theory of consciousness explicit. He sees the thesis that thoughts can be the properties of material objects, as advanced by Locke and William of Occam, as basic to the materialistic view, and he cites the physicalistic psychologies of such figures as Le Roy, La Mettrie, and Cabanis as important contributions to the development of materialism.[16]

Thus we see that in his early criticism of Hegel, Marx advances a materialism which involves empiricism, atheism, realism, and an account of human consciousness as a product of the material body. However, I do not think these four claims exhaust what is involved in this materialism.

In his criticism of Hegel, Marx locates himself within a tradition of materialism in the history of philosophy that is broadly conceived. In addition to Bacon, Hobbes, Locke, and the French materialists of the eighteenth century, Marx mentions such figures as Gassendi, Bayle, and Epicurus. In the absence of any clear disclaimers from Marx, it is reasonable to suppose that his own conception of the nature of matter had something in common with the conception of matter as it developed in this tradition. There are, of course, serious difficulties here. There is no single, clear conception of the nature of matter running throughout the entire materialist tradition. Is matter substantial? If so, in what sense? Is the corpuscular theory correct? Is extension in space the only essential attribute of matter? If not, what are the other essential properties of matter? Is matter finite or infinite? Marx does not clearly address all of these questions in his discussion of the materialist tradition, but he does comment there on one aspect of matter that is significant.

There is a tradition in the history of philosophy, particularly within the dualistic framework, that conceives of matter as passive, inert, and undifferentiated stuff. In his discussion of French materialism, Marx distinguishes between two trends: "There are *two trends* in *French materialism*; one traces its origin to *Descartes*, the other to *Locke*. The latter is *mainly* a *French* development and leads directly to *socialism*. The former, *mechanical* materialism, merges with French *natural science* proper. The two trends intersect in the course of development."[17] Marx appears to understand the Lockean trend as involving the aspect of empiricism that might be called the environmental determination of consciousness. The connection between this strand of materialism and socialism is intriguing, but I want to pass over that now. Here I want to pursue what Marx has to say about mechanistic materialism.

Marx claims that mechanistic materialism rests on an older view of matter which attributes to matter as its foremost property motion "not only in the form of *mechanical* and *mathematical* motion but chiefly in the form of an *impulse*, a vital spirit, a tension."[18] And Marx claims that even Descartes "endowed matter with self-creative power and conceived mechanical motion as the manifestation of its life."[19] Whether or not Marx's reading of Descartes is correct, in this appeal to an older tradition of materialism underlying mechanistic materialism, and in locating himself within the materialist tradition broadly conceived, Marx is endorsing the view that matter has active powers within it and rejecting the view of matter as passive, inert stuff. Motion, broadly conceived as an active power that expresses itself in various ways, is thought by Marx to be a fundamental property of matter.

THE PHILOSOPHY OF PRAXIS AND THE CRITIQUE OF VULGAR MATERIALISM

If this analysts is correct, then it is wrong to say that Marx nowhere commits himself to materialism. But the analysis so far developed is open to a serious objection. My argument so far rests upon construing Marx as locating himself within the materialist tradition that preceded him. I said above that in the absence of any clear disclaimers, it is reasonable to construe Marx as sharing the materialism of the tradition with which he associates himself. A powerful objection to this argument rests on the claim that Marx does clearly distinguish his views from the materialism of his predecessors. It is this apparent separation of himself from all previous materialism that provides the interpretational foundation for the ontological version of the philosophy of praxis confronted in the section in Chapter 5 entitled "The Epistemology of Praxis."

Frederic Bender directly challenges the kind of reading of Marx that I have here presented. He protests that "We cannot interpret Marx's qualified praise for Enlightenment materialism (relative to idealism) in *The Holy Family* as indicative of his own ontological position,'' and he argues that in the period 1844–1845 Marx abandoned ontological materialism in favor of a philosophy of ''revolutionary *praxis*'' for which the traditional questions of ontology appear as empty metaphysics.[20] Bender appeals to Marx's characterization of his own position in the *Manuscripts* of 1844 as a ''naturalism or humanism'' and Marx says that ''a consistent naturalism or humanism is distinguished from both idealism and materialism, and at the same time is the unifying truth of both.''[21] He goes on to distinguish Marx's naturalism from ''naturalism *simpliciter*,'' which reduces man and human experience to a collection of ''unmediated natural or physical processes.''[22] Bender sees Marx's naturalism as a clear rejection of ''Feuerbach's materialist view of the alleged priority of nature-in-itself over man.''[23] And he sees Marx's naturalism as rejecting the dichotomy of subject and object implicit in ontological materialism in favor of the standpoint of *praxis* in which the ''*unity* of man and nature is primary.''[24]

I am in agreement with Bender in thinking that Marx rejects any materialism according to which human experience, social life, or history can be understood in terms of ''unmediated natural or physical processes.'' However, ontological materialism need not maintain any such strongly reductionist explanatory standpoint. Marxism is an emergent materialism. It regards the understanding of human social existence as requiring concepts that are not reducible to concepts of physics, chemistry, or biology. There was indeed a tendency for the late Feuerbach to fall increasingly into the camp of the natural scientific materialists. Bender is correct in seeing Marx as clearly breaking with this degeneration of Feuerbachian materialism into such a strongly reductionist natural scientific materialism. But this of itself does not imply that Marx abandoned ontological materialism.

Nor does the appeal to the unity of man with nature achieved in praxis require a rejection of ontological materialism. Working up some natural object into a form more suitable for human purposes does, in some sense, involve a humanization of nature, but it does not follow from this that the materialist insistence upon the real external existence of objects is denied, or that the materialist insistence upon the temporal priority of nature-in-itself over conscious human existence is denied.[25] Stronger arguments are needed to justify Bender's claim that Marx's naturalism involves a rejection of ontological materialism. The unity of man with nature in which the externality and priority of nature is dissolved must involve more than mundane human labor.

There is, indeed, another powerful argument to which Bender and others who deny Marx's ontological materialism appeal. The argument turns on an interpretation of Marx's *Theses on Feuerbach*. In the first of the *Theses* Marx says:

> The chief defect of all materialism up to now (including Feuerbach's) is, that the object, reality, what we apprehend through our senses, is understood only in the form of the *object of contemplation [Anschauung]*; but not as *sensuous human activity*, as *practice*,

not subjectively. Hence in opposition to materialism the *active* side was developed abstractly by idealism—which of course does not know real sensuous activity as such. Feuerbach wants sensuous objects really distinguished from the objects of thought; but he does not understand human activity itself as objective activity. Hence, in *The Essence of Christianity*, he sees only the theoretical attitude as the true human attitude, while practice is understood and established only in its "dirty Jew" appearance. He therefore does not comprehend the significance of "revolutionary," of "practical-critical" activity.[26]

One plausible and widely influential reading of this passage is in terms of what I will call epistemological activism.[27] On this view the central point of this passage is the epistemic claim that the mind plays an active role in organizing and interpreting the data of the senses. The chief defect of all previous materialisms was their view of the human mind as passive and plastic rather than active. Recognition of this active role of the human mind in the process of cognition has important consequences for our conception of the world. For, if this is true, then the object of consciousness is not simply given in sensory experience but also, in part at least, constituted by the activity of the cognizing consciousness. As Marx says, the object apprehended through the senses is itself "sensuous human activity." It is a form of "practice." It is in this sense "subjective."

The conception of cognition presented here is seen as connected with the conception of cognition developed in the critical revolution of Kant. This is thought to explain why Marx notes that the active side, which remained unrecognized in materialistic philosophy, was developed by idealism. On the interpretation in question, Marx stands within the broad framework of post-Kantian critical philosophy. What distinguishes Marxism from Kantianism is its conception of cognition as only a special kind of praxis. What is fundamental is man's practical relation to the world, where "practical" must be understood not in the specifically Kantian sense of morality but in the sense of labor to satisfy diverse human needs. Feuerbach errs not only in thinking of cognition as the purely passive reception of sensory data but also in failing to see that the theoretical attitude is itself only a special case of our broader practical involvement in the world. It is this same blindness to the nature of the theoretical as a special kind of practical involvement in the world that constitutes the fundamental weakness of idealism. What is of greatest value in Hegel is his conception of human development as labor involving the simultaneous creation of self and world. What is fundamentally misguided is Hegel's idealistically distorted conception of this labor as a purely theoretical activity.[28]

This "epistemological activist" interpretation of the First Thesis has wide implications for the understanding of Marxism. It is of fundamental importance for Marxist epistemology and, as was seen in Chapter 5, appears to offer a basic challenge to the Leninist idea of cognition as "reflection" of an independently existing reality. In the discussion of Marxist epistemology in Chapter 5, I distinguished between a metaphysical and a sociological interpretation of the philosophy of praxis. There I postponed consideration of the metaphysical version of the philosophy of praxis. The epistemological activist interpretation of the First Thesis on Feuerbach provides the foundation for this metaphysical version of the philosophy of praxis. Here I want to focus on the implications of the epistemological activist interpretation of the First Thesis, and the metaphysical version of the philosophy of praxis built upon it, for the question of whether or not Marx was a materialist. For this interpretation, Marx's "materialism" consists in his insistence on the primacy of the practical relationship over the purely theoretical, and in his atheism.[29] Any attempt to attribute an ontological materialism to Marx appears to be fundamentally misguided, and involves a regression to a pre-Marxist and pre-critical position in philosophy. On this view, Leninism represents such a regression to a pre-Marxist ontological materialism.[30]

I believe that the interpretation sketched above has been foundational to most of humanistic Marxism. I also believe it is mistaken. To show why I think it is mistaken, it will be necessary to look at Marx's criticism of Feuerbach in *The German Ideology*, written a few months after the *Theses on Feuerbach*. The central problem is to understand what Marx could have meant by saying that previous materialisms have failed to understand what we apprehend by the senses as "sensuous human activity, as practice." The epistemological activist takes this as an epistemological claim with ontological implications. However, a look at the criticism of Feuerbach in the *German Ideology* suggests that what Marx has in mind is more a sociological than an epistemological claim.

Part of what Marx found valuable in Feuerbach was his placing the social relation of man to man at the center of social theory.[31] But between the writing of *The Holy Family* and of *The German Ideology*, it became clear to Marx that Feuerbach did not think of social relations in quite the same way that Marx did.[32] Even in *The Holy Family* it is clear that Marx was moving toward an investigation of the way social relations differed with time and place, and the importance of this fact for social and historical research.[33] Feuerbach's conception of social relations was more abstract, referring to invariant features of human life. In *The German Ideology* Marx begins with this abstract conception of social relations in formulating for his criticism of Feuerbach: "Feuerbach's whole deduction with regard to the relation of men to one another goes only so far as to prove that men need and always have needed each other."[34]

Feuerbach had called himself a communist. But by the time of *The German Ideology*, it was apparent to Marx that what Feuerbach meant by this was simply that human beings need one another and ought to be conscious of this fact. For Feuerbach, mutual assistance was part of the eternal essence of human beings, and a correct philosophical consciousness would recognize that this is so. Having summarized Feuerbach's position, Marx points out that for Feuerbach actual human relations which fail to conform to man's essence are matters of "unhappy chance."[35] Feuerbach can give no explanation for actual social relations, nor is he interested in doing so. For him, features of actual human relations that fail to conform to the human essence are regarded as accidental and uninteresting phenomena. Feuerbach considers himself an empiricist, in the sense that he believes sensory experience to be the basis of knowledge, including knowledge about man's essence. But this knowledge of what is essential must arise by abstracting from the accidental features of actual human relations. Feuerbach's conception of the human essence is ahistorical.

In taking this approach, Feuerbach neglects the analysis and origins of actual human relations. He fails to realize that the world around him, including actual social relations, is largely a product of human interaction with nature. It is this point that lies behind Marx's charge that Feuerbach fails to understand reality as "sensuous human practice." Following the analysis of Feuerbach's ahistorical approach, Marx continues:

> He [Feuerbach] does not see how the sensuous world around him is not a thing given directly from all eternity, ever the same, but the product of industry and of the state of society: and, indeed, in the sense that it is an historical product, the result of the activity of the whole succession of generations, each standing on the shoulders of the preceding one, developing its industry and its intercourse, modifying its social organization according to the changed needs. Even the objects of the simplest "sense certainty" are only given him through social development, industry and commercial intercourse. The cherry tree, like almost all fruit trees, was, as is well known, only a few centuries ago transplanted by commerce into our zone, and therefore only by this action of a definite society in a definite age provided for the evidence of Feuerbach's senses.[36]

I believe that it is this point which lies behind the claim in the First Thesis that Feuerbach fails to understand the object of sensory experience as sensuous human practice. Marx's point is that the world given to us in experience is largely a product of the activity of generations of human beings. The "active side" pertains to the industrial and commercial activity that has produced this "world," not to the activity of the mind in the process of cognition. Marx's point is a historical or sociological, not an epistemological, claim.

Having advanced this criticism of Feuerbach and developed it with some further examples, Marx comments: "Of course, in all this the priority of external nature remains unassailed, and all this has no application to the original men produced by generatio aequivoca."[37] It the active role of men in constituting the object of sense experience is understood in the epistemological sense, then it ought to apply equally to primeval men. But it does not. Only if we understand the active role in the sociohistorical sense—that the objects of sense experience are almost entirely products of past industrial and commercial activity—can we understand Marx's qualification that his criticism of Feuerbach would not apply to primeval men. Marx's criticism pertains to Feuerbach's neglect of the particular socio-historical determinants of actual social life, not to his neglect of critical epistemology. Though the world we inhabit is largely a partial product of human labor, nature-in-itself exists in some remote places, exists prior to its being an object of human labor or consciousness.[38]

That this socio-historical point is what is involved in the First Thesis on

Feuerbach is clear, I believe, from the passages cited. Further evidence that this is so is suggested by the fact that in the discussion in *The German Ideology*, where Marx is criticizing Feuerbach for his neglect of the historical practice that created the world of experience, he refers to Feuerbach's position as confined to "mere contemplation" and mentions Feuerbach's failure "to conceive the sensuous world as the total living sensuous activity of the individuals composing it."[39] With only slight variation Marx uses the same wording as that in the First Thesis. I conclude, then, that it is this same neglect of the historical production of the world of experience which is at issue in the First Thesis on Feuerbach.

The central criticism of Feuerbach in *The German Ideology* concerns his ahistorical perspective: "As far as Feuerbach is a materialist he does not deal with history, and as far as he considers history he is not a materialist."[40] It is this criticism that Marx sees as applicable to "all previous materialisms." When it came to social theory, Marx believed materialists such as Hobbes, Locke, Bentham, Holbach, and Helvetius adopted an ahistorical perspective similar to that of Feuerbach. They attempted to identify universal features of human nature and work out a theory of society and government conformable to that view of human nature. As with Feuerbach, the real world appeared as an accident or as the result of superstition and ignorance. What was needed, according to these materialists, was men wise enough and virtuous enough to adjust social relations to the real natures of human beings. But, on Marx's view, what was crucially lacking in these materialisms was any account of why actual social relations were as they were. Without an understanding of the roots of the particular features of existing social relations, and an understanding of the forces for change at work within existing social relations, efforts for social change would remain ineffectual. Previous materialisms lacked such an understanding of the dynamics of actual socio-historical processes.

In contrast, Hegel had recognized the peculiarities of social relations in different periods, and that there were connections between historical periods. While with Hegel the historical transformation of social relations is seen as the temporal image of the logic of concepts, and the human actors who produce historical change as personifications of Absolute Mind, there is nonetheless an understanding of social relations as the result of human activity responding to the historical conditions in which it finds itself. Where the materialist moralists saw feudalism as an artificial imposition on human nature, Hegel saw it as the outcome of preceding stages in the development of human consciousness. It is in this sense, then, that Marx says that only idealism had developed the active side of human experience. What is at stake here is historical action, not the action of the mind in the constitution of the object of cognition.

For our purposes, what is important here is that incorporation of this historical perspective, as it was developed by Hegel, does not necessitate an abandonment of the materialist tradition. That the cherry tree in Germany is the product of the activity of previous generations does not make it any less a real external object, existing independently from consciousness in external space and containing within its material nature the "vital spirit" imputed by the materialist tradition to all matter. As Marx said in the passage cited above, "Of course, in all this the priority of external nature remains unassailed." The claim that Marx is not a materialist, so frequently encountered in Western Marxism, is simply mistaken.

DIALECTICAL MATERIALISM

Granted that Marx was a materialist, was he also a dialectical materialist? Since the work of Lukács, Western Marxists have mostly claimed that dialectical materialism, as understood by Engels and the Leninist tradition that follows Engels, is foreign to Marx.[41] The term "dialectical materialism" does not appear in Marx's works, nor does the complex of claims associated with that term anywhere receive systematic treatment by Marx. Systematic statements of dialectical materialism derive from Engels, Plekhanov, and Lenin rather than from Marx. Nevertheless, it is not unusual for views that are implicit and unnamed in one philosopher to receive a name and explicit formulation in another. Dialectical materialism as an interpretation of Marx is not wholly without a basis in his writings. It also provides a way of understanding Marx's acknowledgment of a debt to Hegel's dialectics. If Marx is a materialist and a dialectician, then might he not also be a dialectical materialist?

What is dialectical materialism? In typical textbooks of Marxist-Leninism, "dialectical materialism" is dialectically defined in terms of its opposition to "metaphysical materialism."[42] Each of these opposed terms, "metaphysical materialism" and "dialectical materialism," designates a family of views no one of which appears to be a necessary or sufficient condition for the application of the term. Metaphysical materialism assumes the existence of "a certain primary and immutable material substance as a bearer or 'support' of all the observable properties of phenomena." It often identifies this substance with "structureless and immutable atoms." It adopts a mechanistic view of nature in which all processes are seen as involving the mechanical interaction of particles. It seeks to reduce chemical, biological, and social processes to processes involving the interaction of atoms governed by the laws of mechanics. Dialectical materialism denies the existence of primary and immutable substance. Where the metaphysical outlook views things as fixed and distinct, the dialectical outlook views things as changing and inner-connected. It rejects the view that all processes are governed by the laws of mechanics and advances three fundamental laws of dialectics as universal and fundamental laws of nature: the law of the transformation of quantitative into qualitative change and vice versa, the law of the unity and struggle of opposites, and the law of the negation of the negation.

This distinction between mechanistic and dialectical materialism provides the basis for an interpretation of Marx's First Thesis on Feuerbach. On this Marxist-Leninist view, what distinguishes the materialism of Marx from the materialism of Feuerbach and all previous materialisms is that Marx's materialism is dialectical materialism, whereas all previous materialisms had been metaphysical materialisms. By this contrast, of course, the Marxist-Leninist is not denying the ontological content of Marx's materialism. Rather, here the contrast with "metaphysics" pertains to the features mentioned above.

There are some difficulties with this as an interpretation of the First Thesis on Feuerbach. For one thing, as was seen above, Marx uses the term "mechanistic materialism" as a designation for only one current within French materialism. He does not use it as a designation of all previous materialisms. Second, Marx claims that even this mechanistic materialism rests on an older tradition which attributes to matter a "vital spirit, a tension" that even mechanical materialism thought "endowed matter with self-creative power." Marx did not think of all previous materialisms as conceiving of matter as fixed, unchanging, and inactive stuff. The Heraclitean vision is, perhaps, as old as materialism itself.

In spite of these difficulties, I think we might make some sense of the claim that it is dialectics which distinguishes the materialism of Marx and Engels from previous materialisms. The basic idea would be that though the dialectical point of view can be found in materialisms preceding Marx, it is found there only implicitly and in rudimentary form. In the thought of Marx and Engels this dialectical perspective is made explicit, and is enriched through the inclusion of the three Hegelian laws and the historical perspective that arises out of the Hegelian framework. Hegel's philosophical system exhibits a pattern of development in the apparently unceasing Heraclitean flux. It uncovers the contradictory nature of concepts as unities of opposites, and with the laws of quantity/quality and negation of the negation, offers claims about universal features of the changes produced by these inner contradictions. In transposing this dialectic of concepts to the material world, Marx and Engels preserve these specific understandings of the way change and development occur.

Of course there are difficulties pertaining to this "transposition," and we will consider some of them below. Here the point is that incorporation of these specifically Hegelian viewpoints on the dialectic gives a much more richly developed (and problematic) conception of change in the material world than does the simple Heraclitean flux. For Marx, as well as for Hegel, there is development, and not merely change. Given this Hegelian perspective, Marx and Engels would seek to account for each historical social system as the outcome of what went before it, and would seek to find in actual social systems the direction of real future developments. Thus, the interpretation I advanced of the First Thesis on Feuerbach, in terms of the ahistorical character of previous materialisms, can be understood as part of the more general perspective of dialectical materialism.

All of this proceeds on the assumption that Marx and Engels did transpose the Hegelian dialectic of concepts into a dialectics of the material world. While it is uncontroversial that Engels does attempt such a transposition in his *Anti-Dühring, Ludwig Feuerbach and the End of Classical Philosophy*, and the *Dialectics of Nature*, as we have seen in considering the history of Marxism, many philosophers have denied that Marx himself adopted such a position. On their view, the dialectical materialism of contemporary Marxist-Leninism has its roots in Engels' misunderstanding of Marx's position. There are two principal grounds for this denial of a dialectical materialism in Marx. The first is a conception of Marx's social theory as involving a dialectical method distinct from the method of the natural sciences and centering on a dialectical relationship between subject and object not found in the natural sciences. This is the view of Marxist dialectics stemming from Lukács. The second ground lies in the absence of endorsement of dialectical materialism in Marx's written work. I have discussed the Lukácsian interpretation and my reasons for rejecting it in Chapter 3. Here I shall consider the textual issue.

To begin with, the relationship between Marx and Engels was unusual. They were close, intellectually, politically, and personally, for some forty years. The nature of this relationship itself constitutes a prima facie reason for thinking that Engels' claim to be presenting views Marx shared was probably true.

Second, even if it were true that Marx never endorsed any of the claims of dialectical materialism in his written work, this would not suffice to show that he did not believe dialectical materialism was true. From the time of his move to Paris until his death, he was principally occupied with his work on the theory of capitalism and with matters of political action. Questions of philosophical materialism were not directly pertinent to his theoretical writings.

Third, there is some textual evidence to support the attribution of dialectical materialism to Marx. In considering his criticism of Hegel, we have noted that Marx's materialism includes a belief in a vital force within all material things, and a belief that this force is a source of the self-development of matter. This view is at least implicitly dialectical in the broad sense involved in the Marxist-Leninist contrast between dialectical and metaphysical materialism. Explicit endorsement of the specifically Hegelian perspective developed by Engels appears to occur in at least two of Marx's letters to Engels.[43] There is also a passage in *Capital* in which Marx comments on the applicability of one of Hegel's laws of dialectics to natural science. Having discussed how quantitative increase in the number of laborers employed by feudal guild masters gave rise at some point to the qualitative transformation of the master into a capitalist, Marx comments: "Here, as in natural science, is shown the correctness of the law discovered by Hegel (in his "Logic"), that merely quantitative differences beyond a certain point pass into qualitative changes."[44] And in a footnote to this passage Marx says: "The molecular theory of modern chemistry first scientifically worked out by Laurent and Gerhardt rests on no other law." Here, in claiming the confirmation of Hegel's law by natural science and in saying that molecular theory rests on that law, Marx is committing himself to a dialectics of nature. The claim that there is no textual basis for attributing Engels' dialectical materialism to Marx is false.

My interpretational claim here is directly challenged by Terrell Carver in his book on the relationship between Marx and Engels. Carver argues that the passages in the Marx/Engels correspondence show less than enthusiastic endorsement of Engels' views, and that Marx's responses in the correspondence and the absence of any public criticism of Engels can be explained as due to friendship with Engels, financial dependence upon him, and underestimation of the lasting importance of Engels' views in these matters. On the passage from *Capital*, Carver comments as follows:

> Here Marx cites *Hegel* (not "dialectics") and molecular theory to back up his claim that the qualitative change from master craftsman to capitalist follows from the accumulation of commodities or money beyond a critical quantity. What Marx *never* did was to claim that there are dialectical laws of *matter* in motion forcing their way through these transformations, "the great basic process", as Engels put it in the 1885 preface to *Anti-Dühring*.[45]

That Marx here refers to Hegel and not to dialectics is of no consequence, since the Hegelian principle in question is clearly the dialectical law of quantity and quality. While it is true that Marx does not here commit himself to a dialectics of *matter*, he does appear to commit himself to a dialectics of *nature* and to a dialectics of molecular processes. That Marx saw the dialectical law as applying to nature and to natural science provides strong evidence against the attempt to draw a methodological distinction between dialectical social theory and nondialectical natural science, or a corresponding distinction between a dialectical social world and a nondialectical natural world. Marx's position here might fall short of dialectical materialism if he held a nonmaterialist philosophy of science. However, if we accept the argument advanced above for Marx's materialism, then his claim that the dialectical law applies to molecular processes is in itself an endorsement of dialectical materialism.

Carver's last comment, that Marx's account of the origins of capitalism does not appeal to a dialectical law of matter forcing its way to social expression, is true and important. The explanation of the origins of capitalism that Marx offers is couched in terms not reducible to terms of the natural sciences. But neither does Engels claim any such reduction. In the passage from the *Anti-Dühring* that Carver cites, Engels is discussing the progress that has been made in natural science since the first edition of the book. In particular, he is commenting on the awareness which has been established that the quantity of energy remains constant throughout transformation of form, as from mechanical to electrical form. Engels goes on to say of this awareness, "It serves as the basis which has already been secured for the now much more pregnant investigation into the very process of transformation, the great basic process, knowledge of which comprises all knowledge of nature."[46] It is possible to read this passage as asserting that there is some basic process in physics which would, if known, give us knowledge of all natural processes, including the historical process of social transformation. This appears to be Carver's reading of Engels. But this is not the interpretation of Engels' dialectical materialism commonly found within Marxist-Leninism.

One of the fundamental ideas of dialectical materialism, as understood within the Leninist tradition, is the idea of emergence. In the course of the development of the material universe, processes appear that cannot be fully understood in terms which were appropriate for the understanding of the material world at earlier stages in its development. In contrast with metaphysical materialism, dialectical materialism does not think that all processes are completely understandable in terms of the mechanics of physical particles. Explanatory reductionistic materialism is contrary to the whole Marxist-Leninist tradition. To be sure, the Marxist-Leninist would claim that the three laws of dialectics are universally applicable to all processes of transformation. But these are philosophical laws and not laws of "matter" in the sense in which the laws of physics and chemistry are laws of matter. And the Marxist-Leninist does not claim to be able to reduce all scientific explanations to these laws.

I conclude, then, that Marx is a materialist and a dialectical materialist. These conclusions are of considerable importance within the context of the current study of Marxism because they have both been denied by the humanistic framework that has dominated Western Marxism, and were denied by both the Neo-Kantian and the positivist Marxisms of the time of the Second International. This interpretational conclusion, of course, does not say anything about the truth of materialism or dialectical materialism as a substantive philosophical position, or about their relationship to Marxist social science. As a way of approaching the substantive issues, which I hope will be become clearer as we go along, I want to consider the question of the relation of dialectical materialism to the political economy and historical theory of Marxism.

DIALECTICAL MATERIALISM AND SCIENCE

Dialectical materialism is a philosophical position. It contains an ontology of materialism, a nonreductionist view of the various levels of inquiry, and a claim for the truth of the three laws of dialectics as universal generalizations true for all phenomena in each of the special sciences. According to Marxist-Leninists, dialectical materialism both offers philosophical guidance to the specialized sciences and is confirmed by them. It is the philosophical foundation of Marxist-Leninism, and hence of vital importance for all disciplines within Marxist-Leninist philosophy. It is also that part of Marxist-Leninism which has met with the most hostility in Western Marxism and non-Marxist philosophy. I would like to begin this section with consideration of two of the common criticisms of dialectical materialism.

The first criticism is positivist in nature. According to the positivists, or at least some of them, the philosophical debate between materialism and idealism is irresolvable. It is irresolvable because both the thesis of materialism and the thesis of idealism are metaphysical doctrines that cannot be tested by any possible experience.

This kind of criticism has been directed not only against the ontological position of materialism but also against the three law claims that are central to dialectical materialism. Thus it has been held that the law of quantity and quality is empty, because it does not enable one to say at what point a quantitative increase will give rise to a qualitative change, and so does not enable us to stipulate any possible observations that would disconfirm or confirm the law. And, with respect to the law of the unity of opposites and the law of negation of the negation, it has been claimed that the notions of opposite, unity, and negation involved are so vague as to make impossible any empirical test of the claim.[47] Hence, philosophers in the positivist camp have contended that dialectical materialism is neither true nor false but simply meaningless nonsense.[48]

The second common criticism of dialectical materialism focuses on its role within Marxist-Leninist philosophy. According to the Marxist-Leninist, dialectical materialism is an advance on pre-Marxist materialisms. Further, the Marxist-Leninist argues that this dialectical materialism can and should play a role in founding and guiding the special sciences. But, the critics contend, in reality the philosophical doctrines of dialectical materialism have proven to be a disaster for Marxist-Leninist science. In genetics dialectical materialism is said to have given rise to Lysenkoism. In physics it is said to have blocked acceptance of relativity theory and quantum mechanics. It is also thought to have blocked the development of cybernetics and systems theory. It short, the critics contend, far from enhancing the development of science, the philosophical doctrines of dialectical materialism have inhibited it.[49]

There is a prima facie inconsistency between these two lines of criticism. If dialectical materialism were truly without any implications for experience whatsoever, then it ought not to conflict with any of the results of the specialized sciences. If it is inconsistent with the results of the specialized sciences, then it is not an empty metaphysical doctrine. The theory may be meaningless and it may be false, but it cannot be both.

The conflict between the two lines of criticism is only apparent. Together, they represent a dilemma that positivistically inclined philosophers have seen as fatal to dialetical materialism. Either the theory is patently false or it is empty metaphysics. In his book *Marxism in the USSR*, James Scanlan argues in this fashion. In the classical formulations of dialectical materialism by Engels and Lenin, infinity in time and space, and inexhaustibility in the sense of continuous divisibility, were attributed to the material universe. Scanlan discusses the difficulties raised by modern science for both of these views and surveys various attempts on the part of Soviet philosophers to reinterpret "infinity" and "inexhaustibility" so as to reconcile dialectical materialism with the most widely accepted theories of the specialized sciences. He observes:

> There is nothing that could be called argumentation for these theses in contemporary Soviet philosophy, but at the same time it is difficult to see what facts could possibly contradict them. The trouble with them is not that they are narrow, implausible, and unyielding— as Marxist philosophical theses are often presumed to be—but that they are

so loose and permissive that every imaginable factual finding is consistent with them. Of course this immunity to empirical contradiction has its price: the price is vacuousness, or the failure to make any genuine commitment concerning what will and what will not be found in the real world.[50]

Similar kinds of criticisms can be directed at Marxist-Leninist attempts to reconcile the three laws of dialectical materialism with results of the specialized sciences. Thus, for example the quantity/quality law, which at least in some of its earlier formulations discusses qualitative change in terms of rapid "leaps," has been modified to account for the evolutionary development of new species and to allow for "gradual leaps."[51] For the positivist, this modification of the original theory in the face of a counterexample from the sciences, while it may avoid falsification, does so at the price of rendering the theory vacuous.

The force of objections of this kind has been weakened by developments within post-positivist philosophy of science. The failure of the verificationist theory of meaning is by now well known. On the one hand, it is not clear how the theory satisfies its own criterion of meaningfulness. More important, it is by now clear that paradigm cases of scientific theories include claims that cannot be reduced to claims about immediate sensory experience, and hence cannot be verified in terms of the originally proposed theory of meaning. Attempts to recast the criticism in terms of Popper's falsifiability condition appear equally unpromising. For it is now clear that theories do not face the test of experience in isolation from other theories and beliefs, but instead stand surrounded by a belt of what Imre Lakatos calls auxiliary hypothesis, and by a complex network of factual assumptions.

Given the interconnectedness of theories in what W. V. Quine and others have called the "web of belief," Popper's attempt to demarcate acceptable from unacceptable theories in terms of the falsifiability criterion breaks down. It is always possible to salvage the core of a theory by modifying one of its auxiliary hypotheses in suitable ways. In effect, this is what has happened in the interaction of dialectical materialism with particular scientific theories. Whether we see the modifications of the dialectical materialists' position that have resulted as ad hoc defenses of a vacuous metaphysics, or as creative developments of the philosophical theory on the basis of results in the special sciences, cannot be decided by any formal criterion. Or at least there is no plausible formal criterion on the horizon of post-positivist philosophy of science.

There is another consideration that needs to be mentioned here. Historically, positivist theory of meaning, and various related attempts to solve the demarcation problem in terms of falsifiability, testability, confirmability, and the like, have been wedded to a view of scientific theories as consisting of law claims, where law claims were understood in a fashion that received its clearest expression in the Hempelian "covering law" model of scientific explanation. On this view, a scientific law is a universal conditional of the form "Given conditions $c_1 \ldots c_n$, whenever an event of kind k_1 occurs, an event of kind k_2 will follow."

Given such a law claim, the appropriate conditions, and the occurrence of an event of kind k_1, the occurrence of an event of kind k_2 could be deduced. It was this structure that, problems of the web of belief aside, allowed for testing, falsification, verification, or confirmation of the law claim. In the application of a scientific theory to some object domain, law claims of this kind can be used to force results. We can describe a factual situation to which the law applies, and appeal to the law to explain or predict the occurrence of some phenomenon not contained in the initial description of the situation. It is possible to understand the law claims of dialectical materialism as being of this sort. On this view the law claims of dialectical materialism are supremely general empirical laws. In effect, the kind of criticism of dialectical materialism sketched above views the three laws of dialectics in this way. It tries to show that either the laws are clearly falsified, or they are rendered so vague as to make it impossible to utilize them in the prediction or explanation of any empirically observable phenomenon.

There is some evidence that Marx thought of the laws of dialectics in this way. He does say, as was noted above, that modern chemistry and his analysis of capitalism both "show the correctness of the law" of the quantity/quality transformation, and he does claim that molecular theory "rests on" that law. However, if we look at the relation between the law claim and Marx's scientific work, we see that the role of the dialectical laws in the scientific theory is different from the role of scientific laws in theories of an object domain according to the "covering law" account.

For example, toward the end of the first volume of *Capital*, Marx characterizes the self-destruction of capitalism as "the negation of the negation."[52] This seems to be a clear invocation of the third law of dialectics. If that law were functioning in the manner of an ordinary scientific law in the construction of a theory of capitalist economies, the structure of the argument would be somewhat as follows: (1) Whenever there is a process of change, it follows a pattern whereby the original condition is negated by the second stage and the second stage is then negated by a third stage. (2) Capitalism is the negation of feudalism. (3) Therefore, capitalism will be negated by a form of society that will follow it. But Marx does not argue in this fashion.

The analysis of capitalist accumulation, which lays the basis for the claim of the self-destruction of capitalism, does not appeal to the dialectical principle. The conclusion is independently established. In a letter to the editorial board of a Russian journal, Marx comments on the passage in question. He observes that the claim about the negation of the negation is without proof where it occurs "for the good reason that this statement is itself nothing else but a general summary of long expositions previously given in the chapters of capitalist production."[53] Marx does not appeal to the dialectical law to establish a scientific conclusion. Engels takes the same view of this matter in *Anti-Dühring*. Dühring had argued that Marx's claim about the development of capitalism is proven by appeal to the general law of dialectics. In reply Engels says, "On the contrary. After he has proved historically that in fact this process has in part already occurred, in part that it must yet occur, he adds a description of it as a process which follows a determinate dialectical law. That is all.''[54] Again, Engels views the scientific result as not dependent on appeal to the dialectical law. Just as Marx's attempt to construct a social science of capitalist development did not use the laws of historical materialism to force results, so his theory rests on grounds independent of the laws of dialectical materialism. The scientific results are independently established.

In *The German Ideology*, Marx and Engels claim that, with the development of the individual sciences, all that remains for philosophy is ''a summing-up of the most general results, abstractions which arise from the observation of the historical development of men.''[55] I believe that Marx and Engels saw dialectical materialism in this light as a collection of substantive philosophical generalizations. Such philosophical generalizations are suggested by the results of the specialized sciences and, presumably, like empirical generalizations are in some way testable by experience. But, according to Marx and Engels, results in the various sciences must be independently established. One cannot, as it were, deduce the content of the specialized sciences from the philosophical generalizations.

IS DIALECTICAL MATERIALISM TRUE?

From what has been said thus far, it should be clear that dialectical materialism can be neither confirmed nor disconfirmed by any direct empirical test. In this respect it is not different from other theories in both science and philosophy. This is not to say that empirical observation is irrelevant, just that any appeal to empirical data will have to be mediated by a variety of other considerations. Among the relevant considerations is comparison with philosophical alternatives. In what follows, I will sketch a case for emergent materialism as an alternative to dialectical materialism. Dialectical materialism is a version of materialist realism. In drawing this sketch, I shall assume that there is merit in the resurgence of realism and materialism within analytical philosophy, and focus on dialectics as the central point of contention.

The materialism that has emerged in analytic philosophy is largely a natural scientific materialism. It has mainly concerned itself with problems in the natural sciences, and with the biological theory of consciousness in particular. This natural scientific materialism has often been combined with a reductionist impulse aimed at the ultimate reduction of all scientific theory to physics. On this view, history would ideally be reduced to sociology, sociology to psychology, psychology to biology, biology to chemistry, and chemistry to physics. This reductionist impulse stands in a complex relation to the positivist tradition and is not shared by all philosophers within that tradition. (Comte and Popper are prominent exceptions.)

Insofar as post-positivist materialism is marked by the reductionist impulse of natural scientific materialism, it will be led to view historical, socioeconomic processes in terms of natural scientific processes. Thus we find tendencies toward socio-biology and ecological sociology as natural outcomes of the philosophical bias of natural scientific materialism. Such tendencies, of course, serve to prevent a movement from materialism to Marxism.

One way of understanding this particular barrier to Marxism is in terms of the distinction between materialism and dialectical materialism. The reductionistic impulse of natural scientific materialism contrasts sharply with the dialectical recognition of the qualitative transformations realized in the process of the natural evolution of matter. For a Marxist, the categories appropriate for an understanding of the historical laws of socio-economic development are not reducible to the categories of some lower-level science. What is wrong with natural scientific materialism is that it is not dialectical.

Here the central contrast between natural scientific materialism and dialectical materialism is put in terms of the contrast between reductionist and emergent materialism. This is part, at least, of the contrast between dialectical materialism and natural scientific materialism. On this particular issue, there has been definite movement away from reductionistic physicalism within analytic philosophy of science in recent years. In part this is a result of the failure of various reductionist programs, and in part it is the result of positive work on the analysis of scientific explanation.[56] So here, too, as in the movement from instrumentalism to realism, there is movement within post-positivist analytical philosophy of science toward a position compatible with Marxist-Leninism.[57] And yet, a major difficulty remains.

As a way of getting at this difficulty, I would like to consider some comments by the Hungarian philosopher Andras Gedo on the emergent materialism of Roy Wood Sellars. Sellars' "new materialism" was developed during the ascendency of logical positivism. It was openly critical of positivism; openly materialist, in the sense of asserting the existence of an all-encompassing, mind-independent material world; and it was non-reductionistic, recognizing evolutionary development and multiple levels of causality. Sellars recognized the affinity between his position and dialectical materialism, yet consciously rejected "materialist dialectics." Gedo comments on this: "The spontaneous dialectical moments in his philosophy are not able to defeat his conscious opposition to dialectics. . . ."[58] In a similar vein, Gedo comments on the "logical materialism" of Mario Bunge: "He is at variance with the theoretical results of his own work, which coincide with some ideas of dialectical materialism when he accepts stero-typical anti-Marxist ideas." Gedo goes on to note that part of Bunge's anti-Marxisim includes his opposition to dialectical materialism and that "this opposition comes from the world of positivism."[59]

In his comments on Sellars and Bunge, Gedo seems to be arguing as follows: (1) Both have a materialist standpoint. (2) Both hold an emergent materialism. (3) Both consciously reject dialectical materialism. (4) The basis for their rejection of dialectical materialism lies in positivism. (5) In rejecting dialectical materialism, both are inconsistent with their emergent materialism. I agree with

Gedo on points (1–4), but I disagree with (5). This disagreement gets at what I see to be the central difficulty with dialectical materialism.

The positivist root of Sellars' and Bunge's objection to dialectical materialism is the objection, discussed earlier in this chapter, that dialectical materialism is either false or so vaguely formulated as to be vacuous. We have seen how this kind of criticism is weakened by recognition of the distinction between scientific and philosophical laws and, more important, by criticisms of verificationism, falsificationism, and related formalist attempts to demarcate science from pseudoscience. But recognition of the failure of these formalist attempts does not put an end to positivist-inspired doubts as to the philosophical or scientific value of the laws of dialectics. Vagueness remains an undesirable trait even if it cannot alone provide sufficient grounds for rejecting a theory. If within our comparative approach some theory has all the advantages of dialectical materialism without its disadvantages, then that theory is rationally preferable to dialectical materialism.

Now let us return to Gedo's criticism of the emergent materialism of Sellars and Bunge. Gedo claims that the denial of dialectical materialism involves both philosophers in self-contradiction. But if this is so, then there must be some feature of dialectical materialism, other than emergence, that is implied by emergence. If such a claim could be made out, then Gedo would have succeeded in showing that dialectical materialism is not entirely vacuous. But Gedo nowhere explains just what the supposed contradiction is. And, for my part, I do not see that there is any. In particular, I don't think that emergent materialism implies any of the three laws of dialectics.

I conclude, then, that emergent materialism provides an attractive alternative to dialectical materialism. It retains what is valuable in dialectical materialism without the burden of the three laws that seem to play no positive role.

NOTES

1. James Scanlan, *Marxism in the USSR* (Ithaca, NY: Cornell University Press, 1985), p. 33.

2. Of course Lukács and Korsch were highly critical of Neo-Kantianism and positivism, but they accepted the critique of metaphysical materialism common to Neo-Kantianism and positivism.

3. Among others, by Sidney Hook, *Towards the Understanding of Karl Marx* (New York: John Day, 1933); Z. A. Jordan, *The Evolution of Dialectical Materialism* (New York: St. Martin's Press, 1967); Frederic Bender, "Marx, Materialism and the Limits of Philosophy," *Studies in Soviet Thought* 25 (1983): 79–100; George Kline, "The Myth of Marx's Materialism," *Annals of Scholarship* 3, no. 2 (1984): 1–38.

4. Marx, in Marx and Engels, *The Holy Family*, in their *Collected Works*, vol. 4 (New York: International, 1975), p. 127.

5. Ibid., p. 90.

6. Ibid., p. 126.

7. Ibid., p. 129.

8. Ibid., pp. 125, 127.
9. Ibid., pp. 128, 127.
10. Ibid., pp. 128, 129.
11. Ibid., p. 129.
12. Marx, *Manuscripts of 1844* (New York: International, 1973), p. 181; *Marx Engels Werke* (Berlin: Dietz Verlag, 1968), supp. vol., pt. 1, p. 577. (Hereafter *MEW*.)
13. Marx, *The Holy Family*, p. 127.
14. Ibid., p. 120. Cf. Marx, *Manuscripts of 1844*, pp. 205–207. (I read the naturalism that is here counterposed to materialism as a nonreductive materialism, as opposed to the reductive materialism of earlier French materialists and of the sort advocated by the late Feuerbach and the scientific materialists.)
15. Kline, in "The Myth of Marx's Materialism," denies this. He argues that none of the senses in which Marx uses "material" commit him to an ontological position. While I agree with Kline that many of Marx's uses of the term do not have ontological significance, I think some do. Kline does not mention the passage from *The Holy Family* quoted above.
16. *The Holy Family*, p. 127 (Marx here confuses William of Occam with Duns Scotus). See pp. 125–126 for references to LeRoy, LaMettrie, and Cabanis.
17. Ibid., p. 125.
18. Ibid., p. 128. Consider the materialism of Diderot's *Dream of d'Alembert*.
19. Ibid., p. 125.
20. Bender, "Marx, Materialism and the Limits of Philosophy," pp. 85, 81.
21. Ibid., p. 81; Marx, *Manuscripts of 1844*, p. 206.
22. Bender, "Marx, Materialism and the Limits of Philosophy," p. 82.
23. Ibid.
24. Ibid., p. 83.
25. In this regard, Bender (ibid., p. 83) appeals to a passage in the "Marginal Notes on Wagner" as showing Marx's view concerning the priority of praxis over cognition. Marx writes:

> For the doctrinaire professor [Wagner], man's relation to nature is from the beginning not practical, i.e., based on action, but theoretical. . . . But men do not begin by standing 'in this theoretical relation with the objects of the external world.' Like all animals they begin by eating, drinking, etc., i.e., they do not stand in any relation, but are engaged in activity, appropriate certain objects of the external world by means of their actions, and in this way satisfy their needs (i.e., they begin with production).

I myself see Marx's reference to "objects of the external world" as evidence for a materialist realism alongside his contention regarding the primacy of the practical over the cognitive relation to those external objects. Bender does not comment on the "objects of the external world."
26. Marx and Engels, *The German Ideology* (New York: International, 1966), p. 197; *MEW*, vol. 3, p. 5.
27. Bender, "Marx, Materialism and the Limits of Philosophy," p. 82; Hook, *Towards the Understanding of Karl Marx*, pp. 29–33; Jordan, *The Evolution of Dialectical Materialism*, pp. 27–28; Andrew Arato and Paul Breines, *The Young Lukács* (New York: Seabury Press, 1971), pp. 213–214.
28. This is one of the central points of the section of the *Economic and Philosophical Manuscripts of 1844* entitled "Critique of Hegel's Dialectic and General Philosophy."

29. Cf. Leszek Kolakowski, *Marxism and Beyond* (London: Pall Mall, 1969), pp. 70, 76.

30. Here again, the humanist agrees with the positivist in opposition to Lenin. See the remarks in Chapter 2 on the criticism of Lenin's regressive materialism by Anton Pannekoek.

31. Marx, *Manuscripts of 1844*, p. 172; *MEW*, supp. vol., pt. 1, pp. 569–570.

32. Marx's differences with Feuerbach were forced into the open by Max Stirner's *The Ego and Its Own* (New York: Harper and Row, 1974), which criticized Feuerbach, and by Marx's dissatisfaction with Stirner's reply.

33. E.g., *The Holy Family*, pp. 36–37.

34. *The German Ideology*, p. 33; *MEW*, vol. 3, p. 42.

35. *The German Ideology*, p. 34; *MEW*, vol. 3, p. 42.

36. *The German Ideology*, p. 35; *MEW*, vol. 3, p. 43.

37. *The German Ideology*, pp. 36–37; *MEW*, vol. 3, p. 44.

38. On the existence of nature-in-itself that preceded human history and still exists in remote places, see *The German Ideology*, p. 37; *MEW*, vol. 3, p. 44. Further evidence of Marx's ontological commitment to nature in itself can be found in Philip Kain, *Marx's Method* (Dordrecht: Reidel, 1986), pp. 81–83, and in Henning Ottmann, "Der Begriff der Natur bei Marx," *Zeitschrift für philosophische Forschung* 39 (April–June 1985): 215–228.

39. *The German Ideology*, pp. 34, 37; *MEW*, vol. 3, pp. 42, 44–45.

40. *The German Ideology*, pp. 37–38; *MEW*, vol. 3, p. 45.

41. Gustav Wetter, *Dialectical Materialism* (New York: Praeger, 1961); Jordan, *The Evolution of Dialectical Materialism*; Norman Levine, *The Tragic Deception* (Santa Barbara, CA: ABC-Clio Press, 1975); Terrell Carver, *Marx and Engels* (Bloomington: Indiana University Press, 1983).

42. E.g., V. A. Malinin et al., *The Fundamentals of Marxist-Leninist Philosophy* (Moscow: Progress, 1974), pp. 71–80.

43. Marx to Engels, June 22, 1867 (*MEW*, vol. 31, p. 306), in which Marx discusses the passage on chemistry from *Capital* mentioned below, and Marx's reply of November 27, 1882 (*MEW*,vol. 35, pp. 118–120) to Engels' letter of November 23 on mathematics.

44. *Capital*, vol. 1, p. 309; *MEW*, vol. 23, p. 327.

45. Carver, *Marx and Engels*, p. 133.

46. Frederick Engels, *Anti-Dühring* (Peking: Foreign Languages Press, 1976), p. 15.

47. E.g., Karl Popper, "What Is Dialectic?", *Mind* 49 (1940): 424.

48. H. B. Acton, "Dialectical Materialism," in *The Encyclopedia of Philosophy*, edited by Paul Edwards, vol. 2 (New York: Macmillan, 1967), p. 394.

49. Diane Paul, "Marxism, Darwinism, and the Theory of Two Sciences," *Marxist Perspectives* (Spring 1979): 125, claims that such serious and non-Stalinist thinkers as Kaustsky, Plekhanov, and Bukharin were led to reject the Darwinian account of evolution in favor of the more "dialectical" account of DeVries. David Joravsky, *Soviet Marxism and Natural Science* (New York: Columbia University Press, 1961), and Loren Graham, *Science and Philosophy in the Soviet Union* (New York: Knopf, 1972), have shown that attempts to blame dialectical materialism for problems in Soviet science are often seriously uninformed and oversimplified.

50. Scanlan, *Marxism in the USSR*, pp. 95–96.

51. Ibid., pp. 115–116; Paul, "...Theory of Two Sciences," p. 121, notes that Engels allowed for "imperceptible leaps."

52. Marx, *Capital*, vol. 1, p. 763; *MEW*, vol. 23, p. 791.

53. Lewis S. Feuer, ed. *Marx and Engels: Basic Writings on Politics and Philosophy* (Garden City: Anchor Books, 1959), vol. 19, p. iii.

54. Engels, *Anti-Dühring* (Peking: Foreign Languages Press, 1976), pp. 170–171; *MEW*, vol. 20, p. 125; cf. Allen Wood, *Karl Marx* (London: Routledge and Kegan Paul 1981), p. 199

55. *The German Ideology*, p. 15; *MEW*, vol. 3, p. 27.

56. E.g., Alan Garfinkel, *Forms of Explanation* (New Haven: Yale University Press, 1981).

57. There are other possibilities for convergence, or at least philosophical contact, between analytical philosophy and Marxist-Leninism. I will explore these possibilities further in Part III. There I consider ''subjective'' (methodological) rather than ''objective'' (ontological) dialectics.

58. Andras Gedo, *Crisis Consciousness in Contemporary Philosophy* (Minneapolis: Marxist Educational Press, 1982), p. 198.

59. Ibid., p. 280 n. 38.

7

Ethics

As we have seen in the historical survey, various understandings of Marxism have included widely divergent views as to the nature of ethics and as to the content of Marxist ethics. In the reading of positivistic and Neo-Kantian Marxism, while Marxism contains a descriptive theory of the nature of moral systems as superstructural expressions, Marxism itself is a purely positive science devoid of ethical theory. In contrast, according to some positivistic critics, Marxism is defective science because, contrary to its self-conception, it is contaminated with moral theory. Between these two positivistic positions, both Marxist-Leninism and humanistic Marxism work out interpretations of Marxism that see it as including its own philosophically grounded ethics.

THE POSITIVIST CRITIQUE OF MARX

I will begin with the positivist criticism of Marxism as normatively contaminated science. A typical formulation of this is provided by William Riker:

> The inclusion of normative elements in a descriptive generalization renders it scientifically unfit. This, for example, is where Marx's endeavor to be scientific went astray. The main proposition of *Capital* can be summarized as ''Capitalism is theft''; and since theft, when divorced from a positive legal system, is a normative notion, verification of this sentence as a description of nature is impossible.[1]

It is a measure of the changes which have occurred in analytic philosophy of science that this passage, which appeared in 1965, could seem today so out of date. From the point of view of philosophy of science, the criticism is objectionable for its reliance on a simple verificationist criterion for distinguishing science from pseudoscience. By now it has become clear that such verificationism is untenable. Paradigm cases of genuine science fail the verificationist test.

But this reply does not completely disarm the kind of positivist objection raised by Riker. For even if there are fundamental problems with verificationist solutions to the demarcation problem, it might yet be true that morality has no place in science. If it is the business of science to say how the world is, and the business of morality to say how it ought to be, then if Marxism is fundamentally a moral theory, its claim to scientific status is misplaced. This would be true even if its moral theory claimed verifiability for its moral judgments.

For the moment I will assume that morality has no place in science. We will return to this issue below. Here, however, I want to point out that Riker's criticism of Marx is open to a second kind of objection: that it misunderstands Marxism at a fundamental level. That there is something amiss with Riker's interpretation of Marx is suggested by the fact that the central claim Riker attributes to Marx, "Capitalism is theft," historically is more correctly attributable to Pierre Proudhon, whom Marx criticized for the moralistic nature of his critique of capitalism. Thus Marx complains that Proudhon's moralism has no place in science.[2]

The idea that the central claim of *Capital* is "Capitalism is theft" is not without some foundation in Marx's thought. After all, he does say that labor is the source of all value and that profit arises out of the capitalist's appropriation of the surplus value created by labor. If this idea of labor as the source of value is combined with a Lockean labor theory of property rights, according to which everyone has a right to the full produce of his or her own labor, then the appropriation of the capitalist does appear as theft. This kind of argument was advanced by the "Ricardian Socialists" who preceded Marx.[3] But if Riker's criticism rests on assuming that *Capital* is fundamentally an expression of this argument, it is clearly an untenable interpretation, since Marx explicitly rejected the argument in question. In particular, he rejected the moral premise that the laborer has a right to the full produce of his or her labor.[4]

How, then, are we to understand the Marxist claim that capitalists exploit workers? Is this not a clearly normative claim, and is this not the central point of *Capital*? Positivistic interpretations of Marx would deny that Marxian exploitation is, at bottom, a moral concept. On this view, capitalists exploit workers in the sense that humans exploit natural resources; something of value is extracted. Whether this extraction is morally objectionable is another question.[5] Within the framework of Marxian economics, variable capital, v, is the amount of value necessary to maintain the worker. Surplus value, s, is the amount of value produced in any time period in excess of that needed to maintain the productive process. The rate of exploitation, s/v, is thus an empirically definable quantity.[6] Further, the rate of exploitation functions within Marx's economics as an explanatory variable in the account of the rate of profit. Thus, claims about the rate of exploitation or changes in the rate of exploitation are, in principle, empirically testable. There are, of course, a host of complicating factors due to the network of auxiliary hypotheses at work in any actual test of the theory. But the difficulties here are not different in nature from the difficulties encountered in attempts to test any other scientific theory.

One possible objection to this positivistic Marxism is that while there may be within the Marxian system an empirical component to the claim of exploitation, this claim itself introduces an irreducibly value-laden term, and so contaminates science with ideology.

I do not think this is a serious difficulty. Upon examination, the central idea of "contamination" breaks down in ways that defuse any force the objection might have. Consideration of an example from neoclassical economic theory may make this point clear. In neoclassical models of monopolistic markets, "exploitation" is used to refer to the return in excess of the return that would have been gained in competitive markets. It is no accident that the term chosen to designate this excess return was "exploitation." Indeed, I think it was likely that this term was chosen because it has the moral connotations that it does have. But the moral judgment that prompts this choice of a term does not undermine the positive theory of monopolistic markets in which it occurs. There remains the fact of the higher return that gives the term its empirical content. The moral judgment, that monopoly is an evil, does not influence the positive theory. A paper in physics that includes an impassioned denunciation of certain weapons research is not thereby transformed into defective science. That the moral judgment in the case of monopolistic exploitation is attached to one of the terms of the theory itself does not change things. It remains a kind of moral footnote to the positive theory. In the same way, the positivistic Marxist can grant that "exploitation" is value laden, and also grant that Marx probably chose the term in part because of its moral connotations, without abandoning the understanding of *Capital* as positive science.

MARXISM AND THE HISTORICAL RELATIVITY OF MORALITY

I have been suggesting ways in which the positivistic Marxist might reply to the kind of criticism raised by Riker. So far we have focused on how one might interpret the Marxist claim of exploitation as part of the positive science of capitalist economies. I want to turn now to the case for a positivistic interpretation of Marx's view of the nature of morality. In several places Marx suggests that morality is historically relative. As part of the ideological superstructure, it is determined by the economic base. Thus, the content of moral codes is a function of the mode of production they express. What is right under conditions of slavery is not right under conditions of capitalism. And there is no transhistorical moral principle that permits us to make moral judgments across differing historical epochs.

There is an important sense in which this theory of the nature of morality is not positivist at all. For the logical positivists, or at least some of them, moral judgments were pseudo judgments. They had no truth value. The view of morality as relative to modes of production is not like this. For, on this view, a practice is morally right if and only if it is in accord with the requirements of the dominant mode of production.[7] But this latter is an empirical question, and hence judgments of right and wrong have an empirically determinable truth value. The historical relativist conception of morality is "positivistic" in the sense that it claims the reducibility of moral judgments to matters of fact. In this respect, the historical relativist conception of morality is like "positive" theories of law. The historical relativist conception of morality is also positivistic in the sense that its acceptance makes pointless moral condemnation of a mode of production as the ultimate grounds for altering a social system. Moral criticism can play a historically significant role only during times in which changes in the mode of production have already rendered the existing moral code less than optimally functional for utilization of the available productive forces.[8] At any other time, to attempt to argue on moral grounds for changing a mode of production would be incoherent. Insofar as Marx did hold the historical relativist conception of morality, he would be unlikely to appeal to moral grounds as the ultimate reason for the overthrow of capitalism.

The interpretation of Marx as holding a historical relativist conception of morality has received spirited defense by Allen Wood. In his widely discussed paper of 1972, "The Marxian Critique of Justice," Wood argued that on Marx's view the wage contract between capitalist and worker does not involve any injustice to the worker. He bases his case here on explicit denials of injustice by Marx, and on passages in which Marx claims that justice is determined by correspondence of rules or practices with the functional requirements of the prevailing mode of production.[9] In his 1981 *Karl Marx*, Wood extends this analysis of justice as a general interpretation of Marx's theory of morality. On this view, morality is a part of the ideological superstructure. Given a mode of production, a rule or practice is moral if and only if it sanctions productive relations that are maximally conducive to full utilization of society's productive powers at the existing stage of their development. What is moral at one stage in the development of social productive powers is immoral at another.

Wood's interpretation has provoked a lively discussion. In what follows, I will consider only a few of the points that have been raised.[10] If the historical relativist theory of morality is true, then it appears that there can be no objective transhistorical moral judgments. This is true in two senses. First, there cannot be any universal moral principles that hold for each stage of development. Second, there can be no objective moral judgments comparing the rules of a society at one stage of development with rules of the same or another society at a different stage of development. In each case the reason for this is that the only criterion of morality in virtue of which judgment could be made is a historically relative criterion limited in scope to societies existing at a certain stage of development. Marxism, understood as the historical relativist theory of morality, reduces morality to system optimization. It is in this sense that the position is "positivistic." Thus Wood writes of the "amoralist" or even "immoralist" side of Marx, and a commentator on Wood's position has attributed to Wood the claim that "there is no such thing as Marxian justice or morality."[11]

This denial of transhistorical moral judgments is interpretationally problematic in that Marx does seem to make transhistorical moral judgments in both of the senses identified above. In the first sense, there are qualities, such as sensitivity to others, veracity, kindness, loyalty, and the like, that Marx appears to regard as virtues in each stage of development. Wood recognizes this, and argues that all this shows is that these principles correspond to the needs of every mode of production.[12]

But Marx also seems to make transhistorical judgments of the second kind. For example, he seems to think that socialism is clearly an improvement on capitalism, and this judgment seems to require for its objective validity some criterion not relative to either mode of production. Wood acknowledges that such comparative judgments occur in Marx's work, but treats them as nonmoral evaluative judgments.[13] On Wood's view, what makes a judgment a properly moral judgment is that it formulates some principle of action which it is claimed we have a duty to obey. Judgments concerning nonmoral goods do not make any such claims upon us. To say that happiness, or freedom, or self-realization is good for human beings is not thereby to say that we are obliged to further those ends.

Wood's interpretational stance turns on his distinction between moral and nonmoral goods. It is by means of this distinction that Wood attempts to reconcile his view that Marx held a historical relativist theory of morality, with Marx's apparent view of socialism's superiority over capitalism in the provision of diverse goods. It is this same distinction, then, that underlies Wood's view of Marx as an amoralist in spite of his obvious strong and frequent value judgments. There are at least four sorts of objections to Wood's solution.

First, one might argue that Wood is working with too narrow a conception of morality. Moral theories have traditionally tried to provide some account of the basic principles of morality, of our obligation to obey those principles, and of our motive to do our duty. On Wood's account, Marx's judgments in favor of socialism rest on no effort to show duty or motive to duty with respect to them, and thereby fail to count as properly moral judgments. But one might object that insofar as Marx's value judgments involve appeals to principles of basic or fundamental significance for human beings, this does constitute a "moral" theory. And Wood does say that in this very broad sense Marx does have a moral theory.[14] There is thus a philosophical question of just what constitutes a morality involved here.

Second, there is a question about whether Wood's position is adequate on interpretational grounds. On Wood's view Marx's judgments about the superiority of socialism make no morally binding claim upon us. But there is some evidence that Marx did think some moral duty was involved here, and that those who did not respond to its claims were morally defective.[15]

Third, if we follow Wood in thinking that morality is historically relative because it is part of the ideological superstructure generated by a particular mode of production and restricted in validity to that particular mode, then why are nonmoral valuations not equally restricted in scope? Are not such nonmoral valuations also ideological superstructural forms? If not, why are they different in this respect from properly moral valuations? If they are superstructural forms, why does this fact make morality of historically limited validity and not make nonmoral forms of valuation equally historically limited?[16] One might reply, as Wood seems to do, that for Marx, morality is fundamentally conservative.[17] The function of morality is to bind human beings to the social order by sanctioning the relations of production it requires and demanding individual compliance with the norms it sanctions. Morality is not just a superstructural product of the economic base, but also its specific function is the legitimation and stabilization of the form of social organization.

This brings me to a fourth objection to Wood's position. It is that it fails to understand the possibility, within the framework of historical materialism, for a revolutionary morality.[18] Recall that on the historical relativist view, what makes rules morally right is that they correspond to the requirements of the mode of production for the most efficient use of the available social powers of production. Insofar as a set of rules satisfying this requirement at the same time serves the interest of the dominant class within that mode of production, we may say of a particular moral code that it expresses the interests of a particular class. But what happens when the existing relations of production cease to facilitate the most efficient use of the available productive powers and become, instead, fetters to the further development of those productive powers? What happens when a new class claims for itself the prerogatives of the dominant class and seeks to legislate a new moral code for all of humanity? What happens during periods of revolutionary transformation?

There are at least two ways of looking at such transition periods. On one view, what we find in such situations is conflict between two class-based moralities for which no moral solution is possible.[19] In the case of the transition from capitalism to socialism there is a period of conflict between proletarian morality, binding on the members of the working class, and bourgeois morality, binding on the members of the bourgeoisie. Marx's value judgments can be understood in this way as expressions of proletarian morality. Such a class-based morality may be consistent with the historical relativist account of morality offered by Wood, and fits with his claim that Marx does not offer a moral theory in the traditional sense of a universal code of conduct. Such a class-based view of Marx's moral theory can also agree with the historical relativist idea that there are no transhistorical normative principles which ground a solution to moral controversy between distinct class-based moralities.[20] The principal difference between the class-based interpretation and Wood's is that the former allows for the existence of a revolutionary morality which plays a causal role in the revolutionary process.

A second account of morality within transitional periods is possible. On Wood's account, morality is not primarily a class affair. If a moral code corresponds to the requirements of maximal development of social powers of production, then it is binding on all classes alike. Morality is only contingently connected with class interests. Supposing this is so, whenever the relations of production sanctioned by a moral code cease to serve, and become fetters to the maximal development of the powers of production, then the moral code ceases to be morally binding on any individual, regardless of class. And if a new moral code emerges that sanctions relations which would maximally facilitate development of the growing powers of production, and which coincidentally expresses the interests of a new class, then that new moral code would be binding on individuals within all classes.

If Marx's theory of morality defines what is moral in terms of what best functions to serve development of productive powers, then there is a certain sense in which the theory is not historically relativist at all. And this is not a trivial sense of nonrelativity. Consider a view of morality as culturally relative in the sense that what is right or wrong in any culture depends upon what is thought to be right or wrong in that culture. Supposing the truth of such a view, it would be true to say that it is always morally right to do within any given culture whatever is thought to be right within that culture. Such a principle is an objective transcultural moral principle. It is objective in the sense that any judgment of the rightness or wrongness of an action in a culture is either true or false, and the truth or falsity of the judgment is empirically verifiable. Nor is such a principle entirely vacuous, since its acceptance would greatly simplify moral decision making. The Marxian theory of morality as historically relative is even more "objective" than this simple cultural relativism. For it makes possible comparative judgments between moral codes that are objective, both in the sense that they can be verifiably true or false and in the sense that they refer not just to people's beliefs but also to facts about the world, other than human beliefs, about which human beliefs can be mistaken. That is, they refer to the function capacity of a moral code to serve the social powers of production.

In this way, our view of Marx's theory of morality as a historical relativist theory of morality appears to have (dialectically?) transformed itself into a transhistorical principle that can be used to ground a revolutionary morality of struggle for socialism. In fact, of course, there is no dialectical miracle at work here. It is just that we are now looking at Marx's moral theory with a different sense of "relativism" in view—the sense in which Wood denies that Marx is a moral relativist. But at the same time, our view of Marx has altered. From this perspective Marx's judgments in favor of socialism rests on a genuinely normative principle: that those social arrangements are best which best serve the productive powers of humankind. This principle is not morally trivial nor is it obviously true. It might be that the pursuit of the development of productive powers is ecologically immoral, or disastrous for humanity and therefore immoral. So it is natural to ask what, if any, rational grounding can be provided for accepting such a principle as a moral principle.

Are there any deeper principles that might be used to justify the correspondence-to-productive-powers principle? A number of avenues are open to us here. We might argue for the principle on straightforward utilitarian grounds.[21] On this view, the development of productive powers might be morally right because it produces the greatest human happiness. Or we might ground the productive powers principle in a principle requiring maximal satisfaction of human needs and capacities that would be furthered by development of productive powers.[22] Or the productive powers principle might rest on a general moral principle requiring maximal development of human freedom or self-realization.[23] Each of these positions has both inherent appeal as a doctrine of morality and interpretational appeal as a way of reading Marx. Each presents itself, with some justification, as an interpretation of Marx's substantive moral theory.

Each also provides what is often called "transhistorical moral principle." That is, each provides a criterion for comparing the moral value of distinct moral codes, given a particular mode of production, and each provides a criterion for moral comparison between distinct modes of production across time and space. In this latter respect, each of the theories mentioned conflicts with the "amoralist" aspect of Wood's account of Marx's morality. Insofar as we do take Marx's transhistorical valuations of certain modes of production over others to be moral evaluations, each of these theories provides a way of understanding aspects of Marx's moral theory ignored by Wood's amoralist approach. Each also provides some basis for understanding Engels' acknowledgment of moral progress in history, an acknowledgment that seems incoherent from the strict, historical relativist, point of view.[24]

MARXIST-LENINIST ETHICS

Marxist-Leninist ethics also tries to make sense of the notion of moral progress. Lenin wrote no systematic work on ethics. In his "Address to the Third All-Russian Congress of the Communist Youth" (1920), he characterized the ethical theory of the Communists as the negation of all claims for a transcendental grounding of ethics, and as the development of a new Communist morality, which serves the interests of the working class: "To a Communist all morality lies in this united discipline and conscious mass struggle against the exploiters."[25] This subordination of ethics to class interest appears to be a version of relativism, in the sense that it makes the morality binding on an individual depend upon the interests of his or her class. The claim that all morality consists in such a class morality seems to preclude any trans-class moral principles that would permit comparative judgments of the moral worth of different class moralities.

But this is not the Marxist-Leninist position. First, the Leninist recognizes the existence of certain moral principles that are found in all class moralities, and hence are universal in that sense. But, more interestingly, the Leninist also claims that there is an objective criterion of morality by which certain class moralities can be judged superior to others. The Leninist's position here seems to parallel his or her position on truth. For the Leninist, all ideology, as part of the superstructure, is determined by the economic base. But this does not preclude the possibility that one ideology is nearer the truth than another. Nor does it preclude the possibility of objective knowledge that one ideology is closer to the truth than are others. In the same way, Leninists view moralities as determined by the economic base and economically determined interests of classes, and yet also more or less true and susceptible of objective evaluation as regards truth. This position lays the foundation for subsequent work in Marxist-Leninist ethics.[26]

A considerable portion of this work falls within the descriptive theory of morality contained within historical materialism. Here the effort is to show how certain moral rules are functionally adapted to serve the needs of the economic base and the interests of the dominant class. This part of Leninist moral theory is not normative, but it does have implications for ethics in the Western sense insofar as it involves a non-transcendental account of the origins of morality. This is a theory of the nature of morality, and hence a part of metaethics. Here the account seems similar to the functionalist determinist lines of Cohen and Wood.

The normative foundation of Leninist ethics is its theory of the good. The good is communism. A moral system is more or less true depending upon how closely its rules approximate the social relations of communism. The morality of one class, or of one mode of production, is an improvement on the morality of its predecessors if its rules more closely approximate the social relations of communism. In communism, for the first time, a "really human" morality appears that represents the highest possible moral standpoint.[27] A description of the Communist ideal is as follows:

> Communism is a classless social system with one form of public ownership of the means of production and full social equality of all members of society; under it, the all-round development of people will be accompanied by the growth of the productive forces through continuous progress in science and technology; all the springs of cooperative wealth will flow more abundantly, and the great principle "From each according to his ability, to each according to his needs" will be implemented. Communism is a highly organized society of free, socially conscious working people in which public self-government will be established, a society in which labor for the good of society will become the prime vital requirement of everyone, a necessity recognized by one and all, and the ability of each person will be employed to the greatest benefit of the people.[28]

This theory of the good provides the foundation for an ethics that is teleological, naturalistic, and objectivist.[29] The theory is teleological in the sense that the fundamental principle of morality is a consequentialist principle of maximally realizing the good. The theory is naturalistic in that the good can be defined descriptively. It is objectivist because the good is not fundamentally defined in terms of the subjective states of one or more agents. It is also objectivist in the sense that according to it, moral judgments have verifiable truth values.

Theories of a similar structure are not unknown in the history of Western ethics. Utilitarianism is perhaps the best-known of such theories. A difficulty for any such theory is its justification of the claim that maximal realization of the good is the true principle of morality. In his *Soviet Ethics and Morality*, Richard de George summarizes attempts in the Soviet literature to deal with this problem. Central to his account is an attempt to ground the Communist ideal in a theory of human nature, human needs, and human interests. Human beings are social beings. This is not to say that they are by nature empathetic or altruistic (though it is not to deny this either). Rather, the point is that human beings become the individuals that they are as a result of myriad social interactions. Language is a good example of this idea. Without language, self-consciousness would be nonexistent, or severely truncated. However, language is a social product, and its acquisition depends upon social interaction. In general, human evolutionary survival and development have hinged on the social nature of human existence. The technical and cultural achievements that make possible the satisfaction of diverse human needs and interests, and even create those needs and interests, cannot be maintained except in and through human social existence.

This view of human nature lays the ground for what seem to be two distinct attempts to justify the Communist ideal. The first proceeds by a metaphysical argument concerning the essence of human nature. De George formulates the argument as follows:

> What is reprehensible in these [class] societies is that man, a collective being, is divided against himself. The essence of man is still collective; he is still the ensemble of his social relations. But in a divided society, the individual man cannot express, experience, or enjoy his collective essence. His essence and existence are separated, and he in fact lives the life of a truncated individual man.[30]

This argument presupposes that there is a human essence, that in class societies human beings exist in ways that diverge from their essence, and that this divergence of existence and essence is morally reprehensible.

There is a fundamental problem with the third premise of this argument. Supposing that *x* is some feature of the human essence, it is not obvious that failure to actualize *x* is morally reprehensible. Why should we live in accordance with our natures? If a tendency toward jealousy is natural, ought we to cultivate it?

Concerning the second premise, one of the common objections to any such argument is that it is difficult to see how a thing can exist in a state divergent from its essence. There are at least two ways of making sense of such states.

One possibility is to see the essential nature as involving a potentiality that is not realized in actual existence. But this does not seem to be the appropriate sense for understanding the essence/existence divergence in the case in question. For the working class is not only potentially but also actually social in nature. The individual can exist as wage laborer only in social relations. And this is true, on the Marxists' own view, for all classes.

A second way of making sense of the divergence claim is in terms of the distinction between objective conditions and subjective awareness of those conditions. Thus, in a class-divided society, the individual may be objectively a product of social relations but hold a false consciousness concerning this, and imagine that he or she exists as an individual independent of any social relations. But this subjective/objective distinction provides no solution at all, since it does not really involve divergence between essence and existence. The subjective individualist may be confused about both essence and existence, and the class-conscious worker may be clear about both. But, presumably, even the class-conscious worker remains separated from his essence so long as he or she remains trapped in capitalist relations of production. False consciousness is not the only moral fault of capitalism.

Any satisfactory account of the moral significance of this alienation of existence from essence must move away from the abstract metaphysical terrain to a consideration of specific components of the human essence as it is understood by Marxist-Leninists. What is morally objectionable about class-divided societies is that most human beings are unable to satisfy their basic needs. Human beings are by nature social. Socially organized production is the essentially human way of satisfying human needs. In class-divided societies, the social organization of production is bent to serve the interests of the ruling class. Individuals in the working classes find their needs unsatisfied. This is what is morally reprehensible about class societies.

This brings us to the second way of understanding the link between the theory of human nature, needs, and interests, and grounding of the moral ideal of communism. Here the argument is that only in a communistically organized society can human needs and interests find their maximal satisfaction.[31] This way of understanding Leninist ethics brings it into structural similarity to classical utilitarianism. The difference is that the Leninist view rejects the narrow utilitarian theory of the good in terms of pleasure. As Marx says, to know what is good for man, one must know human nature. What is wrong with Bentham is that he mistakenly projects the psychology of the English shopkeeper onto human nature in general.[32] For the Marxist-Leninist, pleasure is part of the good, but the good also involves self-expression through socially recognized labor, personal freedom, self-realization, security, and knowledge, the widespread realization of which involves the development of social productive powers.

Like utilitarianism, this ethics is open to objections concerning the grounding of the fundamental moral principle of maximizing the satisfaction of human needs and interests. Why should we do this? So far as I know, there is no unique

Leninist solution to this sort of problem. The Leninist is apt to say that there is no transcendental basis for morality and that, hence, an ethics based on human interests is the only possible solution. But this does not answer either moral nihilists or the moralist who, like Nietzsche, tries to ground a new morality on facts other than satisfaction of human needs. For this reason, the frequent Leninist criticisms of Western ethics for moral skepticism seem to me to be unfair.[33]

The Leninist formulation of the good in terms that are multidimensional and more concrete than those of classical utilitarianism seems to me to be an improvement on hedonic utilitarianism, but it is an improvement that is purchased at the price of possible conflicts between component parts of the good. Personal freedom, well-roundedness, and security need not always mesh with social development, or with each other. The Communist ideal thus fails to generate a unique solution for all moral choices.[34] While this is so, the ideal is not devoid of content and may function as the most fundamental principle of moral theory. Perhaps there are no moral principles capable of generating unique solutions for all moral problems.

My sketch of Marxist-Leninist ethics leaves us with a theory of the good as communism, and the basic principle of morality as the duty to bring about the realization of communism. This picture presents Leninist ethics as a variant of familiar Western theories of ethics.[35] Like its teleologically structured counterparts in Western ethics, Leninist ethics can be criticized for its deficiencies with respect to the status of human rights.[36] While it is true that Leninist ethics does not ground inviolable human rights claims, I am not convinced that this is a weakness of the theory, since I do not see how such strong rights claims could be grounded. However, there is nothing in Leninist ethics that would preclude a theory of rights analogous to the theory of rights developed within Mill's utilitarianism. And insofar as the Leninist conception of the good is richer than the utilitarian account in terms of pleasure, I think the Leninist has more powerful resources for combating some of the supposed objections to utilitarianism in terms of rights. If satisfaction of a need for autonomous self-direction is a part of the Communist ideal, then libertarian rights can be defended in terms of that ideal without recourse to tenuous claims concerning the maximization of pleasure.

Leninist ethics is also commonly criticized on the grounds that it requires the subordination of the individual conscience to the decisions of the collective and to the dictates of the Communist Party in particular.[37] De George comments thus on the relationship between conscience and social demands: "However, the Soviet position may be interpreted in either of two ways. Either one's conscience is one's ultimate court of appeal . . . or the source of objective morality is society, and if ever one's conscience goes against what society says is right or wrong, one must subordinate his own convictions to those of society in order to be moral.[38] He goes on to say that on the Soviet view there is no doubt that social demands outweigh conscience, at least in a socialist society.

There are two questions that need to be kept distinct here. The Leninist position is not relativism that identifies right with what is approved either by the majority or by the Party. As De George has made clear, Marxist-Leninism holds an objectivist ethics in the sense that it makes the ultimate criterion of morality depend upon what is conducive to the development of communism. But, this being so, it is possible for any individual, majority, or the Party to be mistaken about what is moral. Hence, neither the individual conscience, nor society, nor the Party can be the source of morality, in the sense that the content of morality is determined by individual or collective beliefs about what is moral. Conscience or Party can be the source of morality only in the sense of being the medium for knowledge about morality. This epistemic issue concerning the source of our knowledge of morality must be distinguished from the metaphysical question as to the nature of morality. Further, there is no direct connection between the Leninist view of the nature of morality and the epistemic claim about the position of the Party.

The argument for the epistemically privileged position of the Party in fact presupposes an independent external and objective source of morality. Because of its objective nature it is possible for each of us to be mistaken in morality. And, the argument would maintain, since each of us, as a product of the bourgeois order, is apt to retain in the inner reaches of his or her conscience the marks of this order, any direct appeal to the dictates of conscience as an indicator of morality is almost certain to produce moral error. The Party, as repository of the collective wisdom of the most informed understandings of the historical process and the requirements for building socialism, is thus most likely to most closely approximate truth in moral judgments. Thus, the duty of a Communist to subordinate conscience to the direction of the Party does not depend upon a definitional link between morality and the actual decisions of the Party. While some Communists and some anti-Communists may have interpreted the Leninist position as involving such a link, this is perversion of the objective element in the Leninist position. On the Leninist view, the Party is not the source of morality, nor is it infallible.

Appreciation of the objectivist nature of the Leninist theory of the good is also key to understanding the relationship between Leninist ethics and historical materialism. It is often said that the Leninist makes a God out of history, and the implication of this is that, for the Leninist, historical progress is identical with moral progress.[39] From what has been said, it should be clear that, however accurate this may be as a picture of degenerate Communist consciousness, this is not a fair statement of the Leninist position. Marxist-Leninism does hold that communism is the inevitable, and in a sense final, outcome of the historical process actually at work, and it does hold a Communist society is morally superior to any other form of social organization. But communism is not morally superior because of its historical finality. What grounds the moral superiority of communism is that it provides maximal satisfaction of the diverse human needs and interests which are basic to human existence. Of course, it is not mere coincidence that the actual historical process should have this happy outcome. Human beings make history, and it is not surprising that they should ultimately mold their social institutions to serve their ends. But historical location and moral valuation are distinct. In terms of the debate within the Second International, the Leninist position is that the cause of socialism does require a moral theory, and that Marxism provides that theory. The Marxist theory of historical materialism explains the economic origins and functions of the various moralities that have appeared, and the theory of Communist morality provides grounds for claiming the moral superiority of proletarian morality over the morality of all previous classes.

DOES HISTORICAL MATERIALISM UNDERMINE MORALITY?

Some philosophers have claimed that there is a contradiction in these two claims. Thus, De George says:

> With respect to morality, a strong claim of economic determinism would similarly undermine the Soviet position. If what a class holds to be good is determined solely by its economic position, then what the classless society holds to be good is similarly determined. But if this were the case, then there would be no moral reason for holding that what the classless society says is good is to be preferred to what any particular class says is good.[40]

I think this argument involves a non sequitur. From the fact that a moral judgment is causally determined, it does not follow that there is no moral reason for holding one moral judgment rather than another. I take it that to have a moral reason for holding one judgment rather than another is to have some rational justification for doing so. But, as we have seen in our discussion of epistemology, the fact of a belief's having a cause is irrelevant to the question of its justification. The argument that historical materialism undermines claims for the moral superiority of communism is a special case of the more general argument to the effect that historical materialism undermines itself. In Chapter 5, I argued for the compatibility of historical materialism as a causal theory of belief formation with claims concerning the rational justifiability of the beliefs formed. If the argument there is correct, then it seems to me also to be coherent to say, with the Marxist-Leninists, that a moral belief is both historically determined and rationally justified. There is no obvious reason why moral beliefs should be especially problematic.[41]

As in the discussion of general epistemology, recognition of the distinction between the causal genesis of beliefs and their rational justification underlies my position here. It is precisely this distinction that underlay the ethical socialists' argument during the debates within the Second International. As was seen in Part I, the ethical socialists argued that even if Marxism were correct in predicting the coming of socialism, this did not suffice to show the moral desirability of socialism. It is no answer to this objection to say, as Karl Kautsky did and as some Soviet philosophers have said, that with the coming of socialism there would be an alteration in the moral superstructure.[42] For this is merely a claim in descriptive ethics. What is needed is a normative justification of socialism.[43] For the Marxist-Leninist, the theory of communism as the good provides the needed justificatory dimension.

I conclude, then, that the philosophical problems with Leninist ethics do not concern historical materialism but, rather, the theory of communism as the ultimate good. Here it seems to me that there are two basic difficulties. The first concerns the attempt to ground the theory of the good on a theory of human nature. It seems to me that this attempt fails for the reasons mentioned above. In this respect, I am sympathetic to the positivistic theme that value judgments, though not wholly irrational, cannot be given any ultimate justification. The second difficulty with the theory of the good is that the ideal of Communist morality includes potentially conflicting goods within it. Freedom, self-realization, security, knowledge, satisfaction of need, and social development can lead in different directions. To the extent that this is true, Leninist ethics fails to provide a universally applicable criterion for moral decision making. I will return to this point at the end of this chapter.

FACTS, VALUES, AND HUMANISTIC MARXISM

In our consideration of Marxist science in Chapter 3, we looked at an argument brought forward by humanistic Marxists which purported to show that all science, or at least all social science, is normative because all observation is theory laden. There I argued that the argument failed. I have also argued that neither Marx's social theory nor his own conception of it involves an essentially normative dimension. Against the humanistic Marxists I held that *Capital* is essentially value-free science. However, a full consideration of humanistic Marxism requires that we look not only at the theory of science but also at the theory of morality embedded in the humanist position.

Philosophers writing on the influence of Lukács' work on Western Marxism have rightly stressed the importance of his theory of morals. There is also general agreement that a denial of the fact/value distinction is somehow basic to Lukács' framework. But there is no clear agreement as to the nature of his position, its relation to the Marxism of Marx, or its value for philosophy. Thus, Kolakowski contrasts Lukács' denial of the fact/value distinction with the assumption of it by the Marxists of the Second International and takes Lukács as correctly interpreting Marx.[44] Lichtheim also sees Lukács' overcoming of the distinction as a breakthrough in Marxist theory, but is less clear about whether this is Marx's own position underneath his "positivist disguise."[45]

Lukács locates the problematics of the fact/value distinction in the Kantian doctrine of the distinction between theoretical and practical reason. For Kant, the world of phenomena is causally determined, and hence "nothing in the world of phenomena can be explained by the concept of freedom," for "the guiding thread in that sphere must always be the mechanics of nature.''[46] Moral value appears only in the practical sphere external to the theoretical framework. But this dichotomy of the theoretical and the practical renders Kantian philosophy incapable of comprehending moral action in the world. If human beings are free moral agents, does this freedom express itself in action in the phenomenal world? If not, then in what sense are human beings moral agents at all? And if so, then are not some phenomena explainable as the consequences of free human action? Lukács formulates the problem thus: ''The task is to discover the principles by means of which it becomes *possible in the first place* for an ''ought'' to modify existence.''[47] He thinks this problem is insolvable within the Kantian framework. He concludes that every theory of the ''ought'' must adopt one of two possible solutions:

> Either it must allow the—meaningless—existence of empirical reality to survive unchanged with its meaninglessness forming the basis of the ''ought''—for in a meaningful existence the problem of an ''ought'' could not arise. This gives the ''ought'' a purely subjective character. Or else, theory must presuppose a principle that transcends the concept of both what ''is'' and what ''ought to be'' so as to be able to explain the real impact of the ''ought'' upon what ''is.''[48]

This passage is not altogether clear about the nature of the alternatives or the reasons for thinking these are the only available alternatives. Lukács appears to think that if one abandons the Kantian doctrine of human freedom, one is left with a meaningless empirical reality. On this view determinism is universally applicable, and hence the ''ought'' is itself the effect of preceding causes. I take it this is what Lukács means in saying that a meaningless empirical reality forms the basis of the ''ought.''

Lukács goes on to say that this gives the ''ought'' a ''purely subjective'' character. This ''purely subjective'' character could be understood in at least two ways. On the one hand, Lukács may mean that the ''ought'' is purely subjective in the sense that it is merely an epiphenomenal effect in consciousness of natural causes. On this view morality is subjective in the sense that it finds no objective expression in the world of human relations and institutions. But there is no reason why we must accept this conclusion. It does not follow from the fact that morality has causes that it has no effects. A second, more plausible understanding of the ''purely subjective'' claim is perhaps that if morality is caused, then it cannot be objective in the sense of being rationally justifiable. But, as we have seen, there is no inconsistency in claiming both that all moral consciousness is causally determined and that some moral codes are objectively knowable as morally superior to others. I conclude that there is no reason to think that universal causation renders empirical reality meaningless.

Lukács does appear to think that the first, ''purely subjective,'' theory of morality is unacceptable, and accordingly embraces the second alternative of a principle that transcends the concept of both the descriptive and the normative.

But what is this principle, and how does it connect the normative and the descriptive?

Kolakowski takes Lukács' position here as a major advance in the interpretative understanding of Marxism. He argues that the debate between the ethical socialists and the historical determinists during the Second International rested upon a misguided acceptance of the fact/value distinction, a distinction that is foreign to Marxism. He maintains that it was Lukács who "was able to clear the matter up." Kolakowski summarizes Lukács' position in these three claims:

> (1) The working class comprehends social phenomena only in the very act of revolutionizing the world; (2) in general, knowledge of society is the self-knowledge of a society; and (3) Therefore the understanding of the world and its transformation are not contrasted with each other (as in the relationship between natural science and its technological application) but are one and the same act, while the distinction between understanding and evaluation is a secondary abstraction that distorts the original unity.[49]

It is clear that the conclusion Kolakowski aims at is the claim that understanding and evaluation are part of an original unity. However, it is less than clear just what argument is supposed to get us to this conclusion.

The first principle of Kolakowski's interpretation of Lukács is the claim that proletarian comprehension comes only in revolutionary action. Why should we think this is true? Indeed, does not revolutionary action presuppose some prior theoretical comprehension? How else does the proletariat know what to do? Did not Marx himself claim that one of the contributions of the Communists to the class struggle was that they brought a practice-directing theoretical "understanding of the line of march" with them?[50] It may very well be the case that revolutionary practice provides the arena for testing and correcting Marxist theory. It is certainly plausible to maintain that correct social theory will be achievable only by reflecting on the experience of such practice. But in this case the connection between revolutionary practice and theoretical comprehension seems very much like the relationship between technological application and natural science. And there seems to be no reason why the theoretician and the revolutionary need be united in one person. What reason, then, is there for thinking that it is only in revolutionary practice that the proletariat can achieve comprehension of reality?

One possible reason for thinking this is the argument from the theory ladenness of all knowledge to the claim that all comprehension is normatively "loaded" so that recognition of the truth of a theory depends upon normative commitments. Given this argument, we might go on to argue that only those who are willing to make the normative commitment to a revolutionary practice will be able to see the truth of Marxism. However, I have already rejected the argument from the theory ladenness of observation to the normative dependence of knowledge claims, both on substantive grounds and as a matter concerning the correct interpretation of Marx. Thus, I am inclined to think that Kolakowski's claim that only in revolutionary practice can social phenomena be comprehended is neither correct as an interpretation of Marx nor true. What, then, of the other two principles?

Is knowledge of society the self-knowledge of a society? I do not see that this need always be the case. What of Martians and anthropologists? And of course "society" is not some conscious being capable of knowledge. But certainly much of knowledge of society is self-knowledge in the sense that certain agents within a society come to have knowledge of the society in which they find themselves. What, then, of the third claim, that such self-knowledge is distinct from the kind of knowledge found in the natural sciences?

Kolakowski introduces this third claim with a "therefore." How should we understand this "therefore"? Is the third claim supposed to follow from the second alone or from the first and second jointly? I am not at all sure about this. In introducing the second claim Kolakowski says that "in general" knowledge of society is self-knowledge of society. One way of understanding this is that the second claim is intended as a generalization of the first claim, that is, the idea is that all knowledge of society is possible only in practice of one kind or another within society, and that it is the fact which makes social knowledge distinct from natural scientific knowledge. So understood, both the second and the third claim depend upon the truth of the first claim. And, if I am correct in rejecting the first claim, then both of the other claims fall as well. I believe that this is correct. I see no reason why only one who is a revolutionary can understand Marx, and hence no reason for thinking that the kind of self-knowledge the theory of capital provides is the self-knowledge of the revolutionary activist. Finally, I do not think the claimed distinction between the natural and social sciences holds. For the revolutionary to use Marx's theory of capital, he or she must first understand it. There is a separation between the theory and its application.

In any case, the whole argument here seems to pertain more to supposed moral requirements for knowledge than to the specifically ethical task of grounding moral judgments. Even if it were true that certain knowledge was possible only given certain moral commitments, this would not ground those moral commitments themselves. Just how the Lukácsian framework is supposed to do that remains a mystery. As best I can make out, Lukács' grounding of the moral commitments of the revolutionary proletariat is bound up with his claim for the privileged epistemic status of the proletariat.[51] Given his insistence on the prior unity of theory and practice, this makes sense. It is the proletarian viewpoint, both as theory and as practice, that is to be justified. And so Lukács' ethical theory collapses into his argument for the privileged epistemic status of the proletariat. In Chapter 5, I considered his arguments on this point and concluded that they fail. However, I would like to return to one argument that tries to provide the justification of the proletarian viewpoint. This is the argument, running throughout critical theory, that the rational grounding of the proletarian viewpoint lies in the fact that only it is independent of ideological mystifications.

Part of the historical materialist view is the idea that in the revolutionary transformation from feudalism to capitalism, the rising bourgeoisie presented its own interests as the universal interests of "the people" and its own morality as a universal morality binding on all people at all times. Part of Marx's critique of capitalism involved a critique of these claims to universality as being in fact masks for particular class interests and legitimations of class domination. In addition, Marx's critique of political economy involved a criticism of certain central claims of the economists. For example, Marx showed that the Smithian prognostication of continual growth beneficial to all classes rested upon a mistaken account of expanded reproduction, and he exposed the fallacies involved in various arguments of the vulgar economists on the impossibility or undesirability of reform of pure capitalism. In these various ways, Marxism involves an overthrow of false consciousness.

This insight forms the basis for an attempt to show that the moral and political principles of the proletarian outlook can be justified by social theory. For, it is argued, all other moral and political principles rely upon certain false beliefs for their justification. Thus, the justification for capitalism depends upon certain demonstrably false beliefs about growth and distribution of wealth and about the absence of exploitation. Insofar as social theory shatters these beliefs, it undermines the legitimacy of the social order and acquires a revolutionary significance. Insofar as only socialist principles can stand on their own without false consciousness to protect them, socialism acquires a justification rooted in truth. Socialist morality acquires a scientific foundation.

There are a number of distinct points here, and each needs to be considered separately. First, while numerous arguments for capitalism having false premises have been put forward, it is not obvious that all arguments for capitalism are like this. For example, there is the argument for capitalism put forward by Storch, mentioned earlier, that capitalism is desirable because in it the working class does all that is unpleasant in order that others may live in ease and leisure.[52] Such a defense of capitalism makes no pretense of universal appeal. It might be true that no such non-illusory defense of capitalism would function to maintain the system in the face of the countervailing interests of the masses of working people. But this is not itself a normative claim. Most socialists would say that Storch's defense is not only ineffectual but also morally deficient. This latter claim is, I think, true, but this shows that maintenance of illusion is not the only form of moral failure.

It may be true that good social theory is revolutionary in the sense that it does undermine the false beliefs that class domination requires to maintain itself, but this does not show that social theory can provide the foundation for any moral principles. Good social theory has revolutionary consequences only because working people have interests and beliefs about the moral legitimacy of those interests. Without such interests and moral beliefs, the unmasking of illusions would have no implications for social change. Insofar as the issue is one of grounding or justifying moral principles, the question is not whether the social theory has revolutionary consequences but, rather, what in the social theory provides justification for the interests and moral beliefs that give rise to the revolutionary movement.

Here, the humanist's idea seems to be that socialist principles are morally superior because they alone are consistent with the truth. But, as the example from Storch shows, this is not so. We might say, then, that Storch's defense of capitalism rests on a principle which says that the interests of some people are morally more important than the interests of other people, and that this is a false assumption in his argument. But how would we show this? Are we not eventually driven to normative judgments that lie outside the domain of descriptive theory? Further, suppose we could show that only socialist principles were consistent with truth. Suppose someone replies that some things other than truth are valuable and that non-socialist principles do better in terms of these other values. Can there not be a noble lie? What these questions show, I think, is that the moral case for socialism cannot rest solely on judgments about the truth or falsity of various views about how the social system operates. Hence the moral case for socialism remains foundationally distinct from social science.

MARXISM AND OVERDETERMINATION IN ETHICS

Positivists have never held that morality is completely independent of science. Insofar as science and the positivist scientific world view based on science involve a critique of metaphysics and various metaphysical systems of ethics, this positivism has far-reaching importance for morality. But positivists have also granted that science has a variety of interconnections with morality that remain, even within a scientific world view. First, to say that Jones murdered Smith is to make a moral judgment, but it is also to imply that Jones killed Smith, which is a factual claim. Even on a purely emotivist metaethics, moral judgments can be refuted by factual claims. Second, insofar as we accept the maxim that "ought" implies "can," then purely scientific judgments have obvious moral import. Third, if we hold any consequentialist theory, we will also see social scientific theories, which clarify the consequences of different practices, as having enormous importance for morality. In this sense, such positivists as Moritz Schlick and Otto Neurath considered a scientific ethics to be possible. Further, understood as a scientifically informed application of independent normative premises, such a scientific ethics is compatible with an emotivist position in metaethics.

If we accept Marx's theory of capitalism, this theory has great moral significance. For, accepting this theory, capitalism fails on a variety of moral theories. It fails on utilitarian grounds, on Kantian grounds of respect for persons, on grounds of maximal human freedom, and on grounds of self-realization and self-development. On each of these dimensions, socialism is superior to capitalism, if we assume that Marx's theory of capitalism is true. Socialism is morally overdetermined. On all plausible viewpoints, it is morally superior to capitalism.

Given the truth of Marxist economics, it is a simple and uncontroversial value judgment to conclude that socialism is morally superior to capitalism.[53]

This moral overdetermination in the case for socialism is important in several respects. In the first place, it helps us to understand some of the difficulties that have appeared in recent work on Marx's moral theory. As has been shown, in considering the limits of a purely historical relativist view of Marx's moral viewpoint, in recent years there have appeared a number of well-researched and well-argued interpretations of Marx's ethics that reach different interpretations of his moral theory. While I think this work has been important in bringing out a variety of moral themes that are present in Marx and in clarifying the substantive issues involved in such themes, I do not think any one of them has succeeded in claiming Marx for itself, and I do not think any single moral theory can succeed as an interpretation of Marx. In part I think this is because of Marx's distaste for certain moralistic socialisms and his own confusion about the significance of this. But I think Marx's own confusion can be at least partially explained as a result of the moral overdetermination of the case for socialism. Because of this moral overdetermination, Marx could appeal to different moral viewpoints without being forced to confront conflicts between them. And because the case for socialism did not rely upon any controversial moral theory, he did not feel compelled to produce a thorough grounding for the moral judgments he clearly did make.

A second point of importance concerning moral overdetermination of the case for socialism is that it makes clear that the Marxist case for socialism does not rest upon any particular socialist morality. There is some merit to Marx's disdain for moralistic theories of socialism. Various attempts have been made to construct a socialist morality that is said to differ from bourgeois morality and to provide the necessary foundations for socialism. It may well be that morality in a socialist society will give weight to principles, such as solidarity and community, that are relatively unimportant within the scheme of bourgeois morality. But to base the case for socialism on a particular moral theory, a theory that claims to be a new moral perspective, is to make an unnecessarily weak case for socialism.

Third, recognition of overdetermination in the case for socialism connects up with our earlier discussion of ambiguity in the Communist ideal within Leninist ethics. In discussing Leninist ethics, I claimed that the Communist ideal functioned as a theory of the good within a teleologically structured moral theory. One of the difficulties for Leninist ethics is that this theory of the good is in fact a theory with a bundle of goods that could, in some circumstances, come into conflict. For this reason I said that the theory of Communist morality did not succeed as a universal criterion for moral judgments. Here I want to make two further observations. The first pertains to the elements of the bundle of goods in the Communist ideal. As I emphasized, in agreement with Richard de George and Herbert Marcuse, the elements in this bundle are in fact the various familiar elements of the good in traditional moral theories: happiness, freedom, self-realization, and so on. The collection of these various goods into the Communist ideal is, in a sense, the representation of moral overdetermination within the theory of the good. My second point here is that though there is a potential for conflict between these elements of the good, this potential conflict is not important in making the case for socialism precisely because of the moral overdetermination of the case for socialism.[54]

Finally, moral overdetermination is important because is clarifies an important sense in which the Marxist case for socialism can be said to be a scientific case. Given moral overdetermination, the judgment in favor of socialism is "objective" in the sense that it does not rest on controversial moral principles. But it does rest heavily on the scientific theory of capitalism. From this point of view, the issue between capitalism and socialism is a scientific question, and the Marxist socialist alternative is scientifically based. In saying this, I do not mean to deny that the normative case for socialism rests on moral premises which are external to descriptive science. It is just that these moral premises are uncontroversial. The case for socialism is no less scientific than the case for inoculation against smallpox.

NOTES

1. William Riker, *Theory of Political Coalitions* (New Haven: Yale University Press, 1965), p. 5.

2. Marx, *The Poverty of Philosophy* (New York: International, 1973), p. 49; *Marx Engels Werke* (Berlin: Dietz Verlag, 1968), vol. 4, p. 81 (hereafter *MEW*) and *Capital* (New York: International, 1973), vol. 1, pp. 84–85 n. 2; *MEW*, vol. 23, pp. 99–100 n. 38.

3. On the Ricardian Socialists, see Maurice Dobb, *Theories of Value and Distribution Since Adam Smith* (Cambridge: Cambridge University Press, 1973), pp. 137–141.

4. This is one of his central points in the *Critique of the Gotha Program*. For some of Marx's comments on the Ricardian Socialists, see *The Poverty of Philosophy*, p. 69 (*MEW*, vol. 4, p. 98) and pp. 78–79 (*MEW*, vol. 4, p. 105).

5. As was seen in Chapter 5, the economist Storch both acknowledged this exploitation and considered it moral.

6. To be sure, Marx does allow that there is a moral factor present in determining the amount of value necessary to maintain the worker (*Capital*, vol. 1, p. 232; *MEW*, vol. 23, pp. 246–247). But this enters the determination of the rate of exploitation only as a matter of descriptive ethics.

7. I ignore here the possibility of ties between incompatible moral codes.

8. I am indebted to Tom Moody for pointing out to me that moral criticism could play a significant role under such conditions even under the theory that morality is relative to the mode of production. Since on the view in question such conditions are historically decisive, this is no minor concession concerning the historical role of moral criticism.

9. Allen Wood, "The Marxian Critique of Justice," *Philosophy and Public Affairs* 1 (1972), pp. 244–282. See also his *Karl Marx* (London: Routledge and Kegan Paul, 1981), pp. 123–140. In his book, Wood denies that on his view Marx is a moral relativist (p. 131). His point is that on his view, moral judgments are objectively true or false

independent of who makes the judgments. This is consistent with the sense of relativism in which moral principles are true relative to modes of production.

10. In "On Marx on Justice," *New Left Review* no. 150 (March–April 1985): 47–85, Norman Geras provides both an excellent survey of the discussion and a powerful contribution to it. See also Marshall Cohen et al., eds., *Marx, Justice and History* (Princeton: Princeton University Press, 1980); and Kai Nielsen and Steven Patten, eds., *Marx and Morality* (Gullph: Canadian Association for Publishing in Philosophy, 1981).

11. Wood, *Karl Marx*, p. 149; John McMurtry, "Critical Notice of Allen Wood's *Karl Marx*," *Canadian Journal of Philosophy* 15 (June 1985): 348.

12. Wood, *Karl Marx*, p. 154.

13. Ibid., p. 128.

14. Ibid., p. 126.

15. In the Introduction to the *Critique of Hegel's Philosophy of Right*, Marx talks about the "categorical imperative to overthrow all those conditions in which man is an abased, enslaved, abandoned, contemptible being." *Karl Marx: Early Writings*, T. B. Bottomore, ed. (New York: McGraw-Hill, 1964), p. 52. However, it is unclear just how deeply theoretical Marx intends this remark to be, and there is also some question as to how far one can extend the moral theory of this period to the outlook of the mature Marx. In a letter to Sigfrid Meyer of April 30, 1867, Marx comments: "If one chose to be an ox, one could of course turn one's back on the sufferings of mankind and look after one's own skin" (Marx and Engels, *Marx/Engels Selected Correspondence* (Moscow: Progress, 1975), p. 173. This is not the language of duty so much as of psychology. In this respect I think the remark supports Wood's view of Marx.

16. Geras, "On Marx on Justice," pp. 61–62.

17. Wood, *Karl Marx*, p. 149.

18. McMurtry makes this criticism in "Critical Notice of Alan Wood's *Karl Marx*" (pp. 352–353). It is also advanced by David Levin in "The Moral Relativism of Marxism," *Philosophical Forum* 15 (Spring 1984): 264.

19. This appears to be Levin's view of Marx. See Levin, "Moral Relativism of Marx," p. 266.

20. Levin (ibid., pp. 276–278) holds that there can be nonnormative principles for judging between moralities. Here his position is similar to Wood's allowance of nonmoral valuations of one mode over another.

21. Cf. Derek Allen, "The Utilitarianism of Marx and Engels," *American Philosophical Quarterly* 10 (1973), pp. 189–199.

22. McMurtry, "Critical Notice of Allen Wood's *Karl Marx*," p. 351.

23. George Brenkert, *Marx's Ethics of Freedom* (London: Routledge and Kegan Paul, 1983).

24. Engels, *Anti-Dühring* (Peking: Foreign Languages Press, 1976), p. 119.

25. Lenin, *Collected Works* (Moscow: Foreign Languages, 1963), vol. 31, p. 294.

26. "The idea of determinism, which postulates that human acts are necessitated and rejects the absurd tale about free will, in no way destroys man's reason or conscience, or appraisal of his actions" (Lenin, quoted by V. Kelle and M. Kovalson, *Historical Materialism* [Moscow: Progress, 1973], p. 245). In the "Address to the Communist Youth," just below the passage quoted above (note 25), Lenin talks about "human society" moving to a "higher level." Clearly this presupposes some criterion by which one level of human society can be judged higher than another. For a discussion of Marxist-Leninist ethics involving the recognition of both elementary moral principles applying to

all stages in social development and objective criteria of moral improvement, see Herbert Marcuse, *Soviet Marxism: A Critical Analysis* (New York: Columbia University Press, 1958), pp. 227, 215.

27. The reference to a "really human" morality is from Engels, *Anti-Dühring*, p. 119. In the "Address to the Communist Youth" (*Collected Works*, vol. 31. p. 295) Lenin says that "Communist morality is based on the struggle for the consolidation and completion of communism."

28. Quoted in Richard de George, *Soviet Ethics and Morality* (Ann Arbor: University of Michigan Press, 1969), p. 41.

29. Ibid., pp. 27–28.

30. Ibid., p. 31.

31. Ibid., p. 48.

32. Marx, *Capital*, vol. 1, p. 609 n. 2; *MEW*, vol. 23, pp. 636–637 n. 63.

33. E.g., O. G. Drobnitskii, "Marxist Philosophy and the Problem of Value," *Soviet Studies in Philosophy* 5 (1966–1967): 17. No more than their Western counterparts do Marxist-Leninist philosophers possess an account of justifiability of fundamental values. Instead, these values appear as "postulates" within moral theory. In this respect see Drobnitskii's helpful "Discussions Between Soviet and British Philosophers on Problems of Ethics," *Soviet Studies in Philosophy* 9 (1970–1971), "postulates," p. 243.

34. De George, *Soviet Ethics and Morality*, p. 43.

35. Ibid., p. 127. The same point is emphasized by Marcuse, *Soviet Marxism*, pp. 201, 217, 232.

36. De George, *Soviet Ethics and Morality*, p. 39.

37. Ibid., p. 79; Marcuse, *Soviet Marxism*, p. 220.

38. De George, *Soviet Ethics and Morality*, p. 79.

39. Leszek Kolakowski, "Responsibility and History," in his *Toward a Marxist Humanism* (New York: Grove Press, 1968), is a classic statement of this position.

40. De George, *Soviet Ethics and Morality*, p. 63.

41. See note 26. The combatibility of historical materialism and the rational justifiability of moral beliefs has also been forcefully argued by William Shaw in his "Marxism and Moral Objectivity," in *Marx and Morality* edited by Kai Nielsen and Steven Patten, pp. 26–29. See also Andrew Collier, "Truth and Practice," *Radical Philosophy* 5 (1973): 11–12.

42. Drobnitskii, "Marxist Philosophy and the Problem of Value," p. 20.

43. Wood, *Karl Marx*, p. 144, suggests rightly that Marx and Engels were wrong if they thought historical materialism absolved them of the need for an ethics.

44. Leszek Kolakowski, *Main Currents of Marxism* (Oxford: Oxford University Press, 1978), vol. 3, pp. 270–271 for Lukács' position, vol. 2, p. 254, for Kolakowski's judgment that Lukács' view is true of Marx.

45. George Lichtheim, *George Lukács* (New York: Viking Press, 1970), pp. 64–65, 70.

46. Kant, quoted by Lukács in his *History and Class Consciousness* (Cambridge, MA: MIT Press, 1971), pp. 160–161.

47. Ibid., 161.

48. Ibid.

49. Kolakowski, *Main Currents of Marxism*, vol. 2, p. 254.

50. Marx, in *Marx and Engels, Manifesto of the Communist Party* (Moscow: Progress, 1977), p. 62.

51. I ignore here the further complication concerning the status of the Party as the location of proletarian class consciousness in Lukács' theory.

52. See Marx, *Capital*, vol. 1, p. 647; *MEW*, vol. 23, p. 677.

53. This point is made by Andrew Collier in "Scientific Socialism and the Question of Socialist Values," p. 146; and by Shaw, "Marxism and Moral Objectivity," pp. 33–35.

54. Through of course tension between conflicting goals embedded in the good becomes problematic in the process of building socialism.

8

Politics

Humanistic Marxism and Marxist-Leninism emerged as a result of the breakdown of the Second International in the face of World War I. Both Lenin and Lukács argued that the political failure of the International was, at least in part, traceable to the philosophical errors of its leaders. At the same time, ''positivistic'' opponents of Marxism, such as Karl Popper, have argued that the political failures of communism have, at least in part, been traceable to philosophical errors. In this chapter I will attempt to look at some of the relevant arguments pertaining to these alleged connections between philosophy and politics.

DIALECTICS, REVOLUTION, AND REFORM

Long before the war, Lenin had claimed that the roots of nonrevolutionary reformism within the revisionist movement grew out of the failure to appreciate the role of dialectics within Marxism.[1] In *The Collapse of the Second International* (written in 1915), Lenin traced the failure of leadership within the International, and in particular Karl Kautsky's failure to the philosophical inadequacy of Kautsky's understanding of dialectics.[2] The crisis of the Marxism of the Second International was thus not entirely unexpected from Lenin's point of view. What was perhaps surprising to Lenin was the extent to which Kautsky and other opponents of revisionism were themselves infected by it. But the basic understanding of the philosophical roots of the problem extended back prior to the collapse.

Nor was Lenin entirely alone in his understanding of the connection between philosophical revisionism, by way of abandonment of Hegelian dialectics, and political reformism. It will be recalled that Eduard Bernstein appealed to this connection in his argument for revisionism. Bernstein was convinced that a violent revolutionary rising would be disastrous. He argued that the costs of violence were so great as to outweigh any gains to be achieved, and that in any case the working class was not ready to govern, and so no gains would be achieved. The rational political course, in Bernstein's view, was a gradual reform of capitalism, accompanied by a gradual development of the abilities of the working class for self-government. Socialism was conceived not as a particular institutional arrangement that could actually be achieved, but as a normative ideal that would guide a never-ending process of reformist approximation. Gradualist evolutionism, not revolution, was the right politics for German Social Democracy. Revolutionism should be rejected. Its appearance in Marx, and hence its persistence in the rhetoric of German Social Democracy, had its roots in the contamination of scientific Marxism with the unscientific dialects of Hegel.

It is thus clear that representatives of both sides in the revisionism debate at the turn of the century accepted the claim of a connection between philosophical dialects and political revolutionism. But it is not so clear just what this connection is. Must the dialectician be a revolutionist? Is right-wing Hegelianism simply inconsistent? Can one be a non-dialectical revolutionist? Exactly what is the connection between dialectics and revolutionism within Marxist thought?

Part of the problem involves clarification of the concept of revolution itself. At least three conceptual contrasts seem to be relevant here. First, there is the contrast between fundamental and nonfundamental change. Revolutionary change involves fundamental change, and reformist change involves nonfundamental change. Second, there is a contrast between fast and slow change. Revolutionary change involves a rapid alteration of the social system, while reformist change involves a slow alteration. Third, there is a contrast between violent change and peaceful change. These three conceptual contrasts mark out, as it were, three distinct dimensions within which historical change can occur. They may, but need not, overlap. Or, at least, some argument is needed to show that the three dimensions must overlap. One might, for example, see the industrial "revolution" as slow and nonviolent but fundamental. Or one might see a military coup as swift and violent but nonfundamental.

As a step in clarification of the problem of the relation between dialectics and revolution, let us take the fundamental/nonfundamental contrast as the dimension most crucial to understanding the Marxist conception of social revolution. This conception finds its content in the historical materialist account of the change from one mode of production to another. There is a continuous and relatively independent development of the forces of production. If the mode of production is stable, the relations of production in existence function to permit the maximally, or at least acceptably, effective use of the available forces of production. The ideological superstructure sanctions these arrangements. Gradually, new forces of production accumulate. Eventually, this growth of production forces reaches a point where the existing relations of production cease to facilitate, and instead come to fetter, utilization of the available forces. At this point a social revolution occurs in which the existing relations of production are replaced by new relations that better serve the effective use of available powers.

This transformation of the relations of production is followed by a change in the superstructure to accommodate and legitimate the new relations. For the Marxist, revolution involves such change in the relations of production. Such a transformation of relations is fundamental in that it involves pervasive, systematic, and relatively enduring change in social relations and the way the society understands these relations. But not all fundamental change is revolutionary. For example, granted that the industrial "revolution" involved basic, important changes in the way people live, on the Marxist view, this change is not revolutionary because it does not involve a change in the relations of production. The industrial revolution occurred within the boundaries of capitalism and its dominant wage labor relation of production.

Perhaps not all Marxists would agree with this way of understanding the concept of revolution, but this way of looking at it is common enough among Marxists. I will take this specific understanding of revolution as the understanding relevant to the question of the relation between dialectics and revolutionism. Social revolution is fundamental social change, and what makes it fundamental is that it involves a transformation of the relations of production which determine the nature of the mode of production.

Given this understanding of revolution, what is the connection between this understanding and philosophical dialectics? Marxist-Leninists contend that revolutionary proletarian class struggle is logically connected with dialectical materialism and historical materialism.[3] There are certain undeniable similarities between the picture of social revolution presented by historical materialism and a dialectical outlook in philosophy. First, both view reality as changing. Second, on both accounts this change involves processes that are internal to the aspect of reality in view. Third, on both views that process of change is developmental. What comes later is not merely different from what came before but also richer, more developed, or at a higher level. There is, in some sense, progress. Fourth, on both views the inner process that gives rise to this change involves the "contradictory nature" of reality. Each mode of production destroys itself in its own peculiar and essential pattern of development. Fifth, on both accounts, reality can be understood as involving the transformation of quantitative change into qualitative change. The gradual quantitative growth in productive forces at a certain point gives rise to a qualitative change in the whole mode of production. Revolution is a kind of qualitative leap in human social development. Reformism rests on a gradualist evolutionism that is undialectical because it denies the necessity of such leaps.

What all of this shows, I think, is that the historical materialist conception of revolutionary change can be understood dialectically. But the precise relationship between philosophical dialectics and political revolutionism is still not clear. Can one be dialectical and reformist? Can one be revolutionary and nondialectical? I believe the answer to each of these questions is "yes." Historically, it might be argued that Kautsky and Georgi Plekhanov accepted dialectics in theory but shrank from revolutionary politics. And, on the other side, Anton Pannekoek and Karl Liebknecht adopted a revolutionary politics in spite of philosophical objections to dialectics.

Let me begin with the possibility of nondialectical revolutionism. Supposing that we fix the idea of revolution as being fundamental change in the relations of production, I see no reason why one could not advocate and pursue such change independently of a dialectical philosophy. Suppose, for example, that one thought that fundamental social change occurred as a result of heroic acts of will forced upon a violent and reactionary power structure. Such a view would lead one to view revolutions as violent, swift, fundamental changes. But it would not be a dialectical outlook because it would not grasp the revolutionary transformation as the outcome of inner contradictory forces governed by the law of quantity and quality. One can be a revolutionist and not a dialectician.

The Marxist-Leninist would not find this conclusion particularly troublesome. If by "revolutionist" one means "person who understands and advocates revolution as fundamental social change," it is clear that one can be a revolutionist and not a dialectician. But what is important is that one cannot be a successful revolutionist without being a dialectician. This is, in effect, the kind of criticism Lenin leveled against the infantile Communist revolutionists and against Pannekoek in particular.[4] Their revolutionism was doomed to disappointment because they lacked the correct understanding of historical processes as dialectical processes.

This answer presupposes that a successful revolutionism requires a correct account of the historical process. This is not obvious and probably false. Did not Lenin himself assume that the October Revolution would fail in the absence of revolution elsewhere in Europe? Further, the reply assumes that the historical process is a dialectical process either of the kind described by historical materialism or some other dialectical kind. This assumption about the process of history is surely questionable. As I tried to argue in Chapter 4, historical materialism is not a well-developed scientific theory. And, as I argued in Chapter 6, it is not at all clear that any substantive hypotheses regarding any actual processes can be derived from the principles of dialectics. Lacking such derivations, it is not at all clear how a dialectical materialist outlook in philosophy could be requisite for successful revolutionary politics.

Can one be a dialectician and a reformist? Let us suppose for the moment that philosophical dialectics is true. Everything is in flux. Change is developmental, powered by inner contradictions, and describable by the laws of quantity and quality and so forth. Does this preclude reformism? I am not convinced that it does. As a dialectical reformist I could argue as follows. Particular reforms are attempts to rectify particular deficiencies of capitalism. The nature of the reform needed, and the time of appearance of the need for the reform, are themselves products of the contradictory inner development of capitalism. Each reform is in effect a determinate negation that stands in a dialectical relation of contradictory unity with the developing inner essence of capitalism.

If we pursue a policy of gradual reformism, we in effect adopt a policy of successive "quantitative" changes. These changes are "quantitative" in the sense that each leaves the essential "qualitative" structure of capitalism intact. But, by Hegel's law of quantity and quality, we know that at some point this quantitative approach will give rise to a qualitative change in the mode of production. This is the qualitative leap expected within a dialectical outlook. The revolutionist mistakes the qualitative leap for a change distinct from the series of quantitative changes. But this is in effect a mechanical separation of the qualitative change from the quantitative changes preceding it. Reform is not an alternative to revolution; it is the process of revolution. Those who contrast reform and revolution are caught up in questions of violence or nonviolence and slow or swift that are not essentially connected to the revolutionary process at all. Revolution is fundamental social change, and this occurs, on a properly dialectical view, as a result of a series of incremental reforms.[5]

I do not see how commitment to philosophical dialectics of itself precludes such an understanding of revolution and reform. And, consequently, I reject both Bernstein's argument from reformism against dialectics and Lenin's argument from dialectics to revolutionism. So far as I can see, philosophical dialectics is consistent with either political strategy. And, of course, if one accepts the standard positivist criticism of dialectics as devoid of content, then this is as one would expect. Consistency with any political strategy is but a special case of the general lack of content. The acceptance by all sides in the turn-of-the-century revisionism controversy of a link between Hegelian dialectics and revolutionism in politics rests on historical association rather than logic.

This is not to say that Lenin's criticism of the leadership of the Second International is without force. His arguments on the limits of bourgeois democracy, the near certainty of violent resistance to change on the part of the ruling class, and his criticism of the rigid attachment to electoral politics have weight, though I am not convinced that alternative strategies would have been any more successful in Germany in 1914. But, in any case, these criticisms do not depend on philosophical dialectics. That the political failure of the Second International derived from its mistakes in philosophy has not been established.

POSITIVISTIC ANTI-REVOLUTIONISM

A political criticism of Marxism coming from Karl Popper presents a defense of reformism as an alternative to Marxist revolutionism. Popper contrasts piecemeal social reform with holistic utopian attempts to remake the social order. He claims that Marxist revolutionism is a version of holistic utopianism and that any such holistic approach is "incompatible with a truly scientific attitude."[6]

Popper's works suggest at least two arguments to support the claim that holistic utopianism in unscientific. The first turns on his denial of the possibility of knowledge of historical laws of development. This argument was considered in the discussion of historical materialism. Given this criticism of Marxism as a methodologically confused historicism, Popper appears to be arguing in the following fashion:

1. Marxism justifies revolution by appeal to the end achieved.
2. That socialism will be the end achieved is guaranteed by Marxist science of history.
3. Marxist science of history is defective on methodological grounds.

Therefore: The Marxist justification of revolution fails.

This argument depends on Popper's methodological critique of historical materialism. But we have seen that such a purely methodological critique fails. However much doubts about historical materialism may impinge upon questions of political strategy, these doubts involve substantive questions of social science and not purely methodological issues.

However, there is another way to understand Popper's argument that does not depend on the specific methodological claim concerning historical materialism's supposed confusion of trends and laws. This construal of the argument turns not on considerations of method but, rather, on a matter of attitude or point of view. The argument seems to go something like this:

1. The holistic utopian is committed to the complete reconstruction of society.
2. This commitment prejudices the utopian against hypotheses such as the one involving the uncertainty of the effects of social change due to the "human factor."

Therefore: "By a rejection *a priori* of such hypotheses, the Utopian approach violates the principles of scientific method.[7]

As I understand it, by the "human factor" Popper means to refer to the complicated and unpredictable nature of human behavior and human social interaction. On this view, the point of premise (2) is that the utopian is unable to maintain a healthy skepticism concerning the adequacy of the theories which guide his actions. It is this hypothesis of uncertainty that the utopian rejects *a priori*. The obvious reply to this argument is that the holistic utopian is not committed to an *a priori* or an *a posteriori* rejection of the hypothesis of uncertainty. The holistic utopian need not reject the hypothesis at all. Indeed, a stock Marxist response to the criticism that Marx nowhere provides a detailed account of the socialist society which is supposed to justify the revolution is that no such detailed account can be given because the future development of socialism is to a large degree uncertain.

Of course, one may find this morally relevant to the justification of revolutionary change. This evils brought about may exceed the known evils of capitalism. Insofar as piecemeal reforms involve changes, the effects of which may be more nearly certain and reversible, such reforms are morally preferable on grounds that we ought not to impose unknown risks. But this is a moral argument, not a matter of philosophy of science. (Are not sweeping and risky hypotheses preferable in science on Popper's own view?) And it is surely not an overriding moral consideration. In some cases—for example, in risky but potentially life-saving medical intervention—it might be immoral not to impose the risk. Further, in situations where one is dealing with a complex and interconnected system of interacting elements, it may be that certain kinds of changes cannot be achieved in a piecemeal fashion. We cannot, for example, introduce markets into a centrally planned socialist system in a piecemeal fashion of one industry at a time.[8] Surely we cannot assume that the risks involved in such sweeping change always morally prohibit the change.

There is a third and related argument here. Popper says, "The piecemeal engineer can attack his problem with an open mind as to the scope of the reform, the holist cannot do this."[9] But surely the answer to this is that the piecemeal engineer is just as closed to the need for reform. It is not obvious that those South African statesmen who are willing to tinker with the structure of apartheid are more open-minded than the revolutionists who want to do away with it altogether.

Richard Miller considers the role of certain political motivations in influencing a number of writers in the positivist camp.:

> They are appalled by the violence and repression to which extremists are prone. They typically regard such extremism as based on people's ill-founded confidence in their knowledge of causes, confidence that is not just founded on inadequate evidence, but based on fundamental conceptual confusions concerning the nature and limits of evidence, causes or explanation.[10]

Miller goes on to suggest that such writers have attempted to use purely methodological principles as a means of showing "that the whole style of thought of extremists on all sides is based on confusions." No doubt much of extremist though does rest on methodological confusion. But so does much middle-of-the-road thought. I would also question the association of extremists with bloodshed and middle-of-the-road thought with peaceful reform. From the point of view of the radical pacifist, that the murderers in power are moderates is of little consequence. And, more important, it is not clear that all "extremist" thought rests on confusion of method. In defending Marxist political theory, Miller defends the expectation of the likely necessity of violent revolution as the only method for achieving fundamental social change, as a view resting on the best available social science.[11] While his defense of this claim rests upon his theory of rational choice between scientific theories ass involving substantive comparative issues, rather than the purely formal criteria of positivist philosophy of science, I do not see how even a purely formalist philosophy of science is to rule out political extremism.

POSITIVISTIC TOTALITARIANISM

There is an opposing argument that runs through much of humanistic Marxism to the effect that positivism in social science leads to totalitarianism in politics. The classic, though nebulous, formulation of this argument is in the *Dialectic of the Enlightenment*. There Horkheimer and Adorno claim that there is an impulse to domination at the heart of the dialectic between myth and enlightenment. This impulse is crystallized in positivist science, with its emphasis on predication and control of nature. The subsumption of human social life under this positivist vision of human emancipation, through domination and control of nature, gives rise to the manipulative mass culture of the modern world, which finds in fascism only a peculiar and horrible exemplar of its own inner logic.[12]

This framework has been used by humanistic Marxists in the critique not only of advanced capitalism but also of existing socialism. The basic points of this criticism are that there is an inherent connection between positivism in philosophy and totalitarianism in politics; that Engels misunderstood the critical nature of Marx's social theory and recast it as a positivistically understood social science; that Engels' misinterpretation became imbedded in orthodox Marxist-Leninism; that this philosophical misunderstanding produced, in the Soviet model, a fundamentally distorted version of socialism; and that, in particular, the philosophical misunderstanding is responsible for the repressive features of the Soviet model.[13]

From what has been said before, it should be clear that I reject the view that Engels' interpretation is a misunderstanding of Marxism. If it is a mistake to understand Marxism as a "positivistic" science, it is a mistake to which Marx himself was prone. One might also question the identification of Marxist-Leninism as a positivistic philosophy. Also, I think it is a serious distortion of political reality to label the Soviet model as totalitarian. But I want to set these questions aside here. For the critical theorist, any understanding of Marxist social theory as a social science analogous in method to the natural sciences is positivistic, and in this sense I think the critical theorist is correct in identifying Marxist-Leninism as positivistic. What I want to question here is the basic claim that there is some inherent connection between positivism in philosophy and totalitarianism in politics.

In *The Dialectic of Defeat*, Russell Jacoby identifies two fundamental schools in the development of Marxism after World War I. One of these, Soviet Marxism, upholds "a regressive scientific Marxism" rooted in "the cult of science and objectivity."[14] Jacoby sees the repressive features of the Soviet experience as products of this cult of science. "Science guarantees success. Marxism inherited this proposition from bourgeois society and hammered it into a deadly weapon. For Marxists, it became the revolver for shooting dissidents and opponents."[15]

The other school that, according to Jacoby, emerged from the ruins of the war, was Western Marxism. Jacoby includes Lukács, Karl Korsch, Antonio Gramsci, Rosa Luxemburg, Paul Levi, and the Dutch Marxists Pannekoek, Hermann Gorter, and Henriette Roland-Holst among the early Western Marxists. What unites them, on Jacoby's view, is an appreciation of the role of the "subjective" side in the revolutionary process and in the building of socialism. They reject the scientistic view of the historical processes as an objective and law-governed affair. And they reject the bureaucratically distorted and repressive socialism of the orthodox Soviet model in favor of a democratic socialism of workers' councils.

Jacoby sees Western Marxism as philosophically based on the retrieval of the Hegelian dimension of Marxism, which was largely lost in the Marxism of the Second International. He says that "unorthodox Marxism is unthinkable without Hegel."[16] To be sure, the orthodox Marxist-Leninism of the Soviet model also grew out of a reappraisal of the importance of Hegel for Marxism. But, Jacoby argues, whereas Western Marxism has its roots in the Hegel of "history, subjectivity, and consciousness," the Hegel of *The Phenomenology of Mind*, Marxist-Leninism has its roots in the scientific Hegel of the *Science of Logic*.[17] In this way, Jacoby connects the political opposition between the Soviet model and the council socialists with the opposition between scientistic and anti-scientistic currents in philosophy.

Attempts to identify Western Marxism as a philosophically and politically interconnected tendency within twentieth-century Marxism are found in a number of other works. For example, Arato and Breines include the council socialists—Luxemburg, Pannekoek, and Max Adler—alongside Lukács as progenitors of Western Marxism, and Stephen Bonner argues that at bottom Rosa Luxemburg belongs with Western Marxism, understood both as a political alternative to the Soviet model and as a philosophical alternative to scientism.[18]

From a purely historical point of view, there are serious difficulties with any such attempt to identify Western Marxism as an integrated political and philosophical tendency. While it is true that Pannekoek and Adler were sympathetic to council socialism as an alternative to the Soviet model, it is also true, as was seen in Part I, that each was an enthusiastic champion of "scientific" Marxism—Pannekoek as a Machian positivist and Adler as a Neo-Kantian. Luxemburg is equally difficult to force into the mold of this understanding of Western Marxism. Setting aside the continuing debate over her political position, there remain serious difficulties concerning the classification of her philosophical views. Like nearly all of the leading Marxists of the Second International, Luxemburg seems firmly committed to the understanding of Marxism as offering an objective social science. Indeed, with her defense of the breakdown thesis, and her frequent references to the "inevitability" of socialism, she appears as almost an archetypal "scientific" Marxist.

Other Marxists of the postwar period provide classificatory difficulties as well. Within the Soviet Union it was the Machist Aleksandr Bogdanov who led the Worker's Truth opposition to the anti-democratic and bureaucratic tendencies within the Soviet Communist Party during 1920 and 1921.[19] And in the late 1920s, it was the "scientistic" Nikolai Bukharin who led the opposition to enforced collectivization of the Soviet peasantry. More recently, council socialism has found support from Lucio Colletti, one of the most profound critics of the Hegelian currents within Western Marxism.[20]

These examples indicate the difficulty faced by any attempt to identify Western Marxism as a coherent political and philosophical tendency in opposition to the Soviet model and to Marxist-Leninist philosophy. From a purely historical point of view, political orientations do not align with philosophical orientations. This suggests that political positions do not flow from philosophical positions and that, consequently, it is a mistake to attempt to blame philosophical viewpoints for political policies. Of course it is possible that actual historical agents were inconsistent. It might be that certain political policies do flow from a certain philosophical position, but that the men and women who held the philosophical standpoint did not see this. This is possible. But some argument is needed to show that this is so. The case for the totalitarian political implications of positivism in philosophy cannot be made by an inductive historical argument. What is needed is some account of the inherent rational connection between positions in philosophy and political orientations.

The claim for an inherent connection can take several different forms. In the *Dialectic of the Enlightenment* the central connection appears in the identification of the scientific domination of nature with political domination of people. There are a number of difficulties with this attempt to show a connection. In the first place, it is disputable whether domination plays an essential role in the positivist conception of science. If we understand positivist science as aimed at the formulation of general laws that allow us to explain and predict, such a science can, in some cases, serve human efforts to control nature and, in this sense, to dominate it. But power over nature is not necessary for positivist science. To see this, it is enough to consider that for positivism one of the paradigm examples of mature science is astronomy. But astronomy does not give us any power or dominance over the heavenly bodies.

Further, even in those cases in which a positivistic science does give humans power to dominate nature, there is a fundamental difference between this kind of domination and political domination. Political domination involves coercive control, which forces people to act contrary to their own wants and desires. Scientific domination involves no such coercion. This argument in the *Dialectic* rests on a confusion of causal necessitation and coercive compulsion so well understood in the literature on freedom and determinism.

In reply, it might be argued that no such confusion is at work in the *Dialectic*. What the *Dialectic* discloses is the pervasive manipulation of public opinion through advertising, propaganda, and the like. Within the modern world, domination is not primarily a matter of coercive political control. Instead, scientific domination is achieved through such manipulation of the souls of human beings.

Supposing that there is some truth to this understanding of modern culture, there remains a big difference between such manipulation of public opinion and the political coercion of prison camps and firing squads. The argument in the

Dialectic blurs this distinction. One cannot claim, as the *Dialectic* appears to do, that fascist violence is the logical outcome of scientism or that, as Jacoby put it in the passage quoted above, scientism "became the revolver for shooting dissidents and opponents."

Finally, even where science does make possible a scientific domination of nature, the decision to employ the scientific knowledge for purposes of domination is external to the science itself. For instance, some people do not spray their dandelions. It may be that scientific advances have produced technological advances which have been utilized for purposes of political domination, but this use of the technology depends upon choices external to the science itself.

A second argument, running throughout the *Dialectic*, concerns a denial of individuality that Horkheimer and Adorno see as connecting positivist science and totalitarian politics. In the positivist vision, science aims at the discovery of universal laws applicable to all phenomena of a certain kind. Science is interested in the individual only as an instance of the kind. In the same way, it is argued, modern totalitarianism views human beings only as instances of kinds: as workers, peasants, Germans, or Jews. This reduction of the individual to a representative of the kind is a dehumanization that both serves the purposes of the state and impoverishes the spiritual life of human beings. Horkheimer and Adorno suggest that this dehumanization is an outcome of positivist social science.

I do not think this argument succeeds any better than the previous one. While it is true that science considers the individual only as an instance of the kind, this is in no sense a denial of the individual. Physics neither denies that some flowers are yellow and others red nor tries to force flowers to give up their coloration. Subsumption of the individual under the kind is not suppression of the individual. No one's individuality is repressed because the law grants freedom of assembly to all citizens.

An alternative attempt to connect positivism and totalitarianism turns on the supposed positivist reduction of politics to technique. Some of the early positivists, such as St. Simon and Comte, appeared to think that all political questions ultimately could be reduced to technical questions of the most efficient social organization. Such a reduction presupposes the development of a social science strong enough to give knowledge of the consequences of various political decisions. Given such social science, questions of policy would admit of scientific solution. Critical theorists have seen in this vision of a scientific politics the totalitarian outcome of positivism in philosophy. For, on this view, to reduce politics to technique is to hand over total political control to a technocratic elite. Scientism in politics is fundamentally undemocratic.

This formulation of the connection between positivism and totalitarianism is open to a number of objections. One problem concerns the nature of the ends that are to guide political action. While neither St. Simon nor Comte is clear on this point, later positivists stressed the clear distinction between descriptive and normative judgments. Insofar as science concerns itself only with descriptive judgments, it cannot by itself give us any ends. Further, even given some end, politics cannot be reduced to a technical question of efficiency in the attainment of that end, since there may be moral constraints on what means are acceptable or on the imposition of costs in the attainment of the end. Far from advocating a reduction of politics to science, positivism, in denying that these normative issues can be scientifically resolved, denies the possibility of such a reduction. The historical link in St. Simon and Comte between positivist philosophy of science and scientism in politics does not represent any essential connection of clear ideas but arises only on the basis of a fundamental lack of philosophical clarity.

Yet another attempt to show an essential connection between positivist philosophy of science and totalitarianism is made by Terence Ball, who claims that there is a "conceptual connection between positivist metascience and positivist programs for social reorganization," and that "there is a logical link between positivist metascience and the political program of such prominent positivists as Saint-Simon and Comte."[21] Ball's case for the supposed connection between positivism and totalitarianism thus assumes, contrary to fact, that the vision of a scientism of politics found in Saint-Simon and Comte is shared by all positivists (or that they are inconsistent in not sharing it). In fact, as I claimed above, the dominant view among positivists is to deny the very possibility of such a scientism of politics. But perhaps these other positivists are mistaken. What is the "logical link" Ball finds here? Ball answers the follows:

> More specifically, the connection between metascientific ideals and political program can be traced to the obvious affinity between nomological explanation and expert manipulation: Those armed with the necessary nomological knowledge are presumably in a position (as others are not) to produce or prevent specific sorts of social and political outcomes. Politically speaking, then, positivism's second pertinent feature is its notion of "scientific politics," understood as rational administration by experts.[22]

Ball goes on to blame positivism for its distrust of democracy and critical thinking. Here the "logical link" becomes the "obvious affinity" between nomological explanation and expert manipulation. But, as I argued before, this "affinity" does not involve any logical connection. Knowledge of nomological explanatory theory is not sufficient for expert manipulation, as the case of astronomy shows. Nor is it necessary. The expert craftsman need not have theoretical knowledge. More important, for consideration of politics, is the missing role of both ends and moral constraints in Ball's discussion. Ball presumably thinks they are missing because positivism excludes them. But the positivist exclusion of values from science is not an exclusion of values from politics. Positivist science can only make judgments concerning the consequences of alternative policies. The determination of ends and moral constraints, which is necessary for human action in general and for political action in particular, lies outside science. There is no contradiction in holding a "positivist" theory of science and at the same time advocating a democratic process for determining both the ends of and the constraints on political action. This was the position of Kautsky, Adler, Liebknecht, Luxemburg, and Pannekoek, and as far as I can see, Ball has shown no inconsistency in their position. His interpretation of positivism involves attributing to it a reduction of politics to science that is in fact inconsistent with its insistence on the distinction between facts and values. The "logical link" is one of inconsistency.

There remains one further argument attempting to link philosophy of science and politics that I want to mention because of its widespread appearance in critical theory and in some Leninist criticisms of positivism. This is the argument that because positivism, and indeed all versions of empiricism, take the observation of facts as epistemologically foundational, this produces an uncritical attitude toward facts that appears in politics as an uncritical acceptance of the factually given status quo. This argument has roots in Lukács.[23] It is connected with the claim that empiricism in philosophy is condemned to false consciousness because it cannot get behind the surface of appearances in order to grasp the essential truth hidden there. Politically, the argument claims that this false consciousness appears as the taking for granted of existing social and political arrangements as facts that cannot be questioned.

I have already criticized the claim that empiricism cannot draw the appearance/essence distinction. Here I will simply add that the political version of the argument appears to rest on an additional confusion of the epistemological and political ways of taking the facts as givens. The medical theory of a disease may take its contagiousness as a factual given in the epistemic sense without thereby committing itself against the possibility of developing a vaccine to combat the disease. To recognize that I am in fact dominated by a capitalist master is not to accept that domination. Kolakowski rightly comments on this argument as follows: "This strange paralogism, equating the observance of empirical and logical rules with fidelity to the *status quo* and rejection of all change, recurs again and again in the writings of the Frankfurt school."[24]

ON THE INDEPENDENCE OF POLITICS

Positivists, Leninists, and humanists have each tried to link their opponents' positions in the philosophy of science with political orientations. In this chapter I have examined a number of the attempts to do this. I have tried to argue that none of the arguments advanced succeeds in showing any such connection. Whatever historical connections there may have been between various schools in the philosophy of science and various political orientations, I do not see that there is any logical connection. There are several reasons for this. For one thing, I believe that the fact/value distinction is philosophically sound, and hence no political program could follow from scientific theory alone. This is not to say that science is politically neutral. Indeed, it seems to me that the scientific theory of capitalism is of great importance in resolving the political questions of our times, since it suggests grounds for thinking that revolutionary change in the relations of production is necessary for human security, peace, dignity, and prosperity. What also makes attempts to argue from philosophy of science to politics misguided is the distinction between science and philosophy of science. One cannot pass from philosophy of science to judgments about the content of science. And, since social science is relevant to public policy, this provides another reason for thinking that attempts to link philosophical views with political policies are doomed to failure. I believe that much of twentieth-century Marxism is misguided in this way. There is no methodological key to politics or science.

NOTES

1. "The professors treated Hegel as a 'dead dog', and while themselves preaching idealism, only an idealism a thousand times more petty and banal than Hegel's, contemptuously shrugged their shoulders at dialectics—and the revisionists floundered after them into the swamp of philosophical vulgarization of science, replacing 'artful' (and revolutionary) dialectics by 'simple' (and tranquil) evolution." Lenin, *Marxism and Revisionism* (1908), quoted in Lenin, *Against Revisionism*, edited by F. V. Konstantinov and G. D. Obichikin (Moscow: Progress, 1976), p. 112.

2. Ibid., pp. 239, 244.

3. E.g., Matthäus Klein et al., eds., *Zur Geschichte der Marxistisch-Leninistischen Philosophie in Deutschland*, vol. 1.2 (Berlin: Dietz Verlag, 1969), pp. 324, 340–341.

4. Lenin, *"Left Wing" Communism—An Infantile Disorder* (Moscow: Foreign Languages Publishers, 1961).

5. Recall here Engels' allowance of the possibility of "evolutionary leaps" (*Anti-Dühring* [Peking: Foreign Language Press, 1976], p. 83). Rilki, *Der Revisionismus* (Zurich: Girsberger, 1936), p. 43 n. 3, goes so far as to suggest that for Marx, all dialectical leaps involve intervening evolutionary processes.

6. Popper, *The Poverty of Historicism*, (New York: Harper, 1964), p. 70.

7. Ibid., p. 69.

8. Alec Nove, *The Economics of Feasible Socialism* (London: George Allen and Unwin, 1983), p. 232, makes this sort of point as a criticism of Popper.

9. Popper, *Poverty of Historicism*, p. 69.

10. Richard Miller, *Analyzing Marx* (Princeton: Princeton University Press, 1984), p. 305.

11. Ibid., pp. 114–126.

12. Max Horkheimer and Theodor Adorno, *The Dialectic of the Enlightenment* (New York: Continuum, 1972).

13. Such a view runs through much of the work of the Frankfurt School critical theorists. More recently, in *The Social and Political Thought of Karl Marx* (Cambridge: Cambridge University Press, 1971), Schlomo Avineri has tried to trace the "cruelty and harshness of Bolshevism" (p. 65) back to Engels' positivistic misunderstanding of Marx. For a particularly clear formulation of this view, see Terence Ball, "Marxian Science and Positivist Politics," in *After Marx*, edited by Terence Ball and James Farr (Cambridge: Cambridge University Press, 1984).

14. Russell Jacoby, *Dialectic of Defeat: Contours of Western Marxism* (Cambridge: Cambridge University Press, 1981), p. 7.

15. Ibid., p. 20.

16. Ibid., p. 37.

17. Ibid., p. 38.

18. Andrew Arato and Paul Breines, *The Young Lukács and the Origins of Western Marxism* (New York: Seabury, 1971), pp. 215–216; Stephen Bronner, *Rosa Luxemburg: A Revolutionary for Our Times* (New York: Columbia University Press, 1987), pp. 97–98.

19. Ruth Fischer, *Stalin and German Communism* (Cambridge, MA: Harvard University Press, 1948), p. 251.

20. Lucio Colletti, "A Political and Philosophical Interview," *New Left Review* 86 (July–August 1971): 6–7.

21. Ball, "Marxian Science," pp. 239.

22. Ibid., p. 240.

23. Lukács, *History and Class Consciousness* (Cambridge, MA: MIT Press, 1971), p. 7.

24. Kolakowski, *Main Currents of Marxism* (Oxford: Oxford University Press, 1978), vol. 3, p. 377.

Part III

Conclusions

9

Analytical Marxism and the History of Marxist Philosophy

In Part I of this study, I argued that the shared core of the various Marxisms of the Second International was the conception that what was valuable in Marxism was social science largely independent of philosophy. Theoreticians of the time sought to rescue Marxism from the attacks of Neo-Kantians and positivists by separating the social scientific content of the theory of capitalism and the theory of historical materialism from confusion with the philosophical ontology of materialism, and by freeing this social scientific content from its apparent reliance upon Hegelian dialectics. While Bernsteinian revisionists might differ with their "orthodox" opponents as to the extent to which this Marxist social science remained tenable, this difference did not flow from any deep philosophical differences as to the nature of social science but, rather, from conflicting viewpoints concerning the adequacy of this science. If Eduard Bernstein appealed to Kant against what he saw as no longer tenable dogma within Marxist thought, other Neo-Kantian Marxists, such as Max Adler and Karl Liebknecht, defended this Marxist "dogma" as good social science. Karl Kautsky's judgment concerning the compatibility of Marxist social science with materialism, positivism, or Neo-Kantianism reflected this shared ground of the theoretical debates of his time.

By the middle of the twentieth century, this understanding of Marxism as "scientific socialism" was defended only by Marxist-Leninists, and only on the basis of a radical change in the understanding of the nature of science and its relationship to philosophy. Outside the socialist world, within "Western Marxism," the understanding of Marxism as "scientific socialism" was nearly universally rejected as a "vulgar Marxism" resting upon a philosophically naive conception of the nature of social theory. In his *Philosophy and Myth in Karl Marx*, Robert Tucker noted this change in the Western view of Marx:

> It seems fair to say that a change in the generally accepted view of Marx has been taking place in the twentieth century. In the new image he appears not as the scientist of society that he claimed to be but rather as a moralist or a religious kind of thinker. The old assumption that "scientific socialism" is a scientific system of thought has tended more and more to give way to the notion that it is in essence a moralistic or religious system.[1]

Tucker's work presented an interpretation of Marxism as fundamentally a religious moralism along the lines earlier developed by Edmund Wilson, Max Eastman, and J. L. Talmon. On this view, the Marxist faith in the coming of socialist salvation rested upon the scientifically unfounded Hegelian teleology of history. In Chapters 4 and 5, I offered some criticisms of the adequacy of this Hegelian interpretation of Marx. Here I want to call attention to the broader theme of the rejection of scientific socialism within Western Marxism.

Tucker's book first appeared in 1961, and the passage quoted appears without alteration as late as 1977.[2] Since that time, there has been a significant revival of interest in "scientific socialism" within English-language philosophy. Gerald Cohen's 1978 work on Marx's theory of history is often mentioned as the opening salvo in the campaign to restore scientific Marxism.[3] In the years since the publication of this work, a number of other works have appeared that have been grouped with Cohen's under the banner of "analytic Marxism." One of the themes that ties these various works together is an interest in the social scientific aspects of Marx's work. Collectively these works have succeeded in casting some doubt on the continuing validity of Tucker's relegation of scientific socialism to the dustbin of history.

ANALYTICAL MARXISM

Identification of analytical Marxism as a tendency in contemporary Marxist thought is relatively unproblematic in terms of constructing a list of thinkers who are taken as representative of that tendency. Gerald A. Cohen, John Roemer, and Jon Elster are perhaps the central figures. Others who have been mentioned as important figures within analytic Marxism include Allen Wood, Norman Geras, Phillipe van Parijs, Adam Prezeworski, Robert Brenner, Pranab Bardhan, and Erik Olin Wright.[4] There is considerably less agreement as to what ideational content identifies this body of work as a distinctive tendency in contemporary Marxist thought.

In his Introduction to *Analytical Marxism*, John Roemer offers some suggestions for identifying analytical Marxism as a school of thought. He tells us that this species of social theory is a Marxism which is "analytically sophisticated."

It is "inspired by Marxian questions" but employs the "contemporary tools of logic, mathematics and model building" that have been developed outside the Marxian tradition. The analytical sophistication of this tendency consists in this application of "state-of-the-art methods of analytical philosophy and 'positivist' social science" to the questions inspired by Marxism. Roemer contrasts analytical Marxism with "conventional Marxism" in three ways. First, analytical Marxism accepts the necessity of abstraction from the actual historical process, which has been shunned by conventional Marxism. Second, it raises foundational questions that have not been raised by conventional Marxism. And third, it is said to be undogmatic and uninterested in exegetical questions, in contrast with the dogmatic and exegetical approach of conventional Marxism.[5]

In the discussions of analytical Marxism, considerable importance has been attached to certain methodological principles and tools of analysis imported from "positivist" (as Roemer put it) social science. Roemer himself mentions the importance of methodological individualism as a methodological "postulate" of analytical Marxism, and the rational choice models of "general equilibrium theory, game theory, and the arsenal of modelling techniques developed by neoclassical economics" as the "tools *par excellence*" of Marxist analysis of capitalism.[6]

The commitment to methodological individualism and the view of rational choice models as privileged tools of analysis are interconnected. Methodological individualism is a principle of method that grows out of an ontological perspective. The ontological perspective is indicated in this passage from Jon Elster: "But capital is not a collective actor with eyes that see and hands that move. On the assumption of methodological individualism capital is only shorthand for the many individual capitalists."[7] The methodological principle is formulated by Elster in this way: "All social phenomena—their structure and their change—are in principle explicable in ways that only involve individuals—their properties, their goals, their beliefs and their actions."[8] If collective agents such as "capital," "society," and "the bourgeoisie" are ontological fictions, if these terms are at best shorthand ways of referring to sets of individuals, then, it seems, the actions attributed to such agents must be ultimately explicable by the actions of individuals. The various rational choice models provide the means for developing such accounts. They provide a way of understanding social outcomes as products of individual goals, beliefs, and behaviors.

In the work of both Elster and Roemer, the commitment to methodological individualism is also connected with a rejection of what is seen, in a pejorative sense, as a speculative theory of history running throughout the work of Marx and conventional Marxism. In their view, Marx became convinced, on grounds of the Hegelian speculative philosophy of history, that the socialist society of the future was the inevitable end toward which the historical process was directed. From this teleological perspective, Marx attempted to explain particular stages of that historical process in terms of the functional role those stages played in the passage toward socialism. And, given the functional necessity of each stage,

Marx applied this teleological and functional approach to the analysis of aspects found within each stage. Thus, for example, Elster sees Marx as attempting to explain hostility between English and Irish workers, within modern capitalism, in terns of the usefulness of this antagonism to capital in its struggle with the proletariat.[9]

Elster and Roemer reject the supposition that socialism is the end at which the historical process aims as an unwarranted intrusion of speculative philosophy into social science. But, without this teleological foundation, the attempted functional explanations are radically defective. For there is no reason to suppose that the functional usefulness of *x* to *y* explains the occurrence of *x* in the absence of some teleological guarantee of *y*. Thus, conventional Marxism's attempted explanation of change in relations of production, in terms of the conduciveness of such change to utilization of increased forces of production, fails. Without the speculative guarantee of historical progress, Elster points out, even if such beneficial change does take place, we have no reason to suppose that its beneficial consequences explain why the change took place.[10] In a similar way, Roemer argues that conventional Marxist attempts to explain sexism and racism in terms of their functional usefulness to bourgeois rule not only fail for lack of an account of how this usefulness is connected to the continued existence of racism and sexism, but also ignore powerful arguments to the effect that profit-maximizing capitalists would act in ways that would result in the elimination of discriminatory wage differentials.[11]

In place of this speculative theory of history and the functional mode of explanation dependent upon it, the analytical Marxists recommended the application of the rational choice models of neoclassical economics and game theory. Such models attempt to explain social outcomes as products of individual behavior. Analytical Marxists think this approach to social theory is exemplified in the Marxism of Marx. In his theory of capitalism, Marx tried to show how certain unintended social consequences, such as concentration and centralization of capital, polarization of the classes, decline in the rate of profit, increasing unemployment, and a tendency to more frequent and deepening crises, were produced by the rational behavior of individual capitalists within the framework of institutions making up the capitalist mode of production.

This approach is independent of the speculative theory of history and of functional explanation. Though they want to replace the labor theory of value with other, neoclassical foundations, analytic Marxists see Marx's theory of capitalism as paradigmatic for further Marxist social theory.[12] An analytical Marxist research program would include attempts to apply rational choice models to problems of collective class action. It would also include game theoretic approaches to collective bargaining between workers and capitalists, as well as attempts to provide accounts of phenomena, such as racism and sexism, that appear to be *prima facie* difficulties for rational choice models of social behavior. In short, analytical Marxism seeks to apply the kind of rational choice analysis of social systems pioneered by Marx to questions and problems that have emerged out of the Marxist tradition.

ANALYTICAL MARXISM AND THE MARXISM OF THE SECOND INTERNATIONAL

In a number of respects, analytical Marxism bears some resemblance to the Marxism of the Second International. Like Bernstein, Elster and Roemer claim to be inspired by Marx. But, also like Bernstein, they are highly critical of Marx and end up throwing out much of what has been thought to be central to Marxism. Like many of the Marxists of the Second International, analytical Marxists are critical of Hegelian ideas at work in Marx's thought, seeing Hegelian dialectics as speculative metaphysics at its worst. Like the Marxists of the Second International, the analytical Marxists are keen on borrowing the latest ideas from bourgeois science and philosophy. Like the Marxists of the Second International, they conceive of historical materialism and the theory of capitalism as social science. And, like the Marxists of the Second International, they conceive of science in the manner in which it is conceived in the academic philosophy of science around them. Like the Marxism of the Second International, analytical Marxism has roots in the academic world outside the socialist movement. Its philosophical orientation is derived from academic philosophy. As with the Marxism of the Second International, the attempt to trim Marxism to fit the requirements of the surrounding philosophical environment has led to a certain blurring of the distinction between Marxism and left liberalism. And, as with the Marxism of the Second International, problems of ethics and the need for a moral validation of socialism have come to play a central role in the development of the analytical Marxism.[13] For the analytical Marxists, Marxism is trimmed to fit the preconceptions of this surrounding philosophy. For them, the defense of Marxism involves a frank revision of fundamental aspects of Marxism as it is conventionally understood.

In his Introduction to *Analytical Marxism*, John Roemer has this to say about the origins of analytical Marxism:

> What produced this search for foundations, which led to asking these perhaps heretical questions, and using state-of-the-art methods of analytical philosophy and "positivist" social science to study them? I think two phenomena of our era are responsible: the chequered success of socialism and the dubious failure of capitalism. These two events are unquestionably *the* serious challenges to Marxism, as it was inherited from the nineteenth century. One response is to retreat to a Talmudic defence of the Word, and to find an interpretation which conforms with history as it has come to pass. Another is to deny what appear to be the historical facts. A third response is to reject Marxism as fundamentally wrong. The fourth response is to recognize that Marxism is nineteenth-century social science. As such it is bound to be primitive by modern standards, wrong in detail, and perhaps even in some basic claims. Yet its power in explaining certain historical periods and events seems so strong that one feels there must be a valid core,

which needs to be clarified and elucidated. . . . This is the intellectual foundation of the trend I am calling analytical Marxism.[14]

Except for the reference to "the chequered success of socialism" this passage could easily have been written by Bernstein. The intellectual project is the same: squarely to face the facts, in particular "the dubious failure of capitalism"; to throw away what is wrongheaded in Marxism; and, utilizing the best tools of more recent science, to build upon the valid core of Marxism that remains.

It is not surprising that some Marxists should feel a little uneasy in considering this project. Like some of Bernstein's critics, Michael Lebowitz worries about the blurring of the distinction between Marxism and left liberalism.[15] And, perhaps with an eye on the unhappy influence of *Kathedersozialismus* on German Social Democracy, Anderson and Thompson worry about the academic roots of analytical Marxism.[16] A critical perception of the resemblance between analytical Marxism and certain currents within the Second International is neatly expressed in a review of *Analytical Marxism* by Ronald Kieve:

This is not so much an attempt to update Marx's supposedly hopelessly antiquated theories and method, as an effort to eviscerate the revolutionary kernel of Marxism and transform it into a safe—and useless—academic exercise. The only thing that the general editors and the various authors in the series have succeeded in modernizing has been the work of Eduard Bernstein, whose effort in the late nineteenth century to turn revolutionary Marxism into counterrevolutionary reformism sparked Rosa Luxemburg's devastating response *Reform or Revolution*. The author's lack of a historical understanding of social theory has condemned Marxists to refight the theoretical battles of a century ago.[17]

This comment suggests an argument against analytical Marxism along the following lines. The position taken by analytical Marxism is the position taken by Bernstein. Bernstein's position was refuted by Luxemburg and others. Therefore analytical Marxism stands refuted. While I believe there is fundamental agreement in the basic intellectual projects of Bernstein and analytical Marxism, I think the proposed refutation of analytical Marxism fails. In the first place, the common intellectual project admits of several different possible realizations. It is not clear that Bernstein and the analytical Marxists agree about what lies within the valid core of Marxism and what does not. It does not seem to me that there is any clear alignment between contemporary analytic Marxists and Bernstein in this regard. Nor is it at all clear that analytical Marxists need align themselves politically with Bernstein.

The central point of Luxemburg's attack on Bernstein is that socialism cannot emerge from capitalism by a series of reforms but requires a revolutionary seizure of power by the working class and a revolutionary transformation of the social order. In particular, she rejects the idea of a gradual replacement of capitalist enterprises by producers' cooperatives. As we have seen, this was an idea championed by the Neo-Kantian socialist, and by Ferdinand Lassalle, that Bernstein appeared in places to endorse.

Underlying Luxemburg's attack on this view is a dialectical outlook. Thus, Luxemburg speaks of the need to understand things dialectically, talks about contradictions, appeals to the law of quantity and quality, and appeals to dialectics to prove the inevitability of socialism.[18] Clearly in Luxemburg's thought, Bernstein's politics is connected to his lack of a dialectical understanding. This suggests an alternative argument against analytical Marxism drawn from an awareness of its historical similarities with Bernsteinian revisionism. Like Bernstein, the analytical Marxists exclude dialectics from the valid core of Marxism. Accordingly, they are doomed to repeat the political errors that, as Rosa Luxemburg demonstrated, flow from a nondialectical standpoint.

While analytical Marxists do agree with Bernstein in throwing Hegel overboard, it is not clear how important this agreement is. For, as was seen in Part I of this study, not all who agreed with Bernstein in rejecting Hegelian dialectics also agreed with his reformist politics.[19] And, if the argument of Part II of this study is correct, there is no logical connection between the reformist politics of Bernstein and his rejection of dialectics. Indeed, Luxemburg's attack on Bernstein's position can be understood independently of her professed dialectics. For example, in attacking the producers' cooperative model, she argues that within the framework of competitive markets, producers' cooperatives will be forced to act just as capitalist firms would act if they are to survive. Here, as in her major work, *The Accumulation of Capital*, Luxemburg utilizes precisely the tool of rational choice analysis championed by the analytical Marxists.[20]

The point of these remarks is not to suggest that there is any contradiction in both criticizing analytical Marxism and utilizing the tools of analysis it recommends. There may be important differences in the understanding of the legitimate role and limit of such forms of analysis. The point here is that analytical Marxism need not embrace Bernsteinian politics and that, consequently, one cannot argue from the failure of those politics to the theoretical deficiency of analytical Marxism. A successful critique of analytical Marxism must build upon specific criticisms of the theoretical analysis and political program advanced by it.

CRITICISMS OF ANALYTICAL MARXISM

A number of such specific criticisms have been advanced. In his article "Is 'Analytical Marxism' Marxism?" Michael Lebowitz has argued that analytical Marxism not only is not Marxism but "indeed, it is in essence *anti*-Marxist."[21] He begins his argument by pointing to an assumption which, he believes, it appears that analytical Marxism shares with neoclassical economics. This is the assumption that theory begins with "the atomistic individual conceived as ontologically prior to the whole, the particular society."[22] Lebowitz contrasts this assumption with the Marxist "organic" viewpoint according to which "parts have no prior independent existence as parts" and private interests are always "socially determined interests" that can be satisfied only within a social setting.

Lebowitz maintains that "there is absolutely no compatibility between the atomistic approach of neoclassical economics and Marxism."[23]

Though Lebowitz excludes the atomistic analysis of neoclassical economics, he does allow for the use, within Marxist theory, of rational choice models such as those studied in game theory. What distinguishes acceptable from unacceptable uses of such models is whether they deal with "collective" or "individual" games. For Marxism, classes, not individuals, are of fundamental significance. Game theoretic approaches to the conflict between capitalists and wage laborers are acceptable. In such a game the actors are classes or representatives of classes. The analysis of such games builds on a foundation of structural analysis that identifies distinct social classes, and understands the central class conflict between labor and capital as the starting point for a genuine understanding of capitalism. The individualist use of rational choice models ignores these historically determinate social structures within which agents act. For the collective game, and for the Marxist, *"epistemological priority is assigned to the determination of the structure within which individuals act."*[24]

But, Lebowitz argues, analytical Marxism, contrary to Marxism, insists upon the explanatory priority of the individual level. "At the core of analytical Marxism is the categorical imperative: *there shalt be no explanation at a level above that of the individual unit.*"[25] Both Elster and Roemer have committed themselves to the principle of methodological individualism. In Elster's formulation, that principle says, "All social phenomena—their structure and their change—are in principle explicable in ways that only involve individuals—their properties, their goals, their beliefs and their actions."[26] Elster points to passages in which Marx appears flatly to reject methodological individualism. In this reading of Marx, Lebowitz is in agreement with Elster. It is at this point, Lebowitz argues, that analytical Marxism exposes itself as fundamentally opposed to a genuinely Marxist outlook.

This critique of analytic Marxism has both an onntological and a methodological dimension. At the ontological level, Lebowitz contrasts the atomistic ontology of neoclassical economics with the organic holism of Marxism. At the methodological level, the contrast is put in terms of whether individual acts or social structures have epistemological priority. These two levels are connected, for both Lebowitz and certain analytical Marxists, in the thesis of methodological individualism that is understood both as an ontological opposition to collective subjects and as an insistence on the reduction of all explanations to explanations in terms of properties of individuals. In considering Lebowitz's critique of analytical Marxism, I will deal first with the ontological dimension and then turn to the methodological aspects.

Ontological Individualism

The view that Marx held an organic, holistic ontology is widely current. It is often thought that this ontological perspective is part of his Hegelian heritage.

In the philosophy of Hegel this holism appears in the speculative philosophy of the Absolute according to which each particular individual and aspect of existence is comprehended as but a moment in the process of Thought coming to self-consciousness of itself. It is clear to all that Marx rejected this speculative ontology of Absolute Spirit.

What has not been so widely appreciated is that Marx's critique of this speculative philosophy appears to involve a critique of other forms of organic holism. Thus, as was seen in Chapter 5, in his critique of Hegel, Marx rejects the theory of internal relations often thought to underlie his organic holistic ontology. Further, in the attack on the Left Hegelians, in *The German Ideology*, Marx and Engels appear to commit themselves to an individualist ontology. Thus, they say that "the premises from which we begin" are "real individuals."[27] They criticize Stirner's claim "that each is all that he is through the State" as "fundamentally the same as the statement the bourgeois is only a specimen of the bourgeois species; a statement which presupposes that the *class* of bourgeois existed before the individuals constituting it."[28] Here Marx and Engels seem to ridicule the collectivist ontology attributed to them by Lebowitz. Elsewhere in the *German Ideology* they criticize the non-individualistic conception of society: "Society, the 'totality of existence,' is conceived by our author not as the interaction of the constituent 'individual existences,' but as a separate existence which undergoes another and separate interaction with these 'individual existences.' "[29]

Lebowitz does not mention these passages in which Marx and Engels appear to embrace the individualism he denies them. Elster does mention Marx's "intermittent" commitment to methodological individualism in the *German Ideology*, but appears to believe that the mature Marx returned to the Hegelian framework he had earlier rejected.[30] Both Elster and Lebowitz appeal to passages from the *Grundrisse* in which capital is personified in various ways and in which Marx argues that competition among individual capitals merely "expresses" or "executes" the inner laws of capital as conclusive evidence for Marx's rejection of methodological individualism.[31] But the anti-individualistic import of these passages is far from clear, and in a criticism of Jean Baptiste Say published after the *Grundrisse*, Marx repeats the kind of criticism cited by Elster as evidence of this intermittent individualism.[32]

In each of the passages cited by Lebowitz and Elster, Marx is arguing against attempts to construct a theory of relative prices on the basis of the notion of competition alone. His point is that we need some explanation of why competitive markets stabilize around the relative prices that they do. For this, he argues, one needs the labor theory of value. Relative prices are determined, indirectly of course, by labor values. Competitive markets merely enforce these relative prices. Just what else is going on in these passages is not altogether clear. But it is far from clear that they should be read as assertions of a nonindividualist ontology. In the first of the *Grundrisse* passages cited by Lebowitz, Marx goes on to say that "capital exists and can only exist as many capitals, and its self-determination therefore appears as their reciprocal interaction with one another,'' which seems to conflict with the nonindividualist ontology Lebowitz claims to find there.[33] Neither the appeal to the inner laws of capital that are expressed in competition nor the personification of capital commits Marx to a nonindividualist ontology.[34]

There is a passage in the *Grundrisse* that says, ''Society does not consist of individuals, but expresses the sum of interrelations, the relations within which these individuals stand.''[35] It is possible to read this as a rejection of an atomistic ontology in favor of an organic holism. But what is this whole? Is it society? This appears to be the viewpoint adopted by Lebowitz. He says, ''Marx's starting point . . . is to develop an understanding of society as a 'connected whole'.''[36] But this seems to contradict the individualism found in Marx's critique of Hegel and the Left Hegelians. And it seems to contradict the criticism of Say voiced by Marx both in the later published version, the *Contribution to the Critique of Political Economy*, and in the draft version of this same material in the *Grundrisse*: ''To regard society as one single subject is, in addition, to look at it wrongly; speculatively.''[37] Here Marx refers back to the earlier philosophical critique of the speculative philosophy of Hegel and the Left Hegelians without apparent revision of his earlier views.

I believe it is possible to understand Marx's comment on society, individuals, and relations without recourse to a nonindividualistic ontology. The real subjects remain human individuals, just as in the *Critique of Hegel's Philosophy of Right*. Society has no ontological standing. It is abstract; individuals are concrete. But these individuals do stand in definite relations to one another. Society is an abstract expression of these definite relations. In this sense, society does not consist of individuals. It does not consist of bare individuals. If the relations between individuals change, society changes. But the individuals remain the same beings. Human beings can alter their social relations. They can change classes. They can revolutionize the social order. But, from the ontological point of view, they remain the same individual human beings. Human beings exist in social relations, but these social relations are not—at least most of them are not—necessary properties for the identity of individuals as the individuals they are.[38] To adopt such a framework is to abandon an ''atomistic'' conception according to which human beings somehow exist prior to their involvement in social relations. But then the individualist need not deny that individuals exist in relations with other individuals. Nor need the individualist deny that individual wants and beliefs are influenced by their relations with others. Even atoms exist in relations with other atoms.

Explanatory Individualism

This ontological framework bears directly on one aspect of the dispute regarding the methodological aspect of methodological individualism. Once we see that an individualist ontology does not preclude interaction and mutual influence between individuals, we see that such an ontology does not prevent neoclassical economics from recognizing that private interests are socially determined. For such interests are not ontologically necessary for the identity of individuals. An individual can pass from one class to another. In so doing his or her (socially determined) interests change, but the same individual remains. So we can not argue, as Lebowitz does, that Marx's recognition of the socially determined nature of individual interests necessarily precludes use of neoclassical models within a Marxist perspective. While it is true that neoclassical economics did, for the most part, simply take individual preferences as givens, there is no reason why the neoclassical economist need deny that preferences are themselves socially determined. Once social determination of preferences, and the importance of this social determination, is granted, it is not obvious that the use of neoclassical models is incompatible with a Marxist perspective. And, of course, the analytical Marxists are quite clear in their recognition of both the fact of the social determination of preferences and the importance of this fact. Roemer, for example, includes this point as one of four ways in which analytical Marxism differs from neoclassical economics, and Elster also discusses the point.[39]

In addition to stressing the social determination of private interests, Lebowitz's critique of analytical Marxism stresses the importance of social structures in Marxist social science. In Lebowitz's view, analytical Marxism, which tries to explain structures by individual properties, should be contrasted with a genuine Marxism in which "*epistemological priority is assigned to the determination of the structure within which individuals act*."[40] In Chapter 3, following the analysis of Daniel Little, I stressed the importance of the analysis of social structures in Marx's theory of capitalism. I am also in agreement with Lebowitz in thinking that this stress on social structures may bring Marxism into conflict with the explanatory individualism of Elster and Roemer. But I do not think this "priority of social structures" has either the foundational significance attributed to it by Lebowitz or the regulative consequences for social theory that he draws from it. I shall return to the question of compatibility of this structural priority with explanatory individualism below. For the moment I want to comment on the foundations of this priority and the regulative implications of it.

In Chapter 3, I discussed the passage from the unpublished "Introduction to the Critique of Political Economy," in which Marx talks about the origins of scientific political economy. There he suggests that a genuinely scientific approach becomes possible only after certain characterizations of the economic process have been attained as a result of abstraction from observation and experience. These abstract characterizations of the economic process serve to define the structures within which individual agents act. Marx says that a genuinely scientific treatment becomes possible only after these structures have been identified, and that such a scientific treatment proceeds by deductive analysis from such abstract structures to the "reproduction" of the concrete facts of experience. What this suggests is that the priority of social structures in Marxist social science is more an explanatory than an epistemic priority. An explanatory theory of capitalism begins with the identification and analysis of the fundamental defining structures of capitalist modes of production, which rests upon a prior foundation of empirical observation and abstraction from that observation.

The theoretical reproduction of the concrete, by way of deductive analysis of the unintended consequences of individual actions within the framework of the basic structures defining the system of capitalism, follows the pattern of successive concretization discussed in Chapter 5.[41] But it is also true that the analysis of the basic structures of capitalism proceeds by way of the method of successive concretization. Thus, in the passage from the unpublished introduction, as examples of the concepts abstracted from experience that become the starting point for scientific analysis, Marx mentions division of labor, money, and value.[42] But each of these is a category that is more general than the category of capitalism. Each applies, for example, to systems of simple commodity production as well as to systems of capitalism. In a similar fashion, Marx's systematic theory of capitalism in *Capital* begins with the analysis of commodities in a fashion that applies equally to capitalism and to systems of simple commodity production. The determinate structures of capitalism are reached only with the discussion in Part II of "The Transformation of Money into Capital." Further, the more abstract discussion of Part I clearly is intended to provide a foundation for the more specific analysis of capitalism that follows it.

These points are significant in assessing the regulative significance of the priority of structures for Marxist social science. At one point Lebowitz criticizes the attempt by Roemer to derive specifically capitalist forms of class exploitation from a more abstract account involving individuals with different holdings acting within competitive markets. Lebowitz appears to think that such an attempt is insufficiently concrete, and he contrasts the attempt with Marx, who, he thinks, "begins from the specification of a particular set of relations of production," which are historical givens.[43] Not only does Lebowitz here fail to provide any substantive objection to the attempt to provide abstract foundations for the analysis of capitalist social structures, he also ignores Part I of *Capital* and Marx's comment that the order of theoretical comprehension does not correspond to the order of historical appearance.[44] So, while it is true that Marx considered the relation between capital and labor to be decisive to the understanding of capitalism, it is clear that he himself saw this specific structural relation as a particular form of more abstract relations, and that the analysis of these more abstract relations, in some sense, constitutes the starting point for Marx's scientific theory of capitalism. There is nothing in Marx's approach which would rule out attempts, like that of Roemer, to provide abstract foundations for the understanding of the specific structural relations of capitalism.

There is yet another point concerning the regulative significance of specifically capitalist social structures that needs to be mentioned here. Recall that Lebowitz allowed for the use of rational choice models in the analysis of the "collective game" played by capital and labor, but that he rejected rational choice models of individual games dealing with intraclass relations. There is no basis for this proscription in Marxism. It is of course true that Marx thought the capital/labor relation was the *differentia specifica* that identified capitalism as a distinct system of commodity production. But there is nothing in that to rule out the use of rational choice models of intraclass relations. Further, Lebowitz's proscription of such use contradicts Marx's own theoretical practice. In the analysis of the tendency for concentration and centralization of capital, in the analysis of the tendency for unemployment to increase, and in the analysis of the tendency for the rate of profit to fall, for example, Marx utilizes individual rational choice models. In each case, the unintended social outcome is traced to the rational decisions of individual capitalists.

In spite of these criticisms, I believe there is an important element of truth in Lebowitz's criticism of certain versions of analytical Marxism. In Chapter 6, I argued that Marx's materialism is a form of emergent materialism which resists the reductionistic physicalism or biologism of natural scientific materialism. In addition, I believe that a Marxist viewpoint would resist any attempt to reduce the social to the psychological. Human action always takes place within an environment of social relations, social roles, and social institutions. This social environment is historically variant. It also influences, as we have seen, the interests and preferences of individuals. Though there may well be some invariant features of human psychology, these are not sufficiently rich to account for the real behavior of human beings. Hence, an adequate account of human behavior must include an analysis of the historically determinant features of the social environment in which the behavior takes place.

This recognition of the importance of the social environment for the account of human behavior appears to contradict Elster's formulation of the explanatory thesis of methodological individualism, which holds that "all social phenomena—their structure and their change—are in principle explicable in ways that only involve individuals—their properties, their goals, their beliefs and their actions."[45] Since an adequate account of human behavior involves not only facts about the psychological states of the individual actors but also facts about the social environment in which they act, it appears that social theory is not reducible to psychology.

The explanatory individualist might attempt to meet this objection by insisting that facts about the social environment must themselves be ultimately reducible to facts about individuals. Social roles, for example, would be reducible to beliefs, aims, values, and expectations of individuals. However, it is not at all apparent that such reductions are possible with respect to every aspect of the social world.[46] Further, it may well be that reductions of the social to the psychological are possible only at the token-token level.[47] If this is so, then sociological laws would be irreducible to psychological laws and the regulative significance of explanatory individualism becomes questionable.

The principle of explanatory individualism says that all social phenomena can be explained in individual terms. But if the social is supervenient on the psychological, then such individual-level explanations, even if they can be achieved, appear to be of little theoretical or practical value because they fail to identify regularities that can be used to explain or control social processes. The principle of explanatory individualism has traditionally been intended as a principle of regulative significance. That is, it is understood as recommending the elimination of social-level explanations in favor of explanations appealing only to the properties of individuals. But if social regularities really are supervenient, then the recommendation to avoid social-level explanations in favor of individual-level explanations appears to be a recommendation of suicide for social science.[48]

Levine, Sober, and Wright agree that if social phenomena are supervenient on individual phenomena, then social science would be wise to reject the explanatory reductionism advocated by some methodological individualists. Nevertheless, they argue that there may yet be some regulative value in Elster's explanatory individualism: ''In defending methodological individualism, Elster advances two reasons why a concern with microfoundations is important in social science. His reasons are sound, even if the reductionist ambition of Elster's overall methodological position is not.''[49]

Elster's first argument for the importance of searching for microfoundations for social processes involves worries about confusions at the social level between genuine laws and mere correlations, and between causal explanation and mere necessitation. Elster thinks that a clarification of the actual microfoundational processes underlying social regularities will increase our confidence in them as genuine causal explanations. But if supervenience holds, knowledge of the microfoundational processes underlying a particular social event cannot be projected to any other instance of a like social event. Microfoundational analysis cannot increase our warrant for belief that social regularities are genuine social laws. Why, then, do Levine, Sober, and Wright think there is merit in Elster's argument here? Having argued for the supervenience of the social macro level on the individual micro level, they comment as follows: ''Nevertheless, since every macro-process must have micro-realizations, the elaboration of the possible microfoundations adds credibility to macro arguments.''[50]

The authors say no more as to how the elaboration of the possible microfoundations adds credibility to macro arguments. The conclusion appears in a context in which the point has been made that there may well be more than one possible microfoundation for any given macro-social phenomenon. This suggests that the authors have in mind the elaboration of various possible microfoundations. But since there are indefinitely many of these, and since many involve relatively uninteresting variations on one another, it is not clear how this sort of elaboration would lend credence to a macro-level account.

However, there is another way of understanding this ''elaboration of the possible microfoundations'' that links Elster's explanatory individualism with his criticism of functionalist explanation. Consider, for example, Elster's criticism of Cohen's functionalist account of change in relations of production in terms of requirements of maximal use of expanded forces of production. Elster argues that even if invariant regularities could be established at this level, the functionalist account is inadequate in the absence of some microfoundational account of how the requirements of the productive forces give rise to change in the relations of production. In part Elster's argument here turns on his critique of functional explanation in general. But Elster notes that the presumed functional explanation is also dubious because it seems to violate the result which would be expected on the assumption that capitalists act to maximize the extraction of surplus value.[51] Similar content-specific problems infect other possible Marxist functional explanations. For example, attempts to explain wage differentials based on race, sex, or nationality appear to contradict the assumption that capitalists act to maximize their individual profits.[52] Where functional explanations or, in general, where any social-level explanation appears to require individual behavior inconsistent with individual behavior assumed by the social theory in question in other contexts, there is clearly a need for micro-level analysis. If a possible microfoundation can be elaborated that eliminates the apparent contradiction, this does lend credibility to the macro-level theory.

This is, of course, a much more restricted claim than the one Elster appears to be arguing for in his case for explanatory individualism. Nevertheless, I think it is a claim of some importance. I believe that Elster is correct in seeing much of Marx's work as involving the tracing out of the unintended social outcome of individually rational acts. This being so, much of Marx's theory of capitalism does rest on (at least partially specified) microfoundations. And, at least sometimes, some Marxists do appear to advance naive functionalist explanations that appear to contradict the microfoundations assumed in the theory of capitalism. Thus theories in which "it is just as if there were a single center of decision in each class, a 'collective' capitalist and a 'collective' worker,"[53] which appeal to Lebowitz, seem to me to be in apparent contradiction with Marx's own work.

A second reason Elster advances in favor of explanatory individualism as a regulative ideal is that microfoundations for a macro-level explanation enhance our understanding of the phenomena explained by providing a mechanism through which the macro-level regularity is produced. Elster appears to think that in the absence of such a micro-level mechanism, any proffered macro-level account falls short of providing a genuine explanation. He says, "To explain is to provide a *mechanism*, to open up the black box and show the nuts and bolts, the cogs and wheels, the desires and beliefs that generate the aggregate outcomes," and he quotes William Blake as saying, "Art and Science cannot exist but in minutely organized Particulars."[54]

There are at least two sorts of difficulties with this defense of explanatory individualism. First, it is not at all clear that mechanisms can be provided for all regularities, whether at the macro level or at the micro level. One does not have to be a Humean to accept the possibility that some regularities may present themselves for which no deeper explanatory account can be offered. The explanatory regress must come to an end at some point. If the regularity is well established, it is not clear why explanations in terms of it are deficient. It might be argued that there must be some mechanism underlying social regularities if ontological individualism is true. However, if the social level is supervenient on the individual level, there is no reason to think that there is any one mechanism underlying all instances of any particular social regularity.

This leads to a second difficulty with Elster's demand for specification of the micro-level mechanism underlying macro-level processes. In any particular case, the micro-level mechanism involved in the explanation of some event or process subsumed under a macro-level law may involve an enormous amount of uninteresting detail. Consider, for example, an explanation of the decline in the price of some commodity by appeal to a decline in demand for it. A full micro-level account of the macro-level mechanisms would involve a psychological explanation of the actions of every actor in that commodity market. It is not clear that a macro-level explanation, unsupplemented by this micro-level detail, is deficient as an explanation.

One might understand Elster as arguing not that macro-level explanations lacking such microfoundations are deficient as explanations, but that provision of microfoundations supplements macro-level explanations and deepens our understanding.[55] This claim, of course, does not outlaw pure macro-level explanations; it merely recommends further research into microfoundations for social processes. But even this recommendation is misguided as a general rule. For if specification of the microfoundations involves the kind of uninteresting detail mentioned above, it is not worth pursuing.

Further, in some cases, the search for microfoundations at work in a causal account of any particular social process may shift attention away from what is really interesting in some macro-level law claim that, applied to the given circumstances, necessitates the social process in question without providing a causal account of it. For example, Richard Miller points out that depiction of the actual mechanisms of individual interaction by which the ruling class defeats a challenge to its rule leaves out something important in the Marxist claim that the ruling class will always act to preserve its domination. For part of what is involved in the Marxist claim is that had the mechanism actually employed not been available, some other mechanism would have produced the same effect. At the causal level, redundant forces are at work. The pursuit of microfoundations may blind one to the greater significance of such necessitation claims.[56]

In spite of these criticisms, I believe that there remains something of merit in Elster's insistence upon the search for microfoundational mechanisms. While it may not be important to search for microfoundations in explaining particular social events, it may still be important to have some understanding of the kinds of micro-level processes that could produce such macro-level events. The Marxist claim that the ruling class will act to defeat (or try to defeat) challenges to its domination does need some understanding of how processes at the individual level can work to produce such processes. There may be redundant causal forces at work in actual cases. Still, it is desirable, both for purposes of explanation and for purposes of strategic interaction, to identify the kinds of mechanisms at work.

ANALYTICAL MARXISM: A BROADER PERSPECTIVE

Rejection of explanatory individualism as a regulative principle of social science does not commit one against analytical Marxism. For one thing, not all who are called analytical Marxists embrace regulative individualism. Cohen and Wood, who have developed similar functional accounts of historical materialism, are prominent exceptions. And even those like Elster and Roemer, who do appear to endorse the principle, might be satisfied with weaker and more defensible positions. For both these authors, the demand for microfoundations is linked to a rejection of naive functionalism.[57] But rejection of naive functionalism does not require the strong principle of regulative individualism. Thus, for example, critics of Elster's regulative individualism have agreed with him in rejecting naive functionalism.[58]

Can we then understand analytical Marxism in terms of a research program centered on the application of rational choice models to traditional problems of Marxism? Roemer's characterization of analytical Marxism suggests some such understanding of it.[59] Such a research program need not include a commitment to explanatory individualism as a regulatory principle. While I agree with Elster in thinking that rational choice analysis is central to Marx's theory of capitalism, and while I agree with Elster and Roemer in thinking that valuable work can be done in applying such models to problems of Marxism, I believe that even this conception of analytical Marxism is too narrow. In the first place, it is too narrow because it excludes the work of such thinkers as Cohen and Wood, who are sometimes considered to be among the analytical Marxists.[60] More important, I believe a narrow conception of analytical Marxism obscures what I see as a historically significant thread running through the work of those theorists who are sometimes identified as analytical Marxists, even those whose work is not centered on rational choice models.

The common thread I have in mind here is a rejection of any claim to the methodological distinctiveness of Marxist social science. "I do not think there is a specific form of Marxist logic or explanation," says John Roemer.[61] And provided this is understood at a sufficiently abstract level, all of the figures associated with analytical Marxism could agree. To be sure, Elster opens *Making Sense of Marx* with the claim that "there is a specifically Marxist method for studying social phenomena."[62] But what Elster means by this is the method of tracing out the unintended social consequences of individually rational action that he sees as pioneered by Adam Smith and Adam Ferguson, and that "has become the standard language of the social sciences."[63] Elster sees this method as involving the rational kernel in Marx's dialectics and as Marx's "central contribution to the methodology of the social sciences."[64] And he tells us that in its valuable parts, "dialectical method can be stated in ordinary 'analytical' language, thus offering no brief to those who believe in a radical divide between these two modes of reasoning."[65] In rejecting the claim to a dialectical method radically distinct from the method of bourgeois science, Elster is distinguishing his outlook both from Marxist-Leninism and Lukácsian humanistic Marxism.[66] In this sense, he, like Roemer, breaks with the conviction that Marxist social theory rests on a distinctive philosophy of science, a conviction that has dominated all sides in the discussions of Marxist social theory in the period since World War I.

I believe that a careful reading of Cohen and Wood shows that these analytical Marxists, who are furthest removed from the research program of Elster and Roemer, share with Elster and Roemer a rejection of the distinct methodology claim of Marxist-Leninism, humanistic Marxism, and the positivist critics of each. Again, one must be careful to consider the question of methodology at an appropriately abstract level. Consider, for example, Cohen's defense of historical materialism. Cohen argues for a functionalist interpretation of historical materialism, and then defends functionalist explanations against methodological criticisms coming from positivist and analytical philosophy. But Cohen's defense does not turn on claiming a radical distinction between Marxist functionalism and bourgeois social science. Instead, Cohen seeks to show that the criticisms advanced are mistaken, and that functionalist explanations are acceptable forms of empirical social science, conformable with the fundamental tenets of positivist philosophy of science.[67]

A similar conception of historical materialism as empirical, functional, social science was independently developed by Allen Wood. His interpretation of historical materialism appears within a broader interpretation of Marx that is sympathetic to the influence of Hegel on Marx. But, contrary to both Marxist-Leninism and humanistic Marxism, Wood rejects the view that Marx's dialectics provides a distinctive method for social thought: "The terms 'dialectical method' and 'dialectical logic' are apt to mislead. Neither in Hegel nor in Marx is dialectical thinking really a set of procedures for inquiry, still less a set of rules for generating or justifying results."[68]

In spite of their differences over the relative importance of rational choice models and functionalist explanations in Marxism, analytical Marxists share a rejection of the view that Marxist social theory is methodologically distinct from bourgeois social theory. For the analytical Marxists, what is distinctive in Marxist social science is its content rather than its methodology.[69] With this orientation, analytical Marxists bypass the philosophical and methodological frameworks of Marxist-Leninism and humanistic Marxism that have dominated Marxism since World War I and the October Revolution. This breakaway from the two dominant traditions is important in several ways. It has helped to shift the focus of discussion from methodological to substantive issues. It has allowed for application of techniques developed in non-Marxist science and philosophy to problems of Marxism. And, most important in my view, by removing the methodological walls surrounding Marxism, it has undercut an ignorant, but ideologically useful, dismissal of Marxism on purely methodological grounds.

This broad construal of analytical Marxism in terms of a rejection of the distinctive methodology claims of Marxist-Leninism and humanistic Marxism would include within analytical Marxism a number of thinkers not ordinarily considered as analytical Marxists. It would include a number of philosophers writing for English-language audiences.[70] It would also include work of the Italians: Galvano della Volpe, Lucio Colletti, Sebastiano Timpanaro, and others.[71] This construal of analytical Marxism would not include Louis Althusser because, though Althusser and his followers defended a scientific Marxism against humanistic Marxism, they also defended the claim that Marxist social science employs a distinctive structuralist methodology which breaks sharply with the methodology of bourgeois science.

THE CONVERGENCE THESIS

In the movement within Western philosophy from positivist sensationalism to scientific materialism to emergent materialism, there is a tendency to approach dialectical materialism that has been noted by several Marxist-Leninist philosophers. Thus, in his "From 'Scientific Materialism' to Emergent Materialism," David Dubrovskii quotes with approval the remark of B. T. Grigor'ian that emergent materialism "is a more developed form of non-Marxist materialism, containing certain elements of dialectical thought."[72] And, of course, this particular point echoes the thinking of the Hungarian philosopher, Andras Gedo considered in Chapter 6. Like Gedo, Dubrovskii argues that versions of emergent materialism now popular in the West still fall short of an adequately dialectical understanding. In particular, he argues that the focus on the mind/body relationship, which has dominated discussion of materialism in the West, has led to a neglect of social factors relevant to the understanding of conscious human action.

In rejecting a reductionist account of the relationship between the psychological and the social, some analytical Marxists are moving Western materialism still closer to the kind of dialectical perspective favored by Dubrovskii.[73] Like Gedo, Dubrovskii argues that a consistent emergent materialism must adopt a dialectical standpoint.[74] I have argued above that this is not so. Emergence is part of the idea of dialectical materialism, but dialectical materialism asserts more than this. In particular, the three laws of dialectics make claims that the emergent materialist need not defend, and that continue to appear as dubious to philosophers with roots in the tradition of logical positivism.

In his *Marxism in the USSR*, James Scanlan points to wide-ranging discussions of the three laws of dialectics that have been ongoing since about 1960.[75] He argues that these discussions can be understood in terms of a re-emergence of the controversy between mechanists and Deborinites in the 1920s.[76] Some of the positions adopted by the neo-mechanists bring their understanding of dialectics to positions less unattractive to Western emergent materialists. For example, Scanlan discusses the controversy between the "antimonist" and the "polarist" understandings of dialectical contradictions in recent Soviet philosophy.[77] The antimonists argue that there are logical contradictions which reflect real features of the world. The polarists, on the other hand, deny that real features of the world can accurately be said to reflect logical contradictions. They argue that the dialectically contradictory nature of reality must be understood not in terms of logical contradictions, but in terms of opposing forces or processes at work in the world. By rejecting the idea of real logical contradictions, the polarist position eliminates one of the most important barriers to Western acceptance of dialectical materialism. This polarist position, and especially versions of it developed within the framework of systems theory in terms of stabilizing and destabilizing forces, appears to be a clear descendant of the understanding of dialectics developed by Karl Kautsky, Aleksandr Bogdanov, and Nikolai Bukharin. This connection with the mechanist positions of the 1920s has been clearly pointed out by opponents of the polarist position within current Soviet philosophy.[78] While the polarist position remains a contested position within Soviet philosophy, and in this sense one cannot speak of tendencies of Marxist-Leninist philosophy as a whole, Scanlan nevertheless characterizes the polarist position as a majority position.[79]

The movement within Western philosophy from positivist sensationalism to scientific materialism to emergent materialism and then, perhaps, toward a dialectical materialism is connected with basic changes in Western philosophy of science. For one thing, the breakdown of positivist philosophy of science removed the methodological barrier to consideration of traditional problems of ontology, and hence allowed for development of materialist positions. The breakdown of the positivist dream has also removed much of the bite from positivist criticisms of Marxist social science. As was seen in Part I, by mid-century philosophers were divided into three mutually antagonistic camps with regard to their understanding and evaluation of Marxism. Against humanistic Marxism, Marxist-Leninists and positivists were agreed in viewing Marxism as "scientific" socialism. But Marxist-Leninists and positivists disagreed about the nature of science, and about whether Marxism was good or bad science. In taking Marxist social science seriously, analytical Marxists have broken both with the dominant humanism of Western Marxism and with the anti-Marxism of their own positivist roots. To be sure, some of the analytical Marxists have clearly indicated their own "positivist" doubts about much of Marxism. And though sometimes, as in the case of Elster, these criticisms are extensive, there remains within analytical Marxism a viewpoint that Marxist social science merits consideration and development. This resurgence of "scientific" Marxism is, at least in part, a result of a general shift in analytical philosophy of science away from the doctrines of positivism that had been invoked in the attack on Marxism as pseudoscience.

Consideration of this shift in analytical philosophy of science, and of a contemporary shift in Marxist-Leninist philosophy, has led Andries Sarlemijn to formulate a thesis concerning convergence between Western and Marxist-Leninist philosophies of science:

There is, I am convinced, convergence between scientific methodology and dialectical philosophy. This is a process that we can observe in Western countries like West Germany and the United States. Also the philosophers of the Soviet Union have become more and more interested in the problems and results of the Western philosophy of science.[80]

Sarlemijn identifies two trends that underlie his claim for convergence. On the one hand, "a gradual conversion of many dialectical philosophers to modern logic has taken place, or at least to a more positive attitude to it." On the other hand, "a better appraisal of dialectical philosophy by a number of leading proponents of scientific methodology exists."[81] What Sarlemijn has in mind by this "better appraisal of dialectical philosophy" is not so much a better-informed or favorable appraisal of Marxist-Leninist philosophy as it is the attainment of a perspective that is, in certain respects, dialectical. Logical positivism adopted a nonhistorical framework for understanding science and scientific method. Problems pertaining to the history of science, to the origin of scientific theories, to the idea of scientific progress, or to the change in meaning of key terms in scientific theories were relegated to the context of discovery that stood outside the arena of investigation. For the logical positivists, the central task was to clarify the relationships between scientific theory and observation states that would prevail in a final and true scientific picture of a field of investigation. Such a framework left no room for dialectics.

With recognition of the underdetermination of theory by sensory data and of the theory ladenness of observation, it became apparent that the ideal of the logical positivists was not attainable. And this recognition in turn led to interest in criteria of scientific progress conformable to the less-than-ideal picture of science that emerged from consideration of the history of science. The post-positivist philosophies of science of Imre Lakatos, Paul Feyerabend, and Thomas Kuhn show a sensitivity to the historical dimension of science, to problems pertaining to the context of discovery, and to the shifts in meaning of key terms within the development of science. And, in doing so, they open Western philosophy of science to a dialectical treatment of these problems. To be sure, there is here only an opening for dialectical treatment of these problems. In their insistence on the difficulties involved in making judgments of scientific progress, Kuhn and Feyerabend stand opposed to the developmental aspect of a dialectical perspective. And, though Lakatos does think judgments of progress are rationally defensible in retrospect, he believes such judgments rest on the overall comparative success of research programs and not upon any inherent, necessary advance in the conceptual transformations underlying shifts in research programs.[82] Nevertheless, there is room here for a dialectical treatment of these problems.[83]

If the introduction of history into the understanding of science has brought Western philosophy of science closer to a dialectical perspective, Sarlemijn finds in Soviet receptivity to formal logic another tendency leading to convergence in philosophy of science. Since the fall of 1946, training in formal logic has been a part of the curriculum in Soviet high schools and universities.[84] In addition, Marxist-Leninist philosophers have shown a lively interest in various formal approaches to the study of social phenomena. In this respect, Roemer's attempt to claim the "state-of-the-art methods" of the social sciences as the private property of analytical Marxism, in contrast with "conventional" Marxism, is either uninformed or unfair. Interests in cybernetics, systems theory, game theory, and other formalist approaches have been strong since 1960.[85]

The revival of interest in formal logic has given rise to a prolonged discussion in Soviet philosophy concerning the relationship between dialectical and formal logic. In the course of this discussion some Soviet philosophers have rejected the idea of a dialectical logic altogether, understanding it as a method of thought that violates rules of formal logic.[86] Other Soviet philosophers have interpreted dialectical logic in ways that preserve dialectics but do not involve it in contradictions with formal logic.[87] Among the conceptions of dialectics proposed is a view of it as applying to problems pertaining to the context of discovery, to the history of science, and to the nature of scientific progress.[88] Such a view permits a more or less wholesale incorporation of Western philosophy of science as synchronic theory of science. Dialectics pertains to the succession of scientific theories in time. Such a solution to the question of the relation of formal logic and dialectical logic would bring Marxist-Leninist discussions of dialectics close to the point, consideration of the history and development of science, at which an opening to dialectics has appeared in Western philosophy of science.

My aim here is not to argue that convergence has been achieved, that it ever will be achieved, or even that it is desirable. There remain serious obstacles to achieving it. Philosophically, dialectics remains the central obstacle to convergence. The understanding of dialectics as pertaining to the history and development of thought, an understanding that provides room for analytical philosophy of science along the lines indicated above, may also provide a framework for fruitful discussion between analytical philosophers and Marxist-Leninists. What such a framework would involve is difficult to say. I am dubious as to the value of the three laws of dialectics. But I am also dubious of formalist attempts to understand progress in science in terms of quantitative judgments about how much was explained, or how many problems were solved, or how many questions answered.[89] The reason for this is that it seems to me that every imperfect theory will have indefinitely many successes and failures. Consequently, I am willing to consider any other sort of proposal for handling these problems. While I am not yet convinced that a dialectical framework can assist in these matters, it seems to me at least worthy of further exploration. It may well be that a "dialectical" approach to the history of science, one that conceives of scientific progress in terms of the concrete, content-specific requirements of particular fields of investigation, will prove more successful in understanding scientific progress.[90]

In any case, these speculative remarks aside, there are also deep-seated institutional factors that make philosophical exchange between Marxist-Leninists and analytical philosophers difficult. The two traditions have developed independently. Each has created its own history, its own fields of investigation, its own paradigms for research in those fields, its own understandings of key terms derived from the shared philosophical tradition, and its own style of interaction with other philosophies. In such circumstances, goodwill on both sides is not sufficient for fruitful philosophical interchange.

SOME FINAL REMARKS

Throughout this volume my principal aim has been to defend a view of Marxism that sees Marx's social scientific theory of capitalism as the centerpiece of Marxist thought. I have agreed that Marxism includes as well defined positions in epistemology, metaphysics, ethics, and politics. However, I have tried to argue that these positions are not such as to sharply differentiate Marxist from non-Marxist philosophy, and not such as to differentiate Marxist science from non-Marxist science. From this point of view, I welcome analytical Marxism as an alternative to the humanistic Marxism that has dominated Western Marxism in recent years. In taking scientific Marxism seriously, analytical Marxism has broken with this humanistic tradition. It has also broken with the shared conviction of humanistic Marxism and Marxist-Leninism that, because Marxism rests upon distinctive philosophical foundations, philosophy is the master key to correct positions in all other scientific fields and in practical political action as well.

Analytical Marxism, as I have broadly construed it, dethrones philosophy. It marks a turning away from the methodological and philosophical themes that have dominated theoretical Marxism in the twentieth century.[91] In doing so, it marks a return to problems of substantive content rather than to problems of methodology. And, in this sense, it marks a return to the vulgar and unphilosophical Marxism of the Second International.

I am inclined to see this turning away from philosophy as a good thing, since it appears to me that both the Marxist-Leninist and the humanist critiques of vulgar Marxism have foundered on untenable connections between philosophical theses and more concrete results. Likewise, I believe that attempts to ground political hostility to existing socialism in philosophical opposition to dialectical materialism are profoundly misguided. It is because I downplay the importance of philosophy that I view this work as a defense of vulgar Marxism. But, of course, I do not advocate a return to the philosophical terrain of the Second International. Neither Neo-Kantianism nor positivism is today a viable option. I have opted in this study for an emergent materialism that seems to me most philosophically tenable but also consistent with Marxist roots. However, if this study is correct, it is not this philosophical orientation, but the theory of capitalism, that is the great contribution of Marxism to our theoretical understanding of the world. At heart, Marxist theory is not esoteric philosophy but empirical science.

NOTES

1. Robert Tucker, *Philosophy and Myth in Karl Marx* (Cambridge: Cambridge University Press, 1961), p. 12.

2. In the 2d ed., Tucker does appear to take Marx's social and economic thought somewhat more seriously. See his comments in the Preface on the relevant revisions in the text.

3. Gerald Cohen, *Karl Marx's Theory of History: A Defence* (Princeton: Princeton University Press, 1978).

4. For relevant bibliographical information, see John Roemer, ed., *Analytical Marxism* (Cambridge: Cambridge University Press, 1986); Alan Carling, "Rational Choice Marxism," *New Left Review* 160 (November–December 1986): 24–62; Michael A. Lebowitz, "Is 'Analytical Marxism' Marxism?" *Science and Society* 52, no. 2 (Summer 1988): 191–214; and W. H. Locke Anderson and Frank W. Thompson, "Neoclassical Marxism," *Science and Society* 52, no. 2 (Summer 1988): 215–228.

5. Roemer, *Analytical Marxism*, pp. 1–2.

6. Ibid., pp. 5 (on methodological individualism) and 192 (on rational choice models).

7. Jon Elster, "Marxism, Functionalism and Game Theory," in *Analytical Marxism*, edited by John Roemer (Cambridge: Cambridge University Press, 1986), p. 210.

8. Jon Elster, *Making Sense of Marx* (Cambridge: Cambridge University Press, 1985), p. 5.

9. On the English and the Irish, see Roemer, *Analytical Marxism*, p. 215. On the speculative theory of history and its relationship to functional explanation in Marx, see Elster, *Making Sense of Marx*, pp. 107–118, 27–37.

10. Elster, *Making Sense of Marx*, pp. 30–31. In "Marxism . . . Game Theory" (pp. 206–207), Elster points out that in fact such change is not what one would expect as the result of attempts to maximize surplus extraction from direct producers.

11. Roemer, *Analytical Marxism*, p. 191.

12. Elster, *Making Sense of Marx*, pp. 3–5.

13. Elster claims that the normative theory built around the concepts of alienation and exploitation "constitutes the *sine qua non* of Marxism" ("Marxism . . . Game Theory," p. 220), and Roemer's work on exploitation is aimed at clarifying the ethical case for socialism. This said, in what follows, I will largely focus on the social scientific side of analytical Marxism.

14. Roemer, *Analytical Marxism*, pp. 1–2.

15. Lebowitz, "Is 'Analytical Marxism' Marxism?" p. 193.

16. Anderson and Thompson "Neoclassical Marxism," p. 215.

17. Ronald Kieve, "Review of Analytical Marxism," *Science and Society* 52, no. 2 (Summer 1988): 232.

18. Rosa Luxemburg, "Reform or Revolution," in *Rosa Luxemburg Speaks*, edited by Mary-Alice Waters (New York: Pathfinder Press, 1970), pp. 53, 59, 77, 76.

19. Prominent exceptions include the Neo-Kantian Max Adler and the positivists Anton Pannekoek and Aleksandr Bogdanov.

20. *Rosa Luxemburg Speaks* (New York: Pathfinder Press, 1970), p. 69. To be sure, more recent work has suggested that producers' cooperatives would act differently than capitalist firms in some respects. See David Schweickart, *Capitalism or Worker Control?* (New York: Praeger, 1980), pp. 72–73, for a discussion of some results in this area.

21. Lebowitz, "Is 'Analytical Marxism' Marxism?" p. 193.

22. Ibid., pp. 193–194.

23. Ibid., pp. 194–195.

24. Ibid., p. 198 (italics in the original).

25. Ibid., p. 199.

26. Elster, *Making Sense of Marx*, p. 5.

27. Marx and Engels, *The German Ideology* (New York: International, 1966), pp. 6–7; *Marx Engels Werke* (Berlin: Deitz Verlag, 1968), vol. 3, p. 27. (Hereafter *MEM*.)

28. Ibid., p. 76 note.

29. Ibid., p. 107. See also the rejection of the theoretical need for the "combination of 'atoms' into an 'organic whole' " (pp. 83–84).

30. Elster, *Making Sense of Marx*, p. 7.

31. Ibid., Lebowitz, "Is 'Analytical Marxism' Marxism?" pp. 195, 199, 201.

32. Marx, *Contribution to the Critique of Political Economy* (New York: International, 1970), p. 199. This same comment on Say appears within the *Grundrisse* itself: *Grundrisse* (New York: Vintage, 1973), p. 94.

33. Marx, *Grundrisse*, p. 414.

34. For a more extended and nuanced discussion of such passages that defends Marx against the ontology and functionalist teleology attributed to him by Elster, but also criticizes Elster's explanatory individualism, see Julius Sensat, "Methodological Individualism and Marxism," *Economics and Philosophy* 4, no. 2 (October 1988): 189–219.

35. Marx, *Grundrisse*, p. 265.

36. Lebowtiz, "Is 'Analytical Marxism' Marxism?" p. 194.

37. Marx, *Contribution to the Critique of Political Economy*, p. 199; *Grundrisse*, p. 94.

38. The ontological individualist cannot accept all properties and relational properties without trivializing the doctrine. On this, see Sensat, "Methodological Individualism and Marxism" pp. 194–199.

39. Roemer, *Analytical Marxism*, pp. 196–197 and 198–199; Elster, *Making Sense of Marx*, pp. 9 and 18–22. Of course, problems pertaining to social determination of preference formation play a significant role in much of Elster's earlier work as well. See his *Ulysses and the Sirens* (Cambridge: Cambridge University Press, 1979) and *Sour Grapes* (Cambridge: Cambridge University Press, 1983).

40. Lebowitz, "Is 'Analytical Marxism' Marxism?" p. 198 (italics in original).

41. Section on "Marx's Philosophy of Science."

42. Marx, *Grundrisse*, p. 100.

43. Lebowitz, "Is 'Analytical Marxism' Marxism?" p. 201–202.

44. Marx, *Grundrisse*, pp. 107–108.

45. Elster, *Making Sense of Marx*, p. 5.

46. Sensat, "Methodological Individualism and Marxism," p. 198–199, raises the possibility that criteria for the individuation of some individual states may be uneliminably social.

47. Andrew Levine, Elliott Sober, and Erik Olin Wright, "Marxism and Methodological Individualism," *New Left Review* no. 162 (March–April 1987): 67–84; see also Alan Garfinkel, *Forms of Explanation* (New Haven: Yale University Press, 1981).

48. For a criticism of the regulative significance of methodological individualism even supposing the reducibility of social level explanations, see Sensat, "Methodological Individualism," pp. 201–202.

49. Levine, Sober, and Wright, "Marxism . . . Individualism," p. 79.

50. Ibid., p. 80.

51. Elster, "Marxism . . . Theory," p. 207; see also his *Making Sense of Marx*, pp. 30–31.

52. Roemer, *Analytical Marxism*, p. 191.

53. Lebowitz, "Is 'Analytical Marxism' Marxism?" p. 197. I do not mean this as a criticism of Maarek, with whose work I am unfamiliar.

54. Elster. *Making Sense of Marx*, p. 5.

55. See Levine, Sober, and Wright, "Marxism . . . Individualism," p. 80.

56. Richard Miller, *Analyzing Marx* (Princeton: Princeton University Press, 1984), pp. 129–136; see Garfinkel, *Forms of Explanation*, pp. 62–63.

57. Elster, "Marxism . . . Theory," p. 203; Roemer, *Analytical Marxism*, pp. 191, 201 (on teleology).

58. Lebowitz, "Is 'Analytical Marxism' Marxism?" p. 212.

59. See his Introduction to *Analytical Marxism*.

60. On this, see Carling, "Rational Choice Marxism," p. 27 n. 7.

61. Roemer, *Analytical Marxism*, p. 191.

62. Elster, *Making Sense of Marx*, p. 3.

63. Ibid.

64, Ibid., p. 48.

65. Ibid., p. 37.

66. Ibid., p. 122. Here Elster endorses the idea of successive approximation against Lukácsian totality.

67. Cohen, *Karl Marx's Theory of History*, chs. 9, 10. It is perhaps in part because this approach bypasses the terrain of the humanism/Leninism debate that Cohen can describe the position he defends as "an old fashioned historical materialism" (p. x).

68. Allen Wood, *Karl Marx* (London: Routledge and Kegan Paul, 1981), p. 190; cf. p. 199. Wood appears to understand Marx's dialectics as an empirically grounded metaphysics along the lines sketched in Chapter 7 of this volume. See Wood, p. 208.

69. See Levine, Sober, and Wright, "Marxism . . . Individualism," p. 67; and Daniel Little, *The Scientific Marx* (Minneapolis: University of Minnesota Press, 1986), p. 31.

70. Among others, this construal would include, in addition to Elster, Roemer, Cohen, and Wood, Daniel Gandy, Russell Keat, Daniel Little, John McMurtry, Richard Miller, D.-H. Ruben, Derek Sayer, William Shaw, and John Urry.

71. Galvano della Volpe, *Logic as Positive Science* (1950) (London: NLB, 1980); Lucio Colletti, *Marxism and Hegel* (1969) (London: NLB, 1973); Sebastiano Timpanaro, *On Materialism* (London: NLB, 1975).

72. David Dubrovskii, "From 'Scientific Materialism' to Emergent Materialism," *Soviet Studies in Philosophy* 27 (Summer 1988): p. 73.

73. The clearest statement of such an irreducibility of the social to the psychological can be found in the thesis of the supervenience of the macro level on the micro level in Levine, Sober, and Wright, "Marxism . . . Individualism." Although he does not commit himself on this point, Sensat ("Methodological Individualism and Marxism") clearly does think that Marxist rejection of the reducibility claim does not impair the scientific status of Marxist social theory. Wood, Cohen, and Miller also appear sympathetic to the irreducibility claim.

74. Dubrovskii "From . . . Materialism," p. 68.

75. James Scanlan, *Marxism in the USSR* (Ithaca, NY: Cornell University Press, 1985), pp. 111–140.

76. Ibid., pp. 107, 120, 142.

77. Ibid., pp. 124–133.

78. Ibid., p. 120 (quotation from Il'enkov).

79. Ibid., p. 133.

80. Andries Sarlemijn, "Convergence in the Philosophy of Science," *Studies in Soviet Thought* 30 (1985): 307.

81. Ibid., p. 305.

82. Sarlemijn compares Lakatos' distinction between theories and research programs to Hegel's distinction between the sciences of the understanding and the science of reason. Sarlemijn contends that there is a correspondence between these two distinctions and he quotes Lakatos concerning "the dialectic of research programmes" (ibid., p. 335 n. 69). On my view, Lakatos' dialectic of research programs remains on the side of the sciences of the understanding. For Lakatos, progress in research programs is determined ultimately by judgments of overall empirical adequacy.

83. See Rüdiger Bubner, *Modern German Philosophy* (Cambridge: Cambridge University Press, 1981), pp. 134–138, for a sympathetic discussion of a dialectical approach to such problems.

84. Scanlan, *Marxism in the USSR*, p. 150. Note that this precedes Stalin's pronouncement in the *Short Course* (1950) that language is class neutral.

85. On cybernetics and systems theory, see ibid., pp. 155–160. Well before the advent of analytical Marxism, the GDR philosopher Georg Klaus argued that Marxist social theory needed the conceptions and methods of game theory in *Spieltheorie in philosophischer Sicht* (Berlin: Deutscher Verlag der Wissenschaften, 1968), p. 228.

86. Scanlan, *Marxism in the USSR*, p. 151 (on Bakradze and Kondakov).

87. Ibid., pp. 151–160.

88. Ibid., pp. 160–173. Scanlan points out that these conceptions of dialectics are mixed with other, more problematic, claims.

89. In greatly simplified form, these appear to me to be the answers of Lakatos, Laudan, and Newton-Smith, respectively.

90. This appears to me to be the view developed by Richard Miller in his *Fact and Method* (Princeton: Princeton University Press, 1987). Miller does not claim a "dialectical" approach to the philosophy of science.

91. Perry Anderson, *Considerations on Western Marxism* (London: NLB, 1976), pp. 52–53, identifies these philosophical themes as peculiar to Western Marxism. It seems to me that a preoccupation with philosophical methodology is characteristic of all Marxism since the time of World War I and the October Revolution.

Bibliography

Acton, H. B. *The Illusion of the Epoch*. London: Cohen and West, 1955.

Addis, Laird. *The Logic of Society*. Minneapolis: University of Minnesota Press, 1975.

Allen, Derek. "The Utilitarianism of Marx and Engels." *American Philosophical Quarterly* 10, 1973: 189–199.

Anderson, Perry. *Considerations on Western Marxism*. London: NLB, 1976.

Anderson, W. H. Locke, and Frank W. Thompson. "Neoclassical Marxism." *Science and Society* 52(2), Summer 1988: 215–228.

Angel, Pierre. *Eduard Bernstein et l'evolution du socialisme allemand*. Paris: Marcel Didier, 1961.

Appignanesi, Richard, and Oscar Zarate. *Lenin for Beginners*. New York: Panthenon, 1978.

Arato, Andrew, and Paul Breines. *The Young Lukács and the Origins of Western Marxism*. New York: Seabury Press, 1971.

Avineri, Schlomo. *The Social and Political Thought of Karl Marx*. Cambridge: Cambridge University Press, 1971.

Ball, Terence. "Marxian Science and Positivist Politics." In *After Marx*. Edited by Terence Ball and James Farr. Cambridge: Cambridge University Press, 1984.

Bender, Frederic. "Marx, Materialism and the Limits of Philosophy." *Studies in Soviet Thought* 25, 1983: 79–100.

Bernstein, Eduard. *Evolutionary Socialism*. New York: Schocken, 1963.

Böhm-Bawerk, Eugen. *Karl Marx and the Close of His System*. New York: Augustus Kelley, 1949.

Bottomore, Tom, and Patrick Goode, eds. *Austro-Marxism*. Oxford: Oxford University Press, 1978.

Brenkert, George. *Marx's Ethics of Freedom*. London: Routledge and Kegan Paul, 1983.

Bronner, Stephen. *Rosa Luxemburg: A Revolutionary for Our Times*. New York: Columbia University Press, 1987.

Bubner, Rüdiger. *Modern German Philosophy*. Cambridge: Cambridge University Press, 1981.

Butterwege, Christoph. "Der Bernstein-Boom in der SPD." *Blätter für deutsche and internationale Politik* 23(5), 1978 579–592.

Carling, Alan. "Rational Choice Marxism." *New Left Review* no. 160, November–December 1986: 24–62.

Carr, Douglas. "Tolerant Empiricism: An Essay on the Philosophy of the Vienna Circle." Unpublished M.A. thesis. University of Alberta, Edmonton, 1977.

Carver, Terrell. *Marx and Engels*. Bloomington: Indiana University Press, 1983.

Cohen, Gerald. "Karl Marx and the Withering Away of Social Science." *Philosophy and Public Affairs* 1(2), Winter 1972: 182–203.

———. *Karl Marx's Theory of History: A Defence*. Princeton: Princeton University Press, 1978.

Cohen, Marshall, et al. *Marx, Justice and History*. Princeton: Princeton University Press, 1980.

Cohen, Stephen. *Bukharin and the Bolshevik Revolution*. Oxford: Oxford University Press, 1980.

Cole, G. D. H. *The Meaning of Marxism*. Ann Arbor, MI: Ann Arbor Paperbacks, 1948.

Colletti, Lucio. "A Political and Philosophical Interview." *New Left Review* no. 86, July–August 1971: 3–28.

———. *From Rousseau to Lenin*. New York: Monthly Review Press, 1972.

———. *Marxism and Hegel*. London: NLB, 1973.

Collier, Andrew. "Truth and Practice." *Radical Philosophy* 5, 1973: 9–16.

———. "Scientific Socialism and the Question of Socialist Values." In *Marx and Morality*. Edited by Kai Nielsen and Steven Patten. Guelph: Canadian Association for Publishing in Philosophy, 1981.

Cunningham, Frank, and Dan Goldstick. "Marxism and Epistemological Relativism." *Social Parxis* 6, 1979: 237–254.

De George, Richard. *Soviet Ethics and Morality*. Ann Arbor: University of Michigan Press, 1969.

Della Volpe, Galvano. *Logic as Positive Science*. London: NLB, 1980.

Dobb, Maurice. *Theories of Value and Distribution*. Cambridge: Cambridge University Press, 1973.

Drobnitskii, O. G. "Marxist Philosophy and the Problem of Value." *Soviet Studies in Philosophy* 5, 1966–1967: 14–24.

———. "Discussions Between Soviet and British Philosophers on Problems of Ethics." *Soviet Studies in Philosophy* 9, 1970–1971: 237–246.

Dubrovskii, David. "From 'Scientific Materialism' to Emergent Materialism." *Soviet Studies in Philosophy* 27 (1), Summer 1988: 51–76.

Dupré, Louis. *The Philosophical Foundations of Marxism*. New York: Harcourt Brace and World, 1966.

Eastman, Max. *Marxism: Is It Science?* London: George Allen and Unwin, 1941.

Edgley, Roy. "Marx's Revolutionary Science." In *Issues in Marxist Philosophy*. Edited by John Mepham and D.-H. Ruben. Vol. 3 Atlantic Highlands, NJ: Humanities Press, 1979.

Elster, Jon. *Ulysses and the Sirens*. Cambridge: Cambridge University Press, 1979.
———. *Making Sense of Marx*. Cambridge: Cambridge University Press, 1985.
———. "Marxism, Functionalism and Game Theory." In *Analytical Marxism*. Edited by John Roemer. Cambridge: Cambridge University Press, 1986.
———. *Sour Grapes*. Cambridge: Cambridge University Press, 1983.
Engels, Frederick. *Anti-Dühring*. Peking: Foreign Languages Press, 1976.
———. *Ludwig Feuerbach and the End of Classical German Philosophy*. Peking: Foreign Languages Press, 1976.
Feenberg, Andrew. *Lukács, Marx, and the Sources of Critical Theory*. Totowa, NJ: Rowman and Littlefield, 1981.
Feigel, H. "Memoir of Rudolph Carnap." In *Boston Studies in the Philosophy of Science*. Edited by Roger Buck and Robert Cohen. Vol. 8. Dordrecht: Reidel, 1971.
Fischer, Ruth. *Stalin and German Communism*. Cambridge, MA: Harvard University Press, 1948.
Gandy, Daniel. *Marx and History*. Austin: University of Texas Press, 1979.
Garfinkel, Alan. *Forms of Explanation*. New Haven: Yale University Press, 1981.
Gay, Peter. *The Dilemma of Democratic Socialism*. New York: Columbia University Press, 1952.
Gedo, Andras. *Crisis Consciousness in Contemporary Philosophy*. Minneapolis: Marxist Educational Press, 1982.
Geras, Norman. "On Marx on Justice." *New Left Review* no. 150, March–April 1985: 47–85.
Geuss, Raymond. *The Idea of a Critical Theory: Habermas and the Frankfurt School*. Cambridge: Cambridge University Press, 1981.
Gneuss, Christian. "The Precursor: Eduard Bernstein." In *Revisionism: Essays on the History of Marxist Ideas*. Edited by Leopold Labdez. New York: Praeger, 1962.
Goff, Tom. *Marx and Mead*. London: Routledge and Kegan Paul, 1980.
Graham, Loren. *Science and Philosophy in the Soviet Union*. New York: Knopf, 1972.
Gramsci, Antonio. *Prison Notebooks*. Edited by Quintin Hoare and Geoffrey Nowell Smith. New York: International, 1971.
Grebing, Helga. *Der Revisionismus*. Munich: Beck, 1977.
Gregory, Frederick. *Scientific Materialism in Nineteenth Century Germany*. Dordrecht: Reidel, 1977.
Gustafsson, Bo. *Marxismus and Revisionismus*. Frankfurt am Main: Europäische, 1972.
Haberiler, Gottfried. "Marxist Economics in Retrospect and Prospect." In *Marxist Ideology in the Contemporary World*. Edited by Milorad M. Drachkovitch. New York: Praeger, 1966.
Habermas, Jürgen. *Knowledge and Human Interests*. Boston: Beacon Press, 1971.
Hegel, G. W. F. *Science of Logic*. London: Allen and Unwin, 1966.
Hook, Sidney. *Towards the Understanding of Karl Marx*. New York: John Day, 1933.
Horkheimer, Max, and Theodor Adorno. *The Dialectic of the Enlightenment*. New York: Continuum, 1972.
Howard, Dic. *The Marxian Legacy*. New York: Urizen Books, 1977.
Hudelson, Richard. "Popper's Critique of Marx." *Philosophical Studies* 37, 1980: 259–270.
———. "Marx and the Theory of Internal Relations: A Critical Note on Ollman's Interpretation of Marx." *Philosophy of the Social Sciences* 14, December, 1984: pp. 505–507.

———. "Marxist Science as Ordinary Science." *Noûs* 20(1), Spring 1986: 53–63.

———. "Review: *The Scientific Marx* by Daniel Little." *The Philosophical Review*, 98, July 1989: 421–423.

Jacoby, Russell. *Dialectic of Defeat: Contours of Western Marxism*. Cambridge: Cambridge University Press, 1981.

Jensen, K. M. *Beyond Marx and Mach: Aleksandr Bogdanov's Philosophy of Living Experience*. Dordrecht: Reidel, 1978.

Joravsky, David. *Soviet Marxism and Natural Science*. New York: Columbia University Press, 1961.

Jordan, Z. A. *Philosophy and Ideology*. Dordrecht: Reidel, 1963.

———. *The Evolution of Dialectical Materialism*. New York: St. Martin's Press, 1967.

Kain, Philip. *Marx's Method, Epistemology and Humanism: A Study in the Development of His Thought*. Dordrecht: Reidel, 1986.

Katkov, George. "Lenin as Philosopher." In *Lenin: The Man, the Theorist, the Leader*. Edited by Leonard Schapiro, Peter Reddaway, and Paul Rosta. New York: Praeger, 1967.

Kautsky, Karl. *Ethics and the Materialist Conception of History*. Chicago: Charles Kerr. 4th ed. of the 1914 translation by John Askew.

Keat, Russell. *The Politics of Social Theory*. Chicago: University of Chicago Press, 1981.

Kelle, V., and M. Kovalson. *Historical Materialism*. Moscow: Progress, 1973.

Kieve, Ronald. "Review of *Analytical Marxism*." *Science and Society* 52(2), Summer 1988: 229–232.

Klaus, Georg. *Spieltheorie in philosophischer Sicht*. Berlin: Deutscher Verlag der Wissenschaften, 1968.

Klein, Horst, et al. *Philosophischer Revisionismus*. Berlin: Dietz Verlag, 1977.

Klein, Matthäus, et al. *Zur geschichte der Marxistisch-Leninistischen Philosophie in Deutschland*. Berlin: Dietz Verlag, 1969.

Kline, George. "The Myth of Marx's Materialism." *Annals of Scholarship* 3(2), 1984: 1–38.

Kolakowski, Leszek. *Toward a Marxist Humanism*. New York: Grove Press, 1968.

———. *Marxism and Beyond*. London: Pall Mall, 1969.

———. *Main Currents of Marxism*. Oxford: Oxford University Press, 1978.

König, Erika. *Vom Revisionismus zum demokratischen Sozialismus*. Berlin: Akademie, 1964.

Korsch, Karl. *Marxism and Philosophy*. New York: Monthly Review Press, 1970.

Kosing, Alfred. "Recent Problems in Marxist Epistemology." *Revolutionary World* 27, 1978: 69–74.

Lange, Oskar. *Political Economy*. New York: Pergamon Press, 1963.

———. "Marxian Economics and Modern Economic Theory." In *Marx and Modern Economics*. Edited by David Horowitz. New York: Monthly Review Press, 1968.

Lebowitz, Michael A. "Is 'Analytical Marxism' Marxism?" *Science and Society* 52(2), Summer 1988: 191–214.

Lenin, V. I. *Collected Works*. Moscow: Foreign Languages Publishing House, 1963.

———. *Materialism and Empirio-Criticism*. New York: International, 1972.

———. *What Is To Be Done?* Moscow: Progress, 1973.

———. *Against Revisionism*. Edited by F. V. Konstantinov and G. D. Obichkin. Moscow: Progress, 1976.

Levin, David. "The Moral Relativism of Marxism." *Philosophical Forum* 15(3), Spring 1984: 249–279.

Levine, Andrew, Elliott Sober, and Erik Olin Wright. "Marxism and Methodological Individualism." *New Left Review* no. 162, March–April 1987: 67–84.

Levine, Norman. *The Tragic Deception*. Santa Barbara, CA: ABC-Clio, 1975.

Lichtheim, George, *Marxism*. New York: Praeger, 1961.

———. *George Lukács*. New York: Viking Press, 1970.

Little, Daniel. *The Scientific Marx*. Minneapolis: University of Minnesota Press, 1986.

Lukács, Georg. *History and Class Consciousness*. Cambridge, MA: MIT Press, 1971.

———. "Interview." *New Left Review* no. 68, July–August 1971: 49–58.

Luxemburg, Rosa. *Rosa Luxemburg Speaks*. Edited by Mary-Alice Waters. New York: Pathfinder Press, 1970.

Malinin, V. A., et al. *The Fundamentals of Marxist-Leninist Philosophy*. Moscow: Progress, 1974.

Mandel, Ernest. *The Formation of the Economic Thought of Karl Marx*. New York: Monthly Review Press, 1971.

Marcuse, Herbert. *Soviet Marxism: A Critical Analysis*. New York: Columbia University Press, 1958.

Markovic, Mihailo. *The Rise and Fall of Socialist Humanism*. Nottingham: Spokesman Books, 1975.

Marx, Karl. *The 18th Brumaire of Louis Bonaparte*. New York: International, 1963.

———. *Early Writings*. Edited by T. B. Bottomore. New York: McGraw-Hill, 1964.

———. *Selected Writings in Sociology and Social Philosophy*. Edited by T. B. Bottomore. New York: McGraw-Hill, 1964.

———. *Theories of Surplus Value*. Moscow: Progress, 1968.

———. *Contribution to the Critique of Political Economy*. New York: International, 1970.

———. *Critique of Hegel's Philosophy of Right*. Cambridge: Cambridge University Press, 1970.

———. *Capital*. New York: International, 1973.

———. *The Economic and Philosophical Manuscripts of 1844*. New York: International, 1973.

———. *Grundrisse*. New York: Vintage, 1973.

———. *The Poverty of Philosophy*. New York: International, 1973.

Marx, Karl, and Frederick Engels. *Basic Writings on Politics and Philosophy*. Edited by Lewis Feuer. Garden City, NY: Anchor, 1959.

———. *The German Ideology*. New York: International, 1966.

———. *Marx Engels Werke*. Berlin: Dietz Verlag, 1968.

———. *Collected Works*. New York: International, 1975.

———. *The Holy Family*. In their *Collected Works*, vol. 4., 1975.

———. *Marx/Engels: Selected Correspondence*. Moscow: Progress, 1975.

———. *Manifesto of the Communist Party*. Moscow: Progress, 1977.

McCarthy, Thomas. *The Critical Theory of Jürgen Habermas*. Cambridge, MA: MIT Press, 1978.

McLellan, David. "Elusive Foundations: Recent Work on Marx and Marxism." *Philosophy* 57(219), January 1982: 119–126.

McMurtry, John. *The Structure of Marx's World View*. Princeton: Princeton University Press, 1977.

Meek, Ronald. *Economics and Ideology and Other Essays*. London: Chapman and Hall, 1967.

Meszaros, Istvan. *Marx's Theory of Alienation*. New York: Harper Torchbook, 1972.

Miller, Richard. *Analyzing Marx*. Princeton: Princeton University Press, 1984.

———. *Fact and Method*. Princeton: Princeton University Press, 1987.

Neurath, Otto. "Sociology and Physicialism." In *Logical Positivism*. Edited by A. J. Ayer. New York: Free Press, 1959.

———. *Empiricism and Sociology*. Dordrecht: Reidel, 1973.

Nielsen, Kai, and Steven Patten, eds. *Marx and Morality*. Guelph: Canadian Association for Publishing in Philosophy, 1981.

Nove, Alec. *The Economics of Feasible Socialism*. London: George Allen and Unwin, 1983.

Nowak, Leszek. *The Structure of Idealization*. Dordrecht: Reidel, 1980.

Oizerman, T. I. "The Problem of the Scientific Philosophical World-Outlook." In *Philosophy in the USSR: Problems of Dialectical Materialism*. Moscow: Progress, 1977.

Ollman, Bertell. *Alienation*. Cambridge: Cambridge University Press, 1971.

Pannekoek, Anton. *Lenin as Philosopher*. New York: Breakout Press, 1975.

Paul, Diane. "Marxism, Darwinism, and the Theory of Two Sciences." *Marxist Perspectives* Spring 1979: 116–143.

Pepperle, Heinz. "Der Determinismus der materialistischen Geschichtsauffassung und die moderne bürgerliche Philosophie." *Deutsche Zeitschrift für Philosophie* 34, 1986: 434–442.

Plamenetz, John. *German Marxism and Russian Communism*. London: Longman's Green, 1954.

Popov, S. I. *Der moderne Revisionismus*. Berlin: Deutscher Verlag der Wissenschaften, 1975.

Popper, Karl. "What Is Dialectic?" *Mind* 49, 140: 403–426.

———. *Conjectures and Refutations*. New York: Basic Books, 1962.

———. *The Open Society and Its Enemies*. Vol. 2. Princeton: Princeton University Press, 1963.

———. *The Poverty of Historicism*. New York: Harper, 1964.

Popper, Karl, and John Eccles. *The Self and Its Brain*. New York: Springer Verlag, 1977.

Rader, Melvin. *Marx's Interpretation of History*. Oxford: Oxford University Press, 1979.

Riker, William. *Theory of Political Coalitions*. New Haven: Yale University Press, 1965.

Rilki, Erika. *Der Revisionismus*. Zurich: Girsberger, 1936.

Robinson, Joan. "The Labor Theory of Value." In her *Collected Economic Papers*. Oxford: Basil Blackwell, 1951.

———. *Economic Philosophy*. Chicago: Aldine, 1962.

Rockmore, Tom. "Lukács on Classical German Philosophy and Marx." *Idealistic Studies* 10(3), September 1980: 209–232.

Roemer, John, ed. *Analytical Marxism*. Cambridge: Cambridge University Press, 1986.

Rossi-Landi, F. "Towards a Marxian Use of Wittgenstein." In *Austrian Philosophy: Studies and Texts*. Edited by J. C. Nyiri. Munich: Philosophia, 1981.

Salvadori, Massimo. *Karl Kautsky and the Socialist Revolution 1880–1938*. London: NLB, 1979.

Sarlemijn, Andries. "Convergence in the Philosophy of Science." *Studies in Soviet Thought* 30, 1985: 305–336.
Sayer, Derek. *Marx's Method*. Brighton: Harvester Press, 1979.
Scanlan, James. *Marxism in the USSR*. Ithaca, NY: Cornell University Press, 1985.
Schilpp, P. A., ed. *The Philosophy of Rudolf Carnap*. LaSalle, IL: Open Court, 1963.
Schmitt, Richard. *Introduction to Marx and Engels: A Critical Reconstruction*. Boulder, CO: Westview, 1987.
Schumpeter, Joseph. *History of Economic Analysis*. Oxford: Oxford University Press, 1954.
Schweickart, David. *Capitalism or Worker Control?* New York: Praeger, 1980.
Sensat, Julius. *Habermas and Marxism*. Beverly Hills, CA: Sage, 1979.
———. "Methodological Individualism and Marxism." *Economics and Philosophy* 4(2), October 1988: 189–219.
Shaw, William. *Marx's Theory of History*. Stanford: Stanford University Press, 1978.
———. "Marxism and Moral Objectivity." In *Marx and Morality*. Edited by Kai Nielsen and Steven Patten. Guelph: Canadian Association for Publishing in Philosophy, 1981.
Sheehan, Helena. *Marxism and the Philosophy of Science*. Atlantic Highlands, NJ: Humanities, 1985.
Smith, Steven. "Review of *Analyzing Marx* by Richard Miller." *Political Theory* November 1985: 662–676.
Steigerwald, Robert. *Anti-Communist Myths in Left Disguise*. New York: International, 1977.
———. *Bürgerliche Philosophie und Revisionismus im imperialistischen Deutschland*. Frankfurt am Main: Marxistische Blätter, 1980.
Steinvorth, Ulrich. *Eine analytische Interpretation der Marxischen Dialektik*. Maisenheim am Glan: Anton Hain, 1977.
Talmon, J. L. *The Origins of Totalitarian Democracy*. Boston: Beacon Press, 1952.
Timpanaro, Sebastiano. *On Materialism*. London: NLB, 1975.
Tucker, Robert. *Philosophy and Myth in Karl Marx*. Cambridge: Cambridge University Press, 1961.
Utechin, S. V. "Philosophy and Society: Alexander Bogdanov." In *Revisionism: Essays on the History of Marxist Ideas*. Edited by Leopold Labedz. New York: Praeger, 1962.
Van der Linden, Harry. *Kantian Ethics and Socialism*. Indianapolis: Hackett, 1988.
Von Wright, G. H. "Ludwig Wittgenstein, a Biographical Sketch." *Philosophical Review* 69, 1955: 527–545.
Vorländer, Karl. *Marx und Kant*. Tübingen: J.C.B. Mohr, 1926.
Wetter, Gustav. *Dialectical Materialism*. New York: Praeger, 1961.
Wilson, Edmund. *To the Finland Station*. Garden City, NY: Anchor, 1940.
Wood, Allen. "The Marxian Critique of Justice." *Philosophy and Public Affairs* 1, 1972: 244–282.
———. *Karl Marx*. London: Routledge and Kegan Paul, 1981.
Zelený, Jindřich. *The Logic of Marx*. Totowa, NJ: Rowman and Littlefield, 1980.

Index

Acton, H. B., 49, 93
Adler, Friedrich, 15, 22
Adler, Max, 14–19, 205
alienation, 66, 177
Althusser, Louis: and analytical Marxism, 229; on empiricism, 119, 131
analytical Marxism: criticisms of, 217–27; defined, 212–13, 227–29; and the Second International, 215–17
a priori categories, 22, 114
Austro-Marxism, 13–21
Avenarius, Richard, 22, 23, 31
Axelrod, L. I., 44–45

Ball, Terence: historical laws, 67; repressive politics of positivism, 204
Bauer, Otto, 15, 19, 20, 21
Bazarov, V. A., 22, 43
Bender, Frederic, 147–48
Berdiaev, Nikolai, 31
Berkeley, George, 31, 124
Bernstein, Eduard: and decentralized socialism, 9–10, 21; disconfirmation of Marxism, 8; on economic determinism, 11–12; ethical socialism, 8–9; Hegel, 10–11; revisionism of, 7–13; revolution, 8–9
Bogdanov, Aleksandr, 22, 23, 43, 47, 201, 230
Bolsheviks, 22, 23, 31
Bukharin, Nikolai, 39, 44–45, 201–2, 230
Bunge, Mario, 162–63

Carnap, Rudolf, 46, 47
Carr, Douglas, 46
Carver, Terrell, 155–56
Chilton, Steve, *x*
Cohen, Gerald A., 90–91, 103, 138, 212, 224, 227
Cohen, Hermann, 13, 20
Colletti, Lucio, 202, 229
convergence thesis, 229–33
council socialism, 41–43, 201
covering laws, 63, 67, 95, 120. *See also* hypothetical deductive science; nomothetic laws
critical theory, 69, 184–86. *See also* emancipatory theory
critique of political economy, 68, 70–71
Croce, Benedetto, 41

Deborin, A. M., 44–45
De George, Richard, 180, 187
Della Volpe, Galvano, *xv*, 229
determinism: Adler on, 17–19; and emancipatory theory, 107–8; humanist rejection of, 40, 104–6; of Pannekoek, 42; Popper on, 134–35; and prediction of socialism, 107
Dialectic of the Enlightenment, 200, 202–4
dialectics: Adler on, 16–17; in *Capital*, 73–80; and formal logic, 229–30, 232; and history of science, 231–32; humanist view of, 39; Marx's critique of Hegel, 117; and prediction of socialism, 160–61; revolution and reform, 33–34, 193–97; and Soviet science, 158
dialectics of nature: M. Adler on Engels, 17; humanist critique of, 39; of Lenin, 35; of Marx, 154–56
dictatorship of the proletariat, 21
disconfirmation of Marxism, 8, 15–16
Dubrovskii, David, 229

Eastman, Max, 212
economic determinism: Bernstein on, 11–12; humanist critique, 38, 65–66, 102–6; and Marx's theory of history, 90–93, 103
Elster, Jon: on dialectical deductions in *Capital*, 78–80; on functionalist explanations, 214; on microfoundations, 224–27
emancipatory theory, 64–73, 107–8. *See also* critical theory
emergence: and convergence thesis, 229; in dialectical materialism, 157; and emergent materialism, 162–63, 229
empiricism: of M. Adler, 16–17; Luckács on, 72, 205; of Marx, 62–64, 117–18; supposed political implications of, 204–5
empirio-critical Marxism, 21–23
Enchmen, E., 43
Engels, Frederick: on dialectics, 35, 45, 160–61; economic determinism of, 90; epistemology of practice, 123; philosophical Marxism of, 24, 153; positivist politics of, 200; on progress in morality, 174; supposed misunderstanding of Marxism, 154–57, 200
epistemically privileged classes, 135–38
epistemological activism, 34–35, 149–50
essence/appearance distinction, 121
ethical socialism: Austro-Marxists on, 18–20; of Bernstein, 8–9
exploitation: Marx on, 167–69; Roemer on, 222

fact/value distinction: humanist critique, 40, 181–86; and scientific politics, 204–5. *See also* value free science; value ladenness; normative contamination
falsifiability, 48, 96
Feenberg, Andrew, 127
Feuerbach, Ludwig, Marx's critique of, 150–52; scientific materialism of, 23, 148; as undialectical, 153–54
Feyerabend, Paul, 231
functionalist explanations, 213–14

game theory, 213, 218, 232
Gedo, Andras, 162–63, 229
Goff, Tom W., 133
Gorky, Maxim, 23
Gorter, Hermann, 41, 201
Gramsci, Antonio, 36–41
Grundrisse: and methodological individualism, 219–20; on science, 63, 118–19
Guiral, Jesús, *x*

Habermas, Jürgen, 129–30
Hegel, G.W.F., 4, 5, 23, 37, 45, 74, 144–46, 149, 152, 213; importance for Marxism, 152; Marx's critique of, 113–18
Hilferding, Rudolf, 15, 21
historical laws, 48–49, 67, 86–90
historical materialism: Acton's critique, 49, 93; of Austro-Marxism, 14–15; Bernstein on, 12; G. A. Cohen on, 90–91; of empirio-critical Marxism, 22; Lenin on, 33; Lukács on, 102–4; R.

Miller on, 91–97; and morality, 180–81; Pannekoek on, 42–43; philosophical status of, 97–102; Popper's critique, 48–49, 86–90; as research hypothesis, 97; as self-defeating, 133–35
humanistic Marxism, 30, 36–38, 50–51
human rights, 178
Hume, David, 31, 32, 74, 118, 124
hypothetical deductive science, 74, 91. *See also* covering laws

idealization, 62
ideas, role of in history, 65, 104–6
inevitability of socialism, 106–7
instrumentalism, 22, 42, 123
internal relations, 71, 116–17, 220–21

Jacoby, Russell, 200–201, 203
Joravsky, David, 44
Jordan, Z. A., 126

Kant, Immanuel, 17, 32
Kathedersozialismus, 4, 13, 216
Kautsky, Karl, 4–7, 33, 37, 65, 180, 196, 205, 230
Keat, Russell, *xv*
Kolakowski, Leszek: epistemology of praxis, 126; on moral theory, 181, 183–84; political implications of empiricism, 205
Korsch, Karl, 29, 36–41
Kuhn, Thomas, 97, 231

labor theory of value, 49–50, 60–62
Lakatos, Imre, 16, 97, 231
Lange, F. A., 13, 20
Lange, Oskar, 62
Laudan, Larry, 97
Lebowitz, Michael, 216, 217–23
Lemke, Dorothy, *x*
Lenin, V. I.: and critique of vulgar Marxism, 30–36, 193, 197; dialectics and revolution, 33–34; on historical materialism, 33; *Materialism and Empirio-Criticism*, 31–32, 34–36; materialism of, 31, 32, 35, 42, 153; *Philosophical Notebooks*, 32, 34–36, 45; reflection theory, 34–35; two Lenins thesis, 34–36
Liadov, M. N., 43
Lictheim, George, 104, 181
Liebknecht, Karl, 196, 205
Little, Daniel, 97, 100, 120, 221
Locke, John: empiricism of, 119; Marx on, 145–46; theory of property rights, 168
Lukács, Georg: and critique of vulgar Marxism, 36–41; on empiricism, 72; epistemic class bias, 136–37, 184; epistemology of praxis, 126–27; Marxism as method, 64–73; on morality, 182–84; on politics of empiricism, 205
Lunacharsky, Anatoly, 22, 23, 43
Luxemburg, Rosa, 200–201, 205, 216–17

Mach, Ernst, 15, 22, 23, 31, 42, 43, 47
Markovic, Mihailo: on determinism, 104–6; epistemology of praxis, 128; moral theory, 128
materialism: emergent, 162–63, 229; humanist critique of, 147–53; Neo-Kantian and positivist critique of, 3–4, 14; of Marx, 144–53; mechanistic and dialectical, 147, 153–54; scientific, 23–24, 148, 161, 229
mechanists, 44–45, 229–30
Mensheviks, 22, 31
methodological individualism: and analytical Marxism, 213–15; as explanatory thesis, 220–27; as ontological thesis, 218–20
microfoundations, 224–27
Miller, Richard: on historical materalism, 91–97, 103; on positivist anti-revolutionism, 199; redundant causality, 226
Minin, S., 43
Moody, Tom, *x*
morality: as class-based, 172–73; and Communist Party, 178–79; and historical marterialism, 180–81; as historically relative, 169–74; and history, 179–80; and human nature, 176–78; Marxist-Leninist morality, 174–80; moral progress, 174; objectivism in ethics, 179, 188; overdetermination in

ethics, 186–88; revolutionary morality, 172

naturalism of classical economics, 69–70
Neo-Kantianism: and Austro-Marxism, 14–15, 17; and Bernstein, 10–11; critique of Marxism, 3–4; and humanistic Marxism, 40–41; and Russian Marxism, 31
Neurath, Otto, 46–47
nomothetic laws, 63. *See also* covering laws
normative contamination, 167. *See also* fact/value distinction
Nowak, Leszek, 62

objectivism: humanist critique of objectivization, 66–67; of Marxist social science, 68; in morality, 179, 188; supposed political implications of, 200–201
Oedipus effect, 86–87, 108
organic ontology, 217–20
Ostwald, Wilhelm, 42

Pannekoek, Anton: empirio-critical Marxism of, 41–43, 47; on Engels on skepticism, 123; on historical materialism, 43; on Lenin, 41–42; politics of, 196, 201, 205
philosophy of science of Marx, 118–21
Piccone, Paul, 64
Plekhanov, Georgi, 23, 37, 42, 65, 104, 123, 153, 196
Pokrovsky, M. N., 43
Popper, Karl: anti-revolutionism of, 197–99; on deterministic materialism, 134–35; on dialectics, 47–49; on historical materialism, 48–49, 86–90
positivism: as anti-revolutionist, 197–99; and Austro-Marxism, 14–15; of Bernstein, 11; critique of Marxism, 3–4, 47–50; and empirio-critical Marxism, 21–23; reactionary politics of, 31, 42; and Soviet philosophy, 43–46; supposed totalitarian implications of, 200–205
practice epistemology, 122–24
praxis: epistemology of, 117–30; in humanistic Marxism, 37; and moral theory, 128–30
primacy of the practical thesis, 125
principle of identity, 37
Proudhon, Pierre, 168

realism, 31, 124, 126, 146
reductionism: and dialectical materialism, 148, 153, 157, 223–24, 229; and Marx's theory of capital, 156; of scientific materialism, 223–24
reflection theory: epistemology of, 130–33, 149; humanist critique, 37; Lenin on, 34–35
reflectivity of social theory, 39–40, 68–70
reification, 68, 102
relativity theory, 42, 43
Renner, Karl, 15, 20–22
revisionism debates, 4, 36
revolution and reform, 8–9, 20–21, 194
Ricardo, David, 60, 63, 67, 74, 119–21
Riker, William, 167–68
Robinson, Joan, 49–50, 62
Roemer, John: on analytical Marxism, 212–13; on exploitation, 222; on functionalist explanations, 213–14; on labor theory of value, 62
Roland-Holst, Henriette, 41, 201

Sarlemijn, Andries, 230–32
Scanlan, James, 53, 229–30
Schmidt, Konrad: on Engels on skepticism, 123; on historical materialism, 125
Schmitt, Richard, 105
science of reason, 113–14
sciences of the understanding, 113–14
Sellars, Roy Wood, 162–63
Sensat, Julius, *x*, 79
Sheehan, Helena, 44
skepticism, 123–24
slow revolution, 20–21
Smith, Adam, 60, 63, 67, 119
social association, 17
social determination of preferences, 217, 221

social structures, 61–63, 221
speculative theory of history, 213–14
Stalin, J. V.: against mechanists, 45; for proletarian science, 136
Steedman, Ian, 62
Stepanov, I. I., 44–45
Storch, Heinrich, 137
Struve, Peter, 31
successive concretization, 62
supervenience, 223–24

Talmon, J. L., 212
teleology, 49, 213–14
tendencies and laws, 15, 48–49, 87–90
theory ladenness of observation: Lukács on, 72; in post-positivist philosophy of science, 231
Timiriazev, A. K., 44
Timpanaro, Sebastiano, 229
totality, 71, 103, 219
transhistorical moral judgments, 170–74
Tucker, Robert, 212

unity of science: and theory of internal relations, 72; Lukács on, 72; Marx on, 64
Untermann, Ernest, 136
utilitarianism, 5, 174, 176–78

Valentinov, N. V., 22
value free science: of empirio-critical Marxism, 22; of Kautsky, 4–5; and Marx's theory of exploitation, 168–69
value ladenness, 72–73, 169, 183–86. *See also* fact/value distinction; normative contamination
Vienna Circle, 46–47
vulgar Marxism: concept of, 29–30; defense of, 233; humanistic critique of, 36–41; Leninist critique of, 30–36
vulgar materialism, 35–37, 42

Western Marxism, *xii*, 200–202
Wetter, Gustav, 44
Wilson, Edmund, 212
Wittgenstein, Ludwig, 47
Wood, Allen, 170–74, 212, 227

Yushkevich, P. S., 22

Zelény, Jindřich, 73–78

ABOUT THE AUTHOR

RICHARD HUDELSON graduated from DePauw University with a B.A. in philosophy in 1968. After being active in the antiwar movement, he returned to the study of philosophy, finishing a Ph.D. in philosophy at the University of Michigan in 1977. Since then Hudelson has published a number of articles and reviews on Marxism and related topics. He currently teaches courses in philosophy and humanities at Duluth Community College Center, the College of Saint Scholastica, and the University of Minnesota-Duluth.

www.ingramcontent.com/pod-product-compliance
Ingram Content Group UK Ltd.
Pitfield, Milton Keynes, MK11 3LW, UK
UKHW020801290926
15470UKWH00003B/884

9 780275 935931